Advanced 3D Game Programming All in One

Kenneth C. Finney

THOMSON

COURSE TECHNOLOGY

Professional ■ Technical ■ Reference

ISBN: 1-59200-733-3

Library of Congress Catalog Card Number: 2005927437

Printed in Canada

05 06 07 08 09 WC 10 9 8 7 6 5 4 3 2 1

Publisher and General Manager, Thomson Course Technology PTR:
Stacy L. Hiquet

Associate Director of Marketing:
Sarah O'Donnell

Manager of Editorial Services:
Heather Talbot

Marketing Manager:
Jordan Casey

Acquisitions Editor:
Mitzi Koontz

Senior Editor:
Mark Garvey

Project Editor/Copy Editor:
Jenny Davidson

Technical Reviewer:
Jacquie Finney

Thomson Course Technology PTR Editorial Services Coordinator:
Elizabeth Furbish

Interior Layout Tech:
Bill Hartman

Cover Designer:
Mike Tanamachi

CD-ROM Producer:
Brandon Penticuff

Indexer:
Katherine Stimson

Proofreader:
Sara Gullion

THOMSON

COURSE TECHNOLOGY ™

Professional ■ Technical ■ Reference

Thomson Course Technology PTR, a division of Thomson Course Technology
25 Thomson Place ■ Boston, MA 02210 ■ http://www.courseptr.com

*This book is dedicated to my father and mother,
Leonard and Jean Finney. I love you.*

Per Ardua ad Astra.

ACKNOWLEDGMENTS

I want to thank all you kind people who bought my first book, *3D Game Programming All in One*. I hope you find that this book fills the bill as well as it did.

I also want to thank my editors, Mitzi Koontz, Jenny Davidson, and especially my wife, Jacquie Finney for their collective patience, guidance, and the occasional kick in my assets. Oh yeah, and for not rolling their eyes at me too many times. Also, I have to thank my two volunteer editors: my sons Indy and Lucas for their biting critiques laced with unabashed boosterism.

I also want to acknowledge Ed Maurina and the great work he is doing with his *Essential Guide to Torque* and the stuff he has written for the GarageGames (GG) online docs.

Speaking of GarageGames, we all owe a debt of gratitude to Ben Garney for his awesome descriptions of some of the inner workings of Torque. When Ben gets his feathers ruffled, it's a thing of beauty to witness him wreaking order and knowledge upon unsuspecting bystanders, leaving whirlpools of understanding in his wake when he goes on a verbal rampage. Then there's the ever-patient, mentally nimble, and coolly competent Josh Williams, who once had the graciousness to check whether I would mind hearing some advice from a kid (him). Well, duh! Good advice is good advice no matter where it comes from. Now go to your room.

A few other members of the GarageGames community contributed to this book in various ways, knowingly and unknowingly. Paul Scott provided useful information in understanding SimSets. Nelson A. K. Gonsalves has some great ideas about how NPC conversations should take place. Mark Holcomb did some really cool things with sliding doors. The entire GarageGames online forums are an invaluable resource in their own right, providing a ton of added value that would be extremely expensive if you had to go out and buy it. There is a tremendous amount of knowledge, skill, and innovation in that group. As I utilized their ideas, I sometimes modified them to suit my own needs, and so any deficiencies are my own.

I would also like to thank the faculty and staff at the Art Institute of Toronto, especially Predrag, Lisa, and Paul, for their support. And I thank my students for their forbearance, especially John and Ali, who've ended up as de facto guinea pigs for everything new I want to try out. Hey look, where'd that stick come from?

Regards,
Ken

ABOUT THE AUTHOR

Kenneth Finney teaches game design, development, and prototyping at the Art Institute of Toronto where he is Lead Faculty Member in the Game Art & Design program. He began programming in 1974 and remembers that old HP-1000 with its paper tape and punch cards with a perverse fondness. Finney had been a software engineer from the mid-'80s until the late '90s focusing on advanced technology development. He was a recipient of the prestigious Conference Board of Canada ITX (Innovation in Technology Excellence) Award in 1997 for his work on "InScan," a high-speed document scanning system. He has been an Associate Professor at Seneca College at York University in Toronto, teaching technical writers how to survive in a software development environment. Ken is the creator of the popular Tubettiworld "Online Campaign" Mod and the "QuicknDirty" game management tools for the *Delta Force 2* game series from NovaLogic. He is currently working on completing a new and unique action/adventure game based on the original Tubettiworld design using the Torque Game Engine.

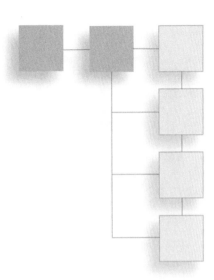

CONTENTS

PART IV
ENHANCED GAME MODELING   393

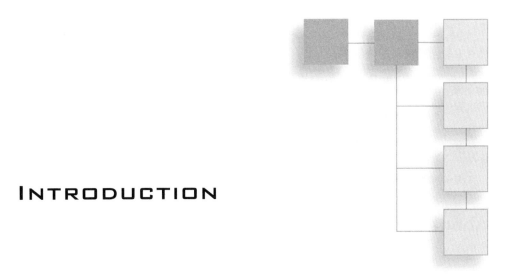

INTRODUCTION

"Hi, I bought your book, and I think it's great! But how come you didn't cover this, and you didn't cover that, and you only briefly touched on the other thing? Huh? Well?"

I've received many complimentary e-mails from satisfied readers of *3D Game Programming All in One* ("3DGPAI1" for short). But more than a few people were beating me up for not covering one favorite topic or another. Fortunately for me they haven't organized—I don't relish the idea of looking out the window one night and seeing a gathering of villagers with pitchforks and torches.

But they aren't just a mob of villagers, they are people like you—people who love computer games and believe that *they* can make a better game than the big game development software houses. They are on the march to change the game development world.

And you know what? You (and they) may be right. The problem until very recently has been that many creative and talented people don't have the cash and other resources required to spend on the development costs and game engine licensing that's needed *just to get to a starting point.*

This is changing, and books like this one and 3DGPAI1, and game engines like the Torque Game Engine are the reasons why this change is happening. The Indie game movement is about empowerment in its rawest form.

That Other Book

If you haven't read 3DGPAI1, let me just bring you up to speed quickly: It will give you a rounded education in using the Torque Game Engine to develop 3D games. It covers programming fundamentals and programming with Torque, 3D basics, 3D modeling using MilkShape 3D and QuArK, audio engineering using Audacity, texture development using Paint Shop Pro, and it gives you a ton of exposure to TorqueScript. Even though there was a comprehensive spread of topics in 3DGPAI1, it was not possible to cover everything in those 800 pages of material, hence the villagers with the torches.

About This Book

This book is going to take the next step, covering many of the more advanced areas, like artificial intelligence and dynamic skins, as well as digging deeper into the workings of a game engine. We'll also rummage around in the TorqueScript goodie-box to discover what mechanisms it has that will give you a boost into the realm of game development.

What You Need to Provide

You can leave the pitchforks and torches at home. However, you will need a reasonably capable computer system. You really should be using Windows XP by now, although other flavors of Windows will work.

And this is not quite a beginner's book like 3DGPAI1 was. If you've bought and used 3DGPAI1 to good effect, then you will certainly be in good shape with this book, but it's not entirely necessary.

Skills

If you are a somewhat accomplished programmer (regardless of the language), or have prior experience with modeling using tools like Valve's Hammer or 3D Max, you will most likely be able to get along just fine in here without being familiar with the introductory level material in 3DGPAI1.

You need to be familiar with finding your way around Windows folders and hard disks, using the Windows command shell (cmd.exe), and creating shortcuts and editing their properties.

System

You need a Windows-based computer to use this book (the following table outlines the minimum system requirements). It is possible for Macintosh and Linux users to use this book to create a game, because the game engine used—Torque—is also available for those platforms. However, not all of the required development tools are available on Mac and Linux, so the book's focus will be on Windows on Intel.

System Requirements

processor	Pentium III/800MHz minimum
operating system	Windows 98/ME/2000/XP
video card	3D graphics accelerated video card, NVidia GeForce 2–32MB equivalent or better
display	17-inch recommended
input devices	keyboard and mouse
memory	128MB minimum with 256MB recommended
hard disk	4GB minimum
CD player	CD-R minimum

I also suggest that you have a decent modern sound card and broadband Internet access.

What the Book Provides

To truly get the maximum benefit from this book, I encourage you to purchase your own license for the Torque Game Engine, at the stunningly reasonable price of $100. If you buy a license, you can go to the GarageGames site (www.garagegames.com) and download the latest versions of community resources offering alternative techniques to those used in this book.

The version of Torque used in this book is based on Torque Release v1.3. It is exactly the same executable and demo code as the downloadable Torque Game Engine demo found at http://www.garagegames.com/makegames/. All of the chapter exercises in the book use TorqueScript—there is no discussion, nor inclusion, of any core engine code or the C/C++ code modules that comprise the Torque Game Engine.

The Companion CD

The companion CD contains quite a few resources, including Torque and several custom builds, TorqueScript game code source and artwork resources, development tools, and demos of Torque-based games.

Source Code

The book's CD contains all of the TorqueScript source code in sample form and final form. The samples will be aligned with the contents of each chapter. The scripts for completed demos will be included in the chapter folders.

Game Engine

The CD contains the complete Torque Game Engine with its executable, DLLs, and all required GUI and support files. The Torque Game Engine is a fully featured game engine that includes advanced networking capabilities, blended animations, built-in server-side anti-cheat capabilities, BSP support, a strong and complete object-oriented C++-like scripting language, and many other advanced features.

Tools

Most of the "standard" set of tools (as established in 3DGPAI1) is also provided on the companion CD, even though we will not be covering their use in detail. They are included for your convenience. These tools include the latest version of MilkShape 3D, QuArK, and UltraEdit-32.

Extras

There is a folder on the companion CD called EXTRAS that contains demos and games made with Torque for Windows, Macintosh, and Linux. Additionally, the Macintosh and Linux v1.3 Torque Game Engine demo installers are included in the EXTRAS folder.

Now Go Make Better Games!

I keep telling anyone who'll listen: If you want to succeed as an independent, you need to be enthusiastic about what you are doing. You aren't going to be a smashingly successful Indie developer if you merely sit back and make cold, calculated, profit- and loss-oriented business decisions. That guy over there with the glint in his eye and the fire in his belly is gonna stomp all over you!

Well, you know what you have to do, don't you?

Stomp all over him *first*, or join forces with him. Armed with the knowledge this book will provide, the choice is yours.

PART I

ADVANCED SCRIPT PROGRAMMING

The workhorse technology in any game engine, including Torque, is its scripting capabilities. In a certain sense, a game engine is a collection of enabling technologies, like a renderer, resource manager, physics code, and so on. Scripts are the glue that connects these technologies to each other in a way to create a workable game environment.

In Part I we'll learn more about TorqueScript and how to apply it to game development situations. We'll look at how to use TorqueScript for mundane things like printing text strings to the console screen and log file, and sexy things like using matrix and vector math to move stuff around in a game world.

1

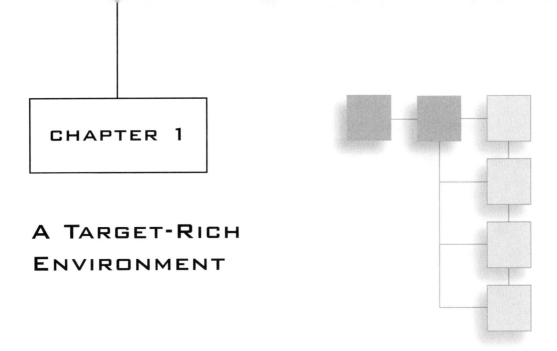

CHAPTER 1

A Target-Rich Environment

In my first book, *3D Game Programming All in One*, we went on a journey of discovery in the wilds of the 3D game development jungle. Starting with an examination of the 3D game industry, we then made our first tentative forays into the fields of programming and three-dimensional concepts. After that we marched across the vast steppe of Torque, using it to create some introductory single-player game environments. We then flanked through the verdant forests of game artwork, building models and textures. All the while we refined our understanding of game development and our appreciation of how Torque can carry us through the rough parts. When we came out the other side, we had seen everything to be seen, and spent a fair amount of time looking at many things we encountered along the way.

However, many of the features and concepts we encountered only received the shallowest glance. This is in no small part due to the richness of the game development scenery. In the chapters to come, we will return directly to some of those places and dwell longer, learn more, and develop a much more complete understanding.

TorqueScript

The workhorse technology in any game engine, including Torque, is its scripting capabilities. In a certain sense, a game engine is a collection of enabling technologies, like a renderer, resource manager, physics code, and so on. Scripts are the glue that connects these technologies to each other in a way to create a workable game environment. In Part I of the book you'll learn more about TorqueScript and how to apply it to game development situations.

Scripts are often used in this way because they allow the *ad hoc* creation of code to do things like manage and control the game engine or to formalize game rules. Programmers don't need to recompile program code to test it. It's a fairly simple operation to change or add a script; tell Torque to reload it, and see the results immediately. Torque, for its part, when told to load a script, will automatically recompile it into a byte-based encoding called p-code, if an encoded version doesn't exist, or if the source version is newer than an existing encoded version. Here is a brief example of some TorqueScript source code:

```
if (%obj.getState() $= "Dead")
   return;
%obj.applyDamage(%damage);
%location = "Body";
%client = %obj.client;
%sourceClient = %sourceObject ? %sourceObject.client : 0;
if (%obj.getState() $= "Dead")
{
   %client.onDeath(%sourceObject, %sourceClient, %damageType, %location);
   return;
}
```

TorqueScript is a very flexible language that offers pretty close to all the features and capabilities of a modern programming language. It incorporates an object-based paradigm alongside a procedural approach and syntax that will be very familiar to those who are already versed in C/C++.

As you will discover, one of the most important concepts in Torque is the *datablock*, and how it works. TorqueScript has intrinsic support for datablocks.

The Torque Engine exposes a great deal of its internal functionality via TorqueScript. All of the programming that we will do in this book will be done using TorqueScript.

3D Math Preview

An important mathematical capability in 3D games is the ability to calculate the coordinates of destinations in 3D space based upon where you are now, how far you want to move, how fast you want to move, and what directions you want to go when you move.

Vectors are the tool to use in most cases where moving from place to place is an issue.

Figure 1.1 shows, in conceptual form, how vectors can be used to navigate a pathway through an obstacle course. We can tell the boat how to get through the barriers by feeding it the needed vectors, from A to B, B to C, and C to D. We determine each new vector by locating the safe turning points, and then calculating the required vector. When we inform the boat of each vector, we basically tell it to point in a certain direction and to sail in that direction for a certain amount of time.

Figure 1.1 Using vectors for navigation.

In geometry, the only properties a vector has are *displacement* and *direction*. Vectors are not bound to any specific location in space. This means we can apply the same vector in an operation to any point, or vertex, of an object and obtain different results. Note that the results will be related in several ways. They will be mathematically related because the same vector was used, and they will be spatially related in exactly the same way they were before the vector was applied, since the vector was the same in each case. The triangle in Figure 1.2 has the same vector (dashed, arrowed lines) applied to each of its vertices. Notice how the resulting triangle has the same shape as the original. It's just been moved.

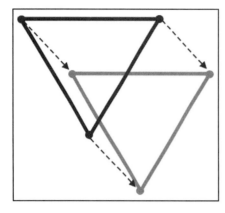

Figure 1.2 Using the same vector three times.

Now, a vector is really a specialized form of a matrix—a single column matrix, in fact. We'll look at matrices in more detail in Chapter 3 when we dive into vectors.

Torque has built-in functions for doing vector math and solving all of the possible vector-oriented problems you can encounter.

Playing Around

There are many aspects to making an interesting and fun game. The game play features that appear in a game can play a huge part in the success of a game. Many times, a game play feature is the factor that makes a game truly unique. An example of this is the "one shot, one kill" capability in the original *Delta Force* game. Prior to its release, first-person shooters tended to merely accumulate "hit points" until enough damage was inflicted on a character to kill it. Now, a player could take a sniper rifle, go hide in the hills, wait for an enemy to appear, and take him out with a single shot to the head.

Making It Hurt

As you've just seen, it's one thing to be able to assess a general damage value for a character, but many games like to be able to assess damage to specific parts of a player's character, like arm injuries, head shots, and so on. We are going to use Torque's built-in ability to track hit locations and use it to provide a more precise form of damage assessment. Figure 1.3 shows an orc model with its collision box outlined in white.

Torque provides us with a way to figure out where on the model a hit occurred. We can also apply the same concept to other objects. Imagine shooting the leaves and branches off of trees.

Figure 1.3 Player model collision box.

We will also discover how to make virtual pyromaniacs happy. We will blow stuff up and set cars on fire. Just your typical sunny summer's afternoon fun and frivolity. Except, of course, nothing real will actually be damaged. We'll show a dune buggy model how to have a really bad day at the races, while you, as the player, use it for target practice!

And what game would be complete without the sound of smashing windows? Figure 1.4 shows what happens when a rambunctious orc waves his exploding-bolt-firing crossbow around indiscriminately

Making 'Bots

Artificial Intelligence (AI) is a big, broad topic; we are generally only interested in computer-controlled game characters and their behavior, and that's the subject matter in Part II of the book. In game development, there are specific areas where the use of AI techniques is well-understood and well-developed. There are other areas that are certainly at the leading edge of AI use, at least in a game context.

How we refer to AI varies a bit depending on the game genre or community we are addressing. In general, the term "AI" is used. However, many action-oriented games use the term *bots* or *'bots* (with the single-quote character in front of the b), which is

Visitor: nope, busy writing
Visitor: and testing
calder: cool

Figure 1.4 Busted windows in the Great Hall.

a shortened form of the word robots. In some places, the term "NPC" is used, especially in the role-playing game world. Here, NPC means *Non-Player Character*—a character within the story of the game, but not one controlled by any player (see Figure 1.5).

Another term is *monster*. It seems odd to refer to a computer-controlled soldier character that is guarding some secret facility as a monster, but some people do. The expression rises from the use of AI monsters in such old-time games as *Doom* and *Commander Keen*. The big monster that you have to beat to make it to the next level is the *Boss*. People still use those terms, even when they seem out of place.

AI Concepts

Simulating characters using computer-controlled AI usually involves simulating three different behavioral modes: *perception*, *action*, and *reaction*.

It is necessary, to varying degrees, to inform the AI character about the world around it. When we do this, we are helping the AI character to perceive its surroundings and the events that occur. It's important to realize that your AI character can only per-

Figure 1.5 'Bots contemplating their next moves.

ceive what you tell it, according to how you've programmed it. An AI character might be programmed to detect players by "looking" around, but unless you've given it the ability to perceive the fact that incoming rockets are hitting nearby, you can fire rockets at the 'bot all day long and it will have no clue that it is in danger.

Sometimes we want to rigidly control AI characters, especially when it comes to specifying where the AI characters can go. We can use a straightforward technique called *path-following*. Torque gives us easy to use visual tools for specifying paths that our AI can follow, as shown in Figure 1.6. In the figure, the path route is specified by the path markers labeled a, b, c, d, and e (marker a's label is obscured by another object). The path is shown as a curvy loop of dots.

Action, to a 'bot, would be the ability to perform specific tasks or a sequence of tasks. A simple task would be to move to another location. Another task would be to fire at an enemy. Our goal as game programmers is to teach, or program, our AI characters to perform an appropriate number of simple tasks. We then want to be able to efficiently tie the simple tasks into larger sequences of compound tasks, and tie the compound tasks into even larger collections of compound tasks, until we get the behavior we desire.

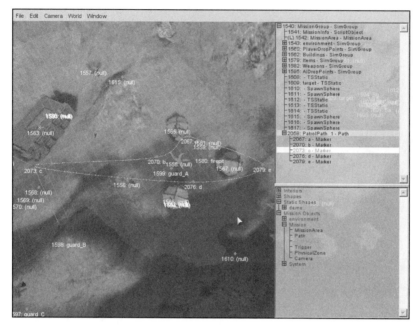

Figure 1.6 An AI path in the World Editor.

Reaction is the process of perceiving states or events, and then acting appropriately based on the perception. Using the example I cited earlier, if we can program our 'bots to sense or perceive that they are being shot at, we can then program them to react by running for cover, shooting back, or crying like a little lost kitten.

Hands On

In this book we are going to write code to invest in our AI characters a realistic ability to find their way around the game world, perceive the game world in ways that matter, act in ways that will hopefully keep players on their toes, and react appropriately to threats and events.

Torque has built-in support for AI, and we will rely on that capability—but it won't be enough. So we will script the behaviors we want. If we do it well, we can witness some really interesting *emergent behavior*—things that the 'bots will do that we didn't plan for or expect. Figure 1.7 shows two fantasy creatures, controlled by a fairly simple AI script, fighting against each other.

Figure 1.7 'Bots settling their differences.

Group Dynamics

Many game genres present the player with groups of computer-controlled players, either playing along with the player or as adversaries or obstacles to the player's advancement. Sometimes groups of computer-controlled critters may be desired simply to provide an appropriate ambience. Picture a flock of seagulls wheeling around a ship at sea.

Swarms, flocks, herds, and packs are a few of the varied group types that might be modeled in a game environment. In Part II, we will explore these concepts and create several scripts that illustrate how they work, as shown in Figure 1.8.

Getting All Artsy-Fartsy

We can't really get by without addressing the more artistic side of game development. There are several topics in the artwork and modeling chapters of *3D Game Programming All in One* that didn't get complete coverage. Part III provides some redress to that situation. Keep in mind that there will be no tutorial sections for art-related tools. You will, however, find shareware and freeware versions of suitable tools

Figure 1.8 Getting swarmed.

on the companion CD. So you will still have easy access to everything needed to do the work. If you really need to learn how to use the tools, then get yourself a copy of *3D Game Programming All in One* to accompany this book.

Details, Details

There is a slick mechanism available for the game developer that goes a long way in reducing the load on a game client's renderer, and it's called level of detail (LOD) switching.

It is similar to the concept of MIP mapping, an approach to texture mapping in which an original high-resolution texture map is scaled and filtered into multiple resolutions before it is applied to a surface. With LOD, we create multiple versions of a model, each version with fewer polygons.

The basic idea is that as we move farther away from a model, two things happen: First, the farther we are from something like a building, the more likely there will be more buildings in our field of view, and this loads down our renderer and video hardware with more and more polygons to draw; the second thing that happens is that we can discern less and less detail on the building as it recedes in the distance. Figure 1.9

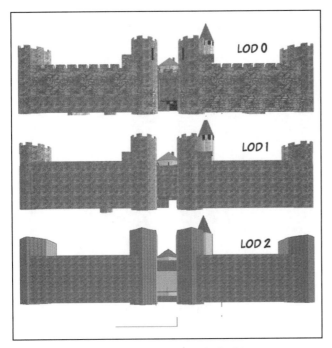

Figure 1.9 Various levels of detail of a building.

shows a building model at full LOD, and then two lesser LOD versions. Note how the least-detailed version is really just a box!

By using LOD switching, we capitalize on the second phenomenon to minimize or even completely eliminate the undesirable effects of the first. As we move away from the building, the game engine examines the apparent size of the building in our view. When the apparent size hits a certain limit, the engine stops rendering the fully detailed version of the model and starts rendering the less-detailed version. And then it monitors the apparent size until it reaches the next limit, and so on. We can take the detail levels all the way down until the apparent size is a single pixel in the distance if we want.

We can do the same things with all of our models—player characters, lampposts, vehicles, trees, and whatnot.

Portals

When modeling interior structures we can use things called *portals* (see Figure 1.10) to help the engine figure out what it has to draw and what it can ignore.

Figure 1.10 Portals in a castle interior.

This provides yet another way to speed up the rendering job and improve your game's frame rates. Portals also provide a mechanism to help control the lighting of your interior scenes. Figure 1.10 shows how portals can be used to divide an interior into multiple *zones* (also called *cells*). The room the player is viewing from is a zone; there are two zones inside the stairwell to the right, and the entire area outside the windows is a zone.

In Figure 1.11, the portals, which are CSG *brushes*, are depicted as thick black lines. A brush in CSG terms is a convex 3D shape.

When the source models are compiled into their Torque-compatible format, the compiler figures out which cells are visible from the other cells and embeds this information into the model's description. The engine then uses that information when deciding how to render the scene with that interior in it.

Let There Be Light!

Absolutely amazing things can be accomplished using judiciously applied lighting effects. Torque has several lighting mechanisms available: fxSunlight, ambient scene lighting, and interior spotlights and omni-lights.

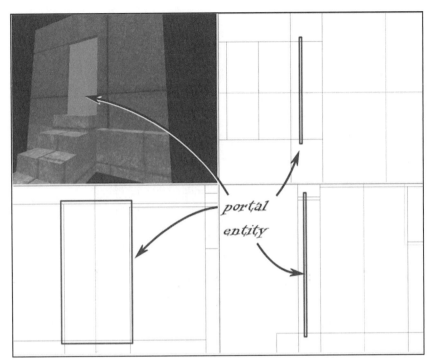

portal

entity

Figure 1.11 Portals in a building interior model.

There are also Torque-community created resources, such as the Lighting Code Pack from Synapse Gaming. You can buy the lighting pack on the GarageGames website (www.garagegames.com). Figure 1.12 is scene rendered using the lighting pack. All of the objects in the scene are lit by the dynamic light emitted by the campfire in the scene.

Using the technology in the lighting pack, one can "bake" lighting information into a scene—things like shadows. This allows for very complex scene lighting with almost no impact on rendering performance. It also makes it possible to generate dynamic lighting for things that are always moving around, and still obtain the realism and vibrancy needed to create an absolutely *killer* game world.

In Part III, we will also explore static and dynamic lights using Torque's built-in lighting capabilities. Strobe lights, runway lights, and colored lights are just a few of the effects we'll implement.

Figure 1.12 Dynamically lit nighttime scene.

Skin Shedding

To obtain variety in a game, it's often a good idea to create a large and diverse collection of models. Obviously, doing this is highly labor-intensive. There is a quicker way to achieve and celebrate diversity than simply grunting through the creation of dozens of models, and that'd be by *skin swapping*.

A simple way to achieve different skins for different models is to simply copy a model a dozen times, and then edit each copy and apply a different skin to each model. While this is certainly doable, there is still a lot of extra work involved in the copying and editing, as well as the fact that each copy of the model (and skins) takes up more disk space and memory when the game is running and the models are loaded.

A better way would be to just create a model and a set of skins once, right? You are so right! In fact, Torque has a built-in mechanism to do just that. Using this mechanism, we can assign any set of skins to a model at any time while the game is running. We can set it up so that players can choose characters based upon a preference for a skin design. We can also set it up so that a player character's skins can be changed to reflect changes in the character—such as injuries, health, new clothing, and so on.

Dynamic skin swapping is ideal for supporting team-based game play. Simply create one model or model set, and then swap in the skins that pertain to the appropriate team.

Moving Right Along

In this chapter we took a quick survey of a host of features and concepts that represent a more advanced and complete understanding of 3D game development than you saw in *3D Game Programming All in One*. As you can see, there is a lot to cover, so we want to get started right away.

In the next chapter, we'll roll up our sleeves and muck around with TorqueScript to achieve a better understanding of it and how to go about abusing it. Err, I mean using it correctly. Honest.

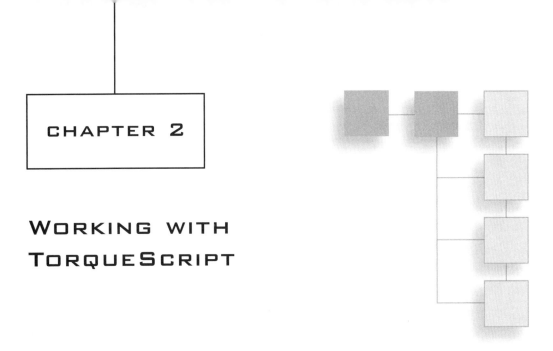

CHAPTER 2

WORKING WITH TORQUESCRIPT

In this chapter, we'll go over some of the features of TorqueScript that don't apply to programming in general. Much of TorqueScript's basic capabilities were covered in *3D Game Programming All in One*, in Chapters 4 to 7, and I won't repeat it all here.

I will, however, go into some of the more advanced and complex features in this chapter, and in later hands-on activities in Parts II and III of this book.

To mangle the words of Ben Garney of GarageGames:

> "TorqueScript occupies this sort of Zen space between procedural and Object-Oriented programming (OOP), just like JavaScript and a few others. The paradigm is 'do what works within the spirit of the system.'"

This is a pretty useful direction from which to approach TorqueScript. You get most of the important things that OOP brings to the table, like encapsulation, data hiding, polymorphism, and inheritance, but perhaps not to the extent that you can with a language like C++.

Torque Project Organization

When working with Torque, we must always keep in mind where we "are" in the code. Figure 2.1 shows the folder layout of the scripts in a typical Torque project.

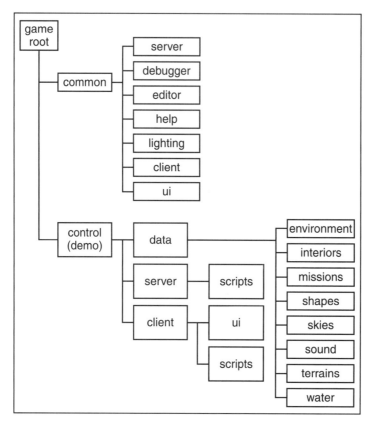

Figure 2.1 Typical TorqueScript project organization.

When we are developing our game, we will likely spend a lot of our time working with the *control code base*. This is the code that defines your game—the game play code, the artwork, and other resources. In this book's Torque folder, called \A3D, there are three control folders: demo, show, and rw.

Whenever we need to keep track of something, measure it, keep score, or make important game play decisions, we need to be writing code for the server. Usually, we will have a subfolder named server in our control folder, where all the server code will be.

When we want to define game-related GUI stuff, display artwork or play audio files, or deal with user input, we need to be writing code for the client. It's conventional to have a subfolder named client where all of the client code will reside.

Then there is that vast body of useful and necessary utility code, called the *common code base*, that is found in the folder named common. This folder has most of the code needed for the everyday, non-game-specific things that you need to make your project work, like the control definitions, server and client management and synchronization code, in-game editors, font caching, and other little odds and ends. For the most part, you won't bother with the code in here, although you might modify some of the graphic images and textures found there to match your overall game appearance.

Installing Torque

The companion CD contains all the materials you will need to follow along with the chapters: the Torque executable, the Torque Game Engine Demo ("Torque demo"), any required art and script resources, plus useful tools. Everything you need will be in the folder called \A3D.

Some of the tools, which will be located in the \A3D\TOOLS folder, may require installation before you use them. Not all of the supplied tools are required in order to follow along in the book. Some are provided as a courtesy in case the reader does not have another suitable tool for a particular task.

If the text absolutely requires you to use a specific tool to complete a procedure outlined in the book, the text will tell you where to find and install it or otherwise use it for that task.

To install Torque for use with the book, insert the companion CD into your CD drive, and follow the on-screen instructions. When you have finished the layout of the hard drive, it will match the layout of the companion CD, so anywhere you see the folder \A3D or any of its subfolders described in the text, you will be able to find it on your hard drive or on the companion CD. The \EXTRAS folder on the CD is *not* needed in order to use the book, however.

For Macintosh and Linux Users

For readers using an operating system other than one of the Windows variants, the companion CD's installation procedure will likely not work for you. The Torque demo executable in \A3D will also not work for you. However, the scripts and artwork from the book's examples *will* work on Macintosh and Linux systems providing you have the correct demo installation from the \EXTRAS folder on the companion CD installed for your operating system.

When using the installers described below, please ensure that your destination directory or folder during the installation is /A3D and not the default installer path. This is to ensure that your installation paths match the paths described in the book.

To do this, first look in the /EXTRAS folder on the companion CD and locate and install the demo for your operating system:

For Macintosh
Use /EXTRAS/Macintosh/TorqueGameEngineDemo_1_3.dmg,

For Linux

Use /EXTRAS/Linux/TorqueGameEngineDemo-1.3.bin.

After installing the appropriate Torque demo variant on your system, you must then copy the contents of the companion CD's /A3D folder into the new directory that the installer created, /A3D on whatever volume you've just installed the Torque demo to on your system.

After that you can then delete the files demo.exe, getdxver.exe, glu2d3d.dll, OpenAL32.dll, and opengl2d3d.dll from your new /A3D folder if you like—they are Windows files that you won't be able to use anyway.

One more thing: In the book, you will sometimes see references to folders that utilize full path names—like \A3D\demo\client\init.cs, for example—and sometimes see partial paths—like RESOURCES\ch2. The drive letter will never be included. This means that the path to the folder will be appropriate no matter which hard drive or volume you install to. With the partial paths, it will be obvious where the folders are. RESOURCES is always a subfolder of \A3D, for instance, as are the TOOLS, demo, common, rw, editor, and show folders.

Note

Throughout the book, you will see references to the "fps demo." This is the Torque Game Engine Demo program, set to run the fps mission. Run the fps demo by double-clicking on demo.exe in the A3D folder. After the splash screen disappears, in the main menu, click on the button near the center that says "Example: FPS Multiplayer." On the next screen, make sure the Create Server box is checked, then click on the right-facing arrow button in the bottom left part of the screen.

Quickie TorqueScript Briefing

For those of you who are new to Torque, here's the cook's tour of TorqueScript that will get you up and running. There are obviously more details behind these few points that will surface and be explained with the fullness of time.

Typelessness   With Torque, variable types are converted as necessary and can usually be used interchangeably. Variables are either *global* or *local* in scope. Global variables are prefixed with the $ character, and local scope variables are prefixed with the % character. You can only have locally scoped variables within functions or methods, but global variables are accessible everywhere.

Caselessness	TorqueScript ignores case when interpreting variable and function names. Keywords *are* case-sensitive. See Appendix A, Table A.3 for a list of TorqueScript keywords, and note that they are all lowercase.
Statement Termination	Code statements are terminated with a semicolon (;) as in many modern programming languages like C/C++ and Java. If you don't include the semicolon at the end of a Torque-Script statement, you'll probably get an error in the console.
Operators	See Appendix A, Table A.4 for a complete list of Torque-Script's operators. You will find most of them to be basic operators common to most programming languages, along with a few more advanced operators. Operator precedence is shown in Appendix A, Table A.5.
Control Structures	Like C/C++ and Java, TorqueScript provides the standard programming constructs: `if-then-else`, `for`, `while`, and `switch`.
Functions	TorqueScript provides the ability to create functions with the optional ability to return values. Arguments can be passed by value and by reference. When you define a function, the statement must begin with the `function` keyword.
Objects	Torque uses a wide assortment of objects and object-types and makes them available for use in TorqueScript, and provides for the creation of ad hoc objects (ScriptObjects). See Appendix A, Tables A.8, A.9, and A.10 for lists of script-accessible objects and Table A.2 for their methods.
Packages	Packages are the mechanism that TorqueScript uses to provide dynamic-function polymorphism. A function defined in a package will override the prior definition of a same-named function when the package is activated. Only functions can be packaged, and a function can exist in more than one package, with a different definition in each. Activating and deactivating packages determines which version will be used.

Problem-Solving Techniques

When working with TorqueScript, as with any programming language, you will eventually run into some intractable problem that you just can't beat into submission. Something isn't working right, and nothing you do seems to change it.

There are a few proven approaches that are useful when you need help beating a problem into the ground and pounding it into tiny little pieces.

Logging

The simplest, and often most effective, debugging tool is the console logging capability. Logging is available in two forms: logging to console and logging to file.

Logging to console is always enabled by the Torque engine, and log messages are visible when using Torque by opening the console window (by pressing the tilde (~) key).

Logging to file can be enabled in one of several ways. The most common method is to include the program statement:

```
setLogMode(n);
```

where *n* is one of the values in Table 2.1, into your script somewhere where it will be executed before the program code that you want to debug. In fact, the Torque demo does this for you already. If you do not otherwise specify a log mode, the Torque demo enables logging with mode 6.

You can also set the log mode through the use of a command line switch. If you launch the Torque demo from a Windows command shell or batch file, then add the `-log n` to your command line, where *n* is one of the mode values from Table 2.1.

Finally, you can turn logging on or off, or change the mode, whenever you like while running the demo by simply opening the console window with the tilde (~) key, and typing the command:

```
setLogMode(n);
```

where again, *n* is one of the modes in Table 2.1. Note that's a semicolon at the end of the command; make sure you press the Enter key after typing in the full command statement.

Logging to the console.log file is enabled by default in the Torque demo, in mode 6.

Table 2.1 setLogMode settings

Setting	Meaning
0	Disables logging to console.log file.
1	Enables logging to console.log in append mode. All entries are appended to existing log file. This means that to remove the logging info from earlier sessions, you need to delete console.log manually via the operating system (using the command shell or Explorer). The log output buffer is flushed and the console.log file is closed after every logging write operation to the file. If the first time that Torque encounters setLogMode(1) in script, it (setLogmode) is setting the log mode to 1, then logging to the console.log file will begin at that first encounter, and the output begins at the point in the script where that first encounter takes place.
2	Enables logging to console.log in overwrite mode. Every time the Torque demo is launched, the old contents of console.log are overwritten with new information. The log file remains open while the Torque demo is running. This yields higher performance, since there is only one log file open operation and one log file close operation per run session of the Torque demo. If the first time that Torque encounters setLogMode(1) in script, it (setLogmode) is setting the log mode to 2, then logging to the console.log file will begin at that first encounter, and the output begins at the point in the script where that first encounter takes place.
3	Not used.
4	Not used.
5	Same as mode 1, except all of the contents of the console window created prior to the point where the setLogMode(5); statement is encountered are flushed out to the log file when this first setLogMode(5); statement is encountered in TorqueScript.
6	Same as mode 2, except all of the contents of the console window created prior to the point where the setLogMode(6); statement is encountered are flushed out to the log file when this first setLogMode(6); statement is encountered in TorqueScript.

Checking for Compiler Errors

The first place to start is ensuring that your modifications are indeed making it into the compile *byte-code* (also called p-code) that Torque uses when it runs script code. The usual process is that Torque compiles your script into a byte-code module, then loads that module and begins execution at the top of that module. If there was already a byte-code version (.dso) of your script (.cs) module, then Torque will replace the old one with the new version it has just created.

However, if Torque discovers an error in your code, it will abort the compilation process, dump an error message into the console (and into the console.log file if logging is enabled), and then move on to the next task. The noteworthy thing is that Torque will *not* delete the old version of the byte-code.

You will then end up in the state where your source code module is different from the byte-code module. You see one thing with your eyes, and Torque sees something different.

The quickest way to detect if a programming error has caused Torque to not compile your changed source code module is to open the console and scroll back up to the beginning of the session, looking for error messages. Serious, fatal messages are printed in the console in red, whereas mere warnings are printed in gray. Look for the red error messages, and if there aren't any, peruse the warning messages to see if anything looks pertinent.

Cleaning Out the Byte-Code Modules

Finally, if you see nothing in the console or the console.log file, then locate the byte-code module in question (the .dso version) and delete it. In fact, you can safely delete all .dso modules in your script folder tree, as long as you don't touch the source files. Torque will simply rebuild all of the byte-code files. If the problem was in your source code, you should now get new behavior, possibly a serious and obvious error message or at least *some* kind of useful error message in the console window.

Using Debug Output Statements

The three functions that send messages out to the console can be used to great effect when debugging:

```
echo(text);
warn(text);
error(text);
```

echo prints *text* to the console with the standard black font; warn does the same thing, but the output is the standard font in the color gray; likewise with error, except the output is in the color red. With all three functions, *text* can be formatted according to the string rules.

With judicious application of an appropriate output message, we can track what is happening in our scripts. In general, you want to make your best guess about where the problem is taking place, and put a debug output message there. You will want to either put in a recognizable marker that can be found when scrolling through a console dump or output some important information related to the code's activity—perhaps the output of a few variables.

In order to have the console output dumped into the console.log file, make sure that you've placed a call to `setLogMode` somewhere in your code where it will be executed before the program reaches the problem areas. A simpler way is to use the `-log` command line switch, followed by a space, and then the number 0,1, or 2. If you use the 0, you will disable logging. Using the 1 enables logging such that each new session is added to the end of the log file. Using 2 enables logging such that the previous log file is overwritten.

To put in a progress marker, you can do something like this:

```
error("*********************************************");
```

This will create a line like this in the console.log file:

```
*********************************************
```

In the console itself, the line of asterisks will be red in color and easier to spot. You could use `warn` to get gray output and `echo` to get black output in the console.

Often, when using debug output like this, if the game hangs or locks up, the last line of output doesn't actually make it to the log file, even though the line has been executed. The way to deal with this is to simply put two identical error lines, one right after the other. If the game hangs, only the first line will be printed, but now you will have narrowed down your bug search. Next, move your two marker lines farther down in the code until they stop appearing in the console log. When that happens, you'll have bracketed the location of the problem.

If you need to examine the contents of important variables, let's say, X, Y, and the player's name, you might use a statement like:

```
echo("player's name:" @ playerName @ "   X=" @ %X @ "   Y=" @ %Y);
```

You would end up with output in your console log looking like this:

```
player's name:bozotheclown  X=123  Y=456
```

Using trace

Torque has a very handy function called trace that can be used to figure out exactly what code is being executed as a script is run. This is especially helpful when you are puzzling out some logic problem. You need to stick in the trace statement well before the code that you are interested in. Enable tracing by using trace(true). Stick in a call to trace(off) to disable tracing when the code is past the area of interest.

You can also enable tracing simply by opening the console and typing

```
trace(true);
```

Take a look at this bit of console output:

```
--------- Initializing MOD: Common ---------
Loading compiled script common/client/canvas.cs.
Loading compiled script common/client/audio.cs.


--------- Initializing MOD: Torque demo ---------
Loading compiled script demo/client/init.cs.
Loading compiled script demo/server/init.cs.
Loading compiled script demo/data/init.cs.
Loading compiled script demo/data/terrains/highplains/propertyMap.cs.
```

When we turn on trace, the output looks like this:

```
--------- Parsing Arguments ---------
Entering [demo]parseArgs()
   Entering [common]parseArgs()
   Leaving [common]parseArgs() - return
Leaving [demo]parseArgs() - return
Entering [demo]onStart()
   Entering [common]onStart()


--------- Initializing MOD: Common ---------
      Entering initCommon()
         Loading compiled script common/client/canvas.cs.
         Loading compiled script common/client/audio.cs.
      Leaving initCommon() - return
   Leaving [common]onStart() - return
```

```
--------- Initializing MOD: Torque demo ---------
  Loading compiled script demo/client/init.cs.
  Loading compiled script demo/server/init.cs.
  Loading compiled script demo/data/init.cs.
  Loading compiled script demo/data/terrains/highplains/propertyMap.cs.
  Entering initServer()
```

Using dump

We can look at the current values of properties for any object in the game if we have the object's handle, or at least a variable that's in scope that contains the handle. We do this by opening the console window with the tilde (~) key and calling that object with its inherited dump method, like this:

```
%player.dump();
```

In this case, assuming %player holds a valid Player object handle, the call to dump will yield the following reams of information:

```
Member Fields:
  dataBlock = "LightMaleHumanArmor"
  position = "202.197 268.211 257.386"
  rotation = "0 0 1 111.172"
  scale = "1 1 1"
Tagged Fields:
  client = "1600"
  invCrossbowAmmo = "10"
  mountVehicle = "1"
Methods:
  applyDamage() -
  applyImpulse() -
  applyRepair() -
  canCloak() -
  checkDismountPoint() -
  clearControlObject() -
  clearDamageDt() -
  clearInventory() -
  clearScopeToClient() -
  Damage() -
  decInventory() -
  delete() -
```

```
dump() -
getAIRepairPoint() -
getCameraFov() -
getClassName() -
getControllingClient() -
getControllingObject() -
getControlObject() -
getDamageFlash() -
getDamageLevel() -
getDamageLocation() -
getDamagePercent() -
getDamageState() -
getDataBlock() -
getEnergyLevel() -
getEnergyPercent() -
getEyePoint() -
getEyeTransform() -
getEyeVector() -
getForwardVector() -
getGhostID() -
getGroup() -
getId() -
getImageAmmo() -
getImageLoaded() -
getImageSkinTag() -
getImageState() -
getImageTrigger() -
getInventory() -
getMountedImage() -
getMountedObject() -
getMountedObjectCount() -
getMountedObjectNode() -
getMountNodeObject() -
getMountSlot() -
getMuzzlePoint() -
getMuzzleVector() -
getName() -
getObjectBox() -
getObjectMount() -
getPendingImage() -
```

```
getPosition() -
getRechargeRate() -
getRepairRate() -
getScale() -
getShapeName() -
getSkinName() -
getSlotTransform() -
getState() -
getTransform() -
getType() -
getVelocity() -
getWhiteOut() -
getWorldBox() -
getWorldBoxCenter() -
incInventory() -
isCloaked() -
isDestroyed() -
isDisabled() -
isEnabled() -
isHidden() -
isImageFiring() -
isImageMounted() -
isMounted() -
isPilot() -
kill() -
maxInventory() -
mountImage() -
mountObject() -
mountVehicles() -
onInventory() -
pauseThread() -
pickup() -
playAudio() -
playCelAnimation() -
playDeathAnimation() -
playDeathCry() -
playPain() -
playThread() -
save() -
schedule() -
```

```
scopeToClient() -
setActionThread() -
setArmThread() -
setCameraFov() -
setCloaked() -
setControlObject() -
setDamageDt() -
setDamageFlash() -
setDamageLevel() -
setDamageState() -
setDamageVector() -
setDataBlock() -
setEnergyLevel() -
setHidden() -
setImageAmmo() -
setImageLoaded() -
setImageTrigger() -
setInventory() -
setInvincibleMode() -
setName() -
setRechargeRate() -
setRepairRate() -
setScale() -
setScopeAlways() -
setShapeName() -
setSkinName() -
setThreadDir() -
setTransform() -
setVelocity() -
setWhiteOut() -
startFade() -
stopAudio() -
stopThread() -
throw() -
throwObject() -
unmount() -
unmountImage() -
unmountObject() -
use() -
```

Whew! That's a pile of stuff. Notice that there are almost 4 pages of methods for the Player class. Many of those are Player class methods, some of them are inherited ShapeBase class methods, and the rest are GameBase class methods. Way back at the front are a bunch of properties ("member fields" and "tagged fields").

There are tons of methods distributed among all the different classes. If you need to know which methods are available for any given class, just use dump.

You can use dump in several ways. As I showed you in the example, you can dump a variable that you know contains a handle to the object. If you happen to actually know the object handle value you can use that instead, like this:

```
1607.dump();
```

You can also use a datablock name to get a dump, like this:

```
LightMaleHumanArmor.dump();
```

Using the In-Game Object Browser

Easier to use than the dump command is the in-game object browser called tree. Again, this is a console command. Open the console window with the tilde (~) key, and then type **tree();** in the console, and two windows will appear, as shown in Figure 2.2.

Figure 2.2 In-game object browser.

Using the browser window on the right, you can rummage through and find any object in the game. When you click on an object to select it, its contents appear in the editor window on the left. You can maneuver the windows around the screen to your best advantage.

Once you've found the object you are interested in, you can change its values in the editor window in real time as the game is running. Hit the Apply button to commit the changes, then close the windows so that you can go look to see how things change.

The TorqueScript Source Debugger

When all else fails, it's time to call in the big guns. Torque has a built-in run-time source code debugging capability that uses *telnet* (an internet communications protocol) to allow you to log into a running server using another instance of Torque as a client. The client and the server can be on the same computer or on different computers halfway across the world from each other.

Take heed! This is not for the faint of heart. The TorqueScript Source Debugger lets you step through program code and execute program statements and function one line at a time. It will also allow you to view and edit the contents of variables at run time, and it gives you full control over the remote game server through a built-in console. Note that the code you want to debug will *need* to be running on the server, whether that server is remote on another computer or running as another instance of Torque (in dedicated mode) on your development computer (along side the client and all your other development tools).

A Tour of the Debugger

The client-side of the debugger presents a graphical interface (See Figure 2.3) with various panes to provide different kinds of information and control, as described in Table 2.2. Some of the panes contain additional internal controls and widgets that are also described in Table 2.2.

The Source Code Viewer pane contains a number of markers that tell you things about the state of the program. Figure 2.4 shows the Source Code Viewer pane, with the markers pointed out.

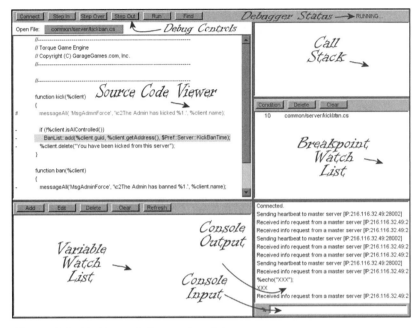

Figure 2.3 The TorqueScript run-time debugger.

Table 2.2 TorqueScript Debugger Panes

Pane	Description	
Debug Controls	Six buttons that control the program execution while the debugger is active:	
	Connect	Connects the client interface to the debugger server.
	Step In	Causes the debugger to enter the next script function encountered, displaying its code.
	Step Over	Causes the program execution to not enter the next function, but to only evaluate any result from its execution.
	Step Out	Causes program execution to run to the end of a function, and then exit to the calling code, returning a value if required. Program execution halts when the program counter is situated at the calling code.
	Run	Causes normal program execution to resume. Program execution will not halt until another breakpoint is encountered.
	Find	Used to locate a string of text within an open source module.

Table 2.2 TorqueScript Debugger Panes (continued)

Pane	Description	
Source Code Viewer	Displays the textual source code of control script (.cs) or interface script (.gui) modules. Also contains several informational widgets:	
	Program counter	Indicates which program statement will be executed next.
	Statement marker	Indicates a valid, executable program statement.
	Breakpoint marker	Indicates a statement that has a breakpoint assigned to it.
	Source File selector	Provides a pop-up list of source files from which to select the file containing the source code to be examined.
Variable Watch List	Five buttons managing and manipulating script variables at run time:	
	Add	Opens a dialog that accepts the name of a variable and adds that variable to this watch list.
	Edit	Opens a dialog that allows you to change the value of the selected variable at run time.
	Delete	Removes the selected variable from this watch list.
	Clear	Sets the value of the selected variable to null.
	Refresh	Updates the values of all variables in this watch list.
Call Stack	This pane displays a list of all functions entered to get to the current point in the program code. The function names are listed in FILO order—the top function in the list is the last function called and will be the function that the program counter is currently in, as seen in the Source Code Viewer pane. The stack refers only to functions entered since the debug session began.	
Debugger Status	Indicates the state of the debugger on the server. Possible values are:	
	NOT CONNECTED	Debugger client is not connected to a server.
	CONNECTED	Debugger client is connected to a server, but has not yet stopped any program execution.
	BREAK	Program counter has encountered a breakpoint and halted program execution at the breakpoint.
	RUNNING	Program code is currently executing and will continue until a breakpoint is encountered.
Breakpoint Watch List	Breakpoints that have been set are listed here. There are three controls:	
	Condition	Opens a dialog in which you can set the conditions under which the selected breakpoint is active. The condition takes the form of a regular valid TorqueScript conditional statement (ie. $\%x > 10$).

Pane	Description	
	Delete	Deletes the selected breakpoint. It has a bug, unfortunately. It will only work to delete a breakpoint if the breakpoint has a condition set. Otherwise the Delete button has no effect.
	Clear	Removes all breakpoints from the list.
Console Output	Works the same as the output window of the regular console, except that it is obviously smaller. Colored output messages work normally.	
Console Input	Works the same as the input field of the regular console, including history recall.	

Figure 2.4 shows the Source Code Viewer pane. You can't edit the source code here; instead, it is used to show you the progress of the program counter (represented by the symbol "=>" on the left side of a statement line). The program counter always points to the next statement to be executed.

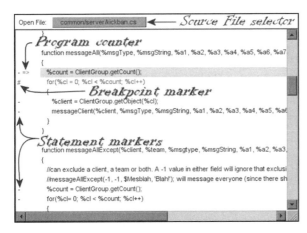

Figure 2.4 The Source Code Viewer pane.

Valid and executable program statements are indicated by the statement marker ("-"), while statements that have a breakpoint set at them are indicated by the breakpoint marker ("#").

To insert a breakpoint, click once on a statement marker, and the marker will be changed to the breakpoint marker. The breakpoint will appear over on the right in the Breakpoint Watch List pane (See Figure 2.5). You can clear that breakpoint if you have to by clicking on it again, or by pressing the Delete button for a selected

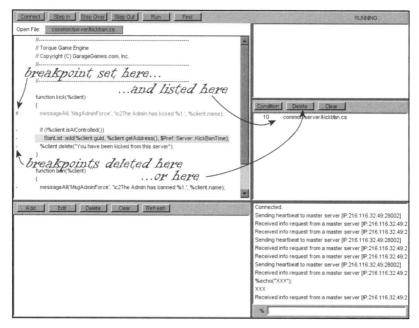

Figure 2.5 Setting breakpoints.

breakpoint in the Breakpoint Watch List pane (although due to a bug, the Delete button only works on breakpoints that have a condition set).

The Breakpoint Watch List pane (Figure 2.6) shows you all of the breakpoints you currently have set. The Condition button is used to turn a regular breakpoint into a conditional breakpoint. Any standard TorqueScript conditional statement can be used here, including comparisons and boolean statements, as long as:

- ▪ the entire expression can correctly evaluate to true or false, and
- ▪ any variables used in the expression are in scope at the time when the watched breakpoint statement has been reached.

For example:

```
%i == 16
(%x <= 800) && (%y <= 600)
Sky.materialList $= "~/data/skies/sky_storm.dml"
```

are all valid breakpoint condition expressions (assuming that their variables are in scope). The expressions are *not* valid program statements as written, and shouldn't be anyway.

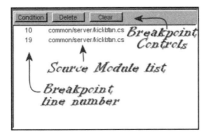

Figure 2.6 The Breakpoint Watch List pane.

N o t e

If ever you were wondering about the usefulness or ability of TorqueScript as a programming language, get a load of this: The TorqueScript Source Debugger is not only for debugging TorqueScript source code—it is also written entirely with the TorqueScript programming language! If you want to take a gander at the code, poke your nose into the file \common\debugger\debugger.cs.

The Variable Watch List is where you can enter variables whose contents you want to examine (see Figure 2.7). The variables can be global or local variables. The only caveats are that the variable must be a valid variable that is in scope at the time you examine it. Typically you would examine the variables when the program counter has encountered a breakpoint and halted program execution.

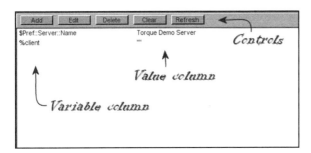

Figure 2.7 The Variable Watch List pane.

You can also change the values of variables by selecting the variable and pressing the Edit button. This is an extremely valuable capability that allows you to quickly try different program execution paths without having to rewrite and reload any source modules.

Enabling the Debugger

To use the TorqueScript Source Debugger, you will need to run two instances of Torque. You will need to launch a server instance of Torque and a client instance. There are a few different ways to go about this.

The Server Debug Host

If you only have one computer, then you really have only one option, and that is to launch a dedicated server version of Torque. This will be your server debugger host.

Step One

To create a dedicated server version of Torque, run a command shell, change to the A3D directory, and launch the dedicated server using this command:

```
demo.exe -dedicated -mission demo/data/missions/fps.mis
```

Of course you can use a different mission file than fps.mis if you like.

Now, it's important to realize that all of the scripts that you will be able to access with the debugger must be loaded on the server. In normal situations, this means that you can only use the debugger on server-side code. However, if you really need to get at some client-side module, then you need to load the module on the server with a call to exec. Fortunately, you can do this manually via the console interface whenever you need to. Not all client-side scripts are necessarily going to work correctly in this way, but most will.

The other server options you have are to run the server on a different computer on your LAN (as long as it has a TCP/IP address), or run the server anywhere else in the world providing there is Internet access.

Once the server is running, you will end up with a standard Windows console window (not the nifty Torque console). This console is less capable than the Torque console, but it will do for our needs.

Step Two

Now you need to turn on the debugger monitor on the server. Do this by entering the following command in the console:

```
dbgSetParameters(5432, "sup");
```

The first parameter, 5432, is the TCP/IP port that the debugger will monitor looking for debugger clients that want to connect. The second parameter is the security password. I suggest that you **don't** use the settings I show you here, since everyone who uses this book will have access to the same information. Pick your own port number and password and record them somewhere; you will need to use them again on the client.

If everything has gone smoothly, you will see this message in the server console:

```
Binding server port to default IP
```

Next up, the client.

The Client Debug Interface

Once the server is set up and running, you then must run the client. You merely need to run the Torque demo as usual and then load the debugger script. The debugger script is written in such a way that the debugger client interface automatically will be invoked after the script loads.

Caution

If you are planning to run both the server and the client on the same computer (and most people will), then you will most likely want to run your dedicated server in the same folder as the client. This is perfectly reasonable and will work just fine. It's the way I do it. There is one small issue though that might matter to you: Only one of the two instances will be able to access the console.log file. The easiest way around this is simple: Make a copy of your \A3D folder, perhaps called \A3DServer (or whatever you choose). You can then run the dedicated server from that other folder and the client from the original folder. That way both instances will have unfettered access to the console.log file. However, if you are using the debugger, you may have little need to use the console log file anyway.

Step Three

Launch the normal Torque demo.

Once the client is running (you only need to go as far as the main menu), open the console with the tilde ("~") key. You can then load the debugger client by typing in this command:

```
exec("common/debugger/debugger.cs");
```

This will bring up the debugger GUI in the back, behind the console window, so you need to close the console window by pressing the tilde key again. There you go! One source code debugger, made to order.

Well, it's cool and all, but not of much use yet. The next step is to connect to the server.

Step Four

Click on the Connect button, and you will get the dialog shown in Figure 2.8.

Figure 2.8 The Connect to Server dialog.

Now's the time to find where you recorded the port and password information you used when running the dedicated Torque debugger server back in Step Two. Enter the values for the port and password.

For the IP Address field, use 127.0.0.1, which is the reserved IP address that represents the *localhost* (the computer you are currently using). If the debugger server is on another computer on your LAN or another computer out there in big scary Internet world, you will need to know the IP address of that other computer and enter that address in the IP Address field instead.

Click on the Open button, and in short order, Lord willin' and the creek don't rise, the Debugger Status field will change from NOT CONNECTED to CONNECTED. We're in!

Using the Debugger

To use the debugger, you will need to open a code module of interest, presumably one that you are having trouble with. Do this by clicking on the Source File selector in the Source Code Viewer pane at upper left. Choose the file to be examined from the pop-up list that appears. For the sake of argument (and who doesn't love a good one, eh?), let's open up the player.cs control script module. Scroll through the Source File selector's pop-up list until you see the entry demo/server/scripts/player.cs, and select that one. It's pretty close to the top of the list.

Once the script appears in the Source Code Viewer pane, scroll through it until you find the method Armor::onEnterLiquid. To insert a breakpoint, click on the statement marker at the line where you want the program execution to stop. Note that you can't insert a breakpoint on a comment-only line. For our purposes now, set the breakpoint on the statement:

```
case 0: //Water
```

If the breakpoint is in the execution path, then the program counter will stop there in short order, and the entire server will be sitting there, twiddling its thumbs waiting for you to make up your mind what you want to do next, and to bloody well get on with it already. However, notice that nothing like that happens right now, and that's solely because the breakpoint's code is *not* in the execution path. So we have to do something about that. Since I told you to put the break in `onEnterLiquid`, I guess we need to find some liquid to enter. Like maybe a risin' creek… stand easy on that little tidbit, we'll get back to it in a minute.

But first, I want to show you something really nifty. You will recall that we connected to the debugger server from our client's main menu. Well, we don't have any pressing need to be in the main menu. Why don't we go and connect to the game server that is being hosted by the debugger server? Yup, we can do that!

You will probably remember that the debugger interface has its own console input and output windows, right? Well that console executes on the debugger server, and not locally on the client. We can still use the regular console on the client by pressing the tilde key. So open the normal console with the tilde key, and then type in this command:

```
Canvas.popDialog(DebuggerGui);
```

Poof! We're back to the main menu! Of course, that pesky console window is in the way, so press the tilde key to get rid of it. Now, click on the FPS demo button there in the menu screen. In the next screen, do *not* click in the Create Server checkbox. Just click on the right arrow. You will come to a server selection screen; press the Query LAN button. You will see your server sitting there, happily serving away. Click on it, and then click the right arrow button. You will soon join the mission being run on the server.

After your guy spawns in, run over towards the water where the pier is. It's right in front of the big gray blocky building (the Great Hall). Run right into the water, and keep going. At some point when you are fully submerged, you will notice everything stop! What happened?

Well, open your console window, and type in the following command:

```
Canvas.pushDialog(DebuggerGui);
```

Poof again! Back in the debugger. Throw away the console, and take a look at the statement where you placed the breakpoint earlier. Notice that there is now a "=>" symbol in front of it. That's the program counter, and program execution stopped when it got here, because we found some liquid to enter, and we entered it. And then everything came to a screeching halt.

Click on the Run button. The program counter will disappear as everything starts chugging away again. Open the console, and flip back to the game view by hitting the up arrow key and recalling the popDialog command you used earlier, and press the Enter key.

Poofaroonie! Back to the game, and notice that we aren't stuck anymore. Move your guy back up out of the water; we're going to do this again, but slightly differently. Take note of your health bar at the left. It should be full up to the top, or pretty darn close.

Let's flip back to the debugger, using the method (pushDialog) I just showed you, and this time move our attention to the Variable Watch List pane. Click on the Add button, and when the Add a Watch Expression dialog appears, type **%type**. A new entry in the watch list will appear, with %type on the left hand side.

Now flip back to the game again, using your newfound powers (popDialog). Run into the water, without a care in the world, not even concerned about sharks. When the game freezes up (sharks?!), switch back to the debugger, and look at the %type entry in the watch list. It will have a value of 1. If you look in the code, you will see that 1 is the value for ocean water, and you will also see that nothing happens when you enter ocean water. You will also recall that after we went in the first time, and then checked our health, it was full, or almost so.

Let's do this: select the %type entry in the watch list, and then press the Edit button. Change the value to 4. Notice from the code that 4 is lava. Press the Edit button in the dialog to submit the change.

Now press the Run button again up in the Source Code Viewer pane. The program counter will disappear, racing off into the innards of your computer. Time to switch back to the game again.

Back in the game, you should be able to move once more and look at that! Your health is way down, almost gone! That's lava for you. Unhealthy.

There's one more handy feature to try out, and that's the conditional break. Go back to the debugger, and select the breakpoint you created earlier in the Breakpoint Watch List pane on the right. Click on the Condition button, and you will get the dialog shown in Figure 2.9. In the top field enter this:

```
%type == 3.
```

Figure 2.9 The Set the Break Condition dialog.

And leave the other fields blank for now. Go back to the game and go into the water. Notice that your movement doesn't freeze, even though you still have the breakpoint set? That's because the breakpoint now will only be operative if the condition of the breakpoint is met. And since the water is ocean water, type 1, the breakpoint will not work. Now go back and delete that breakpoint, and add a new one at the same place. Set the condition the same, but this time set the middle field to 3. Then go back to the game and run in and out of the water at least three times.

Ha!

See that? The movement froze on the third try. Care to guess why? That's right, after the program counter encountered the breakpoint three times, the condition became invalid, so the breakpoint started behaving as if there was no condition attached.

Objects

In a 3D world, pretty well everything is a virtual object, and it behooves a good game engine to allow us to manipulate things in the world as objects. TorqueScript provides flexible and powerful tools and mechanisms for dealing with its objects, which we'll explore in this and subsequent sections.

Creating Objects

The first order of business is to show you the syntax used when we create objects, and see how inheritance can come into play. The general form for creating a new object is

```
variableIdentifier = new ObjectIdentifier(Name[:Provenience])
[{
    [intrinsic_datablock_property] = value;
    [scripted_datablock_property] = value;
}];
```

The new keyword tells TorqueScript that we are creating a new object here, and it is to be called whatever is specified by *ObjectIdentifier*. A couple of optional arguments are available. If we leave them both out, we will have an *anonymous object*. If we do that, then we need to assign the result of the creation to a variable, as specified by *variableIdentifier*. Something like this will do:

```
$myObject = new SomeObjectClass();
```

That assumes that SomeObject is a valid object class. Note that the ensuing code block shown in the general form between the two braces was left out. You can do that if you don't have any properties to create or set. Don't forget the closing semicolon for the statement, though.

The Name term is an optional valid identifier. *Provenience* is an existing datablock that will act as the source for all properties (and their values) that this new datablock will inherit, if you choose to have it do so. The properties that directly belong to the provenience datablock's namespace are simply copied into the new datablock's name space.

For example, let's create a new Item:

```
new Item()
{
};
```

That creates an Item, but doesn't specify a name or any of the properties, so all of the properties will get their values from the default values provided by the C++ Item class constructor. Let's override some properties:

```
new Item(AnItem)
{
   position = "100 100 100";
   friction = 2;
};
```

This time we've created an Item imaginatively named AnItem and positioned it at (0,0,0). If this object is thrown, or collides with something and is propelled across the ground, the friction property will quickly slow it to a stop as the object slides across the surface.

```
new Item(AnotherItem : AnItem)
{
   position = "150 150 100";
};
```

Okay, now we have an Item named `AnotherItem` and it is positioned at (150,150,100). In addition to the redefined `position` property, it will inherit all the properties of `AnItem`, which means it will have the same value in the `friction` property.

```
new Item(SlickItem : AnItem)
{
   position = "200 200 100";
   friction = 0.25;
   volume = 50;
};
```

This time we've created an `Item` named `SlickItem` positioned at (200,200,100). This time we override not only the `position` property but also the `friction` property, giving the object a negligible 0.25 amount of friction—this tends to make items slide for a long, long time. As with `AnotherItem`, this object inherits the remainder of the intrinsic properties and their values that have not been overridden from `AnItem`. Finally, it adds a scripted property named `volume` and initializes it to 50.

Working with Objects

Once we have created an object, we'll probably want to start to do things to it in our game. There are a number of object-related functions and methods available in TorqueScript for working with objects:

- **nameToID(*identifier|string*)** When you pass in an object's identifier variable (or a string name) this function will return the object's handle, like this:

  ```
  %zoneID = nameToID ("FloatySpeedupZone");
  ```

  or

  ```
  %zoneID = nameToID (%zoneName);
  ```

  assuming, of course, that `%zoneName` and `"FloatySpeedupZone"` have indeed been assigned an object.

- **isObject(*identifier|string*)** This function is used to check whether the identifier (or a string name) refers to a valid object or not. When called, it returns `true` if the identifier refers to a real object, `false` otherwise. You can use it like this:

  ```
  if ( isObject(%zoneID) )
     doSomethingCool();
  ```

- **.getName()** When called from an object, this method will return its name, if it has one. Do this:

```
%zoneName = %zoneID.getName();
```

- **.setName(*identifier|string*)** When called from an object, this method will set the identifier (or string name) to be the object's name. Do it this way:

```
%zoneID.setName("FloatySpeedupZone");
```

or this way:

```
%zoneName = "FloatySpeedupZone";
%zoneID.setName(%zoneName);
```

- **.getID()** This is a method common to all objects that is used for the same purposes as nameToID. When called from an object, this returns that object's handle, like this:

```
%zoneIDcopy = zoneID.getID();
```

- **.getClassName()** When called from an object, this method will return the name of its class, like this:

```
%zoneClass = %zoneID.getClassName();
```

Tip

When we call an object's method from that object (or using a namespace, like GameBase), Torque always *implicitly* passes that object's handle into the method as the first argument. So be aware that you need to *explicitly* extract that argument list with a variable. It's purely positional—you can use any locally scoped variable identifier you want, although the convention is to use %this as the identifier since it matches nicely with the C/C++ this keyword. But you could use any identifier. Sometimes people use %obj instead of %this.

When you call MyObject.DoSomething(%anArg), then your object's method needs to be defined this way:

```
Function MyObject::DoSomething(%this, %arg)
{
    //blah blah
}
```

This way, the contents of %anArg that you provided when you called MyObject.DoSomething will arrive in your method cradled in the arms of the %arg variable, with Torque magically putting the handle for MyObject into the variable %this.

All objects in Torque are assigned unique ID numbers. We refer to these numbers as the *handles* of the objects. We will refer to a variable that contains such a number as the *handle identifier* or *object name* as a matter of convenience. In script code we can directly use the handle value when using an object, but it is more common, and useful, to deposit the value into a variable and use that variable's identifier. Assuming 1234 is the ID of a Mexican Jumping Bean object, then:

```
1234.jump();
```

and

```
%beanID = 1234;
%beanID.jump();
```

would do the same thing with the same object. If we use the object's handle value (the number) to work with the object, we will get higher performance—the script executive doesn't have to do as much looking-up in its tables to find the number. However we normally won't know what the number will be when our code runs, so we use the identifiers. We usually get the identifier values from Torque when we create an object programmatically, as a return value from some other function call, or passed into our function by Torque when our function is called.

As you can see, handles can be used to access object elements like properties and methods. For any object, if you want to discover which intrinsic and scripted variables it encompasses, and which methods it has, you can use the `dump` method from the console described earlier.

Datablock Objects

There is a special kind of object that I call a *datablock object* that is used quite a bit in Torque. When we create an object, we can provide it with a property that points to a Torque storage mechanism called a *datablock*. The purpose of a datablock is to provide a "one-stop shopping" location of specific data about an object class.

So, we can have objects that encapsulate all of their intrinsic properties and methods within themselves, and whose properties can change dynamically as a game progresses. And then we can have other objects that have all of those same capabilities, plus contain a property that holds the handle to a datablock that contains more properties and methods whose contents never change! But wait! There's more! A datablock on the server has exactly the same handle on every client! Okay, okay, I'll calm down now, or I will after I point out that normal objects don't carry the same handle as they propagate from the server to the clients—every normal object instance is considered unique.

Why on earth would we want to do this, you might be asking yourself. Simple, I say calmly. It's a nifty feature. You have object data that changes dynamically (normal object properties), and object info that is static or constant and protected from change during the run of a mission (datablock properties).

A few more tidbits: Datablock *names* are not transmitted to clients from a server, only the handles are; datablocks aren't scoped or otherwise culled—if you have a datablock's handle, you can always get at its contents no matter where you are in your program, or whether you are on a client or the server.

Note

It's terminology time! An object is an object—it has properties and methods, and you can make many instances of an object class, with each instance having its own property values. We can call these *normal objects*.

A datablock itself is a kind of object, but we only ever call it a *datablock* and pretend we don't notice its "objectness."

An object that contains a property that holds a datablock handle is called a *datablock object*.

You know, people notice things. Eventually, everyone who works with TorqueScript sits back, rubs the side of his nose, and mutters: "Why are some objects made with datablocks and others aren't?" It's because objects that are placed in the game world always fall into one of two general categories:

A. All of an object's properties are likely to be unique at some time or another to different instances of the object.

B. An object has a substantial number of properties that probably need to be shared between instances of that object class.

Category A describes a set of objects that don't need datablocks so they just aren't created with datablocks. Category B, however, consists of objects that *would* benefit from using datablocks. As I pointed out earlier, unlike normal objects, you are only allowed to have a single instance of any datablock. Furthermore, objects that are created using datablocks all share the *same instance* of that datablock.

Table 2.3 should clarify the difference:

Table 2.3 Normal vs. Datablock Objects

Normal Object	Datablock Object
1. Created directly from a C++ class	1. Created directly from a C++ class
2. Contains intrinsic properties and methods	2. Contains intrinsic properties and methods
3. May contain scripted properties	3. May contain scripted properties
	4. *Requires* a datablock property pointing to an existing datablock

Compare the following normal object declaration of a MessageVector:

```
new MessageVector(TheMsgVector)
{
    lineSpacing = 32;
    lineContinuedIndex = 10
    allowedMatches[0] = "http";
    allowedMatches[1] = "Torqueserver";
    matchColor = "0 0 128";
    maxColorIndex = 16;
};
```

to this declaration of a datablock object of the Item class:

```
datablock ItemData(TheItemData)
{
    category = "Doodads";
    shapeFile = "~/data/things/doodad.dts";
};
new Item(TheItem)
{
    position = "100 100 100";
    rotation = "1 0 0 0";
    scale = "1 1 1";
    dataBlock = TheItemData;
};
```

There you go. In addition to overriding its intrinsic properties, the creation statement for the Item object, named TheItem, sets the value of the dataBlock property with the name of an existing datablock—in fact, the specific datablock is TheItemData. This makes `TheItemData` a datablock object, while the `Item` named `TheItem` and the `MessageVector` named `TheMsgVector` are normal objects.

As you've probably figured out on your own, there are a few different ways we can get our grubby little fingers on the contents of the `TheItemData` datablock. We can simply dereference the `dataBlock` property through the Item class to get the datablock's name, like this:

```
$db = TheItem.dataBlock;
echo($db);
```

This will yield output that looks like this:

```
==>echo($db);
119
```

Then you can access the datablock's properties using the handle 119, like this:

```
Echo(119.category);
==>echo(119.category);
doodads
```

The 119 value is made up, so you should try this out yourself in the console in the fps demo. Look around for something like an ammo box, and get its handle from the Editor Inspector. (Press the F11 key in-game to get the Word Editor, then choose the Editor Inspector from the Window menu.) Instead of using the name `TheItem`, use the handle of the ammo object you found, and then extract the datablock's handle, like this (assuming 123 is a valid handle, which it may not be):

```
$db = 123.dataBlock;
echo($db);
```

and then you get something like this (the number will be different):

```
==>echo($db);
456
```

So now dig into the datablock:

```
Echo(456.category);
==>echo(119.category);
Ammo
```

There is an easier way to do this:

```
Echo(123.dataBlock.category);
==>Echo(123.dataBlock.category);
Ammo
```

We simply drill down through the references to get to the property we are interested in.

Creating Datablock Objects

We'll spend a bit more time on datablocks and datablock objects to reinforce the use of inheritance. This datablock object:

```
new StaticShape(AShape)
{
    position = "0 0 0";
    rotation = "1 0 0 0";
    scale = "1 1 1";
    dataBlock = SomeShapeData;
};
```

creates a StaticShape named AShape. It defines the position, rotation, and the scale. Additionally, it tells the engine to use datablock SomeShapeData to initialize this object's datablock. From now on, this object will always be associated with the datablock SomeShapeData. It's a shame really. Nice object like that getting mixed up with the likes of… oh, never mind. In fact, look here:

```
new StaticShape(AnotherShape: AShape)
{
    position = "0 10 0";
};
```

This time we've created a new StaticShape. This one is named AnotherShape. It inherits all the properties of AShape but overrides the position. The important thing to understand is that it still shares datablock ShapeData with the other instance of StaticShape, AShape. In other words, we have two instances of StaticShape that share one instance of the datablock SomeShapeData.

It's useful to know that in general, for every class that has a datablock property, there is usually a specific datablock class. These datablock classes are usually intuitively named in a manner illustrated by Table 2.4, by tacking the term "Data" to the end of the object class name. You can see a complete list of Torque datablock classes in Table A.8 in Appendix A.

Table 2.4 Example Datablock Names

Object Class Using Datablock	Datablock Name
Item	ItemData
Vehicle	VehicleData
StaticShape	StaticShapeData

Declaring Datablocks

Okay, what do we know? We've seen that datablocks are similar to objects in the game world and that only a single instance of any datablock is created and shared between any number of datablock-using objects.

Interestingly enough, objects are created, but datablocks aren't. No, they don't just spring into being on the seventh day or percolate out of some cosmic chunk of quantum probability. You see, datablocks are declared.

Here's how:

```
datablock DatablockClassIdentifier(Name [:Provenience])
{
    category = "CategoryNameString";
    [intrinsic_datablock_property] = value;
    [scripted_datablock_property] = value;
};
```

Beyond the datablock declaration keyword, we present a datablock class: this would be one of the classes in Table A.8 in Appendix A. The Name term is an optional valid identifier. Provenience is an existing datablock that acts as a source for all properties and methods that this new datablock will inherit, if you choose to have it do so. The properties and methods that directly belong to the provenient datablock's namespace are simply copied into the new datablock's namespace.

Now, category is one of the property identifiers, and it is usually set to a string that identifies the datablock for the Editor Creator.

The rest of the definition is pretty fluid—we can override intrinsic properties just as we did with objects earlier, and we can add our own properties to the datablock definition.

In all cases, once the datablock gets loaded and propagated to all clients at mission load time, the values it carries in its properties are immutable for the duration of the mission.

ScriptObjects

We've seen two kinds of objects, normal objects and datablock objects, both of which are derived from classes generated internally within Torque.

There is a third kind of object, a sort of roll-your-own, chewing gum and bailing-wire object that you can create for yourself in TorqueScript called a *ScriptObject*. A ScriptObject is a way for us to arbitrarily create and use our own objects, if we have a need for one that isn't satisfied by the standard C++ generated objects from Torque.

Creating a ScriptObject

Here's how we can create a simple one property ScriptObject and a simple method for it.

```
$sob = new ScriptObject(MyScriptObject)
{
    someSillyProperty="Bah!";
};
function MyScriptObject::GreetTheWorld()
{
    echo("Hello World!");
}
```

Then, at some point later on, we can use this object and its method or properties by using the saved handle, like this:

```
$sob.GreetTheWorld();
```

Using ScriptObjects

There are as many ways to ScriptObjects as there are programmers to create them. One thing that they are handy for is passing arrays into functions and methods, since Torque does not directly support this kind of operation. Many people have devised workarounds, like stuffing the contents into a string, then extracting each array element as a field within the string once we get inside the function. This is a technique I've used myself many times.

There is a better and tidier way that involves using ScriptObjects.

The basic idea is to create a ScriptObject that encapsulates the array as a property. We then pass that ScriptObject into whatever functions need it. These functions need to be aware, of course, that they are receiving an object containing the array, and need to know how to get at the array. Try this out—enter the following code into the module main.cs located at the root folder of the Torque demo project (which is \A3D if you installed the Torque demo at the suggested location). Put the code near or at the very top. It's probably a good idea to enable logging to console.log, although you can examine the output in the console itself.

```
$sob = new ScriptObject();
for($i = 0; $i < 10; $i++)
{
    $sob.theArray[$i] = $i+10;
}
$sob.cnt = %i;

function testFunction(%container)
{
    for(%i = 0; %i < %container.cnt; %i++)
    {
        %element = %container.theArray[%i];
        echo("The value of array element" SPC %i SPC "is" SPC %element);
    }
}
```

Launch the demo, and when you get to the main menu, open the console by pressing the tilde key (~) and then type:

```
testFunction($sob);
```

You should get output that looks like this:

```
= => testFunction($sob);
   The value of array element 0 is 10
   The value of array element 1 is 11
   The value of array element 2 is 12
   The value of array element 3 is 13
   The value of array element 4 is 14
   The value of array element 5 is 15
   The value of array element 6 is 16
   The value of array element 7 is 17
   The value of array element 8 is 18
   The value of array element 9 is 19
```

If you haven't noticed, it is important to remember to specify how many array elements there are so that you can step through the array. You could work around this by establishing a value to stand for an empty element, and use that to mean that you are at the end of the array. In that case, make sure that the code that populates the array always and only uses that value for the array element after the last valid element.

Working with Files

We often need to be able to read and write data to files—things like settings and preferences, names, tracking information, or what have you. File I/O is an important part of programming complex systems, and games are usually fairly complex systems.

The Export Statement

TorqueScript has several ways to help you deal with files. The easiest to use is the `export` function, whose general form looks like this:

```
export(searchString [, fileName [,append]])
```

This function is commonly used to save preference variables specified by `searchString`, but it will work with any variable that's in scope. We can use the asterisk as the "match anything" character in the search string. Make sure that `filename` shows a complete (and valid) path including the filename plus extension. The `append` switch is set to `true` if we want to append the output to the file, and set to `false` to overwrite the existing file. For example:

```
%result = export("$Pref::Game::*", "./game/prefs.cs", False);
```

Don't forget those double quotes surrounding both the search term and the filename!

In that example, every variable that starts with `$Pref::Game::` will be written to the file in its entirety, with value assignments and all the necessary correct syntax to make a script statement. The syntax needs to be correct because the way you would read a file written this way is with the `exec` function, which will open the file, load it, and begin executing the script statements it encounters. Pretty easy!

FileObjects

Sometimes we need to be able to arbitrarily write and read data to and from files at will. That's easily accomplished using a handy thing called a `FileObject`.

FileObjects are bonafide objects, and all of the things we've seen about objects in general earlier in this chapter certainly apply to FileObjects as well. Type the following two sample functions into the script module \A3D\main.cs, as you've done with earlier code in the chapter:

```
function writef()
{
  %file = new FileObject();
  %file.openForWrite("folder/test.dat");
  %file.writeLine("Tar Fu Fu Bar!!!");
  %file.close();
  %file.delete();
}
function readf()
{
  %file = new FileObject();
  %file.openForRead("folder/test.dat");
  %text = %file.readLine();
  echo("the text is:" SPC %text );
  %file.close();
  %file.delete();
}
```

Re-launch the Torque demo, and when you reach the main menu, open the console and enter writef(); and then press the Enter key, followed by readf(); and the Enter key. You should see the contents of the file displayed for you. You can modify the text by creating the text file with a text editor, and then just running readf();.

Although its obviously more complex than using the export function, it works for any arbitrary data, not just variables.

The data is read in line-by-line. If you need to read multiple lines (or write them), that is easily done by looping the read or write lines, and testing to see if you are at the end of the file using the isEOF method, like this:

```
while (!file.isEOF())
{
   %text = %file.readLine();
}
```

After you've stuffed %text with the contents of a line from the file, you can then hack away at it to your heart's content.

Working with Strings

Standard strings, in double quotes, behave as most of us would expect. Fire up the Torque demo, open the console, and try a few examples. Type in `echo` statements like the following and observe the output:

```
echo("Hello World!");
echo("1.5" + "0.5");
```

Heh. I get a kick out of that second example. In most languages, those two strings would be treated like strings, and an operation like that second one would yield something like:

`1.50.5`

for the output of the `echo` command. But here, Torque recognized that they were numeric values and added them together when told to by the addition operator.

Tagged Strings

Now then, strings that appear in single quotes, like this:

`'abcd'`

get special treatment in TorqueScript. These strings are called *tagged strings*, and they are special because not only do they contain string data, they also have a special numeric tag associated with them. Tagged strings are used for sending string data across a network. The value of a tagged string is only sent once, regardless of how many times you actually do the sending. On subsequent sends, only the tag value is sent. Tagged values must be detagged when printing.

Try these examples:

```
$a="This one is normal";
$b='This one is tagged');
echo("Normal string: "@$a);
echo("Tagged string: "@$b);
echo("Detagged string: " @ detag('$b'));
```

That last line shows a blank because even though we've created the tagged string, it has not been <u>transmitted</u> *to* us. You can only detag a tagged string that you have <u>received</u>. You can't detag it if you've created it. Okay, sorry, it was a trick.

Here are the string operators:

@   concatenates two strings

TAB   concatenation with tab

SPC   concatenation with space

NL   new line

To "concatenate" two strings means, simply, to append them together, end-to-end. If we concatenate the strings "Hello " and "World" we end up with a longer string that says "Hello World".

The basic syntax for these string operations is:

```
"string 1" op "string 2"
```

where op is a string operator. For example, try these in the console:

```
echo("Hi" @ "there.");
echo("Hi" TAB "there.");
echo("Hi" SPC "there.");
echo("Hi" NL "there.");
```

Escape Sequences

There is one last important feature of strings: *escape sequences*.

Escape sequences are shown in Table A.7 in Appendix A.

TorqueScript allows you to create new line and tab characters using the backslash character as the *escape character*, familiar to most programmers. These combinations are called "escape sequences." Escape sequences are used to indicate to TorqueScript that the following character is a special character.

Escape sequences are also used to modify the characteristics of the text that is printed to the console and GUIs. You can colorize by using \c*n*, where *n* is a value between 0 and 9 that represents a pre-defined set of colors (See Table 2.5). Now *n* is an index into a color table defined by the property GUIControlProfile.fontColors[]. The colors 6 to 9 are "system" colors defined in the file common\ui\defaultProfiles.cs. Colors 1 to 5 are "game" colors defined in the file demo\client\ui\defaultGameProfiles.cs. A usage example would be:

```
echo("\c2ERROR!!!\c0 => my bad!");
```

If you type that in the console, you will see that it prints the line "ERROR!!! => oops!" with the part between \c2 and \c0 in red, and the part after the \c0 in black.

Table 2.5 Color Escape Codes

Escape code	rgb value	Description
\c1	4 235 105"	client join/drop, tournament mode
\c2	219 200 128"	gameplay, admin/voting, pack/deployable
\c3	77 253 95"	team chat, spam protection message, client tasks
\c4	40 231 240"	global chat
\c5	200 200 50"	used in single player game
\c6	50 50 50"	dark gray
\c7	50 50 0"	dark yellow
\c8	0 0 50"	dark blue
\c9	0 50 0	dark green
\c0	44 172 181	defined by `GUIControlProfile.fontColor`

Moving Right Along

Whew! That was a bit of a crash course in TorqueScript right there. We covered the essential points, and you should have a better understanding of what you can do with TorqueScript, and what some of its more powerful capabilities are.

We covered how to troubleshoot difficult programs, and the tools you have at your fingertips, along with some techniques that have been proven to be effective.

We learned about the various kinds of objects that Torque makes available to TorqueScript, and how to work with them to great effect.

Then we saw how to save data to disk files and get it back again, stuffing the data into string variables.

And finally, we saw how we can manipulate strings and modify them when printing to the screen.

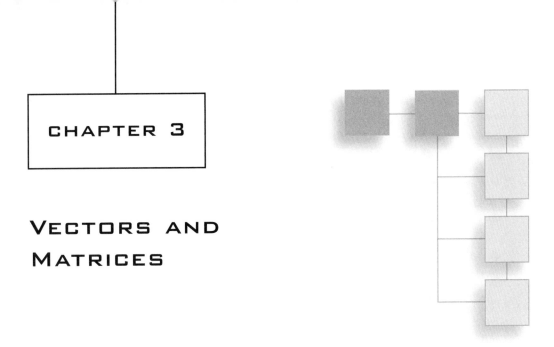

CHAPTER 3

VECTORS AND MATRICES

When we need to manipulate objects in a 3D world, we often need to deal with two spatial characteristics of the objects: location and motion. You may remember from trigonometry classes that you can represent motion by using mathematical constructs called *vectors* and examine locations in mapped spaces using *matrices*.

In this chapter, we will take a look at how we represent and manipulate vectors and matrices in general, and how we can use them specifically in game development using TorqueScript.

I don't expect you to be a math wizard to understand this chapter. The explanations are given in a way that will help you understand how the concepts are applied practically in 3D games. You already should understand coordinate spaces, as well as basic math including square roots and the like.

If you *are* a math wizard, then you'll probably want to skip to the "Applied Techniques Using TorqueScript" section.

Understanding Vectors

You've probably seen and heard something like this on TV or in the movies:

> *"Nowhereville Control Tower, this is Happy Skyways Flight 13. We are lost in a severe blizzard at 10,000 feet altitude, somewhere south or southeast of you. If you can see us on your radar, we need you to give us a vector to the runway!"*

> *"Roger Flight 13, we see you. The vector to the runway is 330 degrees, at 10 miles."*

In this exchange, the tower controller, having spotted the hapless flight on his radar scope, has told the pilot in which direction to point his airplane (330 degrees) and how far away the runway is (10 miles). This combination of direction and distance is precisely what a *vector* is.

The vector's ability to convey direction and distance is the reason that the primary use for vectors and vector math in games is to calculate *translations*, or movements in space.

What's a Vector, Victor?

A very strict and quite terse definition of a vector is a "directed quantity." Those two innocent seeming words embody a constellation of capabilities, as we will see.

We can expand our definition of a vector to: "a measurement having both direction and magnitude." Everyone knows what direction means, and magnitude, of course, refers to the measurement of how much of something (anything) there is. In the prior example, the heading in degrees is the direction, and the distance is the magnitude; from those components, we can assemble a vector to the runway from the airplane's position.

Among the many talents of this creature—the vector—is the ability to disguise itself. Vectors can be represented in several different ways. How we depict a vector depends either on what we want to do with it or what it is used to represent. Figure 3.1 shows a line vector on a two-dimension graph—a geometric representation of a vector.

It's not hard to visualize the Happy Skyways Flight 13 being located at the base of the arrow, where X=2 and Y=-4, with the runway being located at the tip of the arrow, where X=-3 and Y=5. And of course, the direction that the arrow is pointing indicates the direction that the airplane needs to travel to get to the airport.

So, a vector can look like an arrow that tells us how far to go and in what direction.

We can place ourselves at the location of the lost airplane, at the coordinates X=2 and Y=-4, which we depict as a *tuple* like this: (2,-4), as shown in Figure 3.2.

Casting an eye toward our destination, which the diagram places at (-3,5), we can easily see that to get to the runway, we need to move five miles in the negative X direction (ΔX=-5), and nine miles in the positive Y direction (ΔY=9). Therefore, we can also describe the direction and distance we need to travel with a tuple, like so: (-5,9). That's another way to depict a vector. This vector tuple (-5,9) provides us with the same information that the arrow did in Figure 3.1—direction and displacement (or distance), although the information is not as obvious as it is when shown as an arrow.

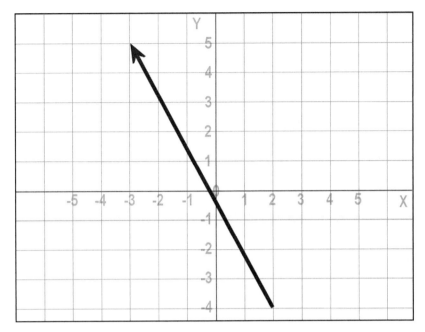

Figure 3.1 A simple 2D vector diagram.

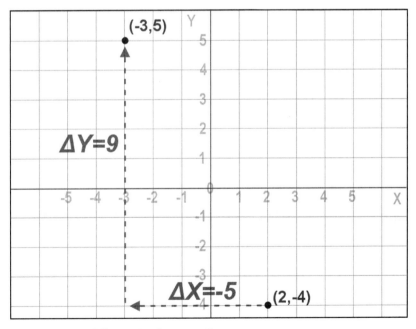

Figure 3.2 A different simple vector diagram.

Note

The triangle (Δ) that you see in Figure 3.2 is called *delta*, and it is used to indicate a change in a value. So when you see ΔX, you should read that as "delta X" or "the change in X." For example, ΔX=5 indicates that the change in X is 5.

So, a vector can also be a series of numbers, or a tuple.

There are also algebraic notations that are used to represent vectors. If you take a quick look at Figure 3.3, you will probably recognize the geometric annotation used, where A and B are end points of the line AB.

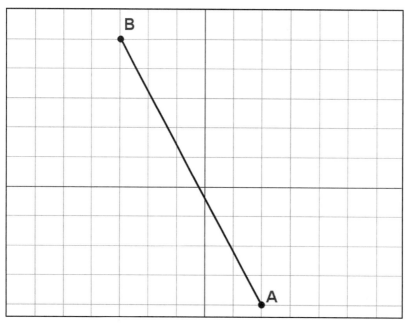

Figure 3.3 Line AB.

Despite the different annotation, you can still see it's the same vector that Figures 3.1 and 3.2 show. If we decide to use that line as a vector then we could specify it algebraically like this:

$$\overrightarrow{AB}$$

So, a vector can be represented symbolically.

Note

The vector diagrams you've seen so far have the 0 point of the axes situated at what amounts to an arbitrary location in space. The reason for this is to provide space in the diagram to show the axis values in both positive and negative directions, and to show how the end points of a vector in a real-world situation can be anywhere within a coordinate space.

We can draw those same diagrams with one of the vector endpoints rooted at 0 in both axes at the location of the airplane, like this:

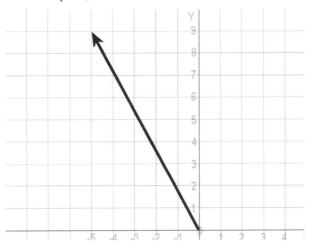

Or from the location of the runway, like this:

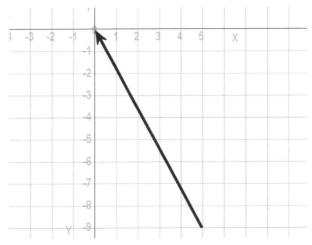

We'll stay with the 0 location being somewhere between the airplane and the runway, however, because it implies a more neutral perspective to the situation.

There are other more complex vector representations, called *vector equations* and *column vectors*, which we employ when we actually want to perform calculations.

You can think of any vector directed in two dimensions, such as the example we have been using that derives from the Happy Skyways flight, as having an *influence in two different directions*. The vector has two parts. I know it seems simplistic to state this so baldly—it seems to be blindingly obvious. But it is an important point.

Each of the parts of this two-dimensional vector is called a *component*. A 3D vector has three components, a 4D vector has four components, and so on. The components of a vector indicate how much total influence that vector has in a given direction. The combined influence of the two components is the same as the influence of the single two-dimensional vector; therefore, the single two-dimensional vector can be replaced by the two components. If we do that, we can use the vector in equations.

A generalized 2D vector equation would be $\mathbf{v} = x\mathbf{i} + y\mathbf{j}$ where $\mathbf{i}$ and $\mathbf{j}$ are called the *unit vectors* of the equation; this means that even though they are parts of components, both $\mathbf{i}$ and $\mathbf{j}$ are vectors for each axis in their own right. We'll see how components can be treated as vectors later in this chapter. By convention, lower case letters are used for vectors.

Note

A unit vector is a vector with a length of 1. The unit vectors for the vector in Figure 3.1 look like this:

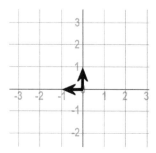

Of course, a unit vector can point in any direction; its length will always be 1. We always consider the unit vectors for a given vector to originate at that vector's origin (tail, or start point). The unit vector for any known vector can be found by dividing that vector by its magnitude. This is called *normalizing* the vector.

In the equation, x and y are the axis coefficients of their respective terms, and indicate the magnitude of the vector in that axis. Each unit vector, combined with its axis coefficient, is a component of the vector.

Fetching back to the earlier Figure 3.1, we can show that particular vector using a vector equation, substituting -5 for x and 9 for y, like this: $\mathbf{v} = -5\mathbf{i} + 9\mathbf{j}$.

So, a vector can also be represented by a vector equation.

For working in three dimensions, we obviously need to incorporate the third dimension into the vector equation. We end up with this for the generalized form: $\mathbf{v} = x\mathbf{i} + y\mathbf{j} + z\mathbf{k}$. In this case, the unit vector for the third-dimensional component is represented by $\mathbf{k}$, and its axis coefficient is represented by z as the magnitude of the component. Returning to the Happy Skyways flight, the third component of the vector, measuring the third dimension, would be the altitude of the airplane: 10,000 feet. This complicates the vector diagram quite a bit. Figure 3.4 shows the problem in a 3D format.

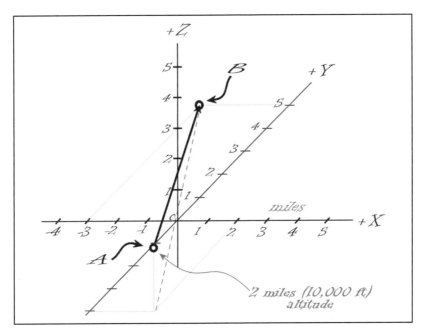

Figure 3.4 3D vector diagram.

For the sake of clarity, I've added in a dashed line to demonstrate the *ground track* of the airplane's vector—this is the tracing of the route of the airplane on the ground, and it should match the 2D vector diagram of the airplane's vector we saw in Figure 3.3. If you mentally subtract the Z-axis from the diagram in Figure 3.4, you will see that the ground track does match the 2D vector in Figure 3.3.

Now 10,000 feet is pretty darn close to two miles, so we will use miles as the unit to match the unit of the other two components. Since the airplane needs to descend from its altitude to the ground level of the runway, we need to ensure that the 2**k** component is a negative value. Therefore, we can expand the earlier vector equation example to look like this: v = -5**i** + 9**j** + -2**k**.

Finally, another vector representation—the earlier mentioned column vector—looks like this:

$$v = \begin{pmatrix} x \\ y \\ z \end{pmatrix}$$

You will recognize x, y, and z as the axis coefficients of the components of the vector from our previous discussion. That means that we can show the vector that guides the Happy Skyways flight safely on to the runway at Nowhereville like this:

$$v = \begin{pmatrix} -5 \\ 9 \\ -2 \end{pmatrix}$$

It is possible that you are now thinking that the column vector looks quite a bit like a *single-column matrix*. Well, you'd be correct if you were thinking that. In fact, we'll dig deeper into that similarity later in this chapter.

So, a vector also can be represented by a column vector, which strongly resembles a single-column matrix.

Which forms you should use for representing a vector depends on how you intend to use it.

Note

An earlier note described how the vector diagrams used an arbitrary location in space for the zero point. Column vectors aren't so arbitrary—implicit in the notation is the notion that each vector has its tail (start point) at zero, and the coefficient values are the head (end point) of the vector.

Using Vectors

It's fairly evident that vector diagrams, like Figure 3.1, are useful visual presentations that can be used to describe a problem that vectors will be used to solve. However, when we need to obtain specific values, we are going to need to use one of the more precise forms.

There are many ways to manipulate and use vectors, but I will focus on how to use them in the context of this book—math for use with 3D game graphics.

Remember when I described what a vector's components were—essentially, the measure of a vector along one of the axes? Well, here's an interesting little twist: Each component of a vector *can itself be treated like a vector*. Once we do that, we can work with the components in vector form, and perform calculations with them.

Figure 3.2, way back there a few pages, shows the components of the example vector we've been working with. Figure 3.5 shows these components now in *vectorized* form. Notice that each of the new vectors, v_w (westerly directed vector) and v_n (northerly directed vector) has no variation in one or the other of its axes.

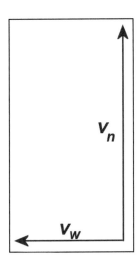

Figure 3.5 Vectorized components.

Vector Addition

If we add the two vectors by placing the two vectors from Figure 3.5 nose-to-tail, we end up with a *resultant* vector, v_r, as shown in Figure 3.6. Note that when we do this, we make the assumption that we are placing the tail, or start point, of the first vector (v_w) at the (0,0) coordinate. Any vectors we add are placed nose-to-tail to this vector. Once we get them placed, the resultant line is drawn with its tail at (0,0) and its nose at the location of the nose of the last added vector. As you know already, that resultant vector is the vector that Flight 13 needs to get to safety.

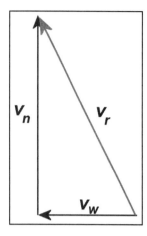

Figure 3.6 Vector addition resultant.

Usually, when doing math with vectors, we work with a numerical form instead of a diagrammatic form. Later, we can use the diagram form to verify our numbers, if we need to. So let's convert our two new vectors, $\mathbf{v_w}$ and $\mathbf{v_n}$, to column vector format, like this:

$$v_n = \begin{pmatrix} 0 \\ 9 \end{pmatrix} \qquad v_w \begin{pmatrix} -5 \\ 0 \end{pmatrix}$$

Now we have a form we can work with, mathematically. We can add the two vectors like this:

$$v_r = v_w + v_n = \begin{pmatrix} -5 \\ 0 \end{pmatrix} + \begin{pmatrix} 0 \\ 9 \end{pmatrix} = \begin{pmatrix} -5 \\ 9 \end{pmatrix}$$

Of course, all we've done is worked our way back to what we already knew. But now you can see that we can add two vectors in column form by simply summing the values in each row as we go across. This applies, no matter how many components there are to the vectors. Here is the 3D version of the addition:

$$v_r = v_w + v_n + v_a = \begin{pmatrix} -5 \\ 0 \\ 0 \end{pmatrix} + \begin{pmatrix} 0 \\ 9 \\ 0 \end{pmatrix} + \begin{pmatrix} 0 \\ 0 \\ -2 \end{pmatrix} = \begin{pmatrix} -5 \\ 9 \\ -2 \end{pmatrix}$$

This resultant matches the resultant that we obtained in Figure 3.6. As you can see, adding vectors is really quite straightforward.

Note

Every vector can be considered to be the hypotenuse of a right triangle. That being the case, we can apply the Pythagorean Theorem to the vector in order to figure out the length of the vector. The theorem states that the square of the length of the hypotenuse is equal to the sum of the squares of the lengths of the two sides adjacent to the right angle, or $a^2 + b^2 = c^2$.

The Happy Skyways vector has an x component of -5 and a y component of 9. The x and y components are the same as the sides adjacent to the right angle, so we should square each value. That yields 25 and 81 which we add together to get 106. That means that 106 is the square of the length of the hypotenuse, which is the vector. The square root of 106 is 10.3 (rounded to one significant digit). Therefore, the length of the vector is 10.3.

The length of a vector is sometimes called the *modulus* of the vector. We write it using a notation like this: $|a|$ or $|v_a|$, or whatever.

Remember that when dealing with game graphics, we use **x** and **y** (and sometimes **z**) to represent the axis components of vectors, instead of a, b, and c, which are used to show the sides of a triangle in general form.

So, for two dimensions,

$$|v| = \sqrt{x^2 + y^2}$$

and for three dimensions,

$$|v| = \sqrt{x^2 + y^2 + z^2}$$

You may breathe now.

Vector Subtraction

Vector subtraction is also quite simple, but there is a twist. You will recall that in basic arithmetic, subtracting **b** from **a** is the same as adding **a** to the negative of **b**. We can, and should, do the same thing when subtracting vectors; negate all of the signs of the coefficients of the vector being subtracted, and then add it to the first vector, like this:

$$V_r = V_w - V_n = \begin{pmatrix} -5 \\ 0 \end{pmatrix} - \begin{pmatrix} 0 \\ 9 \end{pmatrix}$$

This yields:

$$V_r = V_w + -V_n = \begin{pmatrix} -5 \\ 0 \end{pmatrix} + \begin{pmatrix} -0 \\ -9 \end{pmatrix}$$

We can verify the rightness of this approach by doing a quick vector diagram, adding $\mathbf{v_w}$ to the negated $\mathbf{v_n}$, nose-to-tail as shown in Figure 3.7.

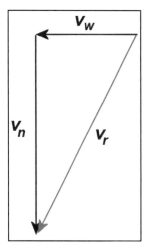

Figure 3.7 Vector subtraction resultant.

You'll notice that $\mathbf{v_r}$, the resultant of subtracting $\mathbf{v_n}$ from $\mathbf{v_w}$, is completely different from the $\mathbf{v_r}$ that you get when adding the same two vectors. And that's as it should be!

Scaling

When scaling a vector, we are simply making it longer or shorter. The direction never changes. We scale a vector by multiplying each component by the same value; this value is called, strangely enough, a *scalar*. A scalar is a value that has a magnitude, but no direction.

You will recall the general form for a single-column vector:

$$v = \begin{pmatrix} x \\ y \\ z \end{pmatrix}$$

When we are scaling a vector, the general form is:

$$kv = \begin{pmatrix} kx \\ ky \\ kz \end{pmatrix}$$

So, if we have the vector

$$v = \begin{pmatrix} 2 \\ -4 \\ 6 \end{pmatrix}$$

and we want to scale it by 2.5, then the result is

$$v = \begin{pmatrix} 2.5 \times 2 \\ 2.5 \times -4 \\ 2.5 \times 6 \end{pmatrix} = \begin{pmatrix} 5 \\ -10 \\ 15 \end{pmatrix}$$

It's also significant to note that if our scalar is negative, then the resultant vector will be pointing in the opposite direction.

Finding Angles

Let us assume that you have two vectors, **u** and **v**, oriented as shown in Figure 3.8, and they diverge by the angle θ (that symbol is pronounced "theta"). Let us further suppose that you're thinking, "It would be mighty nice to actually know what that angle is!"

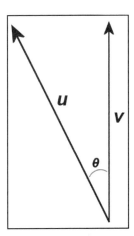

Figure 3.8 Divergent vectors.

Well, don't fret: As long as you know enough about the two vectors, you can calculate that angle using a vector operation known as the *dot product*. The dot product is called that because the symbol used to denote the operation is a "dot"—•.

There are two different definitions for the dot product for two vectors. Which definition you use depends on what you are trying to do.

Assuming two vectors are defined according to these equations:

$\mathbf{u} = a\mathbf{i} + b\mathbf{j}$

$\mathbf{v} = x\mathbf{i} + y\mathbf{j}$

the primary dot product definition is $\mathbf{u} \bullet \mathbf{v} = |\mathbf{u}||\mathbf{v}| \cos \theta$. In words that reads, "the dot product of the vectors $\mathbf{u}$ and $\mathbf{v}$ is equal to the magnitude of vector $\mathbf{u}$ times the magnitude of vector $\mathbf{v}$ times the cosine of the angle theta."

The alternate definition is $\mathbf{u} \bullet \mathbf{v} = a\,x + b\,y$, which reads, "the dot product of the vectors $\mathbf{u}$ and $\mathbf{v}$ is equal to component a times the component x plus component b times the component y."

I'm not going to go into the detailed derivation that shows how we arrive at these equations, but I will show you the 5-cent brief cook's tour of how we use them to find the angle between the two vectors. Figure 3.9 shows the two vectors with their components in more detail.

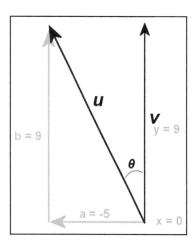

Figure 3.9 Divergent vectors with component values.

Here again are the vector equations for the two vectors:

$\mathbf{u} = a\mathbf{i} + b\mathbf{j}$

$\mathbf{v} = x\mathbf{i} + y\mathbf{j}$

therefore,

$\Rightarrow \mathbf{u} \bullet \mathbf{v} = a\,x + b\,y$

and

=> **u** • **v** = |**u**||**v**| cos θ

therefore,

=> **u** **v** cos θ = a x + b y

and finally,

=> θ = cos^{-1} (a x + b y) / (|**u**||**v**|)

Using this formula, let's plug in some numbers from Figure 3.9: for vector **u**, a = -5 and b = 9, and for vector **v**, x = 0 and y = 9.

so

θ = cos^{-1} ((-5)(0) + (9)(9)) / ((10.3)(9))

θ = cos^{-1} (81/92.7)

θ = cos^{-1} (0.874)

θ = 29.0 degrees

There you have it. The angle between vector **u** and vector **v** is 29.0 degrees. Cool, huh?

Finding Normals

A *normal* is a vector that is at right angles, or perpendicular, to a plane. In 3D geometry, two vectors, like the two we were just working with when we were finding angles, define a plane. A vector that is perpendicular to those two vectors would be the normal for that plane. There are various reasons why normals are useful to us. For example, if you need to know which way is up, compared to the ground, you can compute the normal. There is also a detailed graphic texture rendering technique called *normal mapping* that is used to enhance 3D models.

Figure 3.10 shows the vectors **u** and **v** again, this time visually oriented differently. Vectors **u** and **v** are the same vectors we dealt with when we were looking for the angle using the dot product, except now they are shown in three dimensions. Although you might find it hard to tell, vector **w** is perpendicular to both of the other vectors, therefore vector **w** is the normal vector for the plane **uv**. Also, note that vector **w** is shown to have a length of 1. When we are seeking the normal vector, we are really only interested in obtaining the unit vector for that normal; you already know that a unit vector will always have a magnitude of 1.

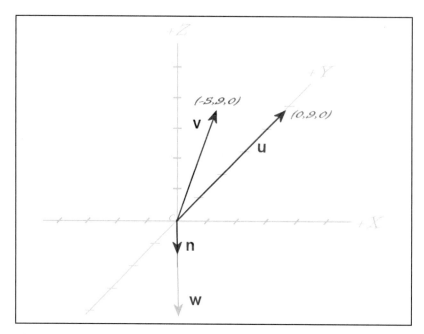

Figure 3.10 Vectors in three dimensions.

We can calculate the information needed to draw that normal from the known specifications of the other two vectors by using the *cross product* operation. The symbol for the cross product is X. So when you see **u** X **v**, you read that as "u cross v"—that *isn't* the times symbol.

The equation for the cross product of two vectors is:

u X **v** = **n** |**u**| |**v**| sin θ

where **n** is the normal vector, and |**u**| and |**v**| are the magnitudes of their respective vectors (just in case you forgot what the | | meant).

The work involved in computing the cross product of two vectors is quite a bit more involved. As I did with the dot product operations, I'll skip some of the proofs and derivative math.

First we need to obtain our values and we can do that using Figure 3.9 again, since the only values we don't have in that 2D diagram are the magnitudes of the Z-axis components. You can see in the diagram that the Z-axis components for both **u** and **v** are zero, so that takes care of that.

For vector **u**: a = -5, b = 9, and c = 0; and for vector **v**, x = 0, y = 9, and z = 0.

Here are our two vector equations; this time it's the 3D version:

u = a**i** + b**j** + c**k**

v = x**i** + y**j** + z**k**

and these can be expressed like this for a cross product operation:

u × **v** = (bz − cy)**i** - (cx − az)**j** + (ay − bx)**k**

So we plug in our values and get:

u = -5**i** + 9**j** + 0**k**

v = 0**i** + 9**j** + 0**k**

u × **v** = ((9)(0) − (0)(9))**i** − ((0)(0) − (-5)(0))**j** + ((-5)(9) − (9)(0))**k**

u × **v** = (0 − 0)**i** + (0 − 0)**j** + (-45 − 0)**k**

u × **v** = (0)**i** + (0)**j** + (-45)**k**

Now since the unit vectors have a magnitude of 1, we can look at the coefficients for i, j, and k, and accounting for the sign of the unit vector in each case, we get a set of coordinates that specifies our normal vector: (0,0,-45) .

So, **w** = (0,0,-45).

Next we need to obtain the magnitude of our vector. Remember Pythagoras?

Well, since two of the sides of **w** have zero length, we can dispense with them in our calculation. And since taking the square root of the square of a number just equals that number, we can forget about the rest of the equation as well, and just take 45 as the magnitude!

So, |**w**| = 45.

Now we need to find **n**, the unit vector for **w**, which we do by performing a scaling operation. As we learned earlier, the unit vector for any known vector can be found by dividing that vector by its magnitude, like this:

$$n = \frac{w}{|w|} = \begin{pmatrix} \frac{0}{45} \\ \frac{0}{45} \\ \frac{-45}{45} \end{pmatrix} = \begin{pmatrix} 0 \\ 0 \\ -1 \end{pmatrix}$$

Whew! Finally, we have our normal vector: **n** = (0,0,1).

One more twist: There are actually two normals, since there are actually two vectors that are perpendicular to a plane. The equations are slightly, but significantly, different if the normal is facing the other way, but there is no need to worry about that here. The purpose of these sections has been to show how vectors are used, but you won't have to do the work manually like we did here. TorqueScript has many useful functions for doing this work that we can call upon to avoid doing the math by hand. Good thing, too!

Understanding Matrices

We've just seen how vectors can be useful when dealing with translations, or movement, of objects in space; similarly, matrices are primarily of interest to us when we need to perform *transformations* and *rotations*—operations that change the shape or orientation of objects. Sometimes, dictated by circumstances, we also use matrices for translation operations.

A matrix is a table of numbers arranged in rows and columns, with brackets (usually square) around the outside like this:

$$\begin{bmatrix} 3 & 6 & 5 \\ 4 & 1 & 2 \\ 5 & 7 & 1 \end{bmatrix}$$

Actually, the *elements* in a matrix can be letters or functions instead of numbers. A matrix is a sort of grid in which we can store such elements in indexed locations. In the matrix above, the number 4 is in row 2, column 1.

However, matrices are not just used to store data. They can be added, subtracted, multiplied, and generally manipulated, so that we can get at much greater information about the data and what it represents.

In fact, you've seen how a column vector is really just a single column matrix. There are also other ways that vector math can be performed with the help of matrices that we didn't cover, since they didn't suit our purposes.

If a matrix has **m** rows and **n** columns, we say it is an **mxn** matrix or that the *size* or *dimension* of the matrix is **mxn**. The example above is a 3x3 matrix.

The general form for a matrix is:

$$A = \begin{bmatrix} e11 & e12 & ... & e1n \\ e21 & e22 & ... & e2n \\ ... & ... & ... & ... \\ em1 & em2 & em3 & emn \end{bmatrix}$$

Matrix **A**, in that example, shows that a matrix can be any number of rows or columns. A matrix where **m** = **n** is called a *square* matrix.

By convention, a matrix is represented symbolically by a capital letter. If we want to write a general matrix **A**, we denote the element in row **i** and column **j** as e_{ij}. Note the use of a lower case letter to specify an element in the array. We can refer to an element with a matrix using standard array notation. For example, the value 7 in this matrix

$$\begin{bmatrix} 3 & 63 & 2 \\ -1 & 45 & 2 \\ 5 & 7 & -6 \end{bmatrix}$$

would be **A(3,2)**. This notation is handy, because it conforms to the standard array notation used in most programming languages.

There is a special matrix, called the *identity matrix* that looks like this:

$$\begin{bmatrix} 1 & 0 & 0 \\ 0 & 1 & 0 \\ 0 & 0 & 1 \end{bmatrix}$$

One of the neat things about the identity matrix is that it shows quite clearly the relationship that can exist between vectors and matrices. If you take the first (left) column, read from top-to-bottom, you have the x,y, and z values for a non-rotated X-axis unit vector! The middle column is for the Y-axis unit vector, and the last column is for the Z-axis unit vector.

The Matrix: Explanations

The handiest feature of matrices, in my humble opinion, is that for each of the fundamental operations that you would want to perform with an object in the 3D world, there is a specific matrix configuration that you can use. Just plug in the numbers, and out pops the result.

Okay, so the result actually doesn't pop out automatically, but there are clear and concise steps to follow, and it's pretty easy to memorize which matrix to apply to a given problem. Matrices have a convenient visual appearance that is a great help to recognizing and remembering them—not at all like gazing at complicated looking and tricky formulas and equations (although you will *never* get away from complicated and tricky formulas and equations in this business).

Using Matrices

Figure 3.11 shows the matrices that can be used for the three transform operations: translation, scaling, and rotation.

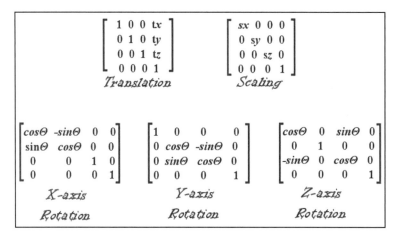

Figure 3.11 Transform matrices.

Moving Stuff

Although you might find yourself thinking in terms of vectors when you need to translate an object, you can also use a matrix to move an object. It's one of the simplest matrix operations, so let's have a peek.

In Figure 3.11 you can see that the translation matrix is essentially a 3x3 identity matrix with an extra column added at the end, with three new terms in the first three rows of the last column. Those terms are our displacement values for the three axes. Basically, a movement vector has been picked apart and dropped into those three spots.

The extra row is a mathematical construct that's used to make sure the math works out right for a larger matrix. We need to have the same number of rows as columns.

Remember Happy Skyways Flight 13? Well it seems those poor bastages haven't made it to safety yet. Let's take their current location as (2,-4,2), and the vector to the runway (including altitude) as (-5,9,-2).

We create our translation matrix by plugging the vector values into the translation matrix like this:

$$\begin{bmatrix} 1 & 0 & 0 & -5 \\ 0 & 1 & 0 & 9 \\ 0 & 0 & 1 & -2 \\ 0 & 0 & 0 & 1 \end{bmatrix}$$

Then, being sneaky like we are, just assume our location to be a vector, and not just any vector, but a column vector (remember those?). That way, our current location coordinates end up looking like this:

$$\begin{bmatrix} 2 \\ -4 \\ 2 \\ 1 \end{bmatrix}$$

Note that I added a 1 as a fourth row. That's simply to make sure that when I use the vector in a multiplication operation, which I will be doing, that the math works out properly. Math guys fudge the numbers *all* the time. Heh. Well, actually it *is* a legitimate way to ensure that the matrix operations work correctly. No actual hanky-panky took place there.

So, when we multiply the vector by the translation matrix, we will perform the operation described by this general form matrix multiplication guide:

$$\begin{bmatrix} a00 & a01 & a02 & a03 \\ a10 & a11 & a12 & a13 \\ a20 & a21 & a22 & a23 \\ a30 & a31 & a32 & a33 \end{bmatrix} \begin{bmatrix} b0 \\ b1 \\ b2 \\ b3 \end{bmatrix} = \begin{bmatrix} a00b0 + a01b1 + a02b3 + a03b3 \\ a10b0 + a11b1 + a12b3 + a13b3 \\ a20b0 + a21b1 + a22b3 + a23b3 \\ a30b0 + a31b1 + a32b3 + a33b3 \end{bmatrix}$$

Figure 3.12 Matrix multiplication guide.

Using real numbers, it looks like this:

$$\begin{bmatrix} 1 & 0 & 0 & -5 \\ 0 & 1 & 0 & 9 \\ 0 & 0 & 1 & -2 \\ 0 & 0 & 0 & 1 \end{bmatrix} \begin{bmatrix} 2 \\ -4 \\ 2 \\ 1 \end{bmatrix} = \begin{bmatrix} 2+ & 0+ & 0+ & -5 \\ 0+ & -4+ & 0+ & 9 \\ 0+ & 0+ & 2+ & -2 \\ 0+ & 0+ & 0+ & 1 \end{bmatrix} = \begin{bmatrix} -3 \\ 5 \\ 4 \\ 1 \end{bmatrix}$$

And look at that! The resulting vector is over there on the right, if you lop off the extra 1 at the bottom (remember I added that in at the start? To make the math work?), then we get our new location vector (-3,5,0).

The matrix rocks.

Note

To be able to multiply matrices, the number of columns in the first matrix must be the same as the number of rows in the second matrix. The product matrix will always have the same dimensions as the second matrix. Pay attention to the matrix multiplication ordering. The position of the matrices are *not* interchangeable. A times B is not equal to B times A.

Sizing Stuff

Changing the size of things is just as easy. Instead of the translation matrix I used in the previous discussion, you use the scaling matrix. This one's on your head. Look at Figure 3.11, get the scaling matrix, and then use the matrix multiplication guide I showed you in Figure 3.12 and apply it in the same way that you did for the translation. Remember that sx, sy, and sz are your scale factors.

Rotating Stuff

Rotation is a bit more complex, though not really any more difficult. The various rotation matrices certainly appear more complicated, as you can see in Figure 3.11.

Rotating around any single axis is accomplished in exactly the same way as the translation or scaling—just multiply the appropriate rotation matrix with the vector.

We can also apply rotations in all three axes at the same time. In order to do this, we need to decide what the order of the rotations will be, and then successively multiply the rotations with each other in that order until we get a product rotation matrix that we can apply to our vector. We need to keep in mind that our vector will be a unit vector that tells us which way our object is facing.

Let's say we are going to rotate our object by 10 degrees around the X-axis followed by 5 degrees rotation around the Y-axis and then 45 degrees rotation around the Z-axis. We need to calculate the cosine, sine, and negative sine of each theta, which we can do by using a calculator or the sine/cosine tables. The calculated values are shown in Table 3.1.

Table 3.1 Sine and Cosine Values for Rotation Example

Operation	$\theta = 5$	$\theta = 10$	$\theta = 45$
Cosine	0.996	0.985	0.707
-Cosine	-0.996	-0.985	-0.707
Sine	0.087	0.174	0.707
-Sine	-0.087	-0.174	-0.707

So our X-axis rotation matrix is:

$$\begin{bmatrix} 0.985 & -0.174 & 0 & 0 \\ 0.174 & 0.985 & 0 & 0 \\ 0 & 0 & 1 & 0 \\ 0 & 0 & 0 & 1 \end{bmatrix}$$

And our Y-axis rotation matrix is:

$$\begin{bmatrix} 1 & 0 & 0 & 0 \\ 0 & 0.996 & -0.087 & 0 \\ 0 & 0.087 & 0.996 & 0 \\ 0 & 0 & 0 & 1 \end{bmatrix}$$

And finally, our Z-axis rotation matrix is:

$$\begin{bmatrix} 0.707 & 0 & 0.707 & 0 \\ 0 & 1 & 0 & 0 \\ -0.707 & 0 & 0.707 & 0 \\ 0 & 0 & 0 & 1 \end{bmatrix}$$

Then we need to multiply (or *concatenate*) our matrices successively. Figure 3.13 shows the general form for multiplying two 4x4 matrices. The product is a little bit dense with values, so it looks quite a bit larger than the other matrices in the picture, but it's still a 4x4 matrix. Essentially what you are doing is multiplying the elements of each column with the corresponding element for each row in the other matrix.

$$
\begin{bmatrix} a00 & a01 & a02 & a03 \\ a10 & a11 & a12 & a13 \\ a20 & a21 & a22 & a23 \\ a30 & a31 & a32 & a33 \end{bmatrix}
\begin{bmatrix} b00 & b01 & b02 & b03 \\ b10 & b11 & b12 & b13 \\ b20 & b21 & b22 & b23 \\ b30 & b31 & b32 & b33 \end{bmatrix} =
$$

$$
\begin{bmatrix}
\begin{array}{l} a00b00+a01b10+ \\ a02b20+a03b30 \end{array} &
\begin{array}{l} a00b01+a01b11+ \\ a02b21+a03b31 \end{array} &
\begin{array}{l} a00b02+a01b12+ \\ a02b22+a03b32 \end{array} &
\begin{array}{l} a00b03+a01b13+ \\ a02b23+a03b33 \end{array} \\[8pt]
\begin{array}{l} a10b00+a11b10+ \\ a12b20+a13b30 \end{array} &
\begin{array}{l} a10b01+a11b11+ \\ a12b21+a13b31 \end{array} &
\begin{array}{l} a10b02+a11b12+ \\ a12b22+a13b32 \end{array} &
\begin{array}{l} a10b03+a11b13+ \\ a12b23+a13b33 \end{array} \\[8pt]
\begin{array}{l} a20b00+a21b10+ \\ a22b20+a23b30 \end{array} &
\begin{array}{l} a20b01+a21b11+ \\ a22b21+a23b31 \end{array} &
\begin{array}{l} a20b02+a21b12+ \\ a22b22+a23b32 \end{array} &
\begin{array}{l} a20b03+a21b13+ \\ a22b23+a23b33 \end{array} \\[8pt]
\begin{array}{l} a30b00+a31b10+ \\ a32b20+a33b30 \end{array} &
\begin{array}{l} a30b01+a31b11+ \\ a32b21+a33b31 \end{array} &
\begin{array}{l} a30b02+a31b12+ \\ a32b22+a33b32 \end{array} &
\begin{array}{l} a30b03+a31b13+ \\ a32b23+a33b33 \end{array}
\end{bmatrix}
$$

Figure 3.13 Multiplying 4x4 matrices.

Performing the actual operation is a bit tiresome; you have to pay close attention to which row and which column in which matrix you are working with, and what you intend to do with it. In short order, the pattern will become clear, and you will be able to zip right along like an old-time expert matrix-multiplyin' fool. Figure 3.14 shows the operation where the X-axis matrix is multiplied by the Y-axis matrix. This has the effect of combining our X-axis rotation and Y-axis rotation.

$$
\overset{\text{X}}{\begin{bmatrix} 0.985 & -0.174 & 0 & 0 \\ 0.174 & 0.985 & 0 & 0 \\ 0 & 0 & 1 & 0 \\ 0 & 0 & 0 & 1 \end{bmatrix}}
\overset{\text{Y}}{\begin{bmatrix} 1 & 0 & 0 & 0 \\ 0 & 0.996 & -0.087 & 0 \\ 0 & 0.087 & 0.996 & 0 \\ 0 & 0 & 0 & 1 \end{bmatrix}} =
\overset{\text{XY}}{\begin{bmatrix} 0.985 & -0.173 & 0.015 & 0 \\ 0.174 & 0.981 & -0.086 & 0 \\ 0 & 0.087 & 0.996 & 0 \\ 0 & 0 & 0 & 1 \end{bmatrix}}
$$

Figure 3.14 XY operation.

Then we need to factor in the Z-axis rotation, which we do by multiplying the XY product matrix by the Z-axis rotation matrix, as shown in Figure 3.15.

$$
\overset{\text{XY}}{\begin{bmatrix} 0.985 & -0.173 & 0.015 & 0 \\ 0.174 & 0.981 & -0.086 & 0 \\ 0 & 0.087 & 0.996 & 0 \\ 0 & 0 & 0 & 1 \end{bmatrix}}
\overset{\text{Z}}{\begin{bmatrix} 0.707 & 0 & 0.707 & 0 \\ 0 & 1 & 0 & 0 \\ -0.707 & 0 & 0.707 & 0 \\ 0 & 0 & 0 & 1 \end{bmatrix}} =
\overset{\text{XYZ}}{\begin{bmatrix} 0.686 & -0.173 & 0.707 & 0 \\ 0.184 & 0.981 & 0.063 & 0 \\ -0.704 & 0.087 & 0.704 & 0 \\ 0 & 0 & 0 & 1 \end{bmatrix}}
$$

Figure 3.15 XYZ operation.

There you go. Now all of the rotations are contained in a single matrix, which you may now proceed to apply to your position vector.

You can also factor in the translation matrix the same way. Except there is a short cut: All you need to do is insert your translation vector into the top three rows of the last column on the right, so that it looks like this:

$$\begin{bmatrix} 0.686 & -0.172 & 0.707 & tx \\ 0.183 & 0.981 & 0.062 & ty \\ -0.704 & 0.087 & 0.704 & tz \\ 0 & 0 & 0 & 1 \end{bmatrix}$$

where the vector would be (tx,ty,tz) in column vector format.

Once you've done that, you can apply the resulting matrix to your object's position vector, and move it through space *and* rotate it around 3 axes, all in one step! Go ahead, grab a pencil and some paper, and give it a try. Meet you in the next section when you're done.

Applied Techniques Using TorqueScript

Now is the time to get down to brass tacks. After all that fooling around with manually manipulating vectors and matrices, what really matters to us in this book is how to actually perform transformations using vector or matrix concepts using TorqueScript. Fortunately, TorqueScript has built-in functions to take all of the drudgework out of this stuff. But then, I'm thinking you've probably already deduced that.

Well, let's see how we would add vectors in Torque. Remember nose-to-tail and all that? Summing the values in the row as we went along? Well no more of that!

Nope, because now we have our handy new VectorAdd function.

```
%resultant = VectorAdd("2 -4 2", "-5 9 -2");
```

Now that was easy. Most of our vector and matrix operations won't be that easy, but they will be pretty close!

Subtracting vectors is about the same:

```
%resultant = VectorSub("2 -4 2", "-5 9 -2");
```

Then there's finding the length of a vector:

```
%resultant = vectorLen(%vector);
```

We're on a roll now! Don't forget about normalizing a vector to get the unit vector:

```
%unitvec = vectorNormalize("5 5 12");
```

I can do this stuff with both the keyboard *and* the mouse tied behind my back! Scaling vectors:

```
%unitvec = vectorScale("2 -7 3", 15);
```

You will find descriptions, syntax, and usage information for these and other vector and matrix functions in Appendix A.

A Moving Program

Let's examine some code that moves an object around the game world. We're going to create a script module and add some code to an existing script module, so you'll need to use a programming/text editor. If you don't have one, the shareware version of UltraEdit-32 using the installer in the uedit-32 zip file can be found on the companion CD in the \A3D\TOOLS\UltraEdit-32 folder.

Warping Your Player Character

Let us say we want to change the position of our player character (or *avatar*—they are interchangeable) by a certain amount, in a certain direction, instantaneously. This is often called *warping*, a term that comes from some obscure science-fiction television program.

This could perhaps be part of some trap or puzzle that the player has to navigate himself through, for example. If the player steps incorrectly, he might find himself farther back down a tunnel whence he came. Or maybe pushed out over 50 feet of water. Or wherever.

What we will do is create a function that will move the avatar 50 world units in whatever direction the avatar is facing, whenever we press the **j** key (I would have used "w" for warp, but it was already taken by the default key binding set up). The algorithm we will use to do this is as follows:

1. Get the current eye transform of the avatar. This yields a unit vector in a string that points in the direction the avatar is looking.
2. Scale the unit vector of the eye transform to have the length of the warp we want—in this case, 100 world units. Call this the warp vector.

3. Add the warp vector to the current position vector of the avatar to get the new position coordinates.

4. Get the current transform of the avatar. This gives us both the avatar position and avatar orientation information in a single string.

5. Extract the orientation information from the current transform and append it to our new position information.

6. Set the transform of the avatar to the new position and old orientation information.

Now that seems like a lot of work, but it really isn't. The actual code will be contained in a function called Warp1, as you will see shortly.

In order to do this, we have to execute the code on the server side, because in Torque the server controls all player avatar motion and status, whether it's a single- or multiplayer game. To help us easily test the code, we will create a key binding for the client that will call the code on the server-side, basically telling the server to execute the warp maneuver.

Step One

Create a new file called myServerScripts.cs, in the folder C:\A3D\demo\server\scripts and add the following code:

```
function serverCmdWarp1(%client)
{
  echo ("We be warpin'!"); // a little feedback for the console log
  %avatar = %client.player;  // 1a
  %eyeVector = %avatar.getEyeVector();  // 1b
  %warpVector = vectorScale(%eyeVector,50);  // 2
  %currentPos = %avatar.getPosition();   // 3a
  %newPos = vectorAdd(%currentPos,%warpVector); // 3b
  %currentTrans = %avatar.getTransform(); // 4
  %orientation = getWords(%currentTrans, 3);//5a(get words 3,4,5,6 from string)
  %newtransform = %newPos SPC %orientation; // 5b - SPC is the same as @ " " @
  %avatar.setTransform(%newTransform);  // 6
}
```

Save your work. Note that the numbers in the comments at the end of the lines refer to the appropriate step in the algorithm. I *won't* be putting statement numbers in comments like this for all of the code in the book. I'm just trying to be nice here. (I know, I know: "don't be nice, just be yourself," they're always telling me that.)

Step Two

Next, open the file C:\A3D\demo\server\scripts\game.cs and locate the function onServerCreated. At the end of the function, *after* the line that says

```
exec("./car.cs");
```

and *before* the line that says

```
// Keep track of when the game started
```

Add in this code:

```
// Book Scripts
exec("./myServerScripts.cs");
```

Save your work.

Take note of this: For any future code modules you add that will execute on the server, you should put your module in the C:\A3D\demo\server\scripts\ folder, and then add the module's name in C:\A3D\demo\server\scripts\game.cs in the same way as I showed you here for myServerScripts.cs. Put them in the same place, after the //Book Scripts comment.

The code in Step Two does this: When the server is created, the script module will be executed, loading its functions and variables (if any) into memory. Also, any code in the script module that is *in-line*, or not part of a function, datablock, or object definition will be executed *immediately* during the load process, as soon as the script executive encounters it.

Step Three

Okay, now we have to create our key binding. Open the file C:\A3D\demo\client\config.cs and go to the end of the file, after everything else. Add the following line of code:

```
moveMap.bindCmd(keyboard,"j","commandToServer(\'Warp1\');", "");
```

Note

You may have noticed that in the key binding

moveMap.bindCmd(keyboard, "j", "commandToServer(\'Warp1\');", " ");

the Warp1 function is surrounded by single quotes, each of which has a backslash in front of it. The backslash serves as an *escape* character. The escape character is used because the single quotes appear inside a pair of double quotes. The single quotes are necessary because the function name needs to be passed to commandToServer as a *tagged string* (see Chapter 2).

You do not *need* to use the double quotes in the binding call, and if you don't, then you don't need to use the backslashes either. However, this is the standard way to do this sort of thing in TorqueScript. In fact, when you exit the demo, the config.cs file is automatically saved back to disk by Torque, and when it is, it will be with the double quotes, and with the backslash-escaped single quotes. So you may as well learn how to do it yourself. Couldn't hurt!

There are several other vector-related functions available to the standard Player object. You can use the %objectID.dump method to get a list of them and other Player methods. Table 3.2 shows a list of vector-related methods:

Table 3.2 Vector-Related Player Methods

Method	Description
getEyePoint	Returns the position of the avatar's eye in a string with three words.
getEyeTransform	Returns the position of the avatar's eye and its rotation vector in a string with three words for the position followed by four words for the rotation.
getEyeVector	Returns the rotation unit vector of the avatar's eye in a string with three words.
getForwardVector	Returns the unit vector of the avatar's eye in a string with three words, with the Z-axis set to 0.
getMuzzlePoint	Returns the position of the specified mounted weapon's muzzle in a string with three words.
getMuzzleVector	Returns the rotation unit vector of the specified mounted weapon's muzzle in a string with three words.
getPosition	Returns the position of the avatar in a string with three words.
getTransform	Returns the position of the avatar and its rotation vector in a string with three words for the position followed by four words for the rotation.
setTransform	Sets the position of the avatar and its rotation using a string with three words for the position followed by four words for the rotation.

Note

You'll notice that the functions that return a transform, return a seven-word string. The first three words of the string are the XYZ position coordinates. The last four words describe what is often called an *angular axis vector* or an *angled vector*. The first three words of the angled vector are a unit vector that points in a particular direction. The final word is a scalar value that specifies, in radians, the rotation around the axis indicated by the unit vector.

Testing the Warp

Once you have edited the appropriate files, you can test the code by running the demo. Launch \A3D\demo.exe, and click on the splash screen to get to the main menu to make the splash screen go away faster. If you leave it be, it will eventually disappear on its own after a time-out. In the main menu, click on the button near the center that says "Example: FPS Multiplayer". On the next screen, make sure the "Create Server" box is checked, then click on the right-facing arrow button in the bottom left part of the screen.

Once the demo game loads, and your player character spawns in, go run around and shoot things with your exploding crossbow until you've had your fill. Table 3.3 shows the default movement control keys that you can use. If you want to change them to suit yourself, press Ctrl+O (that's an "o", as in the first letter of "options"), and then click on the Control tab. To change a key binding, find the movement or action you want in the scrollable list in the Control tab, double-click on it, and then type the key that you want to bind to that action or movement.

Table 3.3 Torque Game Engine Demo Control Keys

Key	Description
w	Run forward
a	Run backward
s	Run (strafe) left
d	Run (strafe) right
spacebar	Jump
z	Free look (hold key and move mouse)
Tab	Toggle player point of view
Escape	Quit game
Tilde	Open console

Once you are through being a tourist, point your avatar in a safe direction—that would be one where you are not looking into or up a hill, and then press the **j** key. You should jump forward 30 world units. You can go warping all around the world like this.

Remember the procedure you followed to get into the game so that in the future, when you are directed to "run the demo game," you'll know what's expected, and I won't have to type so much!

Rotate It

One of the more common capabilities people like to add to their games, or to specific creatures or items in their games, is the ability to rotate and track a player. What we'll do here as our sample rotation program is make an arbitrary object in a map rotate to face your position. Like the warp code, we'll implement it using a key binding. That way you can maneuver your avatar around the map, and then hit the rotate key (we'll use **k** as the key) to make the object turn to face you.

Instead of using some mundane thing like a radar dish or antenna, we're gonna make a whole multi-story building track you! How's that for creepy? The building we will use is the "Great Hall," shown in Figure 3.16.

Figure 3.16 The Great Hall.

Here's the approach we will take:

1. Scan through the Building SimGroup looking for an interior datablock that has the Great Hall's file name in the filename property. There's only one on the demo map.
2. Get the avatar's transform.
3. Get the building's transform.

4. Use the avatar's transform to modify the building's transform to make it face the avatar.

5. Set the new building's transform.

So let's get cracking.

The Code

It's necessary for you to have completed the code in the previous section about warping the player character in order for the code in this section to work. If you haven't completed the warping section and successfully tested it, you should do that now before proceeding.

Now, to get the rotation example code into the program, open the script module called myServerScripts.cs, in the folder C:\A3D\demo\server\scripts and add the following code:

```
function FindBuilding(%filename)
{
   echo ("looking for building:"@%filename);
   %count = Buildings.getCount();
   %target = 0;
   for(%i = 0; %i < %count; %i++)
   {
      %found = Buildings.getObject(%i);
      echo("id:"@%i@"-"@%found.interiorFile);
      if (%found.interiorFile $= "demo/data/interiors/room/greathall.dif")
      {
        %target = %found;
         break;
      }
   }
   return %target;
}
function serverCmdRotate1(%client)
{
   echo ("******* We be rotatin'! *******");
   %avatar = %client.player;  // 1a

   %bldg = findBuilding("demo/data/interiors/room/greathall.dif");
   %newtransform = daRotate(%avatar.getTransform(),%bldg);
   %bldg.setTransform(%newtransform);
}
```

```
function DaRotate(%avatar_xform,%obj)
{
  %obj_xform = %obj.getTransform();
  %rotA = GetWords(%avatar_xform,3,6);
  %matrixA = "0 0 0" SPC %rotA;
  %rotB = "0 0 1 6.28"; // 6.28 = 2PI = 360 degrees
  %matrixB = "0 0 0" SPC %rotB;
  %product = MatrixMultiply(%v1,%v2);
  %transform = getWords(%obj_xform,0,2) SPC GetWords(%product,3,6);
  return %transform;
}
```

Save your work.

Next, open the file C:\A3D\demo\client\config.cs and go to the end of the file, after everything else. Add the following line of code:

```
moveMap.bindCmd(keyboard, "k", "commandToServer(\'Rotate1\');", "");
```

This is the binding for the test key that will invoke the rotation code.

Now, let's have a look at the rotation code and see how it works.

When you press the test key, the code on the client side interprets the key bind and sends a message to the server side telling the server code to locate the server-side command called serverCmdRotate1. It is absolutely necessary to include the prefix "serverCmd" in the function name. Any functions with this prefix will be picked up and tracked by the server when they are encountered when their source modules are loaded. Then when the server receives a message from the client via the commandToServer function, it knows where to look to the find the function. A similar system using commandToClient and a "clientCmd" prefix works for going the other direction: invoking commands on a client from the server.

When serverCmdRotate1 is called, it is automatically passed a handle to the calling client as its first variable, in this case %client. It then outputs a little message to the console just to indicate that the function was invoked. The code then extracts a handle to the player's avatar object from the client object.

Next, we call the function FindBuilding which scans through the mission file looking for the only instance of the Great Hall object that has been placed in the mission file (placed there as part of the Torque Game Engine Demo).

The FindBuilding function uses a loop to look through the Buildings SimGroup, checking to see if there is a building there whose interior file (model file) has a particular name. Once it finds that building, it returns the handle to that building object back to the calling function, which so happens to be `serverCmdRotate1`.

The meat of the code is the function `DaRotate`, which receives the avatar's transform and the handle to the building as parameters. It uses the angled vectors of the avatar's transform and the building's transform to create new rotation matrices. The two matrices are multiplied together, and the product is used to generate the new transformation matrix, which is returned to the `serverCmdRotate1` function and then applied to the building using its setTransform method.

Testing The Rotating Hall

Launch \A3D\demo.exe, and run the FPS Multiplayer in just the same way as you did when testing the warping code earlier.

Once the demo game loads, and your player character has spawned in, make your way over to water's edge, where the Great Hall is located. Check back with Figure 3.16 if you need help with identifying the Great Hall.

Once you have it clearly in your sights, so to speak, its time for the big test. Keep your eyes peeled.

Press "k".

Hah! See that? If you missed it, move your player a large amount one way or the other around the hall, and hit "k" again. Go ahead and experiment with different values for `%rotB` in the `DaRotate` function, and perhaps even different matrix operations to see what the results are.

Moving Right Along

Well, we've looked at vectors and matrices in detail—although not exhaustively. I've concentrated on those characteristics that have the most applicability in games, and are likely to be used in scripted situations.

You've also seen how vectors and matrices can be used to solve typical geometric and navigational problems.

Finally, we've used TorqueScript and some of its built-in vector and matrix methods to manipulate objects in the game world. It is quite evident that Torque provides some powerful tools for the script programmer.

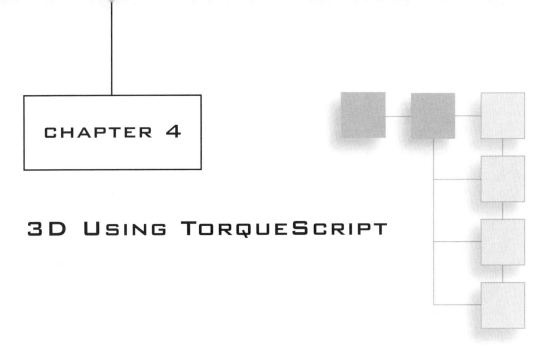

CHAPTER 4

3D USING TORQUESCRIPT

In the previous chapters, you learned some of the more esoteric TorqueScript capabilities. Not *all* of them, mind you—TorqueScript is incredibly powerful and rich with capabilities. If you are skeptical, just take a glance at Appendix A, in the TorqueScript Reference section. There are around *60 pages* of function references for the scripting language, not counting object methods!

In this chapter we're going to solve some fairly common game play problems using some of the 3D manipulation and calculation features of TorqueScript—moving doors, both the swinging and sliding kind, and map warping.

Swinging Doors

As of this writing, the Torque Game Engine (currently at version 1.3) does not have built-in support for doors and elevators and things of that nature. This is a reflection of its heritage as the *Tribes & Tribes 2* game engine, where doors and elevators were not part of the game play design.

This is not really an issue for us, however, since we can easily create our own doors with Torque. There are actually several ways to do this:

1. Create our own door object, derived from a `ShapeBase` object, that understands opening, closing, playing sound effects, tracking its position, locking and unlocking, and so on. This approach requires owning a Torque license and modifying the engine, so I won't go into it here.

2. Create a door Shape object with both an open and close animation. Invoke the animations using a trigger, and use a small amount of TorqueScript code to track state changes. This is a reasonable approach that doesn't require changes to the core engine, but it also doesn't really exercise TorqueScript's advanced features very much at all.

3. Create an ordinary StaticShape door object, and use TorqueScript to rotate and move the door through 3D world space, track its states, and trigger sound effects. This approach is pretty funky, and lets us stretch our minds a bit with TorqueScript, so this is the one we want to tackle.

Now when considering how we'll tackle this task, we sit back and look at the problem. We will need a way to cause the door to open. We can do this several ways: We could just bang into the door and trigger the opening that way, with a collision. Or we could detect when we were near the door, and then trigger the opening. Or we could activate the door opening by pressing a key—"operating" the door, if you will, which is the approach we will take here.

And then there is the actual rotation. In the last chapter we looked at ways to rotate things and move them through space using vectors and matrices. We could certainly take that approach here as well. But whenever I'm looking at solutions to problems or challenges, I also look at ways to optimize the solution, to create the least amount of code. In TorqueScript, the more code you execute, the more work the computer does, which has the potential to bog down a server in a multiplayer situation.

With that in mind, I realize that normal doors only rotate around a vertical axis. Yes, there are hatches, and odd-angled flaps and things that rotate around non-orthogonal axes, but they are much rarer than the everyday door or gate. This limited rotation axis means that we don't actually *need* to use rotation matrices to swing a door open and shut. We just need to add and subtract angles. That will do just fine.

Door Resources

Having settled the question of how we intend to implement the doors, we're going to need a few resources. I've provided them for you in the RESOURCES folder of the CD, under the ch4 folder name. If you want to go about creating your own resources, this is what you'll need to make:

▪ A door model, exported to DTS format for use by Torque. The door can be as ornate as you want, but it must have at least one collision mesh that roughly equals the size of the door itself. Do not include any animations.

- A door skin for your model. Make sure that when you skin your door, you use a skin that doesn't limit how you can place the door. It's best if the skin is symmetrical from left to right, and top to bottom, but failing that, make sure that the front features properly align with the features for the back side. For example, if a door knob appears on the right when looking at the door from the front (see Figure 4.1), make sure that the skin on the rear is mapped so that the rear door handle appears on the *left* side of the back, when looking at the door from the back (see Figure 4.2).

- Three sound effects: for opening a door, closing a door, and slamming when the door actually shuts. You can get away with using the same effect for opening and closing if you want to do that. Torque now supports the Ogg Vorbis file format. This format is better than wav format because it makes a smaller file, and is cross-platform as well. Whenever you can, use this format. The audio engineering tool Audacity supports this format. See Appendix B for pointers about where to obtain Audacity.

Figure 4.1 Door skin, front side.

Figure 4.2 Door skin, back side.

Door Code

Oh boy, now the dreaded code dump. Well, it's going to happen so get used to it! We need to do a little prep-work first, creating a call to exec to load the door code module in, create some key bindings, and other housekeeping activities first.

Step One

Open the file \A3D\demo\client\scripts\default.bind.cs and then place the following line of code at the end of the file:

```
moveMap.bindCmd(keyboard, "o", "commandToServer('Operate');", "");
```

Save your work. This is the key binding for the Operate function that we will be using to open our doors. Now, in the previous chapter we also did key bindings, but we put them in a different module (actually into config.cs). We will also do that, but I'm also asking you to put the binding here because the config.cs file is a preferences-type file that the user can delete. If that file is deleted, the key bindings in there will be lost. By also putting the binding in here, we make sure that it is available if the config.cs file has been deleted. If config.cs *was* deleted, Torque will rebuild it automatically the next time it runs and it will get the info it needs from default.bind.cs.

So, without further ado, open the file \A3D\demo\client\config.cs and then place the following line of code at the end of the file:

```
moveMap.bindCmd(keyboard, "o", "commandToServer('Operate');", "");
```

Step Two

Open \A3D\demo\server\scripts\game.cs and locate where you inserted this line in the last chapter, in the function onServerCreated:

```
exec("./myServerScripts.cs");
```

and add this line after it:

```
exec("./doors.cs");
```

This loads our door control script into memory when the server is created.

Step Three

Now let's copy our resources into the right place. Create the folder \A3D\demo\data \shapes\doors on your hard drive, and then copy the files door.dts and door.png from the \A3D\RESOURCES\ch4 folder into \A3D\demo\data\shapes\doors.

Next, copy from \A3D\RESOURCES\ch4 the files doorslam.ogg, doorslide.ogg, door-swingclosed.ogg, doorswingopen.ogg, and doorthud.ogg to the doors folder \A3D\demo\data\sound. Again, if the folder does not already exist, create it.

Step Four

Now to add the actual door control code. Type in the following contents, and then save as \A3D\demo\server\scripts\doors.cs.

```
$DOORS::RADIANS_PER_DEGREE = 0.017444;
$DOORS::XY_UNIT_VECTORS = "0 0";
$DOORS::PLAYER_REACH = 4.5;
$DOORS::OPEN_INCREMENT = 0.02;
$DOORS::CLOSE_INCREMENT = 0.04;
$DOORS::OPEN_TIMER = 20;
$DOORS::CLOSE_TIMER = 10;
$DOORS::HOLD_TIMER = 2000;
$DOORS::MAX_ANGLE = 90; //  degrees
$DOORS::MAX_SLIDE = 5; //  meters (for sliding doors)


datablock AudioProfile(doorStartOpenSwingSnd)
{
   fileName = "~/data/sound/doors/doorStartOpenSwing.ogg";
   description = AudioClose3d;
   preload = true;
};


datablock AudioProfile(doorSwingClosedSnd)
{
   fileName = "~/data/sound/doors/doorswingclosed.ogg";
   description = AudioClose3d;
   preload = true;
};


datablock AudioProfile(doorSlamSnd)
{
   fileName = "~/data/sound/doors/doorslam.ogg";
   description = AudioClose3d;
   preload = true;
};
```

```
datablock StaticShapeData(ADoor)
{
   category = "Doors";
   shapeFile = "~/data/shapes/doors/door.dts";
};

function ADoor::OnAdd(%theDatablock, %whichDoor)
{
  if(!%whichDoor.doorOpenFlag)
      %whichDoor.doorOpenFlag = false;
  if(!%whichDoor.rotationDirection)
      %whichDoor.rotationDirection = 1;
  if(!%whichDoor.maxOpenAngle)
      %whichDoor.maxOpenAngle = $DOORS::MAX_ANGLE;

  %whichDoor.currentRotation = 0;
  %whichDoor.originalRotation = 0;
  %whichDoor.partialTransform = "";
}

function serverCmdOperate(%client)
{
   %player = %client.player;
   %eye = %player.getEyeVector();
   %vec = vectorScale(%eye, $DOORS::PLAYER_REACH);
   %start = %player.getEyeTransform();
   %end = VectorAdd(%start,%vec);
   %found = ContainerRayCast (%start, %end, $TypeMasks::StaticObjectType, %player);
   if(%found)
      %found.getDataBlock().Operate(%found);
}

function ADoor::Operate(%theDatablock, %whichDoor)
{
  if (%whichDoor.doorOpenFlag == false)
  {
    %theDatablock.StartOpenSwing(%whichDoor);
  }
}
```

```
function ADoor::StartOpenSwing(%theDatablock, %whichDoor)
{
  %whichDoor.doorOpenFlag=true;
  %whichDoor.currentRotation = 0;
  %whichDoor.originalRotation = getword(%whichDoor.GetTransform(),6);
  %z_unit_vector = getword(%whichDoor.GetTransform(),5);
  if ( %z_unit_vector == 0 )
    %z_unit_vector = "1";
  %whichDoor.partialTransform = getwords(%whichDoor.GetTransform(),0,2) SPC
      $DOORS::XY_UNIT_VECTORS SPC %z_unit_vector;
  %whichDoor.openSnd = %whichDoor.playAudio(0,doorStartOpenSwingSnd);
  %theDatablock.IncrementSwing(%whichDoor);
}

function ADoor::IncrementSwing(%theDatablock, %whichDoor)
{
  if ( %whichDoor.currentRotation <
      (%whichDoor.maxOpenAngle*$DOORS::RADIANS_PER_DEGREE))
  {
      %whichDoor.currentRotation  += ( $DOORS::OPEN_INCREMENT *
      %whichDoor.rotationDirection);
      %newrot = %whichDoor.originalRotation + %whichDoor.currentRotation;
      %whichDoor.settransform(%whichDoor.partialTransform SPC %newrot);
      %theDatablock.schedule($DOORS::OPEN_TIMER,"IncrementSwing", %whichDoor);
   }
  else
  {
    %theDatablock.schedule($DOORS::HOLD_TIMER,"StartCloseSwing",%whichDoor);
  }
}

function ADoor::StartCloseSwing(%theDatablock, %whichDoor)
{
  %whichDoor.stopAudio(openSnd);
  %whichDoor.closeSnd = %whichDoor.playAudio(0,doorSwingClosedSnd);
  %theDatablock.schedule($DOORS::CLOSE_TIMER,"DecrementSwing", %whichDoor);
}
```

```
function ADoor::DecrementSwing(%theDatablock, %whichDoor)
{
  if ( %whichDoor.currentRotation > 0)
  {
    %whichDoor.currentRotation  -= ($DOORS::CLOSE_INCREMENT *
      %whichDoor.rotationDirection);
    %newrot = %whichDoor.originalRotation + %whichDoor.currentRotation;
    %whichDoor.settransform(%whichDoor.partialTransform SPC %newrot);
    %theDatablock.schedule($DOORS::CLOSE_TIMER,"DecrementSwing", %whichDoor);
  }
  else
  {
    %whichDoor.doorOpenFlag=false;
    %whichDoor.settransform(%whichDoor.partialTransform SPC
      %whichDoor.originalRotation);
    %whichDoor.stopAudio(closeSnd);
    %whichDoor.slamSnd = %whichDoor.playAudio(0,doorSlamSnd);
    %whichDoor.currentRotation = 0;
    %whichDoor.dump();
  }
}
```

Okay, let's dissect this puppy. At the very beginning of the file are a whole whack of variable definitions that start with $DOORS::. Now, these really are variables—global ones, but I've used them here more in the spirit of *constants*, since I do not intend (cross my heart) to actually change them while running the program. So they are de facto constants, or perhaps *pseudo*-constants, instead of mere variables. This is a fairly important point—Torque doesn't have any way to specify constants, but there is a convention that goes back to the early days of C language that constants (sometimes called *macros* or *#defines* in C/C++) are defined with all caps and underscores as word dividers. So I use that same convention here, and it serves as a reminder to me that I don't want to fiddle with them, although I *can* use them wherever I need their values. Another thing is that they are defined with a namespace prefix, the DOOR:: part. This isn't entirely necessary, but helps me keep things organized. In other places, at other times, this would have been called a *facility* code.

Note

This source code walkthrough and discussion is quite detailed. As the book progresses, I will provide less and less detail. I expect that you will grow more capable at understanding the code you read as you progress, so I can eventually dispense with a large part of the code descriptions.

Anyway, these constants are used to hold values that are used in the code, and by using the value this way, we get something meaningful rather than just some number in the middle of program code. It lends to code readability, which helps reduce bugs.

After the constants, there is a set of datablock definitions for our sound effects. There is nothing particularly special here, but note that I've ensured that the datablock names are meaningful, and closely match the actual filenames of the wave files—this isn't a requirement, but it helps when you are trying to keep track of things. The preload property for each is set to true to ensure that the sound effect data is loaded into memory before Torque tries to play the sound effect. This will minimize any delay between when the script activates the sound effect and when you actually start to hear it on the client.

After the audio stuff, there is a StaticShapeData datablock named ADoor. Inside it are two properties. First is the category which tells the Torque Mission Editor the category under which this object should appear in the Editor Creator, so that the level builder can find the object in order to place it in the world. And then there is the shapeFile property, indicating the path to the actual model of the shape, relative to the *root main* folder of the game (that would be the folder where the game executable—demo.exe—resides).

Next we have the first datablock method, ADoor::OnAdd. This method is called when an instance of a door is added to the mission. This can happen if the door is created dynamically while the game is running, or at load time when the mission is created, if a door that uses this datablock is inserted in the mission's world. The latter is the method we will be using. I'll show you how to add doors to the mission later on in this section. In the meantime, for an example of what an actual door object definition looks like, as found in the mission file for the FPS Multiplayer example after a door was inserted into the mission, look at this:

```
new StaticShape() {
    position = "187.604 -39.4717 198.801";
    rotation = "1 0 0 0";
    scale = "1 1 1";
    dataBlock = "ADoor";
      rotationDirection = "1";
      maxOpenAngle = "90";
};
```

The door object is of the StaticShape class. The first three lines show the transformation information for the object. Then comes the datablock property that points, by name, to the datablock that we just talked about a minute ago: ADoor. So what we have here is an unnamed instance of a StaticShape that uses the ADoor datablock to define its behavior and properties. Now like any StaticShape, it has its own methods and properties as well, which are generally applicable to any StaticShape. By using the ADoor datablock, we can now provide specialized behavior and properties for this shape—and that's what this module doors.cs, is all about. So whenever you see me talk about an instance of a door, or the door object, one of the StaticShapes that was inserted into the mission using the above StaticShape code snippet is what I'm talking about.

Now there are two basic activities in ADoor::OnAdd. First, we are initializing some user-definable *dynamic* variables, as properties of an instance of a door. The user can specify these variables in the mission file by inserting the variables and their values with the Mission Editor, or by editing the mission file manually with a text editor. The series of if statements you see in the first part of this function are checking to see if the user already has defined values for these variables. If he has *not*, then an initial value is assigned to the variable to ensure that they begin in a sensible and known state. These are *conditional* initializations.

After the conditionals, there are a few more initialization statements, but these are subtly different. These are variables that are used during the operation of the doors, just like the earlier conditionals. But we want these variables to always start with specific values, so they are *not* conditional. If the user were to specify values for these variables in the mission file or Mission Editor, whatever settings he created would be wiped out by these statements at the time the object is inserted into the world, because we want to start with these values, and no others.

Turn your attention to the second argument to the ADoor::OnAdd function, %whichdoor. This is the handle to the specific instance of a door that is created, the StaticShape door I told you about. If you look at all of the variable assignment statements, you will notice that it is the property variables of %whichdoor that are being tested or initialized. Now look back a bit to the StaticShape declaration from the mission file I showed you. Notice that the indented properties in the StaticShape declaration are some of the same ones we are testing for in the ADoor::OnAdd? Those are examples of the user creating his own specifications for those variable properties.

Torque Terminology Time!

Like any complex creation of mankind, Torque has its own quirks and foibles. One of these is the nomenclature used by the original GarageGames programmers who created the demo scripts.

First of all, Torque provides a certain handy object reference capability in an object's methods that is similar to the use of the *this* keyword in C++, but not exactly the same. In Torque, if you have a object method like `AnObject::DoSomething`, when you call the method you would call it like this:

```
%objectHandle.DoSomething();
```

Your method's declaration would need to look something like this:

```
AnObject::DoSomething(%theDatablock)
{
}
```

This is because Torque automatically passes the object's handle into the method as the first argument. You need to have a variable there to grab that argument, even if you don't intend to use it. You can use any valid identifier that you like, but by convention established by the GarageGames guys, normally `%this` is used as the first argument's identifier. There are some exceptions: If the object is `GameConnection`, then the first argument is usually called `%client`.

Now be patient with me, I'm slowly working my way to the punch line here.

As you have seen in earlier chapters, Torque uses a special kind of object or data structure called a *datablock*. In some ways, datablocks are treated much like regular objects—they have properties and methods.

Now here comes the rub. This gets a little convoluted, so hang on tight. Here we go!

When we normally create an object method, the first argument to that method is always the handle of its owning object. With any given datablock object, there is only ever *one* instance of that datablock. So every time a reference to that datablock shows up somewhere in the code, it's always the same one, with the same handle. And yet, by convention, the identifier `%this` is used to specify the first argument into any method of that datablock. Can you see it? It can be somewhat subtle: Using `%this` *implies* that there could be more than one version of this datablock, and that you need the handle `%this` to tell them apart. But that just isn't so.

It *would* be the case for any other category of object, but not for datablocks.

Why does this matter? Well, it matters because the identifier usage can quickly lead to confusion, especially when you realize that datablocks are often paired up with related objects with similar names that *do* have multiple instances, sometimes even maybe hundreds of instances running (or standing, crawling, falling, or bouncing) around the game world bumping into each other.

One often gets a situation where there is a `Bozo` class of objects, and a `BozoData` datablock that defines invariant properties and methods that were created for use by the `Bozo` class of objects. For example, you end up with a situation where you can have this object method:

```
Function Bozo::BeepNose(%this ,%obj)
{
}
```

and this datablock method

```
function BozoData::BeepNose(%this ,%obj)
{
}
```

They look almost the same. But in the first case, the `%this` refers to one instance of many possible bozos, and in the second case, the `%this` refers to the *only* instance of `BozoData` that can possibly exist.

But wait, there's more!

Usually what happens is that in the first case, the `%obj` argument is the handle of some object that has just interacted with that particular instance of the `Bozo` class, like maybe another player or a piano that has fallen on the `Bozo`, while in the second case, the `%obj` argument is usually the instance of the `Bozo` class that wants to use the datablock's method!

Arggggggghhhhhhh!!!!! What to do? What to do?

Here's what I've decided to do to help retain what remains of my dignity: When dealing with datablock methods, I call the first argument `%theDatablock` (and not `%this`). And then—because as I said just a moment ago, the second argument to a datablock method is usually a handle to an instance of the object that uses the datablock—I call the second argument a descriptive name like this:

```
function BozoData::BeepNose(%theDatablock,%theBozo)
{
}
```

Using "the" as the prefix in the `%theBozo` identifier takes advantage of English language semantic rules, telling everyone who is paying attention that the second argument refers to a specific (but currently anonymous) Bozo.

So now there is no ambiguity inside the datablock method. The identifiers tell me what I'm dealing with in a much clearer way than before.

And finally, all other categories of objects are treated the same way they always were.

This long sidebar was necessary to explain what might seem to be unusual naming choices in the code I've presented to you for providing opening doors. The same convention will be used at times throughout the rest of this book, but if used, it will only be for new book code—I will *not* be diving into the existing stock Torque demo scripts to change them to match.

After examining the `ADoor::OnAdd` method, we now get to where the action starts, with `serverCmdOperate`. You need to know that this code module is executed on the server-side of things. As you can deduce, when you press the operate key ("o"), you are doing that on the client side. That key was bound in the default.bind.cs module, you might recall. In that module we used the `commandToServer…` *direct messaging* construct to send a command from the client to the server, telling the server to execute the function `Operate` when the bound key was pressed. The server receives that message (and all messages like that) and looks for the function name appended to the end of the string `serverCmd`, so in this instance, it looks for `serverCmdOperate`, and passes the client handle and any transmitted arguments (there aren't any in this case).

What `serverCmdOperate` is going to do is look to see if anything is within reach of the player in the direction that he is looking. If so, and if it is a door, then we'll invoke the door's own `Operate` method on it.

The first thing that `serverCmdOperate` does is extract the player handle from the client handle. Next, we grab the vector that tells us the direction the player's eye is looking. And yes, you are right—`%eye` *is* a unit vector. We take advantage of the fact, and use the reach distance to scale the eye vector, since it is already pointing where we want. So now we have a vector that tells us how far away we can reach, and in which direction to do it. We just need to know where to start our reaching from. We can find this out by getting the transform of the eye, and then with these two values—the transform and the vector—we can figure out where our reach ends (it starts at the eye transform).

All this good data is fed into the magical `ContainerRayCast` function, which pops out the handle of any doors that it finds. `ContainerRayCast` used the `$TypeMasks::StaticObjectType` mask internally, to compare against the types of objects it finds . If the type of the objects `ContainerRayCast` finds matches the specified type, then `ContainerRayCast` returns the details about that object, depositing said details in the `%found` variable. For a list of available type masks, see Table A.1 in Appendix A.

We've also told `ContainerRayCast` to ignore our own player object, by specifying `%player` in the last argument. `ContainerRayCast` is an extremely useful function for game play purposes. What it does is extend a line, or "ray" in the world from the starting coordinates to the ending coordinates in three dimensions (see Figure 4.3). It looks for objects that have the type that is specified in its third parameter, and considers its job done when it has "hit" the first such object.

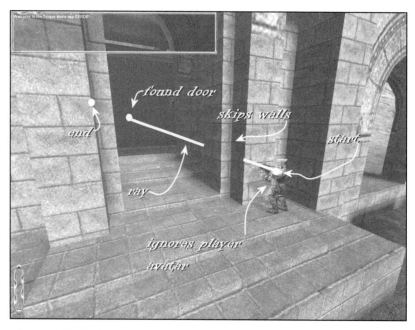

Figure 4.3 Casting a ray.

You can also give it the handle of any object that it should ignore. Usually this would be your own character. In Figure 4.3, the ray being cast is quite long, maybe 30 feet or so. In our code, we are using a 4.5 meter ray. Now I know that is quite a bit farther than people can reach, but I chose it for gameplay reasons—less than that seems to "feel" just too close. But of course, you are free to use any reach that you find suitable, simply by changing the `$DOORS::PLAYER_REACH` constant.

Now, if no object is found that matches the type, then `%found` is stuffed with a big, fat zero. If the right kind of object (a door) is found, then off it goes into the door's own `Operate` method, dragging an argument along the handle of the found door with it. So let's dive right in behind it!

In `Door::Operate` not much happens. This may tempt you to just turn around and head right back out, call a taxi, pass the driver a tenner, and tell him to take you to where the action is. Well, maybe you should take another look. It's true that not much happens in the function, but it's an *important* not much.

First, you check the state of the door to see if it's closed, because if it isn't, that means the door is already being operated. So leave it alone. The `doorOpenFlag` is the variable used during the game to track whether a door is open or closed. At startup, we always want the door set to closed, so `doorOpenFlag` is initialized to `false`, meaning that the door is not open, as you saw back in the discussion about `ADoor::OnAdd`. If we don't watch out for the door state, we can cause some pretty funky things to happen to the door that we want to avoid.

If the door *is* closed, then it's time to get that door swinging, by calling the door's `StartOpenSwing` method. Notice that because this is a method of `ADoor` and therefore part of the `ADoor` namespace, when it is invoked the object's handle is automatically inserted as the first argument in the argument list. Then inside the method we extract it with the variable `%theDatablock`. See the Torque Terminology Sidebar for more exposition on this subject.

`ADoor::StartOpenSwing` is mostly more preparation activity. The very first thing it does is set the door's state flag in order to prevent you or someone else from trying to open the door while it is swinging open (or while it is standing open or swinging closed). Then we initialize our rotation tracking variable, `%whichDoor.currentRotation`. No matter which way a door is facing when it is closed, we consider the rotation to be zero.

Then we extract the current transform rotation, which is the seventh (therefore indexed by the number 6 when zero-based indexing is used, as it is in Torque) value in the transform string returned from `%whichDoor.GetTransform()`. We need this value because we are going to be changing it later in another method. Since it is saved as a property of whichever door `%whichDoor` is pointing to, we can access the value from any method that knows about `%whichDoor`.

Next, we extract the first three values in the transform string, saving them in the `%whichDoor.partialTransform` property for later use. Notice that we only extracted the position information and not the three normal angles that follow (and that precede the rotation value). This is because when you place a `StaticShape` object in the game world using the Mission Editor, by default it assigns the values "1 0 0" for the normals, which would mean that the rotation (which would be 0 at the time of placement) will be applied to a rotation around the X-axis. But this is a door we are dealing with. It only needs to rotate around the Z-axis. So we toss away the default values from the time of placement, and substitute our values: "0 0". But before we toss the three away, we extract the Z-axis rotation value by itself, and then check it, just in case it really was set when the door was placed in the world. If the value is zero, then we will substitute in a 1. Otherwise we will use the setting it had (1 or -1). This will cause the rotation to occur around the axis we want.

Next, we start the audio sound effect playing on channel 0, using the `doorSwingOpenSnd` datablock you saw at the top of the code module. The sound effect is just played once, until it stops. We save a handle to the sound being played as a dynamic property of the door instance in `openSnd`. The handle will be valid as long as the sound is being played. This means that we can do things to the actively playing sound at a later time, like stop it before it runs to completion. Another approach that we could take to generate sound effects would be to use an AudioEmitter, place it in the world at a location of our own choosing, start the sound, and then later delete the emitter when the door stops opening.

Anyway, we finally call `%theDatablock.IncrementSwing`, again passing on the pointer to the actual door instance we're dealing with.

The next method we will examine is that very same `%theDatablock.IncrementSwing`, which is the meat and potatoes of the door control code.

The very first thing we do in `ADoor::IncrementSwing` is check our rotation tracking variable and see if we've exceeded the maximum angle that we will allow the door to open. Since this is our first visit to this bit of code, it's doubtful that the rotation has gone far enough. However, we will be returning here many times over the course of the door opening activity.

Every time through this function we increment the rotation value. By design, our rotation always increments positively. You can see `currentRotation` being incremented by the `$DOORS::OPEN_INCREMENT` constant, which happens to be 0.02 radians, as defined at the top of the doors.cs module. For faster opening, use a larger number. The `rotationDirection` variable is set to either 1 or -1, indicating opposite directions. The positive is for door opening, and the negative is for closing.

The sum of the original rotation angle and the new one we've just calculated is our new total rotation value, saved in the local variable %newrot.

So now that we've computed how far the door has rotated, we need to apply that information to the door's transform. We had saved the door's position information from its transform in partialTransform, so now we can put the whole transform back together again, using the setTransform method. Note that the partial transform and the new rotation are concatenated together using the SPC macro. That's the same as using " "@" " for the string concatenation.

As soon as we set the new transform, the door will rotate a tiny bit to the new position almost instantly. So now, all we have to do is come back and do it again, and again, and again until the door is all the way open. We do that by using the schedule method of the datablock. We give schedule a time period to wait (in milliseconds), the name of a function to call, and the values of any arguments the function needs, and it will go off and count off the milliseconds until the magic moment, and then it will call the function it was told to call, and pass in the arguments it was given.

In our case, we schedule the very method we are in for a wake-up call in 20 milliseconds, and tell it to increment the very same door, all over again.

When we regain consciousness, we find ourselves back in IncrementSwing, where we dutifully perform the calculation, rotate the door a teensy bit, then schedule another wake-up call.

It's like déjà vu all over again! Eventually though, the re-iteration will end when the rotation angle exceeds (by a tiny amount) the maximum angle. At that point, instead of incrementing, we end up in the *else* portion of the code.

In the else block, we now schedule a wake-up call to close the door, but we do it with a longer delay, specified by $DOORS::HOLD_TIMER, which has been set to 2000 milliseconds (two seconds) at the top of the module. This gives players time to get through the doorway. You can set this to anything that suits you. Eventually, the timer expires, and the StartCloseSwing method is called.

ADoor::StartCloseSwing exists for two purposes: to give us a place to stop the door opening sound effect, and to allow us to play the closing sound effect without having it get played every time through the closing loop. So we turn on the sound, and then reschedule a wake-up for ADoor::DecrementSwing in 10 milliseconds.

ADoor::DecrementSwing is almost identical to ADoor::IncrementSwing in the repeating portion, except that it decrements the rotation value.

The one big difference is that `ADoor::DecrementSwing` does more things when the door finally closes. First it sets the `doorOpenFlag` to show that the door is closed. It reassembles the starting transform for the door, and repositions the door exactly as it was before it started opening up. Then it stops the closing sound effect, and plays a final "slamming shut" sound effect. And finally, it resets the rotation counter back to 0.

Well, that's done. There's a lot of stuff happening in there. Next time someone hollers at you: CLOSE THAT DOOR! You can respond with "Do you know how much work that really is?" Unless, of course, it's your mother doing the hollering. Never talk back to your mother!

Now if you want, you can take the code I gave you in doors.cs and expand it to allow for swing doors around axes that have orientations other than purely vertical. A quick trip back to Chapter 3 and a review of rotation matrices should do the trick. You could also do it with vector math, or a combination of both.

Testing the Swinging Door

After all that preparation and code gazing, let's set up a door and test it. Run the FPS Multiplayer demo in the A3D folder. Once you've spawned into the sample mission, run over to the big hall/temple building and plant yourself somewhere in the entrance area. Once there, you can press F8 to switch to fly mode (or camera mode) and fly around the scene divorced from your avatar.

You should position yourself something like five or ten "feet" (estimate by eye) above the ground in camera mode and set your camera speed to the slowest.

Tip

You can adjust the flying speed of the camera mode by opening the Mission Editor (press the F11 key), and then pressing Shift+1 to get the slowest camera speed, or pressing Shift+7 for the highest camera speed, or any of the numbers between 1 and 7. The lower the number, the slower the camera moves. Use Shift+7, or high speed, to move about the map quickly. Once your camera is roughly positioned, you should switch to a slow speed, like Shift+1 to aid in object placement.

Once you've found a suitable place to plant your door, like in the entrance, ensure you stay in fly mode, and then press F11 to invoke the Mission Editor. Once the Editor is up, press F4 to invoke the Creator mode. On the lower right side (as shown in Figure 4.4), you will see the tree view. Expand the Shapes list by clicking on the plus sign, then expand Doors. When you click on ADoor, it will be pasted into the game world at the point on the ground where the center of your screen view is pointing.

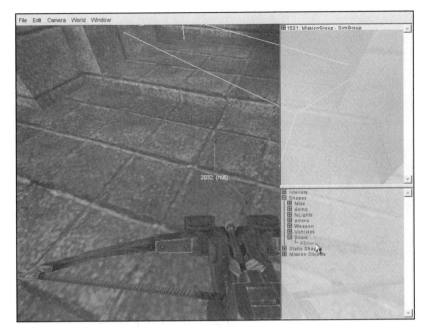

File   Edit   Camera   World   Window

1531: MissionGroup - SimGroup

2032: (null)

Interiors
Shapes
Misc
demo
fxLights
ammo
Weapon
Vehicles
Doors
  ADoor
Static Shapes
Mission Objects

Figure 4.4 Placing a door.

If you are standing in the entrance like Figure 4.4 shows, your door will be inserted below the floor level, since that's where ground level is. When this happens, just move your cursor over the blue line that sticks up from the object, with the Z label on it. When you hover your mouse hand over it, it will become highlighted. Press the mouse button down, then drag the door up to the floor's level by pulling on that Z.

You can position the door to your satisfaction by dragging it by one of the handles. You must make sure you are in fly mode, otherwise you will not be able to grab the axis handles. You can rotate the door around the Z-axis by holding down the Alt key while dragging the Z handle. Try it out for yourself now to see how it works.

Once the door is positioned satisfactorily, press F11 to leave the Editor. Then Alt+C to switch back to player-control mode. Now walk up to the door, fairly close (judging by eye), then press the "o" key. The door will swing open. After standing open for about two seconds, it will swing closed again. If it doesn't open, move closer and try again. If you get right up against the door and it still won't open, press ~ (that's the tilde key) to open the console interface. Scroll upwards looking at old messages in the console looking for messages in red. Not all red text is an error, but if an error occurred, it will be in red text, and will probably have a pair of hash-marks (##) surrounding the spot where the error was detected. Use this and the console log file to debug your program. Also, refer back to Chapter 2 for some pointers on how to go about resolving your code problem.

Sliding Doors

More doors!

This time, let's take on the famous *sliding door* of TV science fiction or *Doom* fame. We won't go into as much detail as with the swinging door code. We'll use some vector and matrix math, which you looked at in the last chapter. We'll make a door that slides up into the ceiling.

Door Resources

We're going to use the same resources that we did with the swinging doors. You'll probably want to change at least the texture and the sound effects to more appropriately match what a sliding door should look like, if you use this for your own game. Most sliding doors that I've seen don't have hinges, for example.

Door Code

What we'll do is apply our changes to the existing door.cs module. But rather than spend pages and pages telling you to change this line, add that one, and remove another one, I'll give you the new code with the sliding door integrated with the swing door, and I'll use a marker on the new lines like this:

```
//   ***new***
```

Also, these next two markers will indicate that there is all new code between them. This one indicates the start of a new block of code:

```
// vvv ***new*** vvv
```

and this one indicates the end of the new code block:

```
// ^^^ ***new*** ^^^
```

That way, you'll know what to add in, and still see it in context. For new methods, I will include the new marker only on the line of the function's declaration, and not the rest of its definition. Then we will take a look at the new code, and how to use it. To refresh your memory, the door module is located at \A3D\demo\server\scripts\doors.cs.

```
$DOORS::RADIANS_PER_DEGREE = 0.017444;
$DOORS::XY_UNIT_VECTORS = "0 0";
$DOORS::PLAYER_REACH = 4.5;
$DOORS::OPEN_INCREMENT = 0.02;
$DOORS::CLOSE_INCREMENT = 0.04;
$DOORS::OPEN_TIMER = 20;
$DOORS::CLOSE_TIMER = 10;
$DOORS::HOLD_TIMER = 2000;
$DOORS::MAX_ANGLE = 90;
$DOORS::MAX_SLIDE = 3.5;    //  ***new***
$DOORS::SLIDE_STEP = 0.05; //  ***new***
$DOORS::MODE_SWING = "swing"; //  ***new***
$DOORS::MODE_SLIDE = "slide"; //  ***new***

datablock AudioProfile(doorSwingOpenSndProfile)
{
   fileName = "~/data/sound/doors/doorswingopen.ogg";
   description = AudioClose3d;
   preload = true;
};

datablock AudioProfile(doorSwingClosedSndProfile)
{
   fileName = "~/data/sound/doors/doorswingclosed.ogg";
   description = AudioClose3d;
   preload = true;
};

datablock AudioProfile(doorSlamSndProfile)
{
   fileName = "~/data/sound/doors/doorslam.ogg";
   description = AudioClose3d;
   preload = true;
};

datablock AudioProfile(doorSlideSndProfile) // vvv ***new*** vvv
{
   fileName = "~/data/sound/doors/doorslide.ogg";
   description = AudioClose3d;
   preload = true;
}; // ^^^ ***new*** ^^^
```

```
datablock AudioProfile(doorThudSndProfile) // vvv ***new*** vvv
{
   fileName = "~/data/sound/doors/doorthud.ogg";
   description = AudioClose3d;
   preload = true;
}; // ^^^ ***new*** ^^^


datablock StaticShapeData(ADoor)
{
   category = "Doors";
   shapeFile = "~/data/shapes/doors/door.dts";
};


function ADoor::OnAdd(%theDatablock, %whichDoor)
{
  if(!%whichDoor.doorOpenFlag)
      %whichDoor.doorOpenFlag = false;
  if(!%whichDoor.rotationDirection)
      %whichDoor.rotationDirection = 1;
  if(!%whichDoor.maxOpenAngle)
      %whichDoor.maxOpenAngle = $DOORS::MAX_ANGLE;
  if(!%whichDoor.maxSlideDistance)                  // vvv ***new*** vvv
      %whichDoor.maxSlideDistance = $DOORS::MAX_SLIDE;
  if(!%whichDoor.mode)
      %whichDoor.mode = $DOORS::MODE_SWING;         // ^^^ ***new*** ^^^

  %whichDoor.currentRotation = 0;
  %whichDoor.originalRotation = 0;
  %whichDoor.partialTransform = "";
}


function serverCmdOperate(%client)
{
   %player = %client.player;
   %eye = %player.getEyeVector();
   %vec = vectorScale(%eye, $DOORS::PLAYER_REACH);
   %start = %player.getEyeTransform();
   %end = VectorAdd(%start,%vec);
   %found = ContainerRayCast (%start, %end, $TypeMasks::StaticObjectType, %player);
```

```
    if(%found)
       %found.getDataBlock().Operate(%found);
}

function ADoor::Operate(%theDatablock, %whichDoor)
{
  if (%whichDoor.doorOpenFlag == false)
  {
    switch$(%whichDoor.mode)                          // vvv ***new*** vvv
    {
      case $DOORS::MODE_SWING:
        %theDatablock.StartOpenSwing(%whichDoor);
      case $DOORS::MODE_SLIDE:
        %theDatablock.StartOpenSlide(%whichDoor);
      default:
        %theDatablock.StartOpenSwing(%whichDoor);
    }                                                 // ^^^ ***new*** ^^^
  }
}

function ADoor::StartOpenSwing(%theDatablock, %whichDoor)
{
  %whichDoor.doorOpenFlag=true;
  %whichDoor.currentRotation = 0;
  %whichDoor.originalRotation = getword(%whichDoor.GetTransform(),6);
  %z_unit_vector = getword(%whichDoor.GetTransform(),5);
  if ( %z_unit_vector == 0 )
    %z_unit_vector = "1";
  %whichDoor.partialTransform = getwords(%whichDoor.GetTransform(),0,2) SPC
     $DOORS::XY_UNIT_VECTORS SPC %z_unit_vector;
  %whichDoor.openSndHandle = %whichDoor.playAudio(0,doorSwingOpenSndProfile);
  %theDatablock.IncrementSwing(%whichDoor);
}

function ADoor::StartOpenSlide(%theDatablock, %whichDoor)  // vvv ***new*** vvv
{
  %whichDoor.doorOpenFlag=true;
  %whichDoor.originalposition = %whichDoor.getposition();
  %transform = %whichDoor.getTransform();
  %rot = getWords(%transform, 3, 6);
```

```
    %matrix = VectorOrthoBasis(%rot);
    %whichDoor.openVector = getWords(%matrix, 6, 8);
    %whichDoor.closeVector = (-1*getword(%matrix,6)) SPC (-1*getword(%matrix,7)) SPC
        (-1*getword(%matrix,8));
    %whichDoor.openVector=vectorscale(%whichDoor.openVector, $DOORS::SLIDE_STEP);
    %whichDoor.closeVector=vectorscale(%whichDoor.closeVector, $DOORS::SLIDE_STEP);
    %whichDoor.openSndHandle = %whichDoor.playAudio(0,doorSlideSndProfile);
    %theDatablock.IncrementSlide(%whichDoor);
}    // ^^^ ***new*** ^^^


function ADoor::IncrementSwing(%theDatablock, %whichDoor)
{
  if ( %whichDoor.currentRotation <
      (%whichDoor.maxOpenAngle*$DOORS::RADIANS_PER_DEGREE))
  {
      %whichDoor.currentRotation  += ( $DOORS::OPEN_INCREMENT *
      %whichDoor.rotationDirection);
      %newrot = %whichDoor.originalRotation + %whichDoor.currentRotation;
      %whichDoor.settransform(%whichDoor.partialTransform SPC %newrot);
      %theDatablock.schedule($DOORS::OPEN_TIMER,"IncrementSwing", %whichDoor);
   }
  else
  {
    %whichDoor.stopAudio(%whichDoor.openSndHandle);
    %theDatablock.schedule($DOORS::HOLD_TIMER,"StartCloseSwing",%whichDoor);
  }
}


function ADoor::IncrementSlide(%theDatablock, %whichDoor)  // vvv ***new*** vvv
{
  if (vectordist(%whichDoor.originalposition,%whichDoor.getposition()) <
      %whichDoor.maxSlideDistance)
  {
    %travel = vectoradd(%whichDoor.getposition(), %whichDoor.openVector);
    %whichDoor.settransform(%travel);
    %theDatablock.schedule($DOORS::OPEN_TIMER,"IncrementSlide", %whichDoor);
  }
```

```
    else
    {
      %whichDoor.stopAudio(%whichDoor.openSndHandle);
      %theDatablock.schedule($DOORS::HOLD_TIMER,"StartCloseSlide",%whichDoor);
    }
}    // ^^^ ***new*** ^^^


function ADoor::StartCloseSwing(%theDatablock, %whichDoor)
{
  %whichDoor.closeSndHandle = %whichDoor.playAudio(0,doorSwingClosedSndProfile);
  %theDatablock.schedule($DOORS::CLOSE_TIMER,"DecrementSwing", %whichDoor);
}


function ADoor::StartCloseSlide(%theDatablock, %whichDoor) // vvv ***new*** vvv
{
  %whichDoor.closeSndHandle = %whichDoor.playAudio(0,doorSlideSndProfile);
  %theDatablock.schedule($DOORS::CLOSE_TIMER,"DecrementSlide", %whichDoor);
}      // ^^^ ***new*** ^^^


function ADoor::DecrementSwing(%theDatablock, %whichDoor)
{
  if ( %whichDoor.currentRotation > 0)
  {
    %whichDoor.currentRotation  -= ($DOORS::CLOSE_INCREMENT *
      %whichDoor.rotationDirection);
    %newrot = %whichDoor.originalRotation + %whichDoor.currentRotation;
    %whichDoor.settransform(%whichDoor.partialTransform SPC %newrot);
    %theDatablock.schedule($DOORS::CLOSE_TIMER,"DecrementSwing", %whichDoor);
  }
  else
  {
    %whichDoor.doorOpenFlag=false;
    %whichDoor.settransform(%whichDoor.partialTransform SPC
      %whichDoor.originalRotation);
    %whichDoor.stopAudio(%whichDoor.closeSndHandle);
    %whichDoor.playAudio(0,doorSlamSndProfile);
    %whichDoor.currentRotation = 0;
  }
}
```

```
function ADoor::DecrementSlide(%theDatablock, %whichDoor)  // vvv ***new*** vvv
{
  if (vectordist(%whichDoor.originalposition, %whichDoor.getposition()) > 0 )
  {
    %travel = vectoradd(%whichDoor.getposition(), %whichDoor.closeVector);
    %whichDoor.settransform(%travel);
    %theDatablock.schedule($DOORS::CLOSE_TIMER,"DecrementSlide", %whichDoor);
  }
  else
  {
    %whichDoor.doorOpenFlag=false;
    %whichDoor.settransform(%whichDoor.originalposition);
    %whichDoor.stopAudio(%whichDoor.closeSndHandle);
    %whichDoor.playAudio(0,doorThudSndProfile);
  }
}                    // ^^^ ***new*** ^^^
```

It looks very much like the swinging door code, as it should since the swinging code is still in there. What we've done is added some methods and audio profiles to handle the sliding doors, and modified a few existing methods to accommodate them. And of course, there are a few more of those pseudo-constants up at the top of the module as well.

There are only two new audio profiles, instead of three. I've chosen to use only one sound effect for when the door is sliding, rather than different ones for opening and closing. The "thud" sound is the slider's version of the swinger's "slam" sound.

You will notice that the new methods parallel the swinging door functions precisely, but with different code. I could have inserted the new code into the original functions, with a test to see if this is a swinger or a slider, but this way it is easier to manage the functionality. In both swingers and sliders, we start opening, then increment, then start closing, then decrement.

As you can see from the new code listing, the new methods that you will have to add are:

```
ADoor::StartOpenSlide
ADoor::IncrementSlide
ADoor::StartCloseSlide
ADoor::DecrementSlide
```

The existing method `ADoor:OnAdd` has an additional initialization step added to it, to ensure that a maximum slide distance is available to limit the door movement, in case the level builder hasn't specified any. There's also a default setting for the operation mode.

And then a new switch block has been added into `ADoor::Operate`. This code checks the value of the `.mode` property and jumps to the appropriate statement depending on the evaluation. Note that there is a default setting, set to the slider mode, just in case no mode value is set, or (more likely) an invalid string is assigned to the mode. A typo could cause that.

Then, because we are chasing slider code here, we jump to the method `::StartOpenSlide`. It's quite a bit different in detail from its swinging brother, but in general it does the same things. It sets the door's status flag, initializes the position tracker to the door's starting position, grabs the transform, and computes the direction of movement for use later in the incrementing method. It also fires off the sound effect before jumping to `::IncrementSlide`.

The real guts of the slider code are the bits in the middle of this function where we use a matrix to obtain the two movement vectors we need: `openVector` and `closeVector`. As you know, when the door is placed in the game world it has a transform that we can grab, and the last four values in that transform are three unit vector axes and a rotation value. With the swinging door, we limited it to only rotating around the Z-axis, but with the sliding doors, we're going to go with no limitation on the orientation of the door when at rest. This means that the door can be facing any which way. And that means we need to be prepared to *slide* it any which way. So this time, we have to use the angled rotation information the way it was meant to be used.

We grab the angled rotation information and stuff it into the local variable `%rot` and then pass that into the function `VectorOrthoBasis`. The return value is a 3x3 matrix that we can use to direct our motion in any direction orthogonal to the door (see Figure 4.5) in its object space.

The matrix is returned as a 9-word string organized like this:

$$\text{"w0 w1 w2 w3 w4 w5 w6 w7 w8"} \qquad \begin{bmatrix} w0 & w3 & w6 \\ w1 & w4 & w7 \\ w2 & w5 & w8 \end{bmatrix}$$

$$\text{return string} \qquad\qquad\qquad \text{matrix}$$

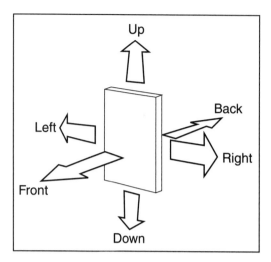

Figure 4.5 The door's orthogonal directions.

The direction I have chosen to move the door when it opens is "up," but you can modify the code to accommodate any of the other five ortho directions. The difference will lie in which part of the matrix to use. Table 4.1 breaks this down for you.

Table 4.1 Movement Vectors

Direction	Words from Return String
up	6,7,8
down	6,7,8
left	0,1,2
right	0,1,2
forward	3,4,5
backward	3,4,5

For the "up" movement, we are interested in words 6, 7, and 8 from the returned matrix string. We take them "raw" to use as our opening vector (the vector that the opening door follows). Then we have to negate them, or take the opposite sign, because the closing motion is precisely opposite to the opening motion. We do this by extracting each of the three axes individually, using the getword script function, and then multiplying each by -1 to change their signs to the opposite of whatever sign they started with. We can do all three operations in the same line, during the assignment statement to `closeVector`. If you have difficulties here, you can break out the work for each vector independently, a statement for each axis, and then stuff them into the `closeVector` string afterwards.

Remember this: Although it may seem like I'm stating the obvious here, "up" and "down" are opposites. Therefore, if you write your own code to implement downward sliding doors, the opening vector for the "down" direction is the same as the closing vector for the "up" direction.

So, after all that excitement, when `::StartOpenSlide`'s moment under the bright lights is coming to a close, it calls `::IncrementSlide` just prior to stepping off the stage.

`ADoor::IncrementSlide`, like its spiritual brother, `ADoor::IncrementSwing`, is tasked with moving the door just a little bit, and then repeatedly leaving itself a wake-up call to come back and nudge the door along a little more until the door has been moved far enough.

It used the `vectordist` script function to find out how far the door is from its original position, and compares that with the maximum distance it is supposed to go. If it still has more distance to cover, it adds the `openVector` value that was computed back in `::StartOpenSlide` to the door's current position, and then sets the door's transform accordingly. This moves the door to the new position. Then it sets its alarm clock with the call to `schedule` and settles back for a short nap.

If the door has reached its destination, the sound effect is stopped, and the hold is scheduled. After the hold, `::StartCloseSlide` is invoked.

`::StartCloseSlide` starts the door slide sound again, and schedules the `::DecrementSlide` method for execution. This is not as dreadful as it might seem at first blush, since in computer talk, execution doesn't mean to kill, but to "run" or "go." Hmmm, slippery words. Anyway, you know what I mean.

`::DecrementSlide` is pretty much the opposite of `::IncrementSlide`, as you have probably already realized. The main difference is that it watches for the travel distance to become zero this time and when it is, it stops decrementing and re-iterating and stuff.

When it does stop, it sets the door's state flag to closed, pops the door on to its exact position before it opens (just in case there were some minor cumulative position errors), turns off the sliding sound, and then finally plays the thudding sound.

Testing the Sliding Door

You can follow the same procedure to get a sliding door into the game world that you did with the swinging door. Don't forget to edit the door's properties, and change its mode property to "slide." You do the editing in the Mission Editor, choosing the World Editor Inspector from the Windows menu (or by pressing the F3 key). Select your door object in the 3D scene by dragging the cursor over it and corralling it with the selection box (or by clicking on it), and then locate the door object's entry in the tree list at the upper right frame. When you have selected the object in the 3D scene, its entry will appear highlighted in the tree list. You may have to scroll the tree list pane down a bit to find the object's entry, depending on the screen resolution you are using. When you have the door object's entry selected, its properties will appear at bottom right. Click on the Expand All button, and scroll down to the Dynamic Fields area. Find the property you need to change there.

Obviously there are several ways to improve the code, which I leave up to you—the various other directions, like "down" and "backward," for instance. In fact, if you lay the door down on its side, with the proper vectors, you can make an elevator!

Another improvement would be to create a combined mode, where the door moves and rotates at the same time, like a one-piece garage door that swings up and back.

A final idea would be code to implement double doors—both sliders and swingers.

Warping

One situation that often comes up in gameplay discussions is what to do in an action game when your player wanders outside the action zone, or off the terrain tile, or otherwise "off the map."

One way to handle this is to give the player warnings that he has left the game area, or the "mission area" as Torque likes to call it. If the player doesn't return to the play area within a reasonable period of time, you could penalize him. For example, in *Battlefield 1942*, the game will actually *kill* your player if you linger too long outside the battle area!

Another approach is to just make it impossible to wander outside the battle area by placing buildings and impassable terrain in the way, or even a force-field-like barrier: invisible, but impassable.

A third way is to treat the map as if it were a spherical world. Then you would have the player "wrap," or "warp" (those words are so much alike, and yet both are used to describe what I'm talking about!) to the far side of the map, just as if he had walked all the way around the world. That's a pretty interesting approach with some significant gameplay impact. So let's tackle that one.

Leaving the MissionArea

In our workup of this problem, we'll use an object built into Torque called the MissionArea. This is an area within your game world that you can define according to your needs; it even has an editor interface in the Mission Editor. When Torque runs, it detects when a player has entered or left the MissionArea object's bounds. When it does this, it makes a call to that player's client connection, to the method ::onLeaveMissionArea. How convenient!

There is a drawback of sorts: MissionArea is a rectangular region. This means that when you travel in a diagonal direction, the distance to cover is greater than if you head off in one of the cardinal directions. But that's a minor drawback in my opinion.

The approach we will take is when the server detects that we've left the mission area, we check to see which side we've gone out on, and then warp the player to the opposite side. It's not a very complex treatment, but it works. In Figure 4.6, if the player leaves the mission area at position A heading north, he is warped to position A', still heading north. Likewise for position B when heading west, the player warps to position B', still heading west. In addition to ensuring that the player's travel vector remains the same, we must allow for changes in terrain height between the starting and ending positions of the warping action.

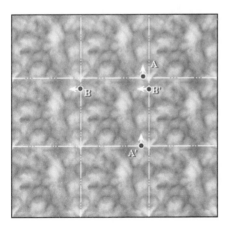

Figure 4.6 Warping across the map.

Getting Ready

To prepare for this, we will use an extra small MissionArea object. This allows us to quickly test the warp code without having to run all over the place for great long minutes at a time.

Run the Torque Demo, and load up the FPS mission in server mode, as you've done before. Then move to a fairly open and flat area in the map, one that visually appears to be about 50 meters square of not too hilly terrain. Then press the F11 key to bring up the Mission Editor. From the Window menu, choose the Mission Area Editor. You will get a frame over on the right like the one shown in Figure 4.7.

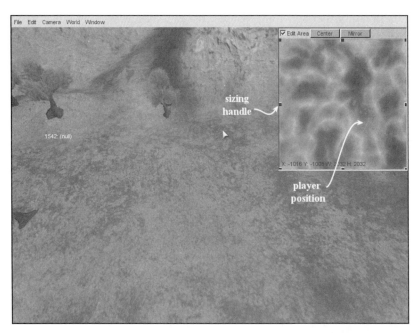

Figure 4.7 The Mission Area Editor.

Inside the editor, your position is marked with a V-shaped indicator. Check the Edit Area box, and a red box with eight *sizing handles* will appear. You may not be able to see all of the sizing handles. If you "grab" one with the cursor, you can change the size of the mission area. If you click and drag your cursor inside the mission area, you can move it around. What we need you to do is resize the mission area until it is really small, as close to 80 units wide and 80 units high as possible. Figure 4.8 shows the resized mission area. Note the coordinates and sizing data in black at the bottom left. You want the "W" and the "H" values to both equal 80, or close to it.

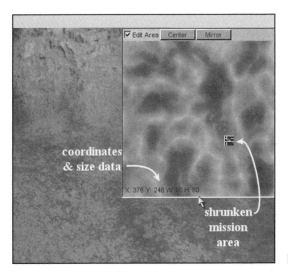

Figure 4.8 The resized mission area.

Caution

Okay, there's a teensy-weensy bug here in the Mission Area Editor. Normally, when you add or change things in the Torque Mission Editor, the engine sets a thing called a "dirty" flag that keeps track of whether or not you've changed anything. If you have changed something, then when you select the File menu, the Save item will be enabled. After you save your work, the Save menu item is disabled (grayed out) so that you can't use it again.

However, the Mission Area Editor sometimes doesn't seem to set the dirty flag when you make changes to it. You have two choices:

a) use File, Save As, which will require you to name your file (you want to use exactly the same name, which is "demo/data/missions/fps.mis")

or

b) make a small, inconsequential change to something else that will set the dirty flag and then use the Save function as described in the text. A simple change would be to locate something in the 3D scene using the World Editor Inspector (F3) and just move it ever so slightly. Then choose File, Save.

If your File, Save menu is grayed out, I recommend using option b, because you won't be able to accidentally misname the file.

Save your mission by choosing Save from the File menu, and then exit the game for the moment.

The Script Code

Next, you need to add in the script code that will accomplish all this magic. Surprisingly, there is very little code involved!

Open the file \A3D\demo\server\scripts\game.cs and locate the method: function GameConnection::onLeaveMissionArea. It's a placeholder method that isn't doing anything very interesting. Okay, it is in fact doing nothing at all. (If you discover that there *is* stuff in there already, then check your code for cooties. Someone's been messing around in there...) Put the following code in between the braces that open and close the function:

Caution

There are two onLeaveMissionArea methods. One is a GameConnection method, and the other is a Game method. You need to use GameConnection::onLeaveMissionArea.

```
%longitude = getword(MissionArea.Area,0);
%latitude = getword(MissionArea.Area,1);
%width = getword(MissionArea.Area,2);
%height = getword(MissionArea.Area,3);

%tf = %this.player.getTransform();
%x = getword(%tf,0);
%y = getword(%tf,1);
%rotation = getwords(%tf,3,6);

if (%x < %longitude)
 %x += %width;
else if (%x > (%longitude + %width))
 %x -= %width;

if (%y < %latitude)
 %y += %height;
else if (%y > (%latitude + %height))
 %y -= %height;

%found = ContainerRayCast (%x SPC %y SPC "1000", %x SPC %y SPC "-1000",
                  $TypeMasks::TerrainObjectType, %this.player);
%newPosition = getwords(%found,1,3);
%this.player.setTransform(%newPosition SPC %rotation);
```

Here is what the code does. The first four statements extract the longitude, latitude, width, and height of the mission area from the `MissionArea` object. Now that's not true latitude and longitude, but it's close enough for our purposes. The longitude and latitude coordinates indicate where the north-west corner of the `MissionArea` object is. The width and height indicate those respective measures for the dimensions of the mission area.

Next, we find out where the player is by grabbing his transform, in an operation you've seen before. We only want the X and Y coordinates of the player's position. We can toss away the Z value for reasons that will become obvious later. We save the rotation information in order to preserve it for later restoration.

Then we go through a series of tests to figure out which face of the `MissionArea` object we have transited. For example, if our X coordinate (our longitude) is less than the longitude of the north-west corner of the `MissionArea` object, then we passed through the western face, heading west, and we need to warp to the eastern side by adding the width of the area to our longitude.

If we aren't on the west side, then we check to see if our X coordinate is larger than the longitude *plus* the width. If it is, then we have passed through the eastern face, heading east. In this case, we want to subtract the width of the area from our longitude.

If we aren't out on the east or west sides, then our longitude is still inside the defined area of the `MissionArea` object.

We go through a similar series of tests for the Y coordinate, using latitude and the `MissionArea` object's height, dealing with the north and south faces adjusting as needed.

When we have adjusted our X and Y coordinates (the actual warping part), then we have to figure out what the Z coordinate of the warped-to position will be. We do this by turning to our friend, the `ContainerRayCast` function. Remember how we used this function to find a door in our line-of-sight? Now we will use it to find the height of the terrain at the X-Y coordinates of our warp destination. Our start and end values will have the same X-Y coords, which are the ones we've just computed. We set the start and end coords' Z value to be really high over the terrain, higher than we know the terrain to be at its highest point, and lower than it can be as well. We set the mask to look for `Terrain`, and also tell it to ignore our player avatar (just in case, even though we know it will not be looking anywhere near where our avatar is).

The return value is a string that contains the id of the found object as the first word. We don't care about that, but the next three words are the X-Y-Z coordinates of the intersection of the ray with the terrain. And *that* is exactly where we want to put our player! *Wooohooo!* So we use the ubiquitous getwords function to grab those coords and stick them into a position variable. We combine that position variable with the preserved rotation data, pass the result into setTransform for our player, and bingo! Instant warp.

Testing the Warp

After you get your code typed in, launch the demo, load the FPS mission, and motor on over to where you created the mini-mission area. You can find your MissionArea object by entering the Mission Editor and looking for the red translucent 3D box that surrounds it. Once you've made your way inside the area, turn and go running off in any old direction. Keep running. More. C'mon, keep on running, now. Eventually you will come to the boundary, and *blink!* You will find yourself on the other side of the area and entering into it again. You can amuse yourself for hours with this little gizmo. Okay, well maybe *you* can't, but I can! Ahem. Another name for this behavior is *teleporting*. At this point, I could easily interject a lame "Beam me up, Scotty!" joke, but I will refrain in deference to your sensibilities.

Oh yes, before I forget—in practical terms, you will probably want to make the MissionArea object at least as big as a single map, and maybe even larger. About 2048 world units on a side.

Moving Right Along

Although we only covered three topics, there was a lot in there. You've seen how we can use an optimized rotation scheme, using a single, fixed axis, to achieve swinging doors.

And then we explored a more general purpose approach to movement, and applied it to creating sliding doors, which have many potential applications, as doors, hatches, and even elevators.

Finally, we saw that there is a quick and easy way to warp a player across a map, to get a sort of "round the world" capability. I don't doubt that a deviously creative mind could quickly come up with several other uses for the warping effect.

PART II

ARTIFICIAL INTELLIGENCE

For quite a long time in the world of computer science, the field of artificial intelligence (AI) was looked upon as one of the Black Arts. Oh, not in any sort of bad way—no association with the Dark Side, or anything like that. But there was a certain sense of mysteriousness and otherworldliness about it.

That's not to say that there was never any negativity, though. Movies like *2001: A Space Odyssey* depicted really, really smart and self-aware computers running amok and killing people. Indeed, intelligent machines often were portrayed as somewhat the stereotypical science fiction bad guys. Even the inestimable Isaac Asimov had his positronic-brain-powered robots that were often in danger of rampaging around the countryside. In fact, he invented his Three Laws of Robotics as a plot device specifically designed to keep artificially intelligent creations fully under the control of human agency.

So it is little wonder that for several decades, those that delved into the real world of artificial intelligence, in contrast to the fictional variation, were looked upon as "way out there" in two, apparently contradictory contexts: sanity and science.

There is a running joke that underlines this dichotomy. Whenever a serious interviewer asked an AI researcher when we would see truly self-aware "thinking" machines, the answer was frequently, "within ten years or so." I still hear that answer from time to time, some 60 years or so after AI research started in earnest!

That research began with Alan Turing and his famous "Turing Test" (see sidebar) and slowly grew through the '50s. AI research received a huge boost at MIT in 1960 with the development of LISP, a language designed specifically for research into artificial intelligence. There was a tremendous amount of optimism in those days, which led to the perennial "ten more years" expression. The optimism was fairly justified. The first computerized mathematical proofs came about in those days as well as the first computer to play chess and the first computerized psychoanalyst—ELIZA. Eliza was a pretty good, but not perfect, Turing Test candidate.

The Turing Test

A human carries on a conversation in his native language with two other parties. One is another human and the other is a machine. If the first human cannot reliably tell which is the machine and which is the other human, then the machine has passed the test. The machine cannot be distinguished from a human. Now the machine has to try to appear to be human. For the sake of universality (testing the linguistic capability of a machine) and simplicity, the dialog is limited to a text-only system like a teletype machine as Turing suggested in the early days or Internet Relay Chat (IRC) in modern times.

With the fullness of time, the field of artificial intelligence filled out and spun off many sub-specialties: expert systems, fuzzy logic, learning systems, least-cost routing or path-finding, path-following systems, image or pattern recognition, and neural networks, to name the biggest areas of research. Many of these specialty areas have something to offer the computer game world, especially when it comes to providing "smarts" for a game's non-player characters (NPCs).

In fact, the game industry now recognizes the importance of AI in games so much that the International Game Developers Association (IGDA) now has a steering committee called the AI Interface Standards Committee (AIISC). The AIISC is attempting to create an AI interface standard similar to OpenAL (for audio) or OpenGL (for graphics) that AI developers can use to hook into a library of low-level AI functions, like path-following or finite-state machines.

In this way, we can raise the bar for game AI development and free up valuable development resources to address more abstract concepts like emotions, complex interactions, or high-level reasoning. However, such an interface is still not on the horizon, and it will probably not be until the end of the decade, 2010 or so, before we'll have a fully featured AI interface library in our bag of tricks. I'd like to be proven wrong in this. Perhaps by then, we'll also have AI routines in hardware as well!

In this part of the book, we'll take a look at how to tackle some of the standard game AI issues, writing our own code, and using Torque's built-in AI features.

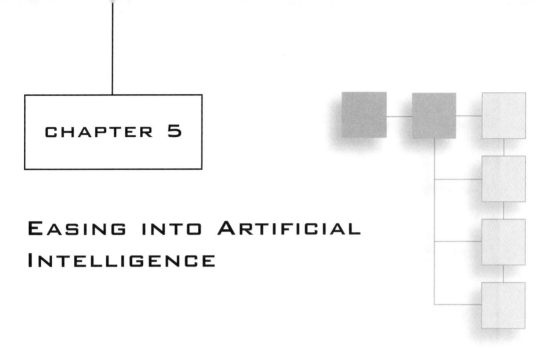

CHAPTER 5

EASING INTO ARTIFICIAL INTELLIGENCE

A s we've seen, artificial intelligence can be as broad a topic as we want to make it, with entire books and multi-volume sets of books written about it. We are talking about computer-controlled characters in a computer game, so remember that when you see the term AI used in the general form in this book.

Our focus in this book will be specific to either areas where Torque provides built-in AI support or useful game-play-specific features that we can cover within the confines of a few chapters. Figure 5.1 shows a scene from *ThinkTanks*, a game from BraveTree Productions LLC that uses the Torque Engine. Six of the seven players shown in this scene from that action game are AI tank characters ('bots).

In this chapter, we will take a brief survey of the areas of AI that are being used, or hold potential for use, in computer games.

Computerized artificial intelligence is mostly about the nuts and bolts of simulating or emulating decisions and decision-making processes that *real* intelligent beings carry out. Some of the techniques, like pattern-matching, try to replicate the function of low-order organic sense systems, like vision or hearing. We try to make sense of the input.

Another approach is to skip to the decision making or data manipulation stages of thought. Rules-based systems and expert systems focus on these areas.

Then there are the esoteric areas like neural nets that are a bit of both—they try to emulate the hardwired connections of our brain's neurons while trying to solve large-scale problems by learning how to solve a series of smaller problems along the way.

Hum [Bot]   2
Ri [Bot]   2
Gum [Bot]   1
CERDIP   0
Gul [Bot]   0
Mal [Bot]   0
Tom [Bot]   0

Gum [Bot]

Gum [Bot] has been eliminated by Ri [Bot]

Figure 5.1 AI tanks in the game *ThinkTanks*.

As of yet, there is no single silver bullet or ultimate answer to the question of artificial intelligence. And there may never be.

What It Isn't... Yet

When the average Joe ponders the idea of artificial intelligence, he probably tends to imagine something along the idea of a "thinking machine." There is a fair amount of debate regarding whether any currently state-of-the-art computer or machine is actually thinking or not. I'm inclined to say they can think—maybe not as well as a paramecium or amoeba can think, mind you! Nonetheless, they are, therefore they think.

However, I don't believe there are any systems anywhere that can *feel* or even present a reasonable approximation of feeling. And there may not be any for quite a long time. In order to experience feelings or emotions, it seems to me that a thinking being needs to be *self-aware*. I can't define that in any specific way that will hold up in the general sense for you, however. Even the heavy hitters in philosophy and AI research can't really define what self-awareness is.

I think we all can recognize self-awareness and feelings when we see them. (If we choose to. Some of us can be hard-hearted bastages, I'll grant you that). Notice that *feeling* in this context should not be confused with *sensing*. We have a dizzying array of sensor systems for robots and machinery that can detect physical surfaces, sound, heat, light, acceleration, and many other natural and physical phenomena. Feelings are more ephemeral and tied into our sense of self and our relationships with others.

Artificial intelligence isn't there yet. Not even close.

What It Is... Mostly

AI capabilities today tend to be automated substitutions, or sometimes simulations, of one or more aspects of what we consider to be the features of intelligence that can be found in humans and other animals. In some cases, some of these artificial capabilities are far more powerful than their human inspirations when employed with sufficiently powerful computer resources. In all cases, though, they remain specializations or subsets of the broader concepts of intelligence and reasoning.

Most of the AI capabilities that have been explored attempt to simulate an overall process rather than try to reproduce every low-level step that organic systems employ. An achingly obvious example of this is the *expert system* which uses computer databases and look-up software to obtain the desired information. The database bears little or no resemblance to an organic brain, and the organization of the data has nothing in common with the way information and data are stored in brains (that scientists are aware of, anyway). And yet many expert systems are able to do a fair job at substituting for specialized professionals, like physicians. It depends on the particular field, and how well it is known, of course.

There *is* some AI research that is endeavoring to mimic the low-level "hardware" aspects of human intelligence. *Neural nets*, for example, try to approach the issue of problem solving using software modules that interact in ways that we imagine neurons in the brain interact. Some approaches to pattern-recognition in imaging systems attempt to use what little is known about how organic vision systems function to identify objects, writing, and drawings.

Even though we have a long way to go before we get to truly intelligent machines or computers, there are still many ways that AI research can benefit us in developing computers games.

Fundamental to most applications of artificial intelligence is the need to solve problems. Notwithstanding my earlier assertion of self-awareness, many people carry the opinion that problem-solving ability is the best measure of intelligence.

Searching and Routing

Least-cost routing and *searching* systems are able to use specialized techniques—some of which are clever and subtle, and some of which are mere brute force—to simulate the intuitive leaps of understanding or recognition that the average human brain can generate, sometimes quite amazingly. Path-finding is a variation of the routing problem.

In any event, one of the most vexing challenges to be met and surmounted when applying AI techniques to real world problems is the scale and complexity of most situations—even those situations that we thinking humans might consider very naïve and simple. A great deal of effort in the early years of AI research was spent developing fast, efficient, and comprehensive search methods. The driving force behind these efforts was the limitation of early computing power.

Many AI researchers consider the activity of searching to be the single-most important aspect of problem-solving, and consequently, artificial intelligence.

When we search for things in lists, databases, or in the big old world out there, we end up creating a map, or path, from where the search began to where whatever we were looking for is found. This path is called a *route*. There can be many different routes to get from one place to another, each with its own particular set of attributes. Imagine plotting a route from your home to work, as shown in Figure 5.2. Some routes can be interesting, and some boring. Some might be hazardous, and some quite safe. Many of them will look almost identical, with only mild variations, while others will vary wildly. Usually, when we search for routes, we want to find the best route that matches criteria that are important to us. In fact, when it comes to the daily commute, most of us would like to find the shortest route, in terms of time.

To find the best route, we would measure the cost of each commuting route in terms of the time it takes to follow the route. More time equals more money; therefore, we are most interested in the *least-cost route*. This also applies to things like airline schedules, with layovers, plane changes at different cities, and so on.

Rules and Expert Systems

Knowledge bases substitute for organic or institutional memory. *Expert systems* and *rules-based decision systems* are stand-ins for years of human diagnostic and analytic experience (and sometimes even for bureaucratic systems) and are used to mine knowledge bases for answers to problems, search for relationships, and dig out patterns and threads of related information.

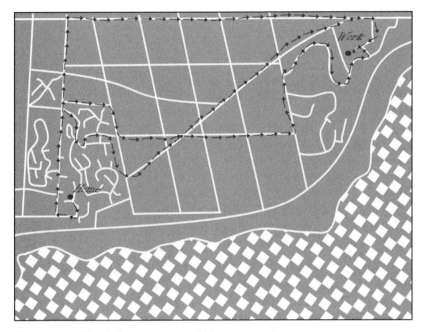

Figure 5.2 The daily commute—which way to go?

One area of games that quickly comes to mind when pondering how to use an expert system in a computer game is the role-playing game (RPG) genre.

Consider the idea that the computerized players used in a role-playing game necessarily have expertise in at least the aspect of the game in which they are used. Many RPG AI characters are there to help players on their various quests. If the game world is broad and rich enough, an expert system would be a great tool for extracting relevant information from the game world. Most expert systems have some kind of learning capability through which information is added to their knowledge, as well. This can be used to build up an understanding of the player's playing style or his pattern of tackling challenges and movement. Based upon this learning, the game's expert system could be used to modify its responses, making the game harder—therefore more challenging and interesting—for players that are romping through the game world too easily. Or, the same approach could be used to temporarily ease up on the player in order to prevent him from becoming discouraged.

In fact, an expert system could even become a game play feature. Imagine a real-time strategy game where you train a cohort of Roman soldiers to attack and defeat a particular enemy. And then you train that enemy to defend against the Romans, and so on.

All of the offensive and defensive capabilities of each of the historical armies would be contained within a representative database. When a particular set of circumstances arises, and an automated defending army needs to figure out which tactics to use, the software would encapsulate those circumstances as a set of parameters for a search through the expert system, looking for the best methods to counter whatever mayhem its enemy is throwing at it.

Logic and Uncertainty

Computer programming is a house built out of bricks of logic. In fact, artificial intelligence programming is often thought of as a specific blended application of two forms of logic called *propositional* logic and *predicate* logic, or predicate calculus. Furthermore, within programming languages we even employ a more specialized form of propositional logic called *Boolean* logic, or Boolean algebra.

Propositional logic frolics in the realm of the truthfulness or falseness of assertions, or *propositions*. Classical propositional logic, or Boolean logic, deals with only two states: something is either true or it isn't.

Predicate calculus (in no way related to regular high school calculus) is a refining extension of propositional logic that embodies the relationships between objects and the truth values of those relationships, in Boolean terms.

The point behind all these ninety-dollar words is that when using these kinds of logic, even in the most complex of logic statements, all we get is a black-and-white world. Something is either true or it isn't. If it isn't on, it must be off. If it isn't evil, it has to be good.

However, many, if not most, problems in need of solving can't comfortably be shoehorned into terms that adapt well to yes or no answers. Notice that I said *comfortably*. We can still do it, and we can often get working results or decisions by the application of classical logic to our problems. And there is a great deal of utility to be had from the simplification of problem statements that happen when we try to squeeze different problem feet into various logical shoes, looking for a good fit.

However, sometimes we need more than just a suitable answer; sometimes we need the *best* answer. It often happens that we can't precisely determine the best answer because some aspects of a problem are unknown. Sometimes we have incomplete data to feed to our problem solver. Sometimes we have no hard data, just a description of the data.

For example, how do we know when we are pressing on the gas pedal just the right amount to accelerate the car as quickly as possible without squealing the tires? Well, look at that problem statement: "just the right amount," "without squealing," and "as quickly as possible." That's not data! How can one solve that problem? We do it by "pressing the gas pedal just enough, but not too much!" Yikes! Pretty clear, huh? Nope. Pretty fuzzy, actually.

Fuzzy logic is a way of controlling processes with imprecise values and approximations where often all we have is a description of data or of valid ranges. It contains mathematical ways to represent concepts like "almost enough," "fast," and "usually," and employ them in computations that mimic human control processes.

Fuzzy logic utilizes a simple, rule-based IF A AND B THEN DO C method for solving control problems, instead of creating a mathematical model of a system (the "old-fashioned way"). Fuzzy logic depends on a user's experience rather than any detailed technical understanding of a system. Rather than dealing with controlling tire slip in terms such as "V = 10", "S < 200", or "150 < SLIP < 300", we use terms like:

> IF (not fast enough yet) AND (tires not squealing)
> THEN (add more gas pedal pressure).

Or, as another example, say, in the shower, terms such as the following are used.

> IF (water is too hot) AND (skin is heating quickly)
> THEN (cool the shower water quickly)

These terms are imprecise and yet very descriptive of what's going on and what needs to be done. If the shower water temperature is too cold, you will fix it very quickly and easily. We use these terms to describe our control solutions, and use the fuzzy logic constructs to convert those expressions into computable solutions.

Natural Language Processing

Whereas problem solving is considered to be the most common task of applied AI, *natural language processing* is usually considered to be the most important. If we can ever achieve the state where computers can unambiguously understand the spoken word of a given natural human language, a whole ton of software development would become unnecessary. Then all us software engineers could retire to a beach in Cancun and sip on banana daiquiris for the rest of our days. Yeah, I wish.

But the reality is (dagnabbit!) that natural language processing is not quite as good at extracting meaning from loosely formatted spoken and written words as humans are, but its limited capabilities are useful in areas that benefit the disabled, translation systems, and word processing spelling and grammar checkers.

The biggest obstacle to the "ultimate" natural language processing system is the utter complexity and size of human language, with its nuances and shaded meanings, confounding and conflicting syntaxes (not to mention spelling and grammar rules for written words).

The objective isn't merely to listen to spoken language and extract or identify words (parsing). That's the easy part. The real holy grail is the ability to extract *meaning*. On top of that, the meaning must be properly in context—a very tall order.

A fair amount of progress has been made using restricted languages, with limited vocabularies, and well-defined and simple grammar rules.

Neural Networks

Neural networks are information processing constructs that try to mimic the way biological nervous systems like the brain process data into information. A neural network is made of many interconnected processing elements called *neurodes* (the functional equivalent to a brain's neurons) and *synapses* that interact to solve specific problems (see Figure 5.3). The network's elements convert *input patterns* into *output patterns*, which themselves can be used as input patterns for other networks. Neural networks learn by example, just like people do. A neural network needs to be configured for specific applications, like image recognition, through learning processes. In living systems we suspect that learning involves adjustments to the synaptic connections that exist between the neurons.

Neural networks can extract meaning from complex and imprecise data; they can be used to identify patterns and trends that are too complex to be noticed by either humans or other AI methods. Trained neural networks are often considered to be "experts" in the realm of data and information they've been used to analyze. They are then used to project into given new situations and areas of interest to resolve "what if" scenarios.

Neural networks exhibit adaptive learning—the ability to learn how to perform tasks according to the data encountered during training or initial experience. They can create their own representation of the data and information they receive while learning.

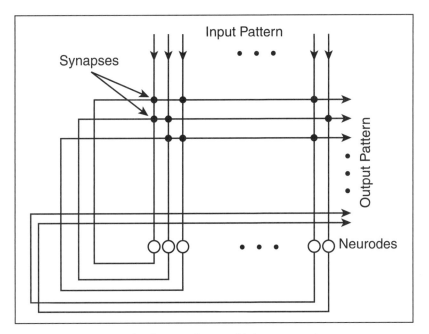

Figure 5.3 An example of a neural network's interconnections.

Neural networks also embody a modicum of *fault* tolerance or *failure* tolerance due to the way they store information. If you partially destroy a network, you will get some degree of performance degradation, but it usually still functions and does its job. Even major network damage will probably not completely cripple a network's capabilities.

Neural networks take a different approach to problem solving than that of conventional computing. Conventional software uses an algorithmic approach—the computer follows a set of instructions to solve a problem. The programmer needs to know the specific required steps before he can create the software to solve the problem. That means that with conventional software, we can only solve problems that we know and understand thoroughly. We call this the *cognitive approach*.

Neural networks process information in a way similar to the human brain. Neural networks learn by example; they can't be programmed to perform specific tasks. The examples must be selected carefully; otherwise, useful time is wasted or even worse, the network might not function correctly. The disadvantage is that because the network finds out how to solve the problem by itself, its run-time operation can be unpredictable.

I believe that neural networks will likely never replace the cognitive approach to solving problems with software, but they do provide an excellent complementary capability.

Implementing a neural network system is no trivial task, however, and I won't be implementing one in this book. Fortunately, there is a great deal of theoretical and practical information available on the Internet, if you think neural networks are the right fit for your needs.

GroupThink

A burgeoning area of research in the AI field is the modeling of groups of intelligent entities as groups—not as a collection of individuals. Group intelligence of this sort is usually called *swarm intelligence*, and it's becoming a busy area of research focusing on the study of different self-organizing processes in nature. The research uses observable natural behavior as inspirational models.

This study is interesting and novel in AI research because such group systems lack a complex single central controller that normally coordinates or directs different tasks in the group system. On the contrary, swarm systems have simple entities that have only local knowledge, but together they form an intelligent system. Researchers have applied this technique to a large number of difficult optimization problems, including traveling salesmen, the quadratic assignment, scheduling, vehicle routing, routing in telecommunication networks (including ad-hoc networks), and in swarm robotics.

Note

I like to think of collective behaviors using a few simple, but everyday terms that describe the collection, and therefore the group behavior.

A *herd* is a collection of members that all have exactly the same goals and predictable behaviors. Each member of a herd is almost exactly the same as the others, with physical capabilities being the only real variation. A herd of sheep or a herd of elephants are good examples. Herds are typically directed by outside influences. Humans, other animals, or environmental considerations (weather, lack of food) determine what the herd should do at any given time. A herd is mostly made up of followers, but there is often at least one permanent leader, and sometimes several. Leaders act more as guides than true leaders, responding to the external stimuli when the situation warrants, but otherwise behaving like the rest of the herd. When the leaders start to move, or react to something, the followers take their cues from the leaders. Absent from any outside influence, a herd is generally semi-active; each member will be engaged in feeding itself, helping groom its neighbors, or caring for offspring. Without an external trigger, the herd will continue this communal grazing behavior forever.

A *swarm* is a collection of members that appear to behave in ways similar to the members of a herd. However, the behavior is more self-serving. Think of a swarm of flies or a school of fish. There are no fixed leaders or followers. Each member makes decisions based upon both external influences *and* the behavior of the other members.

A *pack* is a collection of individuals with common goals, similar and complementary methods, and predictable similar, yet individual, behaviors. A pack of wolves or a pack of mountain bikers come readily to mind. The members of a pack will always cooperate in pursuit of a common goal, but each member usually has a distinct role, depending on capabilities. The distinctions may be subtle, but they are there. Pack members make their own decisions that advance the pack towards its goal, and yet there is usually a long-term leadership structure based on characteristics such as age, strength, aggressiveness, cleverness, and so on. The more capable members are usually the leaders, and the less capable members, the followers, benefit from that leadership. The followers contribute to the success of the pack by their presence and availability to perform more mundane tasks like lookout or scout.

As noted earlier, in general, we use the term *swarm intelligence* when speaking of herd or swarm group systems. Packs are not considered to be part of that paradigm.

Interesting issues in the area of swarm intelligence worth investigation include:

- Self-organization and swarm intelligence in game applications
- Self-organization and swarm intelligence in business applications
- Social insects and animals
- Swarm robotics
- Emergent coordination (coordinator-less coordination)
- Particle Swarm Optimization (PSO)
- Ant Colony Optimization (ACO)
- Multi-Agent Systems (MAS) exhibiting swarm behavior

This is obviously not an exhaustive list, and in this book we won't even delve into the items listed here, except for the first one (obviously). You should consult with something like the Oracle of Google for more information on the other topics, if you want to pursue them. I'm providing the list here to illustrate the richness of opportunity for research and inspiration.

Swarm intelligence can be used in a variety of ways and in genres where the application might be surprising. One example is the use of swarm intelligence in military real-time strategy games. When there are organizations of a large number of similar units, like a division of infantry, swarm techniques can be applied to the attacking modes of the soldiers.

On a practical level, applying swarm intelligence to a problem will generally only require defining the behavior or decision set of a single instance of a swarm member. You would then instantiate (or copy) as many replicas of the swarm member as needed, feed each its own set of initial conditions, and then set it loose. Mayhem and much hilarity ensue.

Until, of course, you get the swarm algorithms and initial condition settings just right—then you can watch in awe as your swarm of flies becomes just as annoying as the real thing. Well, you asked for it!

What the Near Future Holds

The AI Interface Standards Committee of the AI Special Interest Group (SIG) of the International Game Developers Association (IGDA) consists of about 70 experts from game studios, the academic world, and middleware companies. They're trying to conjure up usable and useful interface specifications for game AI functionality (like OpenGL or DirectX do with the graphics). Nowadays, game AI developers rarely have a chance to work on higher-level AI, like believable and interesting NPCs that can learn, that have emotions and complex reasoning and interaction skills, or an automated story-telling system that adapts to a player's interests. It's much more likely that an AI developer will spend his time struggling with things like low-level path-finding details.

Many believe that the next qualitative jump for artificial intelligence techniques in games will be dependent on appropriate interfaces for in-house or external AI middleware, unburdening game AI developers to worry about low-level procedures and enabling them to focus on higher-level creative AI tasks. To make such interfaces and the related middleware feasible, the development of standards for game AI interfaces is necessary, such that the interfaces do not only match a single game but are applicable in a wider scope. Standards in this area may also provide a basis for AI hardware components in the long run.

This focus will avoid an "information overflow" for the participants, makes it possible to go into some details, and allows us to hold a more interactive session than in the past years. The subset of areas that will be covered (the Committee has working groups on "path-finding," "steering," "finite state machines," "rule-based systems," "goal-oriented action planning," and "world interfacing") will be decided one or two months before the session so that the most advanced subset of interfaces can be presented and discussed.

Moving Right Along

In this chapter, you've been introduced to the concepts of artificial intelligence and have been given a picture of the breadth and depth of the subject.

We talked about how AI is not quite all it is sometimes cracked up to be, and yet there does remain great hope for the future in terms of capabilities. Some approaches to artificial intelligence try to emulate low-level human sensory processes, while other approaches try to simulate thinking processes by using information and data to produce results that a human would come up with, but using methods more appropriate to computer technology.

We've seen how AI techniques are used in limited and focused ways in computer games. The point is to re-create the effects of intelligent behavior in the most efficient and directed ways possible to minimize development effort. The areas of research are diverse, covering topics as broadly different as natural language parsing, swarming intelligence, path-finding, and fuzzy logic.

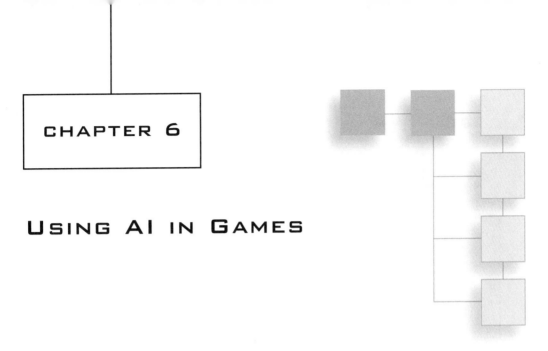

CHAPTER 6

USING AI IN GAMES

I n Chapter 5 we took the five-dollar tour of artificial intelligence and examined the most fruitful area of AI research that can be applied to games. If ever there was opportunity for innovation in game development, AI is the place to be.

In this chapter we will rummage around looking at the ways we can use AI techniques in our games. It's useful to remember that while AI is often used to model real world behaviors, it can also be used to create new gameplay ideas that have no analog in real life.

For example, although an AI chess playing system might model a human chess player, another game could employ an AI expert system in an adventure game to analyze and predict a gameplayer's last and potential next moves, and insert new and more difficult obstacles to challenge the player. This latter approach really has no real world counterpart.

Behavior

When thinking of intelligence, there are four broad types of behavior that are always useful in games and therefore need to be simulated or reproduced in some way:

- Perception
- Action
- Reaction
- Learning

Yes, I know, there are other types of useful behaviors, but these four categories provide a good generalization, especially when considered in the context of computer games.

Perception

Perception is the ability of some nominally intelligent entity to detect what is happening in its world, nearby or from afar. For humans, all the things we can perceive are detected by one of our five senses: sight, touch, smell, taste, and hearing.

For artificial intelligence in a game context, none of these things exist. How could they, it's only software! Heh. Gotcha.

But in our game software, we simulate the senses, and we do that quite easily. As game developers and programmers, we can feed the actual software data or information from one computer construct (audio system, collision system, rendering system, and so on) to the other (player's avatar) on a game server, and then perhaps via a LAN to the player's client computer.

There are a number of gameplay stimuli that should be perceived by AI characters that would provoke a reaction of some kind. These include:

- Visual sighting of the player
- Observation that the player is firing a weapon
- Observation that the player is firing at the AI character
- Observation that the player is firing at an AI ally
- Near miss of weaponry (bullet crack, nearby explosion, and so on)
- Observation that other AI is shooting, being shot, or otherwise engaged in a fight
- Nearby sounds caused by other AI or the player (like footsteps or a window being broken)
- Observation that the player is taking a particular route or is in a particular location

It can be annoying to play a game where the AI doesn't even notice a rocket-propelled grenade (or an exploding crossbow bolt) that detonates five feet in front of it. In Figure 6.1, you can see an encounter between a player and an enemy guard. The good news is that the enemy guard could not be bribed with a nice tasty ear of corn. The bad news is that the enemy guard detected that the player was unarmed and therefore took no action, even though the player is an avowed enemy. Oops. This, my friends, is a case of good perception, but poor reaction.

Figure 6.1 The unbribable guard.

Or maybe it's just a case of the AI guard having a strong moral sense and refusing to kill an unarmed player. Yes, that's it! Cough.

Action

Action behaviors are the sets of those things that an AI chooses (or appears to choose) to do all by its lonesome. The actions are based upon a set of rules, or perhaps "standing orders." The actions may be in response to changes in the state of the game "day" or other variables. But note that these would be merely *responses*, not full-blown *reactions* to gameplay events.

Some actions are timer or schedule driven. Other actions can be simply another step in a series of sequenced steps. In general, an AI action is an action (or response) that was not triggered by player behavior.

Actions are typically generated through *scripted* or *canned* behavior sets. As game designers, we may want to create the appearance of a busy street in a town, with people walking, sometimes running, from place to place, or calling out greetings, entering and leaving buildings, and things like that.

We could write script code to start our AI character on its merry way, walking down the sidewalk, perhaps humming a little ditty to itself, entering a building at the front, and leaving it by the rear, heading up and down a few other streets for a while until it gets to an end point, whereby it is removed from the game world and replaced by some other AI character with a different visual appearance, route, and set of actions. Or, we could have the character circle around to where it began and do the whole thing over again. Or we could have the same character retrace its steps back to where it started, and *then* start over again. You get the point…

Whatever we decide to do, we need to ensure that the set of actions and behaviors matches the sort of things that a player might expect to see happening in the game world. If there are oddball exceptions, like a character that suddenly shimmies up a light pole or maybe whips out a machine gun and starts shooting out windows, there had better be a good gameplay reason for it!

Reaction

Reactions are behaviors triggered by gameplay-related stimuli in the game world, usually something the player has done, like walking in front of the AI's machine gun (you dummy). In addition to getting yourself ventilated, you might spur the AI character to chase you, or call in a warning to its fellow bit-headed players, or offer to sell you a magical sword at cut-rate prices.

Some basic reactions are considered to be "normally" expected. If an AI character is obviously an enemy to the player, then we can reasonably expect the AI character to react in some way. The simplest reaction would be to open fire. It also happens to be the most common! Other reactions include shouting to raise an alarm, proceeding to an alarm switch, or perhaps the AI could lock a door. A more sophisticated system might tell the AI to hide and then try to follow the player unobtrusively, reporting his position back to headquarters, whatever that might be.

Earlier I showed you an AI guard that didn't detect or react properly to the presence of an enemy player. Well, Figure 6.2 shows an effective enemy AI—a rover type (basically it just wanders around looking to cause trouble). The AI rover detected two players driving by in their 4-by-4 trucks and took them out of action. In fact, one disabled truck even rolled into the other disabled truck. Fortunately, the stunt players in that scene were uninjured.

As I pointed out earlier, in order to maintain sanity, we *only* use the word "reaction" to mean something that an AI character does that is triggered by the player's actions.

Figure 6.2 The deadly rover.

If the player or his actions are not the trigger—directly or somewhat indirectly—then how the AI character behaves should be considered to be a response, not a reaction.

This careful delineation may not seem important, but it is a useful conceptual and organizational tool.

Learning

In its rawest form, learning is simply recording information. However, when we think of an AI character learning, we aren't thinking of simply stuffing its electronic head full of facts.

Instead, we usually mean that the AI records, at the very least, which actions work and should be repeated and which things don't work and therefore should be avoided. As mentioned earlier, neural networks are a great tool for this, but they may be overkill for your project.

Many learning systems just record stuff in lookup tables, as a specialized kind of expert system. For example, an AI character fires a pistol at a tank (the weapon, its type, and the target, and its type are well known). If, after the shot is fired, the tank reports little or no damage, then a record of the encounter should be made. The record should include the weapon and type used, the target and type engaged, and the effect it had.

The next time that AI character encounters a tank, it will know not to bother with a pistol.

In general, the learning should be instance-based, meaning that each AI character learns its own lessons, rather than all AI learning at the same time that the player likes to run left after shooting a rocket launcher. A cool gameplay feature might be to have specific knowledge about the player slowly migrate to other AI players over time as the game progresses. Presumably your enemies would be able to communicate with each other and pass the knowledge on to others—just not necessarily instantaneously.

What's a 'Bot?

Once again, that bugaboo of the game development world rears its head: terminology. As in other areas, there are different terms in use to describe the same thing, depending on whom you are working with, what genre you are working with, and where the people you work with learned about AI.

Fortunately, there aren't many contradictions in the uses of descriptive terms and words, although there are a few worth noting. The most notable of these noteworthy notes is the use of the acronym A.I. (or AI).

In many genres, AI was first used for enemy computer-controlled characters. These were often called *monsters* because, well, that's what they looked, sounded, and acted like. Usually there was one monster that was harder to defeat than the others, and defeating him got you to the next level, or gained you extra special powers or abilities, or something else of natural interest and high desirability. This special monster was the *boss monster* or simply *boss*.

Some of these games would eventually evolve and add computer-controlled characters that would *help* the player, rather than hinder him. In order to differentiate these characters from monsters and bosses, they were often simply called AI. So for players who "grew up" playing these games, AI referred to only the friendly computer-controlled characters, and not enemy ones.

Players of other games, like the *Delta Force* series of first-person shooters, usually use AI to describe both friendly and enemy computer-controlled characters.

Also, AI is an acronym, and as such, is not usually pronounced as a word. This is not an issue of contradiction, per se, but does affect communication. So you say "ayy eye" pronouncing each letter, and not simply "ayy" as I have heard once or twice over the years. In fact, I once had a conversation on the telephone where a fellow asked me "do you have any tips on how to get my ayy to shoot at players and not at other ayy?"

> Me: "Ehhh???"
>
> Other Fellow: "Huh?"
>
> Me: "You said 'ayyy'."
>
> Other Fellow: "No I didn't, you did."
>
> Me: "Huh?"

And the conversation went downhill from there.

In some genres, the computer-controlled characters are called *NPCs* (non-player characters), while the smarts behind the behavior they may or may not exhibit is called the AI. Now this approach is one that I heartily approve of. Most notably, it is the role-playing games (RPG) where this terminology is used. However, not everything that the computer controls in a game that might exhibit intelligence of one form or another is necessarily a character.

As discussed previously, another term bandied about is *'bot*. Obviously, this is an abbreviation of the word *robot*. Sometimes it is written with the apostrophe that implies its longer parent word, and sometimes not.

And, of course, the term is also not consistently applied across games, genres, or game communities. In fact, if you listen to two players arguing in a game like *World War II Online*, you might hear the first guy complain about the AI being too *uber*, while the other guy asserts that the 'bots are *nerfed*. It might seem that they are talking about two different things, since they are talking about the same game! But in both cases they are referring to the deadliness of the game's computer-controlled characters.

Note

The term *nerf* is adopted from the soft, foam rubber created by Parker Brothers and used to make safe toys that don't hurt children. Balls are made of the stuff and toy dart guns shoot darts made of the stuff. In computer games, a nerf is a change to either the rules of the game or the behavior of game objects that weakens or reduces power of the object or rule in question. The term may have first surfaced in *Ultima Online*, one of the first online games with a large player base.

The word *uber* is adopted from the German word *über*, meaning over, above, or superior depending on context. In computer games, it is used to mean superior. In fact, not just superior, but greatly superior, perhaps even to the point of being unfairly superior.

The most general usage of the word 'bot encompasses those AI characters that perform certain tasks over and over, somewhat in the manner of an assembly line robot, with little or no ability to interact with the player (other than to be targets or obstacles). They might shoot at whatever crosses their path, but they don't seek out players and attack them. They normally don't take evasive action when fired upon, and in fact, don't even seem to care that they are being or have been shot at.

They are often static, but may be given a path to follow, as if on patrol. In general, a 'bot is like a piece of furniture, put there to get in your way.

'Bots are not necessarily characters, though. A 'bot might be a piece of machinery, like a *Star Wars* probe droid. Or it might be something like an automated mining tool, or a train.

The key point to remember is that 'bots don't make decisions based upon what the players or other AI in the game do; they might react, but the reactions are reflexive, not reasoned or considered. They do not anticipate, and they do not adjust their reactions based upon the success or failure of their previous actions.

Alas, you will encounter game players and developers who will use the word 'bot to describe everything that the computer controls: from representing creatures of varied capabilities to smart (or dumb) machines. It will happen. My best advice is to be nice to them. Smile and nod and go on about your business. Get your game made. Let someone else handle the punishment—I mean, enlightenment—of those errant in the artful ways. That's it.

Opponents

An opponent is any character or creature in your computer game that tries to prevent the player from achieving his goals; we are interested here in the computer-controlled opponents. As noted, many terms are used to describe computer-controlled opponents: monsters, bosses, NPCs and so on.

The range of capabilities of opponents runs from a simple guard 'bot that shoots at whatever walks in front of it to a sophisticated, scheming NPC that employs tactics and learns to anticipate moves and clean the player's clock.

The most important thing to consider when designing your game's AI opponents is whether or not the opponents' capabilities match the player's expectations. It's not your job to outsmart your player, so therefore it is not your AI opponent's job to do that either.

Sure, you want to make it challenging, but you also want to make the game satisfying as well. If players get frustrated, they will drop your game and move on to something else more satisfying and interesting. Too challenging can become boring after a while.

First, have the difficulty presented by your opponents ramp up as the game progresses. This can be done by a combination of adding more opponents as the game moves forward, placing them in more useful and challenging locations as the levels advance, and making them smarter as the player progresses in the game.

Action Opponents

Action games like shooters, some adventure games, and certain kinds of role-playing and strategy games have a natural need for a variety of opponents. It's a good idea to formalize the varieties and think long and hard about the capabilities of each.

You should design your game's computer opponents to be organized into different classes, categories, or types. Whatever terminology you choose to use, your goal is to have predictable *kinds* of opponents; however, depending on the context, their specific behavior should be unpredictable to some degree. Do this by designing several— at least three—different recognizable types of opponents. Make sure that the places and circumstances under which they will be encountered is predictable. Make each type obviously visually different, with different weapons and probably even different sound effects for utterances. You want your player to be able to quickly differentiate between the types.

Create a guard type of opponent that is always found at important entrances and other choke points. Make it behave a certain way, like never leaving its post or at least not wandering too far away. You can insert a little bit of uncertainty by putting guards at unimportant places that might merely *appear* important, but don't overdo it.

Your player will be satisfied if he can learn what to expect from a guard after a few encounters. Then when the player approaches what he thinks is a target of high value, he will expect to encounter a guard. So, always put guards at your high value targets. However, he will expect low value or no value targets to be unguarded. One or two surprise encounters with guards will keep him on his toes, but too many such encounters will no longer be surprises, and will be perceived as tedious, and ultimately, frustrating.

As the levels and the game progress, you can make the guards more alert, or more accurate, or whatever. But they should always behave like guards, and not, let's say, like scouts.

You can create patrol or rover types that will follow a path and look around, engaging any players they encounter. Give them more freedom to pursue the player, but remember to set them back on to their patrol route within a reasonable period of time, or limit of distance. The patrol will force the player to be more circumspect and alert while moving about. The player will need to learn escape and evasion maneuvers in order to stay alive and be successful. But again, it's important that the player know what to expect and to learn that he *can* get away if he goes about it properly.

Create an attack or assault type that, once alerted, has only one thing in mind: hunting down and killing the player. Because the assaulting opponent is different in appearance and sound, as well as behavior, from guards and patrols and other types, the player will be alerted that he cannot expect this character to behave in the same ways. So, the fact that the enemy hasn't given up the chase or stopped firing is less of a surprise. The player will understand that he needs to find another way out of trouble.

We use the term *chasing* to characterize the AI algorithms used to enable a computer enemy to follow and intercept the player or another character or creature. Normally, a successful chase would culminate with an attack of some sort, but not always. You might endow an enemy with the ability to chase with the intent of spying on the player. Or, perhaps the intent is merely to give the player the willies and distract him.

You could also have other types that only respond when provoked, and don't care who they meet, the player or the player's opponents—these are especially useful as animals or other wild creatures.

With each of the different kinds of opponents, there are different algorithms that need to be programmed to achieve the desired behavior. You may be tempted to create a type of opponent that exhibits all of the behaviors. If you do, use them sparingly, with the clear understanding that they should be used in exceptional cases, as bosses, or at the later, more difficult, levels of a game.

Sports Opponents

An important feature of opponents in sports games, whether it be auto racing, downhill skiing, or one of the ball games, is that your opponents will have the same skills as the player (in theory, and maybe also in practice, depending on your game).

The skills will probably all be the same; only the degree of superiority (or inferiority) in using those skills changes. This being the case, the variance in capability of the opponents boils down to their programmed reaction times, accuracy, and tactical decision-making qualities.

In the mano-a-mano sports, like auto racing, each opponent has a different set of strengths and weaknesses, and the proportional quality of each strength and weakness will vary, sometimes widely. In team sports, the variation can be averaged out and mitigated across the team roster.

An important thing to keep in mind is that at the professional level of any sport, the differences between the top, say ten athletes, or top ten teams, can be extremely subtle. There have been Grand Prix races where the entire starting grid has qualified with less than a second separating the fastest car (pole position) from the slowest car on the grid. And that kind of spread can be less than a half of one percent of the total lap time on a track with lap times at around three minutes!

You need to make sure that the proficiency of your game's opponents reflects the real world as much as possible.

Board Game Opponents

If your game is a board game, like chess or Go, then you have a tougher row to hoe. Most players will have had some experience, and many will have a considerable amount of experience playing the game you are making, in a real-world setting.

Your best approach is probably a "brute-force" method, where you analyze the current state of the game board, and then play out, in less than a few seconds, as many variations of moves as far ahead as you think you can get away with. Modern computers are very powerful and quite capable of performing an amazing amount of processing in very little time.

Since board games have clearly defined and limited rules, and a clearly defined and limited play area, very efficient look-ahead algorithms can be created. You also will be able to do things like pre-program every possible move into a lookup database, and using custom-made program code, play through and record hundreds of moves into a lookup table. At that point, your AI routines will amount to not much more than sophisticated database lookups.

You adjust the degree of difficulty for the player by hobbling the AI routines: perhaps by reducing the *depth* of your solution searches (for example, taking the first solution that fits, rather than looking for the best fit) or by reducing the number of moves to look ahead.

Your chess game will likely never be able to beat Gary Kasparov or any other Grand Master, but I'll bet you could give them a run for their money!

Allies

In some games—tactical shooters come readily to mind—you have computer-controlled players that are on your side, helping you complete your mission. In these games, the AI ally capabilities are very similar to those of AI enemies, with the exception that the AI ally is on the player's side and will often be fighting against AI enemies, and sometimes against other players in online games.

You should make sure that your AI allies have access to the same in-game data that your players have. This is not quite as easy as it looks.

Recognition

For example, you can see and recognize an AI enemy when it comes around the corner based mostly upon its appearance. Now, you could do the same thing when you program an AI ally: Give it image recognition software, and have it analyze the scene the same way you do.

Unfortunately, computerized image recognition is not developed to the same degree that it is in humans. *Fortunately*, we can work around this by encoding attributes into the AI characters. It then becomes a simple matter of having the program code that controls the AI ally examine the program code and data of the AI enemy, and based upon those electronic attributes, recognize the enemy. So, using this approach, we can *simulate* our human recognition processes.

Care must be taken to avoid giving our AI allies more capability than a human could possess, however. So, we need to do things like add built-in delays for recognition and reaction times, to simulate the same limitations in humans.

Communication

Also, we might need to enable our players to give orders, directions, or information to their AI allies, and perhaps receive the same in return. The simplest way, on the face of it, is to have the player type in the information and send it to the AI ally. And in terms of player interface, this is certainly the easiest way.

However, making the AI ally *understand* the information is a whole different story. The type-it-in-and-send-it approach invokes the need for *natural language parsing* and *language recognition*. This is a much tougher problem and likely way beyond what a game company really wants to tackle.

First, there is the issue of accuracy and reliability. You really need to make sure that your parser can extract the meaning when a player sends the following command: "Meet me by that big green thing. We'll attack together." And then the player says: "Never mind." Even humans might have trouble. Which big green thing? There's a small green thing; is that it? What are we attacking? You can greatly reduce the problem set by introducing a fixed suite of commands that the player can memorize and limit all typed orders to using those commands. But then there are still the issues of spelling errors and forgetfulness on the part of the players.

Then there's the challenge of timeliness and input speed. It takes time to type in a command. In action games, there is the well-known phenomenon called the *tk* or "typing kill." The player gets shot, stabbed, bent, folded, spindled, or otherwise mutilated while he's typing in the chat window. Combat typing is certainly an acquired skill, and it does tend to separate the cannon-fodder from the stenographers, but players are not going to love you for giving them an interface that gets them killed!

The simplest solution to the speed and danger issues of typing commands is to allow for voice commands. Now you are getting into voice recognition, in addition to language parsing and recognition, and so on. To top it off, many players might not have the requisite hardware, like a microphone or a computer with a powerful enough sound card.

A better way requires more design effort on the player side of things, with less effort on the AI ally side, which yields more reliable results. Use a fixed set of commands, with subcommands or options, and perhaps a pointing system that can extract information about whatever a cursor is pointing at. This way you can ensure that all commands and orders are understandable by the AI.

You can utilize the pointing system in a few different ways. For example, use an onscreen cursor to select who the command is for, choose the command from a popup menu, then use the cursor to point to where the action is to take place or which thing in the game world to attack, run to, or whatever.

The commands can be invoked by a key combination, like a macro, or by selection from a GUI or popup menu in the player's HUD display.

Working from a preset selection of likely commands, options, and information, with a free-form point and select mechanism will save you a lot of development time and grief. There is the risk of the loss of a certain amount of flexibility. But then, who cares if you can't order your AI ally to stand on its head and spit nickels, and have him actually understand it, let alone do it?

Actions

Another ability of an AI ally is the same as an enemy's *chasing* or following capability. At the very least, you are going to want your ally to follow you when directed. It's not any easier for your friends to follow you than it is for your enemies, although at first blush you might think so. After all, you aren't actually trying to elude your friends!

However, it can happen that your ally will lose sight of you, or not be able to figure out how to get around an obstacle to get to you or to where you are going. If this were to happen to an enemy, you would be very glad for it, but you might not know that you've lost the enemy for quite some time. The same could happen with an ally, but this time you *do* want to know if he's been held up!

So you need to enable your AI allies to do two things: detect when they are unable to follow you any longer (they might be stuck, or they might be on the wrong side of a locked gate or something) and then notify you of their predicament by sending you a message of some kind. The best way to send the message would be by some in-game system that already exists. If you have a "radio chat" window, then use that. Or maybe have them holler something with a 3D sound effect. Or probably a combination of both.

Path-finding and *path-following* are also important. At the very least, you need your players to be able to indicate to their allies where they should go, by pointing-and-clicking, typing in coordinates, or clicking on a spot in a GUI map. You could then invoke a path-finding algorithm to enable the AI to actually travel to that location.

You may also want to give your players the ability to outline a path for the AI to follow. This can be done in several ways. One method is to have the player point-and-click to create waypoints in the game world, simply by looking at the locations and clicking the mouse cursor. In a first-person shooter, this might be difficult, since some of the waypoints may not be within the player's line of sight. In that case, use a GUI map and have the player point-and-click on that, setting up a series of waypoints to be followed.

Card Carrying Party Members

Many role-playing games use the concept of the *party*, a group of people who are closely associated with the player's character, who move through the game with the player. An example of this is shown in Figure 6.3, a screenshot from a game currently in development, *Minions of Mirth* (which uses the Torque Game Engine), by Prairie Games. Usually, each member of the party has different sets of skills, experience, and other attributes, and all (except the player) are computer controlled.

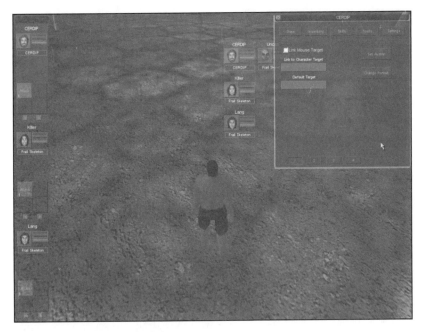

Figure 6.3 *Minions of Mirth* party.

Most of the AI aspects of these players are covered in the earlier sections entitled "Opponents" and "Allies." A critical factor to consider is the balance between the capabilities of the party and the capabilities of the player.

You don't want your party members to be dead weight. I have played some role-playing games, which shall remain nameless, where the party members are pretty much useless in terms of advancing in the game. They become nothing more than a burden, something you have to defend and protect to keep alive, and then harangue and cajole to keep moving. This becomes an unintended and highly frustrating challenge for the player. You need to keep the party members moving along with the player, and they need to be net contributors to the success of the player—not drains.

However, you also need to be mindful of making the party members too capable or powerful. Remember, the fantasy is the player's, not the AI's! You don't want a situation where the AI is pulling the player through the game and defeating all the monsters. This becomes little more than a guided tour.

Group Behaviors

In Chapter 5, I pointed out that AI work in the area of group behavior—swarming intelligence—attempts to mimic natural group dynamics. This is all well and good, but what practical game-related possibilities are there?

Swarms

When I think about using swarms in games, two applications come instantly to mind: The first is always swarms of flies buzzing around corpses that litter a battlefield, acting as a kind of atmosphere-enhancing decoration; the second is schools of fish that can be mere decorations or can be used as part of the gameplay in a game that includes the ability to catch fish for food, sport, or profit.

Some of the interesting characteristics of swarm intelligence are the appearance of *emergent behaviors*, behaviors that are observable and unambiguous, and yet not at all anticipated by the game designers. Sometimes the observant behavior is predictable, once enough observations have been made. *Emergent coordination* is an example of this, where the swarm reacts to some stimulus in a way that shows that different members of the swarm influence other members to behave in specific supportive ways. For example, a school of sharks that surrounds a larger prey without attacking, and then they attack all at once from all directions, making it very difficult for the prey to defend itself effectively.

An adventure game might throw you into a room full of swarming spiders, or a science-fiction based shooter might inundate you with a swarm of mechanical ants. With lasers. Ouch.

I think an under-addressed area of game design is the idea of analyzing player's actions in multiplayer games. Many games can have dozens or even hundreds of players working together in concert towards a common objective. Swarm intelligence techniques could potentially be turned around and used to *predict* the actions of the players, as a group (or swarm), and therefore tweak or otherwise manage resources, balance servers, generate quests or maps, or any of a number of other possibilities.

Herds

Herd intelligence, as a variant of swarms, obviously exhibits the same parallels with real-life models. Many games that may benefit from decorative use of herds of cows and sheep, or even people, will employ herd intelligence.

Additionally, a game can even be all about herding. Imagine a game where you are a cowboy on the open range, trying to get 10,000 head of cattle up to the stockyards in

Kansas on the long open trails. Obviously, your challenge will be to overcome the obstacles of terrain, weather, predators, rustlers, and other undesirables.

We all know how hard it is supposed to be to herd cats. Well, there's a game idea right there! If you don't know how hard it is to herd cats, I'm told that it's likely the same level of difficulty as herding independent game developers.

Again, herd intelligence technology potentially might be used to predict player behavior, especially in games where the players cooperate in a formalized structure of some kind with designated leaders.

A Pain in the 'Bot

Now, I need to address a touchy subject that surfaces often when I talk to people about 'bots. The dark underbelly of the online computer gaming world is inhabited by another kind of 'bot—the *cheatbot*.

A cheatbot can be any one of many different kinds of 'bots. Probably the most ubiquitous and famous cheatbot is the *aimbot*. An aimbot is a computer program that is written to run in memory in conjunction with a game, and it uses a *screenscraper* program to try to identify targets on a game screen (using very primitive image pattern recognition). An aimbot automatically moves the aiming cursor for a weapon's sights to overlay a target, and track it. Some aimbots will even lead moving targets and automatically fire for you as well.

Sometimes, the 'bot is not a separate program but actually written with the game's own scripting language and implemented as part of the game's client by the cheating player!

There are few ways to prevent this kind of cheating, but the good news is that most of the cheatbots, the aimbots in particular, are really only useful in a narrowly defined range of gameplay types. Deathmatch is the gameplay type that is the easiest target for an aimbot because every player on the screen is an enemy. More complex gameplay types, like capture the flag, flag ball, search and destroy, and so on are harder targets for cheaters because there is either less information available for the 'bot to analyze, or there is too much.

The aimbot in particular usually requires that the cheating player change the skins (image textures) for enemy players on his client computer to make them stand out on the screen so that the primitive image pattern-recognition software in the 'bot can detect the enemy. Usually the skins are created as one solid, rarely used color, like bright pink or bright orange.

Moving Right Along

As you've seen in this chapter, a key component of AI design for games revolves around perceiving or detecting changes in the game state and then acting or reacting based upon the circumstances. If our AIs have the ability to learn, then the challenge of the game can increase dramatically.

We've explored the main issues surrounding computer-controlled game opponents and allies, and what approaches we can take to communicate with them and control them. There is a lot of similarity between AI opponents and allies, but some key differences, mostly related to communication between players and the AI characters.

Parties are made up of a special kind of AI ally that is always under the player's direction. Party members need to carry their own weight without doing the player's job for him. Otherwise, where's the fun?

We've poked a bit at swarm intelligence, noting its usefulness in various ways as both a tool to help create atmosphere or peripheral activity in a game (enhancing immersion) and as a gameplay mechanism in its own right.

We've also explored some of the ways that AI-related terminology is used in different game genres. There are many different meanings and usages for some words and many different words that mean the same things, plus variations in between. Most of the confusion springs from emergent usage of terminology in different disciplines (AI research, software development, and game development) and game genres. There is little standardization of terms, and this is not likely to change any time soon. Perhaps when AI-acceleration hardware (the AI analog of 3D video adapters) and standardized AI software libraries start surfacing, the terminology will settle down.

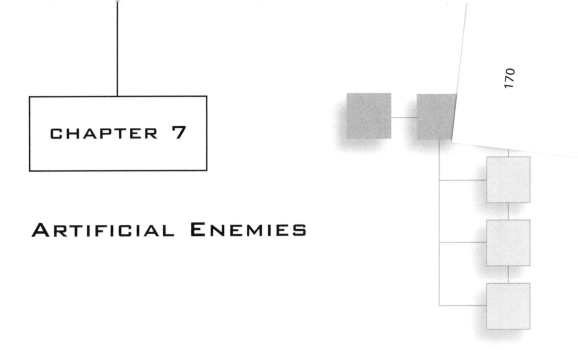

CHAPTER 7

ARTIFICIAL ENEMIES

As you probably gathered from Chapter 6, the range of AI behaviors that could be encountered in enemies or opponents in computer games is a wide one. If we toss them all into the pot and let it boil down, eventually we will get a fairly short, but widely applicable list of behaviors:

- Stationary (guards, spies)
- Follows paths
- Free roaming
- Chases

Most of the other behaviors depend on one or more of those core behaviors, with perhaps some modifications or enhancements.

In this chapter, we'll implement each of these behaviors using TorqueScript, so sharpen your keyboard.

Keep in mind that I will be addressing each of these techniques on its own. You probably should consider enhancing the capabilities with your own solutions. You probably should also consider generalizing the routines and applying them in the form of a library of functions or a set of modified player classes. If you do this, you will want to obtain a license for the Torque Game Engine and directly modify the AIPlayer class, or derive new ones.

Stationary AI

Stationary AI is more useful than it might seem at first blush. Many games have things like guard towers or shacks, pillbox gun turrets, and similar things that don't need to find their way around a game world. They just need to be able to patiently wait for an appropriate target to wander into their sights so they can proceed to blast them into oblivion—or at least give those targets the kind of headache that makes a fine substitute for a "No Trespassing" sign.

So, let's see if we can define some basic attributes of an AI guard. In my estimation, they need to *at least* be able to:

- Visually detect potential threats (sense)
- Determine friend or foe (sense)
- Determine the level of threat (sense)
- Maintain a scan (assigned scan area) (action)
- Engage hostiles (players) (reaction)
- Detect when being engaged by hostiles (sense)

Now each of these capabilities will need some enabling script code, and in some cases they will require certain properties to be assigned to either the AI character or to the real player avatar objects, depending on the circumstances.

Notice that most of the capabilities are senses, with only one action and one reaction.

I want to talk about the ability to visually detect potential threats a bit. Of course, the term "visually" is euphemistic at best. It really just embodies the *notion* of visual detection—a simulation. The sense should operate as if the computer characters were visually detecting things. Sometimes it is too easy for us as game designers to slip into a state of mind where we treat software constructs as real beings. However, when we are talking about simulating or modeling real-world behaviors, it is completely necessary for us to work that way if we expect to achieve any degree of success.

Now, first we need to decide what constitutes a potential threat. In this case, we will assume that all avatars, whether that of a player or those of the AI characters, are potential threats. In the demo, we have only one kind of avatar, which will be used by either the player or the AI, so this is an easy one: All avatars are potential threats. Also, there needs to be a maximum range beyond which another player can't possibly be a threat and therefore is not even a potential threat.

So this sense needs to do one thing: detect when another player avatar is within the potential threat range (maximum sense range). This is easy enough to do by employing a 360-degree scan and looking for player avatars out to the maximum sense range. The technique we will use to accomplish this is to simply loop through the list of players, check their positions, and compare each to the position of the AI guy.

To support the sensing capabilities, we want each AI player to carry some attributes:

- Maximum vision range (some characters should be able to detect farther than others)
- Minimum vision range (less than this and detection is 100%)
- Alertness (some characters are better at detecting things than others)
- Attention level (attention wanes as time passes without any action)
- Aggressiveness (some characters may try harder than others)

These attributes will be assignable on an individual basis and backed up by default values if not specified for individual AI characters.

Preparation

We will also need to be able to specify where the guards will be placed. The best way to do this is to place markers in the game world using the World Editor Creator, and then from within TorqueScript, look up the positions of those markers and place an AI character there. The advantages to this approach are manifold; here are a few:

- It is easy to visually assess the suitability of a placement location.
- Using the World Editor Creator, the level or map designer can assign attribute values to AI characters using dynamic properties.
- It is easy to tweak and adjust placements after script code has been written and testing starts.

And—even with a visual placement method—you still have a textual reference in the mission file that is saved or created if it is necessary to view actual placement coordinates.

1. To get going, start by launching the Torque demo program and run the FPS demo, making sure to check the Create Server checkbox.
2. Once you are deposited in the game world, press the F11 key to open the Mission Editor, and then press F4 to switch to the World Editor Creator interface.
3. On the lower right side, open the selection tree by clicking on the little plus signs and drilling down into Mission Objects, System, as shown in Figure 7.1.

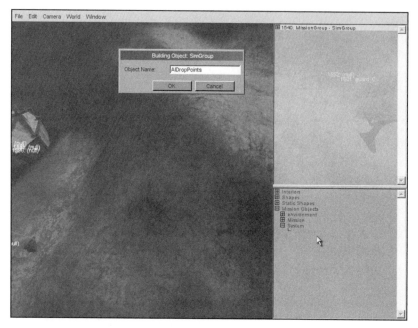

Figure 7.1 Creating the AIDropPoints SimGroup.

4. Click on SimGroup, and you will get the Building Object dialog shown in Figure 7.1. Type **AIDropPoints** into the Object Name field, and then click OK.

Now press the F3 key to switch to the World Editor Inspector and take a look at the tree list at upper right. You will now see an entry called AIDropPoints. This is the new SimGroup.

What we want is to have the SpawnPoints that we create automatically inserted into that SimGroup. All new objects inserted in the game world will be inserted into the Instant Group, which by default is assigned to be the MissionGroup. We can assign any SimGroup to be the Instant Group. So, let's assign AIDropPoints to be the Instant Group:

5. Hold down the Alt key and click on the AIDropPoints entry. This will set AIDropPoints to be the Instant Group and highlight its entry in the list in light gray, as shown in Figure 7.2.

Now, with AIDropPoints set as the Instant Group, repeat steps 1 to 5 above and create another SimGroup as a subgroup of AIDropPoints. Call this new Instant Group "Guard," and set it to be the Instant Group, as shown in Figure 7.3.

Figure 7.2 AIDropPoints as Instant Group.   **Figure 7.3** Guard as Instant Group.

Tip

This technique of assigning SimGroups to be the Instant Group by using Alt+Click is a very useful mission organization method, so you should practice it and use it as much as possible.

Guard is the only sub-SimGroup we will create inside the AIDropPoints for now. If you create other AI types, you can use AIDropPoints and create your own SimGroups in there.

Next up, let's place some markers at which we will be programmatically placing AI characters. As luck would have it, Torque provides a shape, an octahedron, called a *SpawnSphere* that we can use:

1. Press the F11 key to exit the Mission Editor, and then press F8 to enter camera fly mode.
2. Maneuver your way to a likely location to place an AI character. Make sure you place yourself about 20 "feet" (about 3 or 4 character models worth) high off the terrain, looking down at an angle to the spot where you want to place a character spawn.
3. Switch back to the Mission Editor using F11.

Tip

You don't really need to keep switching back and forth between the Mission Editor and camera fly mode. You can use camera fly mode from within the Editor. You just need to make sure you *right-click* (press the right mouse button) and hold the button down while you move the camera to change your view (remember that when you're *not* in the Editor, you *don't* press the right mouse button to change the camera view). The camera fly keys remain the same.

4. Enter the World Editor Creator by pressing F4 key.

5. In the tree list at bottom right, drill down to Shapes, Misc.

6. After ensuring that you are looking at exactly the spot in the game world where you want to place the spawn marker, click once on SpawnSphere-Marker. The marker will appear in the game world, surrounded by a huge red wire-frame sphere, as shown in Figure 7.4. Note that in Figure 7.4, the actual marker is the small item at center-screen with the ID label "2301 (null)". The number ID of your markers will likely be different.

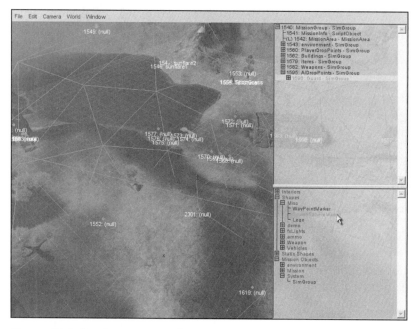

Figure 7.4 Creating a spawn sphere.

Place your markers around the game world wherever you want. After you have them positioned, you will probably want to reduce the size of the sphere that surrounds each of the markers. Do this by selecting them all:

1. Switch to World Editor Inspector by pressing the F3 key.

2. Hold down the Ctrl key while clicking on their tree view entries in the tree list at upper right until you have all of the spheres selected. Figure 7.5 shows two spheres being selected.

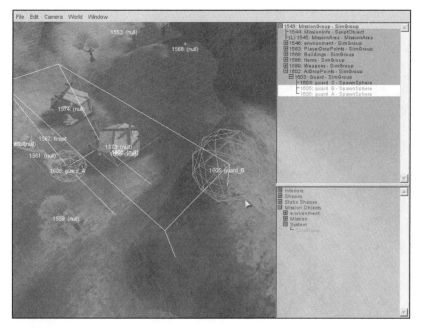

Figure 7.5 Selecting multiple spawn spheres.

3. Once you have the spheres selected, click on the Expand All button at the top of the lower right panel.

4. Using Figure 7.6 as a guide, find the radius field in the dimensions group for a selected spawn marker, delete whatever number is there, enter the value **10**, and press the Apply button. The radius entry for all of the spheres selected will now have the new value.

Note

The radius of the spawn sphere creates an area within which the game engine will automatically choose a set of X, Y, and Z coordinates at which to place the newly spawned player (or in this case, AI character). The larger the sphere, the more potential places there are, and the more random the placement of each individual character will seem.

When I want to be precise about where a player is spawned, I use a radius of 1. When I want to be fairly certain where the player will appear, but want to ensure that the *exact location* is never the same, I go with a radius of 10.

Always make sure that the bottom of your spawn sphere is higher than the midpoint of the spawning character. Otherwise, there is a chance that the character will spawn underground. For best results, be even more careful and make sure that the bottom of the spawn sphere is higher than the *top* of the character it will spawn.

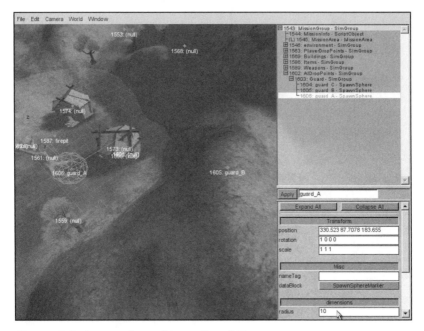

Figure 7.6 Spawn sphere with a radius of 10.

Next, you need to add some dynamic variables, or properties. Hopefully, you still have all of your spawn markers selected; if not, please select them again in World Editor Inspector (F3) mode. Scroll to the bottom of your properties list and add the dynamic fields and values shown in Table 7.1, by pressing on the Add button, and filling in the fields in the Add dynamic field dialog that appears (assuming you created three spawn markers).

Table 7.1 AI Guard Dynamic Field Values

Name	Value
aggression	100
range	100
attention	100
alertness	100

Save your work by choosing File, Save Mission from the Mission Editor's menu, then exit the Editor by pressing F11and hit the Escape key to exit the mission. Exit all the way out of the demo back to your desktop before proceeding.

Code Modifications

Later, we will add a TorqueScript code module to support our AI guard characters, but before we do that, we need to make some small modifications to the demo in order to use our new code module.

In the file \A3D\demo\server\scripts\game.cs, in the function onServerCreated, after the line

```
exec("./crossbow.cs");
```

add

```
exec("./aiGuard.cs");
```

This will cause our new code module, aiGuard.cs, to be loaded when the server is launched. Seeing as how our new code module is a server-side module (only runs on the server, not on the client), this seems like an eminently good idea!

In the same file, game.cs, at the very end of the function startGame, after the line

```
$Game::Running = true;
```

add this line:

```
schedule( 3000, 0, "CreateBots");
```

This will kick off the process of creating and placing AI 'bots in the game at the locations specified by the spawn markers we inserted earlier. The command schedules a call to the CreateBots function to be called 3000 milliseconds, or 3 seconds, after the game is started. The CreateBots function is defined in the aiGuard.cs module.

The aiGuard Module

Next, type in the following code using your favorite text editor, and save it as \A3D\demo\server\scripts\aiGuard.cs.

```
$debugSwitch[onStuck] = false;
$debugSwitch[unBlock] = false;
$debugSwitch[checkForThreat] = false;
$debugSwitch[DoScan] = false;
$debugSwitch[openFire] = false;
$debugSwitch[ceaseFire] = false;
$debugSwitch[onTargetEnterLOS] = false;
$debugSwitch[onTargetExitLOS] = false;
$debugSwitch[spawn] = false;
```

```
$debugSwitch[Equip] = false;
$debugSwitch[GetTargetRange] = false;
$debugSwitch[getClosestEnemy] = false;
$debugSwitch[CreateBots] = false;
$debugSwitch[pickAISpawn] = false;
$debugSwitch[GetBearing] = false;
$debugSwitch[GetHeading] = false;
$debugSwitch[GetRelativeBearing] = false;
$debugSwitch[CheckArcOfSight] = false;
$debugSwitch[Misc] = false;

$ARC_OF_SIGHT = 120;

$MIN_SCAN_GAP = 1000;
$MAX_SCAN_GAP = 20000;
$MIN_TRIGGER_HOLD = 100;
$MAX_TRIGGER_HOLD = 200;
$MIN_ITCHY_FINGER = 2000;
$MAX_ITCHY_FINGER = 10000;
$MAX_THREAT_ENGAGE_RANGE = 100;
$MAX_AGGRESSIVENESS = 100;
$MAX_ATTENTION_LEVEL = 100;
$MAX_ALERTNESS = 100;
$STATIONARY = 0.0;

$cardinalDirection[0] = "0 10000 0";    // N
$cardinalDirection[1] = "6000 6000 0";  // NE
$cardinalDirection[2] = "10000 0 0";    // E
$cardinalDirection[3] = "6000 -6000 0"; // SE
$cardinalDirection[4] = "0 -10000 0";   // S
$cardinalDirection[5] = "-6000 -6000 0";// SW
$cardinalDirection[6] = "-6000 0 0";    // W
$cardinalDirection[7] = "-6000 6000 0"; // NW
$NUM_CARDINALS = 8;

datablock PlayerData(AIGuardDB : LightMaleHumanArmor)
{
   className = "NPC";
   maxInv[CrossbowAmmo] = 500000;
};
```

```
function AIGuardDB::checkForThreat(%this,%obj)
{
  DebugPrint( "%this:"@%this@"~AIGuardDB::checkForThreat  (from:"@%obj@")",
     "checkForThreat");
  if(!isObject(%obj))
    return;

  if (isObject( %obj) )
  {
    %idx = %obj.getClosestEnemy();
    if (%idx < 0)
      return 0;
    %target = ClientGroup.getObject( %idx ); /// player objects as targets
    if ( !%obj.CheckArcOfSight(%target.player) )
      return;
    if (%obj.attentionLevel>0)  // if attentionLevel is non-zero, keep looking at
      max range
    {
      %testRange = %obj.range * (%obj.aggression*2);
    }
    else
    {
      %testRange = %obj.range;
    }
  }
  else
  {
    return 0;
  }

  if (%target.player == %obj.currentTarget)
  {
    if (isObject( %obj) )
    {
      if ( %obj.GetTargetRange(%target.player) <  %testRange)
      {
        return %target.player;
      }
    }
```

```
      else
         return 0;
   }
   else     /// new threat
   {
      if (isObject( %obj) )
      {
         if ( %obj.GetTargetRange(%target.player) <  %testRange)
         {
            return %target.player;
         }
      }
      else
         return 0;
   }
   DebugPrint( "no threat (from:"@%obj@")", "checkForThreat");
   return 0;
}

function AIGuardDB::DoScan(%this,%obj)
{
   DebugPrint("%this:"@%this@"~AIGuardDB::DoScan (from:"@%obj@")", "DoScan");
   if(!isObject(%obj))
      return;
   cancel(%this.scheduledCheck);
   if (%obj.attentionLevel<=0)  // if attentionLevel is non-zero, keep looking in
      same direction
      %obj.attentionLevel=0;
   else
      %obj.attentionLevel--;
   if (%obj.attentionLevel==0)  // if attentionLevel is non-zero, keep looking in
      same direction
   {
    %look = getRandom($NUM_CARDINALS-1);
    if (%this.look != %look)
       %this.look = %look;
```

```
  else
  {
     %this.look = %look + 1;
     if (%this.look < $NUM_CARDINALS-1)
        %this.look++;
     else
        %this.look = 0;
  }
}
%obj.setAimLocation($cardinalDirection[%this.look]);
if ( (%tgtPlayer = %this.checkForThreat(%obj)) != 0)
{
  if (%obj.currentTarget)
  {
     if (%obj.currentTarget==%tgtPlayer)
     {
             DebugPrint( "STILL A THREAT (from:"@%obj@")", "DoScan");
        %obj.setAimObject( %tgtPlayer );
        %obj.attentionLevel = %obj.attention;
     }
     else
     {
             DebugPrint( "CHANGED THREAT (from:"@%obj@")", "DoScan");
        %obj.currentTarget =  %tgtPlayer;
        %obj.setAimObject( %obj.currentTarget );
     }
  }
  else
  {
          DebugPrint( "NEW THREAT!! (from:"@%obj@")", "DoScan");
     %obj.setAimObject( %tgtPlayer );
     %obj.currentTarget =  %tgtPlayer;
     %obj.attentionLevel = %obj.attention;
  }
}
```

```
    else
    {
      if (%obj.getAimObject)
      {
        %obj.clearAim();
            DebugPrint( "> %obj.clearAim (from:"@%obj@")", "DoScan");
        %obj.currentTarget = 0; // forget this target
      }
      %this.nextScan =
        %this.schedule($MIN_SCAN_GAP+getRandom($MAX_SCAN_GAP/%this.alertness),
        "doScan", %obj);
    }
}


function AIGuardDB::onTargetEnterLOS(%this,%obj)
{
    // If an aim target object is set, this method is invoked when
    // that object becomes visible.
      DebugPrint( "%this:"@%this@"~AIGuardDB::onTargetEnterLOS LOS TARGET !
      (from:"@%obj@")", "onTargetEnterLOS");
    if(!isObject(%obj))
        return;
    %obj.attentionLevel = %this.attention;
    %this.schedule($MIN_ITCHY_FINGER+getRandom($MAX_ITCHY_FINGER), "pauseFire",
        %obj);
    %this.schedule($MIN_SCAN_GAP+getRandom($MAX_SCAN_GAP/%this.alertness), "doScan",
        %obj);
    %obj.setImageTrigger(0,true);
}


function AIGuardDB::onTargetExitLOS(%this,%obj)
{
    // If an aim target object is set, this method is invoked when
    // the object is no longer visible.
    DebugPrint( "%this:"@%this@"~AIGuardDB::onTargetExitLOS Fuhgetaboutit
      (from:"@%obj@")", onTargetExitLOS);
    if(!isObject(%obj))
        return;
    %obj.setImageTrigger(0,false);
```

```
    %obj.clearAim();
        DebugPrint( "> %obj.clearAim (from:"@%obj@")", "onTargetExitLOS");
    %obj.currentTarget = 0;   // forget this target
    %this.schedule($MIN_SCAN_GAP, "doScan", %obj);
}


function AIGuardDB::pauseFire(%this,%obj)
{
        DebugPrint("%this:"@%this@"~AIGuardDB::ceaseFire (from:"@%obj@")",
        pauseFire);
    if(!isObject(%obj))
        return;
    %obj.setImageTrigger(0,false);
    %this.schedule($MIN_TRIGGER_HOLD+getRandom($MAX_TRIGGER_HOLD), "ceaseFire",
        %obj);
}


function AIGuardDB::ceaseFire(%this,%obj)
{
        DebugPrint( "%this:"@%this@"~AIGuardDB::ceaseFire (from:"@%obj@")",
        ceaseFire);
    if(!isObject(%obj))
        return;
    %obj.setImageTrigger(0,false);
    %obj.clearAim();
    %obj.currentTarget = 0; // forget this target
}


function spawnbot(%index,%role)
{
    DebugPrint( "%index:"@%index@"%role:"@%role@"~", spawnbot);
  %thisBot = new AIPlayer() {
    dataBlock = AIGuardDB;
    aiPlayer = true;
  };
  MissionCleanup.add(%thisBot);
  AIGroup.add(%thisBot);
```

```
%thisBot.setAimObject( 0 );
%thisBot.look = 0;
%thisBot.range = 100;
%spawn=pickAISpawn(%index,%role);
%thisBot.range      = %spawn.range      < $MAX_THREAT_ENGAGE_RANGE ? %spawn.range
    : $MAX_THREAT_ENGAGE_RANGE;
%thisBot.attention = %spawn.attention  < $MAX_ATTENTION_LEVEL     ?
    %spawn.attention/5         :  $MAX_ATTENTION_LEVEL/5;
%thisBot.alertness = %spawn.alertness  < $MAX_ALERTNESS           ?
    %spawn.alertness/10        :  $MAX_ALERTNESS/10;
%thisBot.aggression  = %spawn.aggressiveness < $MAX_AGGRESSIVENESS  ?
    %spawn.aggressiveness * 0.015 :  $MAX_AGGRESSIVENESS * 0.015;


%thisBot.index = %index;
%thisBot.setTransform(%spawn.getTransform());
%thisBot.setEnergyLevel(60);
%thisBot.role = %role;
%thisBot.setShapeName(%thisBot.getName() SPC %thisBot.role);
%thisBot.SetName(%spawn.getName() SPC %bot.role);
%thisBot.SetShapeName( %thisBot.getName());
%thisBot.attentionLevel = 0;
%thisBot.nextBlockCheck = 0;
%thisBot.conformToGround = 0;
%thisBot.Equip(CrossBow,CrossBowAmmo);
%thisBot.setMoveSpeed($STATIONARY);

echo("Added [" SPC %thisBot SPC "] :" SPC %thisBot.role SPC "#" SPC
    %thisBot.index );

%thisBot.setAimLocation( $cardinalDirection[%thisBot.look]);
%thisBot.getDataBlock().schedule(2000, "doScan", %thisBot);

return %thisBot;
}

function AIPlayer::Equip(%this,%weaponDBName,%ammoDBName)
{
    DebugPrint( "%this:"@%this@"~AIPlayer::Equip", Equip);
    %weapon = new Item() {
        dataBlock = %weaponDBName;
    };
```

```
  %ammo = new Item() {
      dataBlock = %ammoDBName;
  };
  DebugPrint("weapon:"@%weaponDBName, "Equip");
  DebugPrint("ammo:"@%ammoDBName, "Equip");
  MissionCleanup.add(%weapon);
  MissionCleanup.add(%ammo);
  %weaponImageName = %weaponDBName @"Image";
 %this.mountImage(%weaponImageName,0);
 %this.setInventory(%ammoDBName,1000);
 %this.use(%weaponDBName);
}


function AIPlayer::GetTargetRange(%this, %target)
{
   DebugPrint( "%this:"@%this@"~AIPlayer::GetTargetRange", GetTargetRange);
   %tgtPos = %target.getPosition();
   %eyePoint = %this.getWorldBoxCenter();
   %distance = VectorDist(%tgtPos, %eyePoint);
      DebugPrint("Actual range to target: " @ %distance , GetTargetRange);
   return %distance;
}


function AIPlayer::getClosestEnemy(%this)
{
   DebugPrint( "%this:"@%this@"~AIPlayer::getClosestEnemy", getClosestEnemy);

   %index = -1;
   %botPos = %this.getPosition();
   %count = ClientGroup.getCount();
   for(%i = 0; %i < %count; %i++)
   {
      %client = ClientGroup.getObject(%i);
      if (%client.player $= "" || %client.player == 0 )
         return -1;
      %playPos = %client.player.getPosition();
```

```
      %tempDist = VectorDist(%playPos, %botPos);
      if(%i == 0)
      {
         %distance = %tempDist;
         %index = %i;
      }
      else
      {
         if(%distance > %tempDist)
         {
            %distance = %tempDist;
            %index = %i;
         }
      }
   }
   return %index;
}


function CreateBots()
{
   new SimSet (AIGroup);
   warn("# # # # # # # # # # # # Creating NPC characters # # # # # # # # # # # #
      ");
   if ( (%role=nameToID("MissionGroup/AIDropPoints/Guard")) >= 0 )
   {
      %count=%role.getCount();
      for ( %i = 0; %i < %count; %i++)
      {
         spawnbot(%i,"Guard");
      }
   }
}


function pickAISpawn(%index,%role)
{
   %groupName = "MissionGroup/AIDropPoints/" @ %role;
   %group = nameToID(%groupName);
```

```
    if (%group != -1)
    {
       %count = %group.getCount();
       if (%count != 0)
       {
         // %index = getRandom(%count-1);
          %spawn = %group.getObject(%index);
          return %spawn;
       }
       else
            DebugPrint("No spawn points found in " @ %groupName, "pickAISpawn");
    }
    else
        DebugPrint("Missing spawn points group " @ %groupName, "pickAISpawn");

    return %spawn;
}

//  Return the bearing angle of a target's position (%there)
//  from an object's position (%here)
function AIPlayer::GetBearing(%this, %that)
{
  DebugPrint("%this:"@%this@"~AIPlayer::GetBearing",GetBearing,AI_Whisper);
  %here = %this.getPosition();
  %there = %that.getPosition();
  %xHere = getWord(%here,0);
  %yHere = getWord(%here,1);
  DebugPrint("xhere:"@%xHere SPC "yHere"@%yHere,GetBearing,AI_Whisper);
  %xThere = getWord(%there,0);
  %yThere = getWord(%there,1);
  DebugPrint("xThere:"@%xThere SPC "yThere"@%yThere,GetBearing,AI_Whisper);

  %x = %xThere - %xHere;
  DebugPrint("x:"@%x,AI_Whisper);
  %y = %yThere - %yHere;
  DebugPrint("y:"@%y,AI_Whisper);
```

```
  if (%x!=0 )
  {
    %slope = %y/%x;
     DebugPrint("slope:"@%slope,GetBearing,AI_Whisper);
    %angle=mRadToDeg(mATan(%slope,-1) );//-1 is only 2nd arg that works
    DebugPrint("Angle in:" SPC %angle,GetBearing,AI_WhisperLoud);
  }
  else
  {
    DebugPrint("vertical",GetBearing,AI_Whisper);
    %angle = 90.000;
  }
  if( (%x>=0) && (%y>=0) )    // target in quadrant 1, 0-89.999 degrees
    %adjustment = -90;
  else if( (%x>=0) && (%y<0) )  //quadrant 2,  90-179.999 degrees
    %adjustment = 270;
  else if( (%x<0) && (%y<0) ) // quadrant 3, 180-269.999 degrees
    %adjustment = 90;
  else                              //quadrant 4, 270-359.999 degrees
    %adjustment = 90+360;
  %angle += %adjustment;
  return %angle;
}


function AIPlayer::GetHeading(%this)
{
  DebugPrint("%this:"@%this@"~AIPlayer::GetHeading",GetHeading,AI_Whisper);
  %hdg = GetWord( %this.rotation,3);
  if (GetWord( %this.rotation,2)$="-1")
    %hdg = 360-%hdg;
  return %hdg;
}


function AIPlayer::GetRelativeBearing(%this,%that)
{

      DebugPrint("%this:"@%this@"~AIPlayer::GetRelativeBearing",GetRelativeBearing,A
      I_Whisper);
  %azimuth = %this.GetBearing(%that);
  DebugPrint("ANGLE:"@%azimuth,AI_Alert);
```

```
  %heading = %this.GetHeading();
  DebugPrint("HEADING:"@%heading,GetRelativeBearing,AI_Alert);
  if (%heading >= %azimuth)
  {
    %bearing = %heading - %azimuth;
    %bearing *= -1;
  }
  else
  {
    %bearing = %azimuth - %heading;
  }
  DebugPrint("BEARING:"@%bearing,GetRelativeBearing,AI_Alert);
  return %bearing;
}

function AIPlayer::CheckArcOfSight(%this,%that)
{

      DebugPrint("%this:"@%this@"~AIPlayer::CheckArcOfSight",CheckArcOfSight,AI_Whis
      per);
  DebugPrint("%that:"@%that,GetRelativeBearing,AI_Whisper);
  %relbearing = %this.GetRelativeBearing(%this,%that);
  DebugPrint("relbearing:"@%relbearing,CheckArcOfSight,AI_Alert);
  if ( (%relbearing > -($ARC_OF_SIGHT/2)) && (%relbearing < ($ARC_OF_SIGHT/2)) )
    %result = true;
  else
    %result = false;
  DebugPrint("result:"@%result,CheckArcOfSight,AI_Alert);
  return %result;
}

function showDebug(%which)
{
  echo($debugSwitch[%which]);
}
function showAllDebug()
{
    echo("onStuck:"@$debugSwitch[onStuck]);
    echo("unBlock:"@$debugSwitch[unBlock]);
```

```
    echo("checkForThreat:"@$debugSwitch[checkForThreat]);
    echo("DoScan:"@$debugSwitch[DoScan]);
    echo("openFire:"@$debugSwitch[openFire]);
    echo("ceaseFire:"@$debugSwitch[ceaseFire]);
    echo("onTargetEnterLOS:"@$debugSwitch[onTargetEnterLOS]);
    echo("onTargetExitLOS:"@$debugSwitch[onTargetExitLOS]);
    echo("spawn:"@$debugSwitch[spawn]);
    echo("Equip:"@$debugSwitch[Equip]);
    echo("GetTargetRange:"@$debugSwitch[GetTargetRange]);
    echo("getClosestEnemy:"@$debugSwitch[getClosestEnemy]);
    echo("CreateBots:"@$debugSwitch[CreateBots]);
    echo("pickAISpawn:"@$debugSwitch[pickAISpawn]);
    echo("GetBearing:"@$debugSwitch[GetBearing]);
    echo("GetHeading:"@$debugSwitch[GetHeading]);
    echo("GetRelativeBearing:"@$debugSwitch[GetRelativeBearing]);
    echo("CheckArcOfSight:"@$debugSwitch[CheckArcOfSight]);
    echo("Misc:"@$debugSwitch[Misc]);
}
function clearAllDebug()
{
$debugSwitch[onStuck] = false;
$debugSwitch[unBlock] = false;
$debugSwitch[checkForThreat] = false;
$debugSwitch[DoScan] = false;
$debugSwitch[openFire] = false;
$debugSwitch[ceaseFire] = false;
$debugSwitch[onTargetEnterLOS] = false;
$debugSwitch[onTargetExitLOS] = false;
$debugSwitch[spawn] = false;
$debugSwitch[Equip] = false;
$debugSwitch[GetTargetRange] = false;
$debugSwitch[getClosestEnemy] = false;
$debugSwitch[CreateBots] = false;
$debugSwitch[pickAISpawn] = false;
$debugSwitch[GetBearing] = false;
$debugSwitch[GetHeading] = false;
$debugSwitch[GetRelativeBearing] = false;
$debugSwitch[CheckArcOfSight] = false;
$debugSwitch[Misc] = false;
}
```

```
function setAllDebug()
{
$debugSwitch[onStuck] = true;
$debugSwitch[unBlock] = true;
$debugSwitch[checkForThreat] = true;
$debugSwitch[DoScan] = true;
$debugSwitch[openFire] = true;
$debugSwitch[ceaseFire] = true;
$debugSwitch[onTargetEnterLOS] = true;
$debugSwitch[onTargetExitLOS] = true;
$debugSwitch[spawn] = true;
$debugSwitch[Equip] = true;
$debugSwitch[GetTargetRange] = true;
$debugSwitch[getClosestEnemy] = true;
$debugSwitch[CreateBots] = true;
$debugSwitch[pickAISpawn] = true;
$debugSwitch[GetBearing] = true;
$debugSwitch[GetHeading] = true;
$debugSwitch[GetRelativeBearing] = true;
$debugSwitch[CheckArcOfSight] = true;
$debugSwitch[Misc] = true;
}

function DebugPrint(%theMsg,%facility,%priority)
{
  if ($debugSwitch[%facility])
  {
    %theMsg = %priority@"~~~"@%theMsg;
    if (%priority $= "")
    {
      echo(%theMsg);
    }
    else
    {
      switch$ (%priority)
      {
        case "AI_Panic":
          error("~~~~~~~~~~~~~~~~~~~~~~~~~~~~~~~~~~~~~~~~~~~~~~~~~~~~~~~~~~");
          error("~~~~~~~~~~~~~~~~~~~~~~~~~~~~~~~~~~~~~~~~~~~~~~~~~~~~~~~~~~");
```

```
        error(%theMsg);
        error("~~~~~~~~~~~~~~~~~~~~~~~~~~~~~~~~~~~~~~~~~~~~~~~~~~~~~");
        error("~~~~~~~~~~~~~~~~~~~~~~~~~~~~~~~~~~~~~~~~~~~~~~~~~~~~~");
      case "AI_Alert":
        error(%theMsg);
      case "AI_AlertLoud":
        error("~~~~~~~~~~~~~~" SPC %theMsg SPC "~~~~~~~~~~~~~~");
      case "AI_Normal":
        echo(%theMsg);
      case "AI_NormalLoud":
        echo("~~~~~~~~~~~~~~" SPC %theMsg SPC "~~~~~~~~~~~~~~");
      case "AI_Whisper":
        warn(%theMsg);
      case "AI_WhisperLoud":
        warn("~~~~~~~~~~~~~~" SPC %theMsg SPC "~~~~~~~~~~~~~~");
      default:
        echo(%theMsg);
    }
  }
 }
}
```

While you take a few minutes to let your fingers cool off, let's have a look at what's in that module. As elsewhere in this book, I'll start with a fairly detailed examination of what the code does. Later on in the chapter, with other code, the examination will be less detailed, focusing only on the major points of interest.

To begin with, we have a long list of array assignments to an array called $debugSwitch, where each array element is assigned the value false. This array is indexed by the names of the functions in the modules. The purpose of this array is to provide a mechanism to control debugging output in runtime using the DebugPrint function we'll encounter later in this module. For example, the line

```
$debugSwitch[onStuck] = false;
```

will *disable* debugging output from the DebugPrint function in the onStuck function only (a method of the AIPlayer class)—debugging output in other functions or methods is controlled by array entries for those other functions. If we want to enable debugging output for the onStuck method, then we would assign true to that array entry.

After that, there are a series of pseudo-constants that are used to hold values for use later in the code, so they will be described as they are encountered in the operational code.

Then there is another array that contains string entries for cardinal directions. This is used as a handy look-up table to specify XYZ vectors for directions that AI characters will look when they are scanning the horizon.

After the cardinal directions, there is a datablock definition for the AI Guard type. Note that the datablock's name is `AIGuardDB` and it is derived from the `LightMaleHumanArmor` datablock, so it automatically inherits all of the properties of `LightMaleHumanArmor`.

Tip

> To access the methods of a parent datablock, use the `Parent::` prefix when you call the method. If the parent datablock has a method called `Foobar`, then you can invoke that method with the statement
>
> `Parent::Foobar();`
>
> This will work even if you define your own version of the parent's methods for your derived datablock.

In this new datablock, we redefine two properties to new values more suited to our purposes.

The method `AIGuardDB::checkForThreat` provides a means for an instance of an AI guard (passed in via the parameter `%obj`) to find out if threats exist that need to be acted on. The method `getClosestEnemy` is called for the instance. In case you hadn't noticed, in our implementation here, human players are the enemy!

It's important to realize that every instance of an AI guard can have a *different* closest enemy, and therefore a datablock method is not suitable for the job of finding the closest one; this is why the `getClosestEnemy` method is defined for the instance of the AIPlayer object and *not* the `AIGuardDB` datablock.

If a potential enemy is found, then we check to see if that enemy is within the arc of sight (similar to field of view) for this AI object. Of course, the arc of sight is based upon the direction the AI is looking at this particular point in time. The actual size of the arc, in degrees, is defined by the pseudo-constant `$ARC_OF_SIGHT`, currently set to 60 at the beginning of this module. If this value is not satisfactory for your purposes, you can easily change it, even at runtime in the game world, by using the console—which is why it's handy that it is a pseudo-constant and not a real constant!

Next, we use the `attentionLevel` property to test whether we should keep looking. It's used in a simple fashion here: when non-zero, keep looking; otherwise, stop. The `attentionLevel` property is slowly lowered elsewhere in a fashion to simulate the onset of boredom. Highly attentive guards will look all the way to super-duper maximum range. Bored ones will only look as far as they have to. Of course, this is simplistic, and you can use this mechanism to implement a much more realistic and sophisticated scan algorithm based upon the AI's attention level.

Assuming the guard is paying close attention, his maximum range of interest (`%testRange`) is dictated by the standard set range (`%obj.range`) and the particular guard's aggressiveness (`%obj.aggression`). The more aggressive the guard, the farther away he will look for threats.

The AI always deals with the nearest threat before moving on to any others, which is what the code following the attention level code handles.

Note that sprinkled throughout this module, you will find statements like this:

```
if (isObject( %obj) )
```

As the game progresses, threat objects might be killed and removed from the game world, perhaps by other players or AI. Or players might exit the game. Using the `isObject` function is a way to ensure that the enemy we are dealing with really does still exist, just before we try to do something to or with it.

The following method, `AIGuardDB::DoScan`, is the one that actually does the looking around, but more importantly, it's where the AI's avatar is moved to simulate the scanning process. In our version, all we do is rotate the avatar to point at one of the cardinal directions. (Remember the array at the start of the module?)

When we arrive in the `DoScan` method, it is as a scheduled call, so one of our first actions is to cancel the scheduled call, so that we won't end up back here before we are finished!

After that, we decrease this AI's attention a little bit, moving him back towards his normal state of boredom, eventually. However, as long as we *do* have his attention, we make sure he keeps looking in the direction he is looking and actually *doesn't* continue to scan around the horizon. This is a way to simulate *focus*.

If the AI is not focused, then the scan proceeds with a random direction being chosen every time through this method. An improvement would be to implement an orderly scan around the horizon, interspersed with intermittent random direction changes. Perhaps even a "paranoia" property, which causes more random scan direction changes the higher the paranoia is. Just a thought.

The actual task of turning our avatar to face a direction is carried out by the AIPlayer method `setAimLocation`, which is fed the vector from our cardinal direction look-up table.

Once the AI has changed his stance, we use `checkForThreat` to find any new threats, the new closest one, or if the old threat still exists. If a threat exists, we aim at the threatening object using the AIPlayer method `setAimObject`.

Now, we treat new threats as different from known threats in this code, even though there is not much difference in what we do. In a practical way, having the differentiation between new and old threats is useful for debugging purposes so even absent any other reason, it's a good thing.

But the main reason for tracking new versus old threats is that if the threat has changed, we need to change where we are aiming, and if the old threat is no longer of interest, but a new one hasn't come along, we need to "forget" about aiming at the old threat, using the AIPlayer method `clearAim`.

The last thing we do in `DoScan` is schedule another scan for later. How much later depends on a few things. There is a minimum scan time defined by `$MIN_SCAN_GAP`. We add a random amount of time to that, which is based on the AI's alertness. The more alert the AI is, the shorter the additional gap, and the shorter the gap between scans, the more frequent the scans are.

So, how do we get our AI to actually shoot at a target, you wonder? Well, I'm glad you asked. Torque provides a datablock callback function that we use for this. `onTargetEnterLOS` is called by the engine when:

a) an aim target object has been set (using `setAimObject`)

and

b) the target has become visible to the AI.

Becoming visible means that the line of sight (LOS) from the AI to the target is unobstructed by things like terrain or buildings.

When we arrive in `onTargetEnterLOS`, after the usual object validation stuff, one of the first things we do is set the AI's attention level back to its starting value. Hey, we've just seen the enemy! *Of course* we're paying attention now! We then start shooting at the enemy as fast as we can, using the statement that appears at the end:

```
%obj.setImageTrigger(0,true);
```

This enables the trigger of the weapon image mounted in slot 0. How *long* we continue our rapid-fire shooting is determined by a scheduled call to a method called `pauseFire`. How long before the pause happens depends on our "itchy finger." A minimum and maximum value for our itchy trigger finger dictate the minimum schedule time and the maximum possible (randomly selected) schedule time. The schedule calls the `pauseFire` method when the time comes, and the AI's finger is lifted from the trigger, temporarily. Without doing this, the AI wouldn't be able to fire again, because the "finger" needs to be off the trigger before another shot can be fired.

We also schedule another call to the `doScan` method at this time, before exiting this method. Note that these two scheduled calls occur in the code *before* we actually start shooting.

If a target that an AI has been shooting at happens to leave its line of sight, then the AI should stop shooting in order to conserve its ammo. That condition is captured via the datablock callback `onTargetExitLOS`. In this method, the shooting is halted, the aim is cleared, and the target is "forgotten." Then another call to `doScan` is scheduled, for the shortest possible interval.

Tip

> When you are designing your AI and trying to determine what your scan intervals should be, you should keep in mind how many AI characters you intend to have in the game world. The more you have, the more scan processing will need to be done, consuming valuable CPU cycles. Therefore, the more AI you have, the longer the minimum gap between scans should be, to ensure that everyone gets a reasonable kick at the can without dragging down the server performance.

We already know the main job of the `pauseFire` method—temporarily pauses firing (releases the trigger finger) so that we can fire again shortly. It also schedules a call to the `ceaseFire` method, based upon the maximum amount of time the trigger should be held down. The `ceasefire` method stops all firing, clears the aim, releases the trigger finger, and "forgets" the target.

So, that is the meat and potatoes of our AI's actions, reactions, and sensing. The rest of the module is all about placing the AI in the game world and math and other utility functions.

Instead of proceeding function-by-function, I'll now walk through the rest of the module in sequence. The first AI function called (in demo/server/scripts/game.cs) is

CreateBots. In this function, we loop through all of the spawn markers that have been inserted in the game world. Notice the string MissionGroup/AIDropPoints/Guard; that's the sub-SimGroup in which we placed the spawn markers, remember? They are called "roles" here for a reason. When other roles for the AI have been defined, we can create new sub-SimGroups for them, like "Attack" or "Rover" or "Patrol." We can then extract the spawn markers for each of those other roles in the same way.

For each spawn marker we find for a given role, we call the AIPlayer method spawnbot, passing in the index to the spawn marker and the name of the role.

In the spawnbot method, we've got a whole whack of things to do. First we create a new AIPlayer instance, using the AIGuardDB datablock. If we were to use another datablock, maybe an AIPatrolDB, then we would want to make sure that the AIGuardDB was not hardcoded, but carried in a variable.

We add the AI object reference to the MissionCleanup object, so that at the end of the mission, this object will be removed from memory, and we also add it to the AIGroup SimGroup.

Next we initialize a bunch of properties, just in case the mission designer or builder didn't set the appropriate dynamic field in the mission file. Then we use the index to the spawn marker and the role name to pick a suitable spawn marker. When we get the handle to the spawn marker back, we can use it to access the dynamic fields of the spawn marker, as well as its position.

Note that the actual attention, aggression, alertness, and range settings are derived from the spawn marker dynamic fields, but not without checking to make sure that the spawn marker values are legal (according to our pseudo-constants). Also, some of the attributes are tweaked a little here in order to put them into more sensible ranges (a "fine-tuning" process).

The next really important action is the call to Equip, which arms the AI and gives him ammo. Equip would also be a good place to give the AI other trinkets, like a lucky rabbit's foot or something. Hey! I'm just sayin'.

Finally, we echo some information out to the console for audit purposes. Set the AI to look in a direction and schedule his first scan. After that, he's on his own!

You should be able to clearly understand everything that is in the Equip method now—no surprises there, really.

One method worthy of note that I have discussed is the AIPlayer method getClosestEnemy. There are other ways to accomplish what this does that bear no resemblance at all to my technique. The method I use is quite efficient as long as the AI enemies all belong to a few distinct groups. Basically, the approach is to cycle through all the members of the list of possible enemies, find the one that is closest to the AI, and return the index to that member. This way, of all possible enemies, we always know which one is closest.

Another approach would be to use initContainerRadiusSearch or a similar function to search a specified area, masking out those object types of no interest (like trees and rocks), and finding the nearest object of the type of interest—a player. Each way has its pros and cons, and I'm sure there are other useful techniques as well.

The math-bound function GetBearing is noteworthy in that I use a different way to get the angle between two vectors. Earlier in Chapter 3 we looked at vector and matrix math. In GetBearing, the technique used is quite simple. Find the slope between two points, and use the arctangent (mAtan) to obtain the angle in radians, convert it to degrees, adjust it according to the quadrant it's in, and off we go. Basic high school math, really. There is also a GetRelativeBearing function that gets the difference between the heading of an object and the bearing of another object. The difference is always in the range from -180 degrees to +180 degrees. A minus relative bearing is to the left, and positive relative bearing is to the right.

Finally, there is that bunch of debug routines. You may use them if you like, or not. When dealing with AI behavior, the more information you have, the easier it is to solve problems so that you can carry on to create new ones.

Oops, I meant create new *features*, there. Well, maybe I was right the first time!

Standing on Guard for Thee

Right then, let's see what kind of stuff these suckers are made of. Your mission, should you choose to accept it, is to test the aiGuard defenses.

After you've made the code changes, and created the aiGuard.cs module, run the demo. After you spawn in, trot on over to near the area where you placed the guards' spawn markers. Don't rush right in though—angels fear to tread there. Get to within about 50 feet (measured by eyeball) and then start to zigzag in. Zig one way, trot for a bit, then stop. Then zag the other way, and stop. Keep an eye on the guards. See how close you can get before they deliver you an explosive crossbow bolt sandwich.

Take note of not only how close you can get before you are spotted, but how quickly they change their scan arc. Also note how long they maintain contact with you after they've spotted you. Then (assuming you aren't totally dead yet) try to move away, and see how long it takes for them to lose interest in you.

Also try moving in an arc, not directly away, to try to get out of their fields of view. See how long you can keep that up.

Good luck.

Following Paths

One of the easiest forms of directed AI behavior is *path-following*. Path-following is not precisely the same thing as the path-finding concept that I mentioned earlier—in this case, the path is already known (although it *could* have been discovered by using a path- or route-finding technique), and in most cases, paths are specified at world or map creation time by a developer. This puts path-following one rung up the evolutionary ladder. The AI is not held in one place, but its route is very tightly constrained by the path.

We use the path-following approach when we know the routes or paths that we want our AI character to follow. It doesn't mean that the characters always have to take the same routes; we can easily specify several routes and make the character pick one of them either at random or based upon a calculation triggered by some stimulus.

The Torque demo comes with a built-in path-following script, contained in \A3D\demo\server\scripts\aiPlayer.cs. However, the code is not invoked actually in the demo with the Torque Game Engine Demo version 1.3. So in this section, we'll use it.

First, we have to create the path to be followed. Then we want to place an AI character in the game world and tell him programmatically to follow the path. For the sake of clarity, I have *not* included code that combines the path-following feature with the aiGuard method we worked with earlier in this chapter. It isn't that difficult, and I leave it up to the reader as an exercise.

Making the Path

Open up the Torque demo, Press F8 to put yourself in camera fly mode, and enter the World Editor Creator in the Mission Editor.

Our first task is to create a new SimGroup called Paths. Do this the same way you created the AIDropPoints SimGroup back in the "Stationary AI" section, in the "Preparation" subsection. Just remember to give your SimGroup the name Paths and that this new SimGroup should be directly under the MissionGroup SimGroup, just as AIDropPoints was.

After that, you need to add some paths to the Paths SimGroup. In the pane at lower right, expand the Mission Objects group, and then expand the Mission entry in the Mission Object group.

You will see two entries: Path and PathMarker. Click on the Path entry and type in **PathA** in the dialog that appears; then click OK. PathA will appear in the tree view at upper right. Make PathA an Instant Group (Alt+Click on it) and then move your camera view above the ground and face the location where you would like to put a path waypoint—anywhere the ground is reasonably level and uncluttered will do. Click on the Mission, PathMarker entry at bottom right. When the dialog appears, type in **wp1**, and click OK. Repeat this PathMarker placement routine for at least two more waypoints, naming them "wp2" and "wp3" respectively. Notice the dotted lines appear connecting the waypoints. You should get something pretty close to Figure 7.7, except the locations of your choices are probably different.

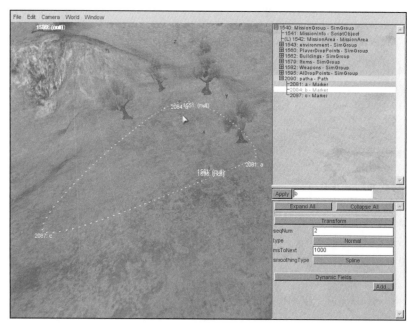

Figure 7.7 A path with three waypoints.

Note how smoothly curved the transitions are from waypoint to waypoint. This is because the waypoints all have their smoothingType set to "spline." You could set the smoothingType to be "linear" instead; you would end up with something like Figure 7.8.

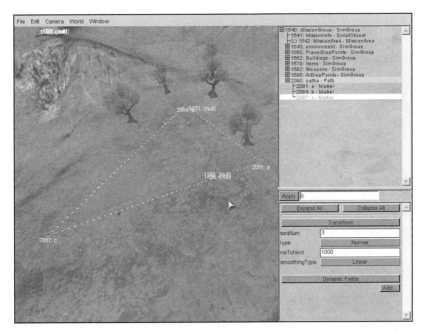

Figure 7.8 A path without spline smoothing.

Of course, you can mix and match the types from one waypoint to another to suit your needs. Once you have your path and waypoints in place, save your mission file. It might be a good idea to exit the demo to the desktop, since we're going to add some more code to the scripts.

Using the Path

Next, open the file \A3D\demo\server\scripts\aiPlayer.cs and add the following code to the very bottom of the file:

```
function InsertPathedAI()
{
    %player = AIPlayer::spawnOnPath("Follower","MissionGroup/Paths/PathA");
    %player.mountImage(CrossbowImage,0);
    %player.setInventory(CrossbowAmmo,1000);
    %player.followPath("MissionGroup/Paths/PathA",-1);
}
```

Save your work. Now run the demo, and once you've spawned in, use camera mode to move to a location over where you placed the path, and look down at the area. Open the console (using the ~ key) and type in

```
InsertPathedAI();
```

and press the Enter key. An AI guy will spawn in and start running around the path. Key method here is the call to:

```
%player.followPath("MissionGroup/Paths/PathA",-1);
```

The second parameter indicates what *node* on the path to proceed to. A node is the path's version of the path markers we placed earlier; each path marker becomes a node in the path. The -1 indicates that the AI guy should go to the nearest node (which will be the first in the path, and coincidentally it will be the same node that he will spawn at), and then just keep running around the path following the spawn markers in order.

Run AI guy, run!

As invigorating as a good run can be, we need him to be a bit more active. So, add the following code to the end of \A3D\demo\server\scripts\aiPlayer.cs:

```
function InsertPathedAIShooter()
{
    %player = AIPlayer::spawnOnPath("Shooter","MissionGroup/Paths/PathA");
    %player.mountImage(CrossbowImage,0);
    %player.setInventory(CrossbowAmmo,1000);

    %player.pushTask("playThread(0,\"celwave\")");
    %player.pushTask("followPath(\"MissionGroup/Paths/PathA\",2)");
    %player.pushTask("aimAt(\"MissionGroup/target\")");
    %player.pushTask("wait(5)");
    %player.pushTask("fire(true)");
    %player.pushTask("wait(1)");
    %player.pushTask("fire(false)");
    %player.pushTask("wait(1)");
    %player.pushTask("followPath(\"MissionGroup/Paths/PathA\",1)");
    %player.pushTask("aimAt(\"MissionGroup/target\")");
    %player.pushTask("wait(1)");
    %player.pushTask("fire(true)");
    %player.pushTask("wait(1)");
```

```
%player.pushTask("fire(false)");
%player.pushTask("playThread(0,\"celwave\")");
%player.pushTask("done()");
}
```

Unfortunately, there is a bug in the AI script code supplied here by the wrenches at GarageGames. Fortunately, we can fix it! Find the method `AIPlayer::aimAt` at around line 208 in aiPlayer.cs. Inside that function find the line:

```
%this.setAimObject(%object);
```

and place this line after it:

```
%this.setAimLocation(%object.getPosition());
```

This change makes the AI guy point directly at the coordinates of the target.

Okay, now make sure that you've exited the demo program completely after the previous test, then relaunch the demo and spawn in to the game world.

Before proceeding with the test, we need to add the target. Use the Mission Editor Creator to add a tree to the scene. Trees can be found in the Static Shapes, demo, data, Shapes, trees group in the Creator. Make sure the tree belongs to the Mission SimGroup and no other SimGroup. Name the tree "target" (remember, put the name in the field next to the Apply button in the Mission Editor Inspector view of the tree object). Exit the Mission Editor and, after positioning yourself to view the path area you created earlier, open the console and type:

```
InsertPathedAIShooter();
```

Watch the frolicking AI monster!

Take a look through the aiPlayer.cs module. You will notice that some of the functions there are similar to functions I provided in aiGuard.cs. Obviously there are many ways to accomplish similar goals, as underlined by the differences between these two modules.

Notice too, the utility functions added in aiPlayer.cs for managing AI tasks. In the `InsertPathedAI` function, the player is simply told to follow the path, and that's it. But in `InsertPathedAIShooter`, the tasks are pushed onto the queue. The first task onto the queue is the first task executed when the appropriate time arrives. This way you can pile up a bunch of tasks to be executed all at once, as a scripted sequence, and then just let the functions like `nextTask` and `wait` look after executing the tasks at an appropriately scheduled time.

Chasing

You can combine some of the code in aiGuard.cs with code in aiPlayer.cs to create an AI guy who will chase you once he's detected you. If you want to do that, I'll provide you with some help in this section. Your biggest challenge will likely be making sure that you don't have any duplicate methods or other operations between aiGuard.cs and aiPlayer.cs.

First, you should probably create another role. In the Mission Editor (or manually in the mission file with a text editor), create another sub-SimGroup and call it, say, "Chaser".

After detecting an enemy, you will need to obtain his position. In aiGuard.cs, this information is available in the function AIGuardDB::checkForThreat. Once a threat has been found, and you've obtained a handle to the threat object, you can get its position by calling the threat object's getPosition method. You can then feed that position data in string form directly into the AI's setMoveDestination as its parameter.

You should also check the role of the AI to make sure that you aren't sending a stationary guard wandering away from his post!

The following code fragment will work if inserted in each of the three places in checkForThreat where the setAimObject method is called.

```
if (%theRole !$= "Guard")
{
   %obj.setMoveSpeed($MAX_CHASER_SPEED);
   %obj.setMoveDestination(%tgtPlayer.getPosition());
   %obj.nextBlockCheck = %this.schedule($MAX_SCAN_GAP*2, "unBlock", %obj);
}
```

What this code does is check to see if the AI is a guard, and if it isn't, then it's assumed to be a chaser. Now, if you have more than just guards and chasers, then this test of roles needs to be more specific, obviously.

Then the movement speed of the chaser needs to be set. You will need to define the pseudo-constant $MAX_CHASER_SPEED yourself near the top of the file. A value of 0.2 is a good place to start. Adjust as needed.

Then the move destination is set, and as you can see, it is set to the current position of the target. As soon as this is done, the AI will trot off in that direction. He may even open fire if the target enters the line of sight.

The last statement in the code fragment is very important. Sometimes AI guys can get stuck. Yup, I know this is hard to believe, but it does indeed happen. The last statement schedules a call to a function that will attempt to unblock the AI by telling him to run off in a random direction. Here is a simple function for the un-blocking work:

```
function AIGuardDB::unBlock(%this,%obj)
{
   if(!isObject(%obj))
      return;
   cancel(%obj.nextBlockCheck);
   %this.setRandomDestination(%obj);
}
```

Now, you've already encountered enough in this chapter to write your own setRandomDestination function. Just remember that you need to give the AI a destination *and* a movement speed, or he simply is not going to go anywhere.

If you keep sending the blocked AI in different directions, eventually he will become unstuck and move on his way.

But hang on—how will the AI know if it's stuck? Well, that's what the scheduled call to unblock was all about. The scheduled time was far enough in the future that the AI certainly would have been able to make it to its movement destination in half that time. And you will need an onReachDestination method to cancel any call to the scheduled unblock routine. It can do this by calling

```
cancel(%obj.nextBlockCheck);
```

exactly as the unblock routine itself does. So now if the unblock function is called, it means that the destination was never reached! So the AI *must be stuck*. And that means going through the "unsticking" effort involving random destinations and so on.

Instead of random destinations, you also can try some kind of reasoned approach. Perhaps rotating the AI first 180 degrees. Since the hapless guy presumably wandered straight into his mess, then he might be able to wander straight out. If that doesn't work, maybe try 90 degrees to the left and then 90 degrees to the right. And if those directions don't all work, then try random directions. Unless he fell into a pit, he's going to get out sooner or later.

Moving Right Along

This chapter gave you a good idea why AI work can be so time-consuming. Look at the amount of code in aiGuard.cs and aiPlayer.cs with the understanding that the capabilities embodied are really only very rudimentary.

At the same time, once the AI guys are bopping around doing their own thing, they can seem amazingly intelligent at times. Whenever we see them do something unexpected, we tend to think that maybe they really *are* intelligent after all!

The code in aiGuard.cs implemented a simple stationary enemy with a number of "internal characteristics" that would help determine how the different AI characters respond. A variety of response behaviors and action variations can be scripted simply by changing things like alertness and aggressiveness.

Then we saw simple path-following capabilities, with an AI player moving from waypoint to waypoint along a path.

Finally, some hints and clues have been provided to help you implement your own chasing AI player.

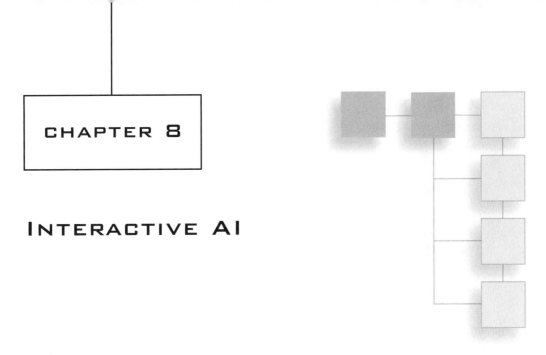

CHAPTER 8

INTERACTIVE AI

A I monsters running around killing players and blowing up stuff may be exciting, especially if you aren't on the receiving end, but using AI in games doesn't need to stop there. Indeed, it doesn't.

Some game genres—role-playing and adventure games come to mind immediately—need the player to interact with the AI characters. Sometimes the AI characters are enemies, sometimes they are neutral, and sometimes they are the player's friends. You (as the player) won't know necessarily until you've met them, perhaps not even after you've chatted with them a bit.

In fact, you may not even know how you stand with an AI character until you've done some things and have "known" the character a while. In a really sophisticated game, *even the AI character* may not know whether to treat you as a friend, enemy, or whatever, until you've done something to prove yourself.

The key to all this is the ability to interact with the AI character. You need to be able to approach an AI and strike up a conversation, receive tips and information, and ask and answer questions. The most efficient way to approach this is through the use of a graphical interface of some kind that becomes available when you want to interact socially with an AI character. (As opposed to, say, engaging him in a knife fight. Sure, that's an interaction, but combat is not generally considered a particularly fruitful form of interaction when it comes to learning important things.)

In this chapter, we'll build a system that we can use to carry on dialog-like interactions with AI characters.

The Approach

What we'll do is create a GUI that will pop up when we want to either talk with or simply query an AI character. Here is a basic list of specifications for the AI GUI interface system:

* Must be configurable to be either key-based *or* automatic.
* Allows the player to select queries or responses from a menu.
* Must provide a means for AI to *respond* to all player inputs, if desired.
* Must provide a means for AI to *act on* all player inputs, if necessary.
* Must provide a means to display a detailed graphic image of the AI character (like a portrait).
* The AI should turn to face the player addressing it.
* Should recognize when a character is not an AI player, and *not* activate.
* Use a configurable database or "flat files" to contain tables of queries and responses.

That will do for now. There's enough work ahead just to meet that specification. There's enough complexity here that we need to take a few minutes to think about the architecture.

Architecture

It might seem trivial to point out that we need to implement this system with client/server in mind. It's important to note this because some of our solution, like the GUI, will have to run on a client and some of it on the server. So don't go like, "Well, duh!" on me, okay?

For lack of a better name, I'll call this AI interaction system the "AI Talk" system or *AIT*.

There needs to be a little bit of effort expended in figuring out exactly what goes where in AIT. We know the client will include the actual GUI. Since our system is expected to be able to send queries from the player to the AI, and since we are going to "can" our queries in files for use in the GUI, then those queries will need to be on the client as well. Then there will be some supporting code to send the queries to the server, which will control the AI responses.

Now, from a security perspective, we're in good shape if the canned queries (the selections that the player will be able to choose from to send to the AI) are on the client, since it's not the queries that really matter, from an anti-cheat point-of-view (especially if the AI system is used in a multi-player game). It's the responses and actions taken by the AI that matter.

And if the responses and actions are on the server, then we're good to go; they're safe from hackers. Okay, okay, unless the server itself gets hacked, but if it does, it won't be through Torque, but through the operating system somehow. So what are ya gonna do, hide the AI server code in invisible ink on paper taped to the underside of the top drawer of your desk? Of course not. We will just have to assume that all server hosts have secured their systems appropriately.

Figure 8.1 is a simple block diagram that shows the separation of responsibilities of the AIT system between the client and server, just to put a graphic image to the idea—*queries* on the client, *actions* on the server.

When we combine the table files for each side—the query table on the client, and the action table on the server—we end up with an *AITScript*. For example, the AITScript foobar would have two parts: foobar.qry on the client, and foobar.rsp on the server.

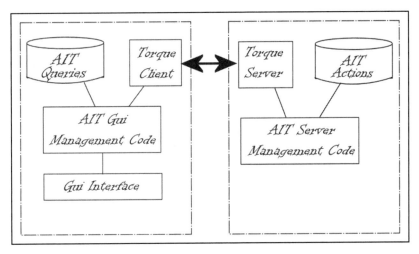

Figure 8.1 The AIT system.

The Code

There are four code modules and a couple of definition files that need to be created. But before we tackle those, there are some changes that need to be made to existing Torque demo modules.

Preparation

At the end of the file \\A3D\demo\client\defaults.cs, add the following lines:

```
$pref::AIT::DataPath = "demo/data/AIT/";
$pref::AIT::MaxOptions = 100;
$pref::AIT::QueryColour = "\c1";
$pref::AIT::ActionColour = "\c5";
```

These are a few global variables we will need access to in various places in different code modules.

Next, add the following code to the end of \\A3D\demo\client\scripts\default.bind.cs.

```
function TalkTo(%val)
{
 if(%val)
   commandToServer('AITCOntact');
}

moveMap.bind( keyboard, q, TalkTo );
moveMap.bindCmd(keyboard, "1", "SelectAnswer(1);", "");
moveMap.bindCmd(keyboard, "2", "SelectAnswer(2);", "");
moveMap.bindCmd(keyboard, "3", "SelectAnswer(3);", "");
moveMap.bindCmd(keyboard, "4", "SelectAnswer(4);", "");
moveMap.bindCmd(keyboard, "5", "SelectAnswer(5);", "");
moveMap.bindCmd(keyboard, "6", "SelectAnswer(6);", "");
moveMap.bindCmd(keyboard, "7", "SelectAnswer(7);", "");
moveMap.bindCmd(keyboard, "8", "SelectAnswer(8);", "");
moveMap.bindCmd(keyboard, "9", "SelectAnswer(9);", "");
moveMap.bindCmd(keyboard, "0", "SelectAnswer(10);", "");
```

```
function OutOfAITFunction(%Number)
{
   switch(%Number)
   {
      case 1: commandToServer('use',"Crossbow");
      case 2: %Number=0;
      case 3: %Number=0;
      case 4: %Number=0;
      case 5: %Number=0;
      case 6: %Number=0;
      case 7: %Number=0;
      case 8: %Number=0;
      case 9: %Number=0;
      case 0: %Number=0;
   }
}
```

The MakeContact function is bound to the Query key ("q"), so that when the player presses the Query key, a request is sent to the server to see if contact can be made with an NPC that is presumably somewhere in front of us. There is no guarantee that contact will be made. We need to be within the minimum distance for that to happen. The contact code is contained in the AITserver module, which we will visit in a later module.

Then there are a number of key bindings. The intent is to reserve the number keys for use as keyboard responses to the onscreen GUI, in addition to mouse browsing and clicking.

The OutOfAITFunction is used to ensure that when we aren't in an AIT query dialog, the number keys get used for their original purpose (selecting weapons).

Next, open \A3D\demo\server\defaults.cs and add this line to the end:

```
$Pref::Server::AITPath = "demo/data/AIT/";
```

Then, in \A3D\demo\server\scripts\game.cs, in the function onServerCreated, after this line:

```
   exec("./crossbow.cs");
```

place these two lines of code:

```
exec("./AITServer.cs");
exec("./AITCommands.cs");
```

And in the file \A3D\demo\client\init.cs, in the function initClient after this line:

```
exec("./ui/playerList.gui");
```

place this:

```
exec("./ui/AITGui.gui");
```

and after this line:

```
exec("./scripts/centerPrint.cs");
```

place this:

```
exec("./scripts/AITClient.cs");
```

Oh, and one more thing: Because we've created new preference entries in the defaults.cs modules for both client and server as well as new default key bindings, we need to delete a few files before continuing. These are the dynamically generated preference files that Torque writes to disk automatically every time the engine exits. We need to delete them so that the engine won't use them when it starts back up and leave us stuck with the old values. In fact, we want to delete their .cs versions *and* their compiled .dso versions. So without further ado, delete these files:

Client-side
```
C:\a3dgpai1\demo\client\config.cs
C:\a3dgpai1\demo\client\config.cs.dso
C:\a3dgpai1\demo\client\prefs.cs
C:\a3dgpai1\demo\client\prefs.cs.dso
```
Server-side
```
C:\a3dgpai1\demo\server\prefs.cs
C:\a3dgpai1\demo\server\prefs.cs.dso
```

In fact, any time you change one of the default files, you should delete the six files listed above.

The AITServer Module

Type up the following code, and save it as \\A3D\demo\server\scripts\AITServer.cs

```
function GetActionEntry(%file,%responseNumber)
{
  %entry="";
  while(!%file.isEOF())
  {
    %ln=%file.readLine();
    %tag = getword(%ln,0);
    if ( !strcmp(%tag,"<"@%responseNumber@">") )
    {
      %entry= getwords(%ln,1,99);
      break;
    }
  }
  return %entry;
}


function GetAction(%responseFile,%queryNumber,%responseNumber)
{
  %file = new FileObject();
  if(isFile($Pref::Server::AITPath@%responseFile@".rsp") &&
     %file.openForRead($Pref::Server::AITPath@%responseFile@".rsp"))
  {
    for(%i=0;%i<%queryNumber;%i++)
    {
      %response=GetActionEntry(%file,%responseNumber);
      if(%file.isEOF())
         return "<Invalid Query>";

    }
  }
  %file.close();
  %file.delete();
  return %response;
}
```

```
function AITMessageClient(%client,%sender,%npcFile,%queryNumber)
{
  %senderName=%sender.getshapename();
  %Mugshot=%sender.AITMugshot;
  %playerName=%client.player.getshapename();

  %sender.AITBusy=true;
  %sender.AITTalkingTo=%client;
  %sender.setAimObject(%client.player);


    commandToClient(%client,'AITMessage',%sender,%senderName,%Mugshot,%npcFile,%qu
    eryNumber,%playerName);
  CheckAITStatus(%client,%sender);
}

function serverCmdAITAnswer(%client,%sender,%queryNumber,%responseNumber)
{
  trace(1);
  if(%client==%sender.AITTalkingTo)
  {
    %npcFile=%sender.AITScript;
    %response=GetAction(%npcFile,%queryNumber,%responseNumber);
    if(%response!$="<InvalidQuery>")
    {
      %ParamStart=strPos(%response,"(")+1;
      %ParamEnd=strPos(%response,")")-%ParamStart;
      %Param=getSubStr(%response,%ParamStart,%ParamEnd);
      %response=getSubStr(%response,0,%ParamStart-1);
      if(%Param!$="")
      {
        eval(%response@"("@%Param@","@%client@","@%sender@",\""@%npcFile@"\");");
      }
      else
      {
        eval(%response@"("@%client@","@%sender@",\""@%npcFile@"\");");
      }
    }
```

```
    else
    {
    echo("ERROR::Invalid Query/Answer!!\nnpcFile = "@%npcFile@"\nQueryNumber =
      "@%queryNumber);
    }
  }
  trace(0);
}

function serverCmdAITContact(%client)
{
  %player = %client.player;
  %eye = %player.getEyeVector();
  %vec = vectorScale(%eye, 5);
  %start = %player.getEyeTransform();
  %end = VectorAdd(%start,%vec);
  while(!%ai.aiPlayer)
  {
    %hit = ContainerRayCast (%start, %end, $TypeMasks::PlayerObjectType, %player);
    %ai = GetWord(%hit,0);
    if(!%ai.aiPlayer)
      %player = %player SPC %found;
  }

  while(%ai != 0 )
  {
    if(%ai.aiPlayer && %ai.AITScript!$="")
    {
      if(!%ai.AITBusy)
      {
        AITMessageClient(%client, %ai, %ai.AITScript,%ai.AITStartQuery); //start
      dialog.
        return;
      }
      else
      {
        if(IsAITBusy(%ai))
        {
```

```
        if(%client!=%ai.AITTalkingTo)
        {
          messageClient(%client, '', %ai.AITBusyText,
    %ai.AITTalkingTo.player.getShapeName());
          return;
        }
        else
        {
          return;
        }
      }
      else
      {
        AITMessageClient(%client, %ai, %ai.AITScript,%ai.AITStartQuery); //start
    dialog.
        return;
      }
    }
  }
}

function IsAITBusy(%AiPlayerID)
{
  InitContainerRadiusSearch(%AiPlayerID.getTransform(), 3,
    $TypeMasks::PlayerObjectType);
  %rayCastBusyCheck=ContainerSearchNext();
  while(%rayCastBusyCheck != 0 )
  {
    if(%rayCastBusyCheck==(%AiPlayerID.AITTalkingTo).player)
    {
      return(true);
    }
    %rayCastBusyCheck=ContainerSearchNext();
  }
  return(false);
}
```

```
function CheckAITStatus(%Client,%Sender) //Checks if the player has moved since he
    started the dialog, moving too far from the sender will cancel the dialog
{
  InitContainerRadiusSearch(%Sender.getTransform(), 2,
    $TypeMasks::PlayerObjectType);
  %rayCast=ContainerSearchNext();
  while(%rayCast != 0 )
  {
    if(%rayCast==%Client.player)
    {
      schedule(1000,0,"CheckAITStatus",%Client,%Sender);
      return;
    }
    %rayCast=ContainerSearchNext();
  }
  CommandToClient(%client,'CloseAIT');
  %Sender.AITBusy=false;
  %Sender.AITTalkingTo=0;
  %Sender.clearAim();
}

function SpawnAI(%Name,%Script,%Mugshot,%startQuery,%location)
{
  %player = new AIPlayer() {
    dataBlock = LightMaleHumanArmor;
    aiPlayer = true;
    AITScript = %Script;
    AITMugshot = %Mugshot;
    AITStartQuery = %startQuery;
    AITBusy = false;
    AITBusyText = 'Sorry but I\'m busy talking to %1 right now.';
    AITTalkingTo = 0;
  };
  MissionCleanup.add(%player);
```

```
// Player setup
%player.setMoveSpeed(8);
%player.setTransform(%location);
%player.setEnergyLevel(60);
%player.setShapeName(%Name);
return %player;
}

function TestAIT()
{
  %player = new AIPlayer() {
    dataBlock = LightMaleHumanArmor;
    aiPlayer = true;
    AITScript = "elf";
    AITMugshot = "elf.png";
    AITStartQuery = 1;
    AITBusy = false;
    AITBusyText = 'Sorry but I\'m busy talking to %1 right now.';
    AITTalkingTo = 0;
  };
  MissionCleanup.add(%player);

  // Player setup
  %player.setMoveSpeed(8);
  %player.setTransform(pickSpawnPoint());
  %player.setEnergyLevel(60);
  %player.setShapeName(%player);
  return %player;
}
```

So, let's see what's going on in these nine functions. At the top, the two routines GetActionEntry and GetAction conspire to extract response actions from a response table file. The response table file (like the query table file) is organized by *entries*. Each entry is delimited by a marker string that looks like this: "<->". The GetActionEntry function scans through, collecting everything it finds into an entry until it finds that marker string; then it bundles it up and tosses it out to its big brother GetAction, who has been told to find a particular action by using an index number that it's been given. GetAction keeps track of how many action entries have been found and keeps discarding them until it gets to the one it wants, where it stops and returns the action entry text back to whatever function called it. It's a fairly straightforward *file parser*.

`AITMessageClient` is pretty important—it's the function that sends stuff to the AITClient code on behalf of the AI guy that the player is talking to. Note the call in there to `setAimObject`.

No, it's not because the AI guy went to the Ronald Reagan School of Diplomacy where the motto is: "Trust But Verify." It's because we want the AI guy to turn and face the player. *Look at me when I'm talking to you!* And, well, this was the simplest way to do that. We programmers are indeed lazy sods.

Then we have `serverCmdAITAnswer`, which is one of the places where all of the grunting and heavy lifting happens. For example, the call to `GetAction` originates here, and the reason is this: The client is the one who sends the message to the server to invoke `serverCmdAITAnswer` and waits to find out what the response will be to the query. The response is passed back in the form of a query number—an index into the action table. Whatever that action turns out to be, the action text is assembled into the form of script code (yes, that's right, *Torque* script code) and passed into the `eval` function, where it is treated like any other TorqueScript script.

The function `serverCmdAITContact` is where it all begins! When the Query key is pressed on the client, `serverCmdAITContact` is summoned remotely. It essentially pokes a big virtual stick (actually, it's a call to the function `ContainerRayCast`, but hey...) straight out in front of the player until it finds something of interest. If it's a Player object, and if it has its `aiPlayer` flag set, then it's probably what we are looking for.

At that point, we either send the `AITScript` for the found AI back to the client, or, if the AI is busy talking to his manicurist, we send a "busy" message back.

And look here: `IsAITBusy` just so happens to be the next function. It's actually a specialized busy check. Normally, back in the function `serverCmdAITContact`, to check if the AI was busy, we'd just look at his `AITBusy` flag. If the AI isn't busy, then off we go, doing AI stuff with him. However, if the AI *is* busy, then we can't just leave it at that. The AI actually may be saying it's busy because it's talking *to us!* Aha! So the `IsAITBusy` check is designed to go out and actually find out who the AI might be talking to. After all, if it's the player he's talking to, then he's not really busy, or at least not in the sense that means we shouldn't be bothering him.

The `CheckAITStatus` function checks to see if the player has left the company of the AI, and if he has, closes down the AIT system. If the player hasn't left yet, we come back and check in another second.

In order to get AIT-system-aware AI into the game, we can use SpawnAI. It sets up a datablock for the AI, with fields that point to the script, the mugshot, starting query, and other goodies, before spawning an actual AI player object into the game world. You've seen code like this before back in Chapter 7. You can use the function practically anywhere to get custom configured AI into the game.

Finally TestAIT is the simple test routine we will be using later. It's full of preset values prepped to use the artwork and sample AITScript script that you will encounter later in this chapter.

The AITClient Module

Type the following code and save it as \\A3D\demo\client\scripts\AITClient.cs.

```
new AudioDescription(AITAudio)
{
  volume    = 1.2;
  isLooping= false;
  is3D      = false;
  type      = $MessageAudioType;
};


new AudioProfile(elf)
{
  filename = "~/data/AIT/elf.wav";
  description = "AITAudio";
  preload = false;
};


new AudioProfile(orc)
{
  filename = "~/data/AIT/orc.wav";
  description = "AITAudio";
  preload = false;
};
```

```
function GetQueryEntry(%file)
{
  %entry="";
  while(%ln !$= "<->" && !%file.isEOF())
  {
    %ln=%file.readLine();
    if (%ln !$= "<->")
      %entry=%entry@%ln;
  }
  return %entry;
}
function GetQuery(%queryFile,%queryNumber)
{
  %file = new FileObject();
  if(isFile($pref::AIT::DataPath@%queryFile@".qry") &&
     %file.openForRead($pref::AIT::DataPath@%queryFile@".qry"))
  {
    for(%i=1;%i<%queryNumber;%i++)
    {
      GetQueryEntry(%file);
      if(%file.isEOF())
          return "<Invalid Query>";
    }
    %query=GetQueryEntry(%file);
  }
  %file.close();
  %file.delete();
  return %query;
}

function clientCmdCloseAIT()
{
  Canvas.popDialog(AITGui);
  AITQuery.settext("");
  AITAnswer.settext("");
}
```

```
function
     clientCmdAITMessage(%sender,%senderName,%Mugshot,%npcFile,%queryNumber,%player
     Name)
{
  $AIT::Sender=%sender;
  $AIT::QueryNumber=%queryNumber;
  onAITMessage(%npcFile,%queryNumber,%senderName,%Mugshot,%playerName);
}

function OnAITMessage(%npcFile,%queryNumber,%senderName,%Mugshot,%playerName)
{
  if(%Mugshot!$="" && isFile($pref::AIT::DataPath@%Mugshot))
  {
     AITMugshot.setbitmap($pref::AIT::DataPath@%Mugshot);
  }
  else
  {
     AITMugshot.setbitmap($pref::AIT::DataPath@"default.png");
  }

  if(%npcFile!$="")
  {
    %queryAnswer=GetQuery(%npcfile,%queryNumber);

    if(%queryAnswer!$="<InvalidQuery>")
    {
      %AnswerStart=strPos(%queryAnswer,"<AnswerStart>");
      %query=getSubStr(%queryAnswer,0,%AnswerStart);
      %answer=getSubStr(%queryAnswer,%AnswerStart+13,strLen(%queryAnswer));
    }
    else
    {
    %query="ERROR::Invalid Query!!\nnpcFile = "@%npcFile@"\nQueryNumber =
     "@%queryNumber;
    }
  }
```

```
if (%query!$="")
{
  %query=strreplace(%query,"<<Name>>",%senderName);
  %query=strreplace(%query,"<<PlayerName>>",%playerName);


  if ((%soundStart = playAITSound(%query)) != -1)
    %query = getSubStr(%query, 0, %soundStart);

  AITQuery.settext(%query);
  ChatHud.addLine($Pref::AIT::QueryColour@%senderName@":
    "@StripMLControlChars(%query));
}

if (%answer!$="")
{
  %answer=strReplace(%answer,"<<Name>>",%senderName);
  %answer=strReplace(%answer,"<<PlayerName>>",%playerName);
  %answer=strReplace(%answer,"<BR>","\n");

  %line=%answer;
  %i=1;
  while(%i<=$Pref::AIT::MaxOptions) //lets number the options
  {
    %Start=strpos(%line,"<a:AIT "@%i@">");

    if(%Start<0)
    {
      %i=$Pref::AIT::MaxOptions+1;
    }
    else
    {
      %line=getSubStr(%line,%Start,strlen(%line));
      %End=strpos(%line,"</a>")+4;
      %line=getSubStr(%line,%End,strlen(%line));
      %answer=strReplace(%answer,"<a:AIT "@%i@">","<a:AIT "@%i@"> "@%i@" - ");
      %i++;
    }
  }
  AITAnswer.settext(%answer);
}
```

```
    else
    {
      AITAnswer.settext("<a:AITNoAnswer>Continue...");
    }
    AITAnswer.Visible=true;

    Canvas.pushDialog(AITGui);
}

function AITAnswer::OnURL(%this, %url)
{
//same as AITQuery::onURL, so just forward the call
  AITQuery::onURL(%this, %url);
}

function AITQuery::OnURL(%this, %url)
{
  if(firstword(%url)!$="AIT" && firstword(%url)!$="AITLink" &&
     firstword(%url)!$="AITNoAnswer")
  {
    gotoWebPage( %url );
  }
  else if(firstword(%url)$="AITLink")
  {
    %Answers=%this.gettext();
    %AnswerHeaderSize=strlen("<a:AITLink "@restwords(%url)@">");
    %AnswerStart=strpos(%Answers,"<a:AITLink
      "@restwords(%url)@">")+%AnswerHeaderSize;
    %Answers=getSubStr(%Answers,%AnswerStart,strLen(%Answers));
    %AnswerEnd=strPos(%Answers,"</a>")+4;

    ChatHud.addLine($Pref::AIT::ActionColour@"You:
      "@StripMLControlChars(getSubStr(%Answers,0,%AnswerEnd)));

    CommandToServer('AITAnswer', $AIT::Sender, $AIT::QueryNumber,
      "QL"@restwords(%url));

    Canvas.popDialog(AITGui);
    AITQuery.settext("");
    AITAnswer.settext("");
  }
```

```
  else if(firstword(%url)$="AITNoAnswer")
  {
    Canvas.popDialog(AITGui);
    AITQuery.settext("");
    AITAnswer.settext("");
  }
  else
  {
    %Answers=%this.gettext();
    %Answers=strReplace(%Answers,restwords(%url)@" - ","");
    %AnswerHeaderSize=strlen("<a:AIT "@restwords(%url)@">");
    %AnswerStart=strpos(%Answers,"<a:AIT "@restwords(%url)@">")+%AnswerHeaderSize;
    %Answers=getSubStr(%Answers,%AnswerStart,strLen(%Answers));
    %AnswerEnd=strpos(%Answers,"</a>")+4;

    ChatHud.addLine($Pref::AIT::ActionColour@"You:
      "@StripMLControlChars(getSubStr(%Answers,0,%AnswerEnd)));

    CommandToServer('AITAnswer', $AIT::Sender, $AIT::QueryNumber, restwords(%url));

    Canvas.popDialog(AITGui);
    AITQuery.settext("");
    AITAnswer.settext("");
  }
}

function PlayAITSound(%message)
{
  %soundStart = strstr(%message, "~Sound:");
  if (%soundStart == -1)
  {
    return -1;
  }
  if(alxIsPlaying($AITSoundHandle))
    alxStop($AITSoundHandle);

  %sound = getSubStr(%message, %soundStart + 7, strLen(%message));
  $AITSoundHandle = alxPlay(%sound);

  return %soundStart;
}
```

```
function SelectAnswer(%Number)
{
  if(strPos(AITAnswer.getText(),"<a:AIT "@%Number@">"))>=0)
    AITAnswer.OnURL("AIT "@%Number);
  else
    OutOfAITFunction(%Number);
}
```

Looking at this module, the first things we notice are the audio description and the two audio profiles—nothing new here. And then there are the two functions GetQueryEntry and GetQuery. These are exactly the same as GetActionEntry and GetAction over on the server side.

The next function is short and to the point: clientCmdCloseAIT. Its only job is to shut down the AIT GUI when ordered to by the server. And it does that with great efficiency.

Next up, clientCmdAITMessage is called by the server and does little more then post the information that it's been given by the server onto the GUI.

Most of the client's grunting and groaning is done in the OnAITMessage function. It starts out by locating the bitmap image that serves as the mugshot for the character. If it can't find a custom one, it uses a default image.

Then it tries to find the AITScript file. If it can't find it by name, it looks it up using the query number index. The OnAITMessage code digs through the query table looking for the answer, which is served up if found. Then the function plays an associated sound effect, if one exists.

If an answer to the query has been found, it is assembled and formatted in the proper way and thrown up on the GUI screen.

AITAnswer::OnURL is the method attached to the AITAnswer GUI object responsible for directing URL clicks. For now, they are all directed to AITQuery::OnURL, who spends all of his life assembling the information to go into the GUI. If there really was a URL passed to us, then the player is sent off to the URL's webpage. Otherwise, all of the answer info is accumulated and organized for display in the GUI.

If a sound effect has been attached to a query, then PlayAITSound will look for the specified wav file and play it.

Finally, SelectAnswer is that function we encountered back when we did the key bindings a few sections ago. Either a GUI "answer" will be selected or if the GUI is not actually on the screen, then the number key can revert to its original purpose.

The AITCommands Module

Type the following code and save it as \A3D\demo\server\scripts\AITCommands.cs

```
function GotoQuery(%QueryNumber,%client,%sender,%npcFile)
{
    AITMessageClient(%client, %sender, %npcFile, %QueryNumber);
}


function CloseDialog(%client,%sender,%npcFile)
{
    %sender.AITBusy=false;
    %sender.AITTalkingTo=0;
}


function MoveTo(%position,%client,%sender,%npcFile)
{
    %sender.setAimLocation(%position);
    %sender.setMoveDestination(%position);
    CloseDialog(%client,%sender,%npcFile);
}


function KillPlayer(%client,%sender,%npcFile)
{
    %client.player.kill("Sudden");
    CloseDialog(%client,%sender,%npcFile);
}


function KillSender(%client,%sender,%npcFile)
{
    %sender.kill("Sudden");
    CloseDialog(%client,%sender,%npcFile);
}


function DamagePlayer(%DamageAmount,%client,%sender,%npcFile)
{
    %client.player.damage(0, %sender.getposition(), %damageAmount, "Sudden");
    CloseDialog(%client,%sender,%npcFile);
}
```

```
function DamageSender(%DamageAmount,%client,%sender,%npcFile)
{
   %sender.damage(0, %sender.getposition(), %damageAmount, "Sudden");
   CloseDialog(%client,%sender,%npcFile);
}


function TeleportPlayer(%Pos,%client,%sender,%npcFile)
{
   %client.player.setTransform(%Pos);
   CloseDialog(%client,%sender,%npcFile);
}


function TeleportSender(%Pos,%client,%sender,%npcFile)
{
   %sender.setTransform(%Pos);
   CloseDialog(%client,%sender,%npcFile);
}


function RenamePlayer(%NewName,%client,%sender,%npcFile)
{
   messageAllExcept(%client, -1, 'MsgPlayerRenamed', '\c1%1 is now known as
      %2.',%client.player.getshapeName(),%NewName);
   messageClient(%client, 'MsgPlayerRenamed', '\c1You are now known as
      %1.',%NewName);
   %client.player.setshapeName(%NewName);
   CloseDialog(%client,%sender,%npcFile);
}


function RenameSender(%NewName,%client,%sender,%npcFile)
{
   messageAll('MsgAIRenamed','\c1%1 is now known as
      %2.',%sender.getshapename(),%NewName);
   %sender.setshapeName(%NewName);
   CloseDialog(%client,%sender,%npcFile);
}
```

```
function ChangeStartQuery(%NewQuery,%client,%sender,%npcFile)
{
   %sender.AITStartQuery=%NewQuery;
   CloseDialog(%client,%sender,%npcFile);
}

function ChangeStartQueryAndOpen(%NewQuery,%client,%sender,%npcFile)
{
   %sender.AITStartQuery=%NewQuery;
   AITMessageClient(%client, %sender, %sender.AITScript,%NewQuery);
}

function ChangeStartQueryAndGoto(%NewStartQuery,%GoTo,%client,%sender,%npcFile)
{
   %sender.AITStartQuery=%NewQuery;
   AITMessageClient(%client, %sender, %sender.AITScript,%GoTo);
}

function ChangeAITScript(%NewScript,%StartQuery,%client,%sender,%npcFile)
{
  if(%NewScript!$="" && isFile($pref::AIT::DataPath@%NewScript@".rsp"))
  {
    %sender.AITScript=%NewScript;
    %sender.AITStartQuery=%StartQuery;
    CloseDialog(%client,%sender,%npcFile);
  }
}

function ChangeAITScriptAndOpen(%NewScript,%StartQuery,%client,%sender,%npcFile)
{
  if(%NewScript!$="" && isFile($pref::AIT::DataPath@%NewScript@".rsp"))
  {
    %sender.AITScript=%NewScript;
    %sender.AITStartQuery=%StartQuery;
    AITMessageClient(%client, %sender, %NewScript,%StartQuery);
  }
}
```

```
function ChangeMugshot(%NewMugshot,%client,%sender,%npcFile)
{
  %sender.AITMugshot=%NewMugshot;
  CloseDialog(%client,%sender,%npcFile);
}

function ChangeMugshotAndGoto(%NewMugshot,%QueryNumber,%client,%sender,%npcFile)
{
  %sender.AITMugshot=%NewMugshot;
  AITMessageClient(%client, %sender, %sender.AITScript,%QueryNumber);
}
```

These commands are pretty straightforward. They've been carefully named to reflect their purposes and parameters.

The AITGui Module

And finally, the last bit of program code—the GUI definition. Type the following code and save it as \A3D\demo\client\ui\AITGui.gui

```
new GuiControlProfile ("AITQueryProfile")
{
    fontType = "Arial Bold";
    fontSize = 16;
    fontColor = "44 172 181";
    fontColorLink = "255 96 96";
    fontColorLinkHL = "0 0 255";
    autoSizeWidth = true;
    autoSizeHeight = true;
};

new GuiControlProfile ("AITAnswerProfile")
{
    fontType = "Arial Bold";
    fontSize = 16;
    fontColor = "44 172 181";
    fontColorLink = "255 96 96";
    fontColorLinkHL = "0 0 255";
    autoSizeWidth = true;
    autoSizeHeight = true;
};
```

```
new GuiControlProfile ("AITScrollProfile")
{
   opaque = false;
   border = false;
   borderColor = "0 255 0";
   bitmap = "./demoScroll";
   hasBitmapArray = true;
};

new GuiControlProfile ("AITBorderProfile")
{
   bitmap = "./chatHudBorderArray";
   hasBitmapArray = true;
   opaque = false;
};

//--- OBJECT WRITE BEGIN ---
new GuiControl(AITGui) {
   profile = "GuiModelessDialogProfile";
   horizSizing = "width";
   vertSizing = "height";
   position = "0 0";
   extent = "640 480";
   minExtent = "8 8";
   visible = "1";
   helpTag = "0";

   new GuiControl() {
      profile = "GuiDefaultProfile";
      horizSizing = "center";
      vertSizing = "bottom";
      position = "120 300";
      extent = "400 300";
      minExtent = "8 8";
      visible = "1";
      helpTag = "0";
```

```
new GuiBitmapBorderCtrl(AITBorder) {
   profile = "ChatHudBorderProfile";
   horizSizing = "width";
   vertSizing = "height";
   position = "0 0";
   extent = "400 300";
   minExtent = "8 8";
   visible = "1";
   helpTag = "0";
      useVariable = "0";
      tile = "0";

   new GuiBitmapCtrl(AITBackground) {
      profile = "GuiDefaultProfile";
      horizSizing = "width";
      vertSizing = "height";
      position = "8 8";
      extent = "384 292";
      minExtent = "8 8";
      visible = "1";
      helpTag = "0";
      bitmap = "./hudfill.png";
      wrap = "0";
   };
   new GuiScrollCtrl(AITScrollQuery) {
      profile = "AITScrollProfile";
      horizSizing = "width";
      vertSizing = "height";
      position = "89 8";
      extent = "303 94";
      minExtent = "8 8";
      visible = "1";
      helpTag = "0";
      willFirstRespond = "1";
      hScrollBar = "alwaysOff";
      vScrollBar = "dynamic";
      constantThumbHeight = "0";
      childMargin = "0 0";
```

```
        new GuiMLTextCtrl(AITQuery) {
            profile = "AITQueryProfile";
            horizSizing = "width";
            vertSizing = "height";
            position = "1 1";
            extent = "303 16";
            minExtent = "8 8";
            visible = "1";
            helpTag = "0";
            lineSpacing = "0";
            allowColorChars = "0";
            maxChars = "-1";
        };
    };
    new GuiScrollCtrl(AITScrollAnswer) {
        profile = "AITScrollProfile";
        horizSizing = "width";
        vertSizing = "height";
        position = "8 100";
        extent = "384 190";
        minExtent = "8 8";
        visible = "1";
        helpTag = "0";
        willFirstRespond = "1";
        hScrollBar = "alwaysOff";
        vScrollBar = "dynamic";
        constantThumbHeight = "0";
        childMargin = "0 0";

        new GuiMLTextCtrl(AITAnswer) {
            profile = "AITAnswerProfile";
            horizSizing = "right";
            vertSizing = "bottom";
            position = "1 1";
            extent = "384 14";
            minExtent = "8 8";
            visible = "0";
            helpTag = "0";
```

```
                lineSpacing = "2";
                allowColorChars = "0";
                maxChars = "-1";
            };
        };
        new GuiBitmapCtrl(AITMugshot) {
            profile = "GuiDefaultProfile";
            horizSizing = "right";
            vertSizing = "bottom";
            position = "8 8";
            extent = "80 94";
            minExtent = "8 2";
            visible = "1";
            helpTag = "0";
            wrap = "0";
        };
        };
    };
};
```

Also nothing of particular note here—all of the GUI elements are standard controls, although there are a few custom profiles for adjusting things like control colors.

AITScript Files

Next, we need to create the actual AITScript Query-Action definitions. These are not standard Torque files, but rather specially formatted text files. The first is the query table file (.qry) for the client GUI. Type in the following code and save it in \A3D\demo\data\AIT\elf.qry, after first creating the folder \A3D\demo\data\AIT:

```
Hello <<PlayerName>>, I'm <a:AITLink 1><<Name>></a>, How can I help you? ~Sound:elf
<AnswerStart>
<a:AIT 1>Kill me!.</a><BR>
<a:AIT 2>Hurt me!</a><BR>
<a:AIT 3>Go the center of the world!</a><BR>
<a:AIT 4>Beam me to the center of the world!</a><BR>
<a:AIT 5>Something Else...</a><BR>
<a:AIT 6>Oops, sorry to bother you!</a><BR>
<->
Yes, I'm <<Name>>, do you want me to change my name to something else? ~Sound:orc
<AnswerStart>
```

```
<a:AIT 1>Yes, please.</a><BR>
<a:AIT 2>Nope... </a><BR>
<a:AIT 3>Change MY name instead!</a><BR>
<->
<AnswerStart>
<a:AIT 1>Change your start query screen to this query screen.</a><BR>
<a:AIT 2>Change your Mugshot!</a><BR>
<a:AIT 3>Change your Mugshot and come back to this question!</a><BR>
<a:AIT 4>Change your script...</a><BR>
<a:AIT 5>Change your script and open it</a><BR>
<a:AIT 6>Go back to the first query screen.</a><BR>
<a:AIT 7>Go back to the first query screen and set it as default.</a><BR>
<->
```

Please note that the closing "<->" is absolutely necessary. Those three characters comprise a marker that indicates when a GUI entry definition is finished.

Next comes the response table file (.rsp) that matches the previous query table file but resides on the server. Type the following code and save it in \A3D\demo\ data\AIT\elf.rsp

```
<QL1> GotoQuery(2)
<1> KillPlayer()
<2> DamagePlayer(10)
<3> MoveTo("0 0 0")
<4> TeleportPlayer("0 0 500")
<5> GotoQuery(3)
<6> CloseDialog()
<1> RenameSender("Inhuman")
<2> GotoQuery(1)
<3> RenamePlayer("Goofball")
<1> ChangeStartQuery(3)
<2> ChangeMugShot("default.png")
<3> ChangeMugShotAndGoto("default.png",3)
<4> ChangeAITScript("orc",1)
<5> ChangeAITScriptAndOpen("orc",1)
<6> GotoQuery(1)
<7> ChangeStartQueryAndOpen(1)
<->
```

Note that when you have a file named "fred.qry" you will always have a file called "fred.rsp". Taken together, the two halves are considered to be one AITScript.

There are a number of commands that can be used in the AIT system, and they are listed in Table 8.1. You are, of course, entirely free to build on the list to suit your needs. The AIT commands that are implemented should be more than sufficient to show you what can be accomplished using this approach.

Table 8.1 AIT Commands

Command	Parameters
GotoQuery	QueryNumber
CloseDialog	
MoveTo	Position
KillPlayer	
KillSender	
DamagePlayer	Amount
DamageSender	Amount
TeleportPlayer	Position
TeleportSender	Position
RenamePlayer	NewName
RenameSender	NewName
ChangeStartQuery	QueryNumber
ChangeStartQueryAndOpen	QueryNumber
ChangeStartQueryAndGoto	StartQuery, GotoQuery
ChangeScript	ScriptName, QueryNumber
ChangeScriptAndOpen	ScriptName, QueryNumber
ChangeMugshot	NewMugshot
ChangeMugshotAndGoto	NewMugshot, QueryNumber

AIT Resources

In addition to the query and action AITScript files, we need to put some image resources in the AIT folder—a default image for any AI characters that have no portrait, plus a portrait for the elf character.

To do this, copy the files RESOURCES\AIT\default.png, RESOURCES\AIT\elf.png, RESOURCES\AIT\default.wav, and RESOURCES\AIT\elf.wav to the folder \A3D\demo\data\AIT. If you add any other portrait image files or .wav sound effect files in the future, they should go into \A3D\demo\data\AIT as well.

Making an AIT Script

The process is fairly simple as long as you keep a few things in mind. You are creating a *query screen* for the AI to use to talk to you—in fact, the query screen is how the AI asks you what you want to do. It can also be used to present you with information, as well as asking you for some kind of direction.

Each of the questions that appear in the GUI that can be clicked on is a *response action*. When you click on a query, you are *responding* to the AI's query. These responses are tied into commands that run in TorqueScript.

The Query File

Take a look in elf.qry.

The first line contains both information and a hyperlink to another query screen via the `<a:AITLink 1><<Name>></a>` construct. The `<<Name>>` tag is replaced by the name of the AI you are talking with (or its object ID). Clicking on the name will send a *querylink* message to server, which will locate the appropriate link in the response file and execute the command attached to that link. In this case, the querylink has the parameter 1.

Each query screen is separated from the others with the `<->` tag.

The contents of the GUI that you see when the AI sends you the query come from the lines that start with `<a:AIT n>`, where n is the index number of the query line.

Once you have your GUI created, you need to specify how it is handled with a response file. The response file for a given query file has the same name as the query file with the extension .rsp.

The Response File

The first line of elf.rsp contains the tag `<QL1>` followed by a script command. This is where the querylink with parameter 1 is handled. If there had been more than one querylink, then we would have more lines like this, but with the appropriate parameter number and the relevant action to be taken.

The rest of the file contains the list of response actions that would be performed by each of the queries (when the player clicks in the GUI) from the .qry portion of the AITScript. Each of the response actions is preceded by a numeric tag ⟨*n*⟩, where *n* is the appropriate sequence number that matches the response action to the entry in the query file. The numbers need to be in order as they appear in the GUI. The numbering starts at 1.

Also very important: There should always be a single space after the tag. The commands are drawn from the command in AITCommands.cs. The command syntax is identical to that found in AITCommands.cs, except that they do not take a semicolon at the end.

Testing the AI Talk System

Okay, let's slam the doors and kick the tires on this puppy.

Launch the demo, and after you spawn in, open the console and type

```
testAIT();
```

This will create an AI non-player character and spawn him in at one of the player spawns. I can't tell you which one, because it's a secret, so you'll just have to go looking for him. You can speed up the process by opening the Mission Editor and selecting the player spawns with the World Editor Inspector to locate the spawn markers and then zip over there and check for an AI guy standing around looking important.

Once you've found him, you need to park your avatar in front of him. Move to within a meter or so, and while facing him, press the Query key ("Q"). You should get the dialog shown in Figure 8.2, with the selection of possible queries listed in the dialog.

You should also have the mugshot for the AI guy there in the dialog. Now back away from the AI guy. The dialog should disappear. Go back up to him again, but this time get so close you bump into him. The dialog should appear again.

Next, select one of the queries, like the "Kill me" one. See what happens. No, really go ahead, try it, it won't hurt.

Heh, not much anyway.

Table 8.2 contains a list of the queries that can be encountered in the GUI provided in the test setup, and what effect they should have. Try each out and see how it goes.

Figure 8.2 The AIT system in action.

Table 8.2 AIT Testing Queries

Query	Result
GotoQuery	QueryNumber
CloseDialog	
MoveTo	Position
KillPlayer	
KillSender	
DamagePlayer	Amount
DamageSender	Amount
TeleportPlayer	Position
TeleportSender	Position
RenamePlayer	NewName
RenameSender	NewName
ChangeStartQuery	QueryNumber
ChangeStartQueryAndOpen	QueryNumber
ChangeStartQueryAndGoto	StartQuery, GotoQuery
ChangeScript	ScriptName, QueryNumber
ChangeScriptAndOpen	ScriptName, QueryNumber
ChangeMugshot	NewMugshot
ChangeMugshotAndGoto	NewMugshot, QueryNumber

Now, as you saw with the study of the code in the earlier section, you can create your own set of actions. In fact, you can use code from Chapter 7 that allows you to sequence actions together and stitch that stuff together with this interface code to create some pretty sophisticated AI control regimes.

Moving Right Along

Well, now you've seen how much effort goes in to creating a fairly flexible AI interaction system (AIT). In addition to the amount of program code involved, don't forget the importance of carefully examining the division of labor between the client and the server. It's not always an issue of performance; sometimes, especially with multiplayer games, it's important to ensure that the server has ultimate control over what happens.

There really is no limit, other than server resources, to how big the query and response tables can get. Obviously, a far more sophisticated implementation, such as might be found in a massively multiplayer online role playing game (MMORPG), will have many times more queries and responses. But the core system is there, ready for you to enhance for your own uses.

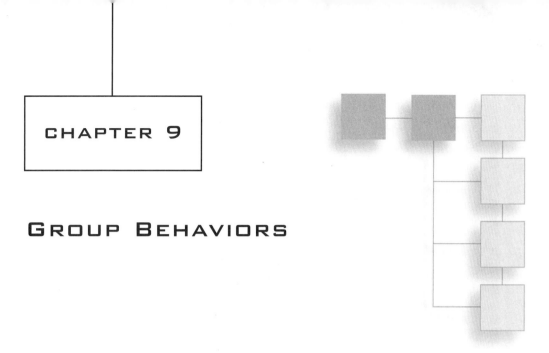

CHAPTER 9

GROUP BEHAVIORS

Y ou will recall from Chapter 5 the discussion about packs, herds, swarms, and other group behaviors. One of the most basic behaviors is the swarm, and it happens to be one that nearly everyone over the age of two is intimately familiar with. Having spent many a summer as a kid being chased around on my bicycle by swarms of black flies, I consider myself somewhat the aficionado. Also, to this day, I wonder now and then why they wanted my bicycle. Or, maybe it's because of that swarm of mid-June mosquitoes that just tried to carry me away back to their lair a few minutes ago. What's worse is that I didn't even have a bicycle.

Swarm behavior is quite simplistic in result, but not exactly as simple as it might seem in the implementation. Years of research in areas such as artificial intelligence and *autonomous steering* (the study of how autonomous—self-directed—vehicles or creatures, um, direct themselves) have yielded a fairly strong, elegant, and tidy little rules set for swarm behavior:

1. The members of the swarm should avoid bumping into each other (collision avoidance).
2. Each member of the swarm should attempt to maintain position with respect to the center of the swarm (swarm centering).
3. Each member of the swarm should attempt to match its velocity with the average velocity of the other members (velocity matching).

Now, we are in a way obligated to limit ourselves to following only these rules. However, if this is all we implement, it's quite amazing to see how well the results simulate real swarm behavior. And to prove it, we're going to create our own swarm of monsters!

Then we're going to enhance our code and see what other interesting group behaviors we can generate with a little bit of hand-waving (and keyboard clacking).

A Perfect Swarm

The first step is to create our own handy-dandy little spawn-a-swarm program. After watching it run for a bit, you can try tweaking a few of the parameters different ways to observe any tiny or gross changes in behavior. But let's get it made first.

Preparation

We will need to add some spawn markers into the game world. In Figure 9.1 you can see that I've added seven of them in a fairly level area north of the little village. You can add as many as you like, but don't add too many. The code has a function that will allow you to repeatedly spawn in more swarmers as desired, so there is little need for a big passel of spawn markers.

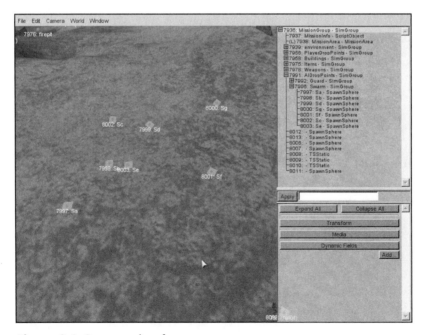

Figure 9.1 Spawn markers for a swarm.

So let's get busy with the spawn markers. This process will hopefully be somewhat familiar to you by now. If you already have an AIDropPoints SimGroup in your mission, leftover from previous work in Chapter 7 or Chapter 8, you can skip the five-point procedure that follows:

1. Launch the Torque demo program and run the FPS demo, ensuring you check the Create Server checkbox on the way.

2. After landing in the game world, press the F11 key to open the Mission Editor, and then press F4 to get the World Editor Creator interface.

3. Open the selection tree on the lower right side by clicking on the little plus signs, and then drill down into Mission Objects, System.

4. Click on SimGroup, to get the Building Object dialog. Type **AIDropPoints** into the Object Name field, and then click OK.

5. Locate the new AIDropPoints SimGroup by clicking the plus sign next to MissionGroup. Once you've found AIDropPoints, hold down the ALT key and click on the AIDropPoints entry. This will set AIDropPoints to be the Instant Group and highlight its entry in the list in light gray.

With AIDropPoints set as the Instant Group, repeat steps 1 to 5 and create another SimGroup as a subgroup of AIDropPoints; call this new Instant Group "Swarm," and set it to be the Instant Group.

Next, go into camera fly mode and zoom up a bit and over the top of a suitable location for your swarm spawn markers. Double-check to make sure that AIDropPoints, Swarm is set to be the Instant Group—it should be highlighted in light gray.

You will find the spawn marker, named SpawnSphereMarker, in the tree list in the lower right panel, under Shapes, Misc. Place the markers in random locations fairly close to each other, something like what I've done in Figure 9.1. As you place each marker, give it a name. That name will be transferred to whatever swarm 'bots are spawned at that marker. Also, give each marker a little tweak by rotating it around its Z-axis. Do this by holding down the ALT key and clicking the cursor on the Z-axis indicator of a selected marker and dragging the mouse left or right, to rotate the marker as you like.

Tip

In case you've forgotten, you can name objects in the game world by changing to the World Editor Creator, selecting the object (either in the 3D scene, or from the tree list), and then typing the name into the field to the right of the Apply button.

Save your work.

Next, as always, we need to add a wee bit of setup code. In the file \A3D\demo\server\ scripts\game.cs, in the function onServerCreated, after this line:

```
exec("./crossbow.cs");
```

place this line of code:

```
exec("./swarm.cs");
```

As you've seen in previous examples, and as you will see in other examples in later chapters, this code is used to load any new server-side script modules that we create and want to use with the demo. In general, it doesn't really matter where in the onServerCreated function the "exec" call is placed, as long as the module that's being exec'd doesn't depend on code in other modules being executed before the new module loads. If that case does exist, just make sure that your module is exec'd later. The convention is to add new exec lines for new modules towards the end of the onServerCreated function just to make sure there are no conflicts or missed dependencies.

Caution

For this exercise, you need to make sure to disable the server-based AI related code from Chapters 7 and 8. Do this by looking in the file demo/server/scripts/game.cs and locating the statements:

```
exec("./aiGuard.cs");
exec("./AITServer.cs");
exec("./AITCommands.cs");
```

You would have added them in game.cs while working on Chapters 7 and 8. They will be in the function onServerCreated. Comment the lines out so that they look like this:

```
// exec("./aiGuard.cs");
// exec("./AITServer.cs");
// exec("./AITCommands.cs");
```

Now we don't have to worry about them interfering with our fun and games.

The Swarm Module

Type the following code, and save it as \A3D\demo\server\scripts\swarm.cs

```
$MIN_SCAN_GAP = 1000;
$MAX_SCAN_GAP = 3000;

$cardinalDirection[0] = "0 10000 0";    // N
$cardinalDirection[1] = "6000 6000 0";  // NE
$cardinalDirection[2] = "10000 0 0";    // E
$cardinalDirection[3] = "6000 -6000 0"; // SE
$cardinalDirection[4] = "0 -10000 0";   // S
$cardinalDirection[5] = "-6000 -6000 0";// SW
$cardinalDirection[6] = "-6000 0 0";    // W
$cardinalDirection[7] = "-6000 6000 0"; // NW
$NUM_CARDINALS = 8;

$MAX_LEADER_RANGE = 100;
$MIN_LEADER_RANGE = 10;
$CATCH_LEADER_SPEED = 0.6;
$JOIN_SWARM_SPEED = 0.4;
$SWARM_SPEED = 0.5;
$LOST_SPEED = 0.2;
$STATIONARY = 0.01;


datablock PlayerData(SwarmBotDB : LightMaleHumanArmor)
{
   className = "NPC";
   maxInv[CrossbowAmmo] = 500000;
};

function SwarmBotDB::DoScan(%thisDB,%thisBot)
{
  if(!isObject(%thisBot))
    return;
  cancel(%thisBot.nextScan);

  %buddy = %thisBot.FindNearestSwarmer();
  if (isObject(%buddy))
  {
    error("SWARM BUDDY FOUND!:"@%buddy@" from:"@%thisBot);
    if (%leader.aiPlayer)
```

```
      {
        %thisBot.leader = %buddy;
        %thisBot.SetAimObject( %thisBot.leader );
        %thisBot.SetMoveSpeed($SWARM_SPEED);
        %thisBot.Avoid();
        %thisBot.CentreOnSwarm();
      }
    }
    else
    {
      %thisBot.SetMoveSpeed($LOST_SPEED);
      %loc = $cardinalDirection[getRandom($NUM_CARDINALS-1)];
      %thisBot.SetAimLocation( %loc);
      %thisBot.Avoid();
      %thisBot.SetMoveDestination(%loc,0);
      error("friendless..:^(...from:"@%thisBot);
    }
    %thisBot.nextScan = %thisDB.schedule($MIN_SCAN_GAP+getRandom($MAX_SCAN_GAP),
        "doScan", %thisBot);
}

function InitSwarm()
{
    new SimSet (AISwarmGroup);
    SpawnASwarm();
}

function SpawnASwarm()
{
    if ( (%role=nameToID("MissionGroup/AIDropPoints/Swarm")) >= 0 )
    {
        %count=%role.getCount();
        for ( %i = 0; %i < %count; %i++)
        {
            spawnbot(%i,"Swarm");
        }
    }
}
```

```
function spawnbot(%index,%role)
{
  %thisBot = new AIPlayer() {
    dataBlock = SwarmBotDB;
    aiPlayer = true;
  };
  MissionCleanup.add(%thisBot);
  AISwarmGroup.add(%thisBot);

  %thisBot.SetAimObject( 0 );
  %spawn=pickAISpawn(%index,%role);
  %thisBot.index = %index;
  %thisBot.SetTransform(%spawn.getTransform());
  %thisBot.SetEnergyLevel(60);
  %thisBot.role = %role;
  %thisBot.SetName(%spawn.getName() SPC %bot.role);
  %thisBot.SetShapeName( %thisBot.getName());

  echo("Added [" SPC %thisBot SPC "] :" SPC %thisBot.role SPC "#" SPC
      %thisBot.index );

  %thisBot.SetMoveSpeed($LOST_SPEED);
  %thisBot.SetAimLocation( $cardinalDirection[getRandom($NUM_CARDINALS-1)]);
  %thisBot.nextScan = %thisBot.getDataBlock().schedule(2000, "doScan", %thisBot);

  return %thisBot;
}

function pickAISpawn(%index,%role)
{
   %groupName = "MissionGroup/AIDropPoints/" @ %role;
   %group = nameToID(%groupName);

   if (%group != -1)
   {
     %count = %group.getCount();
     if (%count != 0)
     {
       // %index = getRandom(%count-1);
        %spawn = %group.getObject(%index);
```

```
        return %spawn;
      }
      else
          DebugPrint("No spawn points found in " @ %groupName, "pickAISpawn");
  }
  else
      DebugPrint("Missing spawn points group " @ %groupName, "pickAISpawn");

  return %spawn;
}



function AIPlayer::CentreOnSwarm(%thisBot)
{
  //get the loc for every AI in the group.
  //average the heading
  //turn to new heading

    %maxx=0;
    %minx=100000;
    %maxy=0;
    %miny=100000;
  %count = AISwarmGroup.getCount();
  echo("count:"@%count);
  for (%i=0;%i<%count;%i++)
  {
    %pos=AISwarmGroup.getObject(%i).GetPosition();
    %x=Getword(%pos,0);
    %y=Getword(%pos,1);
    if (%x<%minx)
      %minx=%x;
    else if (%x>%minx)
      %maxx=%x;
    if (%y<%miny)
      %miny=%y;
    else if (%y>%miny)
      %maxy=%y;
  }
```

```
    %dx = %maxx - %minx;
    %x = %minx + (%dx/2);
    %dy = %maxy - %miny;
    %y = %miny + (%dy/2);
    %thisBot.SetMoveDestination(%x SPC %y SPC "0",0);
    %thisBot.SetMoveSpeed($JOIN_SWARM_SPEED);
}

function AIPlayer::Avoid(%thisBot)
{
  if (isObject(%thisBot) && isObject(%thisBot.leader) )
  {
    %distance = VectorDist(%thisBot.getPosition(), %thisBot.leader.getPosition());
    if (%distance < $MIN_LEADER_RANGE)
    {
      %thisBot.SetMoveSpeed($STATIONARY);
    }
  }
}


// only a buddy if he's within range
function AIPlayer::FindNearestSwarmer(%thisBot)
{
  %result = -1;
  %swarmer=%thisBot.GetClosestSwarmAI();
  if ( isObject(%thisBot) && isObject(%swarmer) )
  {
    echo ("looking for buddy!");
    %tbp = %thisBot.getPosition();
    %sp = %swarmer.getPosition();
    echo ("%thisBot.getPosition():"@%tbp SPC "%swarmer.getPosition():"@%sp);
    %distance = VectorDist(%tbp, %sp);
    echo ("%distance :"@%distance );
    if ( (%distance <= $MAX_LEADER_RANGE) && (%distance > $MIN_LEADER_RANGE) )
    {
      %result = %swarmer;
       echo ("found a possible!");
    }
  }
  return %result;
}
```

```
function AIPlayer::GetClosestSwarmAI(%thisBot)
{
    %index = -1;
    %botPos = %thisBot.getPosition();
    %count = AISwarmGroup.getCount();
    for(%i = 0; %i < %count; %i++)
    {
        %ai = AISwarmGroup.getObject(%i);
        if (%ai == %thisBot)
          continue;
        if (isObject(%ai))
        {
          %aiPos = %ai.getPosition();

          %tempDist = VectorDist(%aiPos, %botPos);
          if(%i == 0) {
              %dist = %tempDist;
              %index = %i;
          }
          else {
              if(%dist > %tempDist) {
                  %dist = %tempDist;
                  %index = %i;
              }
          }
        }
    }
    return AISwarmGroup.getObject(%index);
}
```

Now this code, while quite different, has a lot in common with the code in Chapter 7. It uses roughly the same architecture and organization. At the top are some pseudo-constants and the array containing our cardinal directions.

The significant variables that you will want to consider tweaking are $MAX_LEADER_RANGE, $MIN_LEADER_RANGE, $CATCH_LEADER_SPEED, and $SWARM_SPEED. Swarm 'bots will not be able to choose any leaders beyond $MAX_LEADER_RANGE. Whenever a 'bot approaches to less than $MIN_LEADER_RANGE, he will have been deemed to have "almost collided" with the leader, and per the three swarm rules from earlier in this chapter, the collision will be avoided. The other variables are self-explanatory.

Again, we have a datablock definition—this time for the `SwarmBotDB` datablock.

Next comes the heart of the module: `DoScan`. This version is significantly different from the earlier version for the `aiGuard` datablock.

The primary job of `DoScan` is to find a leader for this 'bot, if one can be found. Then, depending on what was found, the 'bot will be directed what to do. If the leader was found, then the 'bot sets it as his aim object. This ensures that the 'bot will always face towards the leader. The movement speed is set to the swarming speed immediately after the `Avoid` function is called. If the 'bot comes too close to another 'bot (swarm member), then the avoidance routine kicks in.

After that, the `CentreOnSwarm` routine calculates the geometric center of the swarm mass and directs the 'bot to head in that direction.

If no leader was found, the 'bot is leaderless, and then sets its movement according to a randomly selected cardinal direction. The movement speed is set to a lower value. Again, the `Avoid` routine checks for, and avoids, collisions. Then the 'bot is sent off to its new destination.

Finally, the `DoScan` routine is scheduled to be revisited shortly.

The next function, `InitSwarm` is the means by which we get everything going. We call it only once.

The function after that, however, `SpawnASwarm`, can be called as often as desired to add more 'bots in to the world, by however many spawn markers you created. Just make sure you wait for about five seconds or so between each time you call it to give the 'bots time to move away from the spawn point. Otherwise, they run the risk of spawning inside another 'bot and really mucking things up.

Most of the next few functions are quite similar to those in Chapter 7, so I'll skip down to `CentreOnSwarm`. It steps through the entire group of swarm 'bots and finds the east-west and north-south limits of the positions of the other swarm 'bots, and uses that to calculate the geometric center of the swarm. It then points the 'bot at that center and sends it on its way using `SetMoveDestination`.

The `Avoid` routine is a very simple one. If the 'bot gets too close to whatever it is to avoid, it just stops. Simple, but effective. A better version would be to change its velocity vector to point away from the object about to be run into. That's a good exercise for the reader to implement!

`FindNearestSwarmer` works the same way as the human-centric version in Chapter 7 worked.

Testing the Code

To test the code, dive into the FPS demo. Once you've spawned in, open the console and type:

```
InitSwarm();
```

You should see a bunch of AI guys spawn in at the place where you created the swarm's spawn markers. Watch them for a while and notice how they move around, and yet stay in a roughly defined group (see Figure 9.2). You can adjust the tightness of the swarm by fiddling with the ranges and speeds.

Figure 9.2 A swarm of 'bots.

You can also add more 'bots by going into the console and typing:

```
SpawnASwarm();
```

You can keep doing this until you get so many monsters running around that your computer comes to its knees. That happened for me at around 240. Of course, I noticed a slow down at around 120 or so, but the demo was still playable at that number.

And remember—all of this behavior was programmed in TorqueScript!

A Chasing Swarm

Now this is cool. We will keep all of our existing swarm code, but add some more to it to make the swarm follow a real player around as a leader, if a real player is in the area.

Replace the DoScan function with this one:

```
function SwarmBotDB::DoScan(%thisDB,%thisBot)
{
  if(!isObject(%thisBot))
    return;
  cancel(%thisBot.nextScan);

  %leader = %thisBot.FindLeader(%thisBot);
  if (isObject(%leader))
  {
    error("LEADER FOUND!:"@%leader@" from:"@%thisBot);
    if (!%leader.aiPlayer) // real player, not ai
    {
      if ( (%leader != %thisBot.leader ))
      {
        %thisBot.leader = %leader;
        %thisBot.SetAimObject( %thisBot.leader );
        %thisBot.SetMoveSpeed($CATCH_LEADER_SPEED);
        %thisBot.Avoid();
        %thisBot.SetMoveDestination(%leader.getTransform(),0);
        error("GONNA CATCH LEADER!...from:"@%thisBot);
      }
      else if (isObject(%thisBot.leader))
      {
        %thisBot.Avoid();
        %thisBot.SetMoveDestination(%leader.getTransform(),0);
        error("TRYING TO CATCH LEADER!...from:"@%thisBot);
      }
    }
    else
    {
      %thisBot.leader = %leader;
      %thisBot.SetAimObject( %thisBot.leader );
      %thisBot.SetMoveSpeed($SWARM_SPEED);
      %thisBot.CentreOnSwarm();
```

```
        error("nearest object must be an AI!...from:"@%thisBot);
    }
  }
  else
  {
    %thisBot.SetMoveSpeed($LOST_SPEED);
    %loc = $cardinalDirection[getRandom($NUM_CARDINALS-1)];
    %thisBot.SetAimLocation( %loc);
    %thisBot.Avoid();
    %thisBot.SetMoveDestination(%loc,0);
    error("leaderless..:^(...from:"@%thisBot);
  }
  %thisBot.nextScan = %thisDB.schedule($MIN_SCAN_GAP+getRandom($MAX_SCAN_GAP),
      "doScan", %thisBot);
}
```

Next, add in these functions:

```
// only a leader if he's within range
function AIPlayer::FindLeader(%thisBot)
{
  %result = -1;
  %idx=%thisBot.GetClosestHuman();
  %client = ClientGroup.getObject(%idx);
  if ( isObject(%client.player) )
  {
    %distance = VectorDist(%thisBot.getPosition(), %client.player.getPosition());
    if ( (%distance <= $MAX_LEADER_RANGE) && (%distance > $MIN_LEADER_RANGE) )
    {
      %result = %client.player;
    }
  }
  else
  {
    %idx=%thisBot.GetClosestAI();
    %result = AISwarmGroup.getObject(%idx);
  }
  return %result;
}
```

```
function AIPlayer::GetClosestHuman(%this)
{
   %index = -1;
   %botPos = %this.getPosition();
   %count = ClientGroup.getCount();
   for(%i = 0; %i < %count; %i++)
   {
      %client = ClientGroup.getObject(%i);
      if (%client.player $= "" || %client.player == 0 )
         return -1;
      %playPos = %client.player.getPosition();

      %tempDist = VectorDist(%playPos, %botPos);
      if(%i == 0) {
         %dist = %tempDist;
         %index = %i;
      }
      else {
         if(%dist > %tempDist) {
            %dist = %tempDist;
            %index = %i;
         }
      }
   }
   return %index;
}
```

This new code adds in searches for human players to be leaders of the swarm. In DoScan, the new code gives priority to finding a human leader and then following or rallying to his position using the same approach we used in the AI swarm-oriented code.

Testing the Code

We can test this revision to the code in exactly the same way as before, except this time, stick around with your avatar, on the ground.

Spawn in as many 'bots as you need—but don't forget to start everything off with a call to:

```
InitSwarm();
```

And call up more 'bots using:

SpawnASwarm();

Then try things like running your character right through the swarm and out the other side. Watch them follow (eventually). Also, see how far you can run away from them before they all give up trying to follow you. As you can see in Figure 9.3, if you give them the right (or wrong) settings, the 'bots can really find ways to cramp your style!

Figure 9.3 My 'bots love me! They really, really, love me!

Moving Right Along

In this chapter, you've seen how to implement swarm-like behavior with TorqueScript. Note that the three rules of swarms are also considered to be three rules of locking behavior:

1. Swarm members should avoid bumping into each other (collision avoidance).
2. Swarm members should maintain position with respect to the center of the swarm (swarm centering).

3. Swarm members should attempt to match their velocity with the average velocity of the other members (velocity matching).

After spawning in and testing the code for a while, you will have noted what appears to be unplanned and undesigned intelligent behaviors at various times, even with that simple three-part rubric.

Then you learned how easy it can be to add additional behavior on top, like a layer cake, by adding leader chasing to the mix.

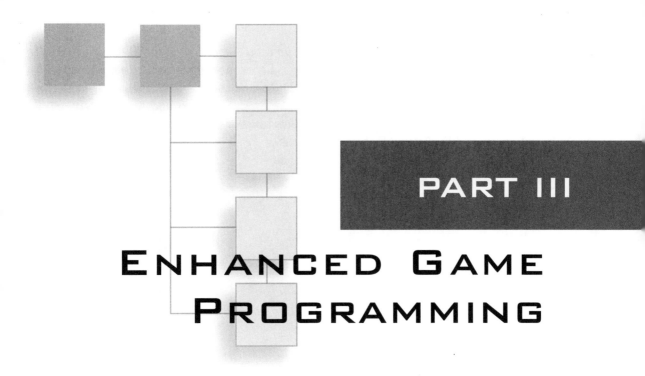

PART III

ENHANCED GAME PROGRAMMING

There are a number of gameplay-related topics that come up time and again when I talk to other game developers using Torque. Of course, gameplay is only limited by the designer's imagination, and it's often one of those unique characteristics that sets one game apart from all the others.

However, there are some common gameplay themes that many 3D game developers and designers tend to take for granted, which then have a tendency to surface as needing attention at the most inopportune times. In this part of the book, we'll pin some of these things down so that we understand what's involved when a specification says "It's gotta have features A, B, and C!"

Issues related to damage and damage management, whether player or AI character related, are hot topics. Many games require more than simply applying damage based on hitpoints. We'll address that point, while learning about Torque's lesser-known built-in damage tracking capabilities.

The real world is figuring into games more and more—terrain and the environment in general. For example, transferring real world data into games is a challenge that many need to overcome. We'll tackle taking DEM data and converting it for use in a 3D game with Torque. We'll also be looking at things like water and sunlight, with the intention of spicing things up. Taken alone, none of these topics is likely to generate a great deal of "gee whiz" response, but they are all issues that cumulatively add up to making a fully featured and complete game.

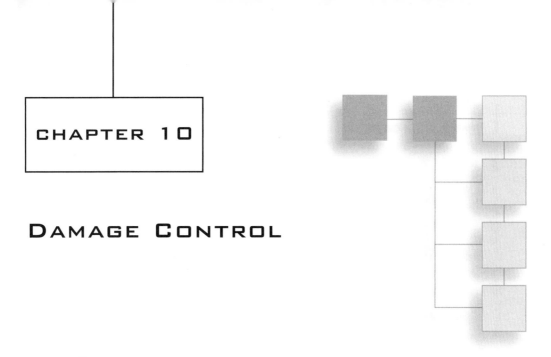

CHAPTER 10

DAMAGE CONTROL

Most action games and real-time strategy games, many role-playing games and adventure games, and *all* first-person shooter games (by definition) have some means by which players can inflict injury or damage on other players, AI characters, vehicles, buildings, or other items in the game world. It's often necessary for the genre, storyline or plot, or game play. On top of that, it's just plain fun to blow stuff up and break things—virtually speaking, of course!

So, in pursuit of the higher calling of blowing up stuff and breaking things, in this chapter we're going to examine areas like accumulating hitpoints, exploding items like barrels and cars, and breaking windows. A veritable vat of virtual vandal value!

There is a lot of typing required in this chapter, so without further ado, on with the show.

Torque Source Code, GarageGames, and Licenses

None of the techniques I discuss in this and other chapters requires changes to the Torque Game Engine itself. Changing the engine would mean using the Torque SDK (C++ source code), and *that* means you need to own a Torque license. A license for the Torque SDK is *not* included with this book. You will have to obtain it on your own; it isn't hard, and it is most certainly *not* expensive! It also means, unfortunately, that I can't present in this book techniques that use source code for the core engine without violating the agreements I have with GG (GarageGames). These agreements allow me to use the engine with the book, and utilize the script source code and all the artwork that accompanies the Torque demo.

vever, what I *can* do is present information in such a way that doesn't violate the letter or the spirit of agreements, protects GG's intellectual property rights and expectations, yet still gives you all the knowledge you need to implement these certain techniques in Torque yourself, whether or not you decide to buy a Torque license.

The optimal license for you to obtain depends on your circumstances. Most likely you will want to get the "Indie" license that allows you, and you alone, to get the source code, as well as make and sell games, royalty free. Stop by at www.garagegames.com, click on the Make Games button near the top of their home page, and look up the SDK licensing information to make your choice. Note that the Indie license requires that you display a GG logo splash screen at the start of your game. A small concession to make to obtain the source code for an AAA game engine for about a hundred bucks!

If you have a company or organization of more than about three or four programmers, all of whom need to be able to work with the source code, then you probably want to get the "Commercial" license, at a price point somewhat higher than the Indie license, but not much. This allows you to have an unlimited number of people in your company work with the source code, and also removes the splash screen restriction.

There are other details in the licenses, and GG is always fine-tuning their material in response to customer feedback, so make sure you don't just take my word for what the license terms are—check them out for yourself.

Hitpoints

You are sneaking through the grass near an enemy outpost. You trip a booby-trap! Scrambling to your feet you race away, while the timer ticks down, but you don't escape unscathed. The booby trap mine detonates lacing your body armor with shrapnel. Fortunately you were far enough away that the explosion had only a minor effect on you. You dive behind a row of crates 10 meters away. Alive, but not unscathed. Perhaps they'll think a rabbit tripped the booby trap. Does this game support Varmints 1.1 with the booby-trap upgrade? Checking your health bar, you see you've lost 10-percent health in the incident—your energy is down by 3 percent. Not good, but not so bad either. You settle into a secure place within the gaggle of crates and begin watching the movements of the enemy in his base.

That basic scenario, in hundreds of variations on game servers all around the world, is played out everyday, in one game or another. The system of tracking health (sometimes called damage) and energy (or power) as simple totalized values is one of the first ever devised for use in computer games.

In some game engines, it's the damage that is being tracked by the engine internals with zero damage being the equivalent of full health. Other engines track health—it can be a distinction without a difference, depending on your damage management approach.

The simplest approach is to merely take damage to your player character as the enemy inflicts it upon you, until your avatar guy is pushing up the daisies, with no way to reverse the process. Examples of games like this are the early games in the *Delta Force* series by NovaLogic—*Delta Force* and *Delta Force 2*. Later releases in that series, starting with *Delta Force: Landwarrior* introduced the Medic character, which could be used to heal players by reducing or eliminating damage.

Games that are health-oriented typically have a selection of *health power-ups* and drain health from the player by means other than inflicted damage or injury alone. Health-oriented games often reduce health based upon the exertions of the player, like running and jumping, and time-based drain (simulating hunger and starvation), in addition to received damage.

In any event, regardless of the approach you wish to take with your game, you are going to need a system to detect personal injury, evaluate the extent, and apply it to the player character.

Managing hitpoint damage generally involves evaluating these things, in this order:

1. Detecting collisions.
2. Evaluating the type of weapon that has been fired to establish its lethality, or damage rating.
3. Calculating the amount of damage caused, and its effect on the player's energy rating.
4. Applying the damage to the target's data.
5. Modifying the target according to the amount of damage received.

The straightforward approach to hitpoints involves extracting a damage value from an interaction between a projectile and its target, based upon a damage value assigned to the projectile.

All of the potential targets in the game, player avatars, vehicles, buildings, items, and anything else of interest, have a health value that is usually directly related to damage.

We then reduce the health (or increase the damage level) of the target by the amount of the damage value of the projectile at the time of the collision between the two. Sometimes a factor is applied to increase or decrease the damage. The value of the factor may be varied according to a random algorithm. Randomness simulates those hard-to-model real-world effects that change the outcome of a traumatic impact. A bullet might tumble sideways, a cross-wind might induce a less-than-optimal glancing blow, or perhaps even deflect the full force of a nearby blast. Often more deterministic influences, like the force of the collision, are used as damage modifiers.

The standard Torque demo has a hitpoint-based damage system. It is implemented as a simple health- and energy-reduction operation combined with a timed-recharge option. Figure 10.1 shows the default health bar in the player HUD (heads-up display). The demo does not include an energy bar in the player GUI, but we will look after that shortly.

Figure 10.1 Default health bar.

Key Features in the player.cs Script Module

Pretty well everything we need to implement hitpoint-based damage is already provided in TorqueScript form in the Torque Game Engine demo. The module that contains the most hitpoint-based damage management code is the \A3D\demo\server\scripts\player.cs. Damage-related portions of player.cs are listed below for examination, in its default, out-of-box form. This is *not* the entire module, only the parts that matter to this discussion—redacted portions are marked with ⟨snip⟩. **Don't type this into any file!**

```
<snip>

// Damage Rate for entering Liquid
$DamageLava      = 0.01;
$DamageHotLava   = 0.01;
$DamageCrustyLava = 0.01;

// Death Animation Indices

$PlayerDeathAnim::TorsoFrontFallForward = 1;
$PlayerDeathAnim::TorsoFrontFallBack = 2;
$PlayerDeathAnim::TorsoBackFallForward = 3;
$PlayerDeathAnim::TorsoLeftSpinDeath = 4;
$PlayerDeathAnim::TorsoRightSpinDeath = 5;
$PlayerDeathAnim::LegsLeftGimp = 6;
$PlayerDeathAnim::LegsRightGimp = 7;
$PlayerDeathAnim::TorsoBackFallForward = 8;
$PlayerDeathAnim::HeadFrontDirect = 9;
$PlayerDeathAnim::HeadBackFallForward = 10;
$PlayerDeathAnim::ExplosionBlowBack = 11;

// Player Pain Audio Profiles

datablock AudioProfile(DeathCrySound)
{
   fileName = "~/data/sound/orc_death.ogg";
   description = AudioClose3d;
   preload = true;
};
```

```
datablock AudioProfile(PainCrySound)
{
   fileName = "~/data/sound/orc_pain.ogg";
   description = AudioClose3d;
   preload = true;
};

<snip>

// Player Impact Audio Profiles

datablock AudioProfile(ImpactLightSoftSound)
{
   filename    = "~/data/sound/replaceme.ogg";
   description = AudioClose3d;
   preload = true;
   effect = ImpactSoftEffect;
};

datablock AudioProfile(ImpactLightHardSound)
{
   filename    = "~/data/sound/replaceme.ogg";
   description = AudioClose3d;
   preload = true;
   effect = ImpactHardEffect;
};

datablock AudioProfile(ImpactLightMetalSound)
{
   filename    = "~/data/sound/replaceme.ogg";
   description = AudioClose3d;
   preload = true;
   effect = ImpactMetalEffect;
};
```

```
datablock AudioProfile(ImpactLightSnowSound)
{
   filename    = "~/data/sound/replaceme.ogg";
   description = AudioClosest3d;
   preload = true;
   effect = ImpactSnowEffect;
};

datablock AudioProfile(ImpactLightWaterEasySound)
{
   filename    = "~/data/sound/replaceme.ogg";
   description = AudioClose3d;
   preload = true;
};

datablock AudioProfile(ImpactLightWaterMediumSound)
{
   filename    = "~/data/sound/replaceme.ogg";
   description = AudioClose3d;
   preload = true;
};

datablock AudioProfile(ImpactLightWaterHardSound)
{
   filename    = "~/data/sound/replaceme.ogg";
   description = AudioDefault3d;
   preload = true;
};

<snip>

// Player datablocks

datablock DebrisData( PlayerDebris )
{
   explodeOnMaxBounce = false;

   elasticity = 0.15;
   friction = 0.5;
```

```
   lifetime = 4.0;
   lifetimeVariance = 0.0;

   minSpinSpeed = 40;
   maxSpinSpeed = 600;

   numBounces = 5;
   bounceVariance = 0;

   staticOnMaxBounce = true;
   gravModifier = 1.0;

   useRadiusMass = true;
   baseRadius = 1;

   velocity = 20.0;
   velocityVariance = 12.0;
};

datablock PlayerData(LightMaleHumanArmor)
{
   renderFirstPerson = false;
   emap = true;

   className = Armor;
   shapeFile = "~/data/shapes/player/player.dts";
   cameraMaxDist = 3;
   computeCRC = true;

   canObserve = true;
   cmdCategory = "Clients";

   cameraDefaultFov = 90.0;
   cameraMinFov = 5.0;
   cameraMaxFov = 120.0;

   debrisShapeName = "~/data/shapes/player/debris_player.dts";
   debris = playerDebris;

   aiAvoidThis = true;
```

```
minLookAngle = -1.4;
maxLookAngle = 1.4;
maxFreelookAngle = 3.0;

mass = 90;
drag = 0.3;
maxdrag = 0.4;
density = 10;
maxDamage = 100;
maxEnergy =  60;
repairRate = 0.33;
energyPerDamagePoint = 75.0;

rechargeRate = 0.256;

runForce = 48 * 90;
runEnergyDrain = 0;
minRunEnergy = 0;
maxForwardSpeed = 14;
maxBackwardSpeed = 13;
maxSideSpeed = 13;

maxUnderwaterForwardSpeed = 8.4;
maxUnderwaterBackwardSpeed = 7.8;
maxUnderwaterSideSpeed = 7.8;

jumpForce = 8.3 * 90;
jumpEnergyDrain = 0;
minJumpEnergy = 0;
jumpDelay = 15;

recoverDelay = 9;
recoverRunForceScale = 1.2;

minImpactSpeed = 45;
speedDamageScale = 0.4;

boundingBox = "1.2 1.2 2.3";
pickupRadius = 0.75;
```

```
// Damage location details
boxNormalHeadPercentage      = 0.83;
boxNormalTorsoPercentage     = 0.49;
boxHeadLeftPercentage        = 0;
boxHeadRightPercentage       = 1;
boxHeadBackPercentage        = 0;
boxHeadFrontPercentage       = 1;

// Foot Prints
decalData   = PlayerFootprint;
decalOffset = 0.25;

footPuffEmitter = LightPuffEmitter;
footPuffNumParts = 10;
footPuffRadius = 0.25;

dustEmitter = LiftoffDustEmitter;

splash = PlayerSplash;
splashVelocity = 4.0;
splashAngle = 67.0;
splashFreqMod = 300.0;
splashVelEpsilon = 0.60;
bubbleEmitTime = 0.4;
splashEmitter[0] = PlayerFoamDropletsEmitter;
splashEmitter[1] = PlayerFoamEmitter;
splashEmitter[2] = PlayerBubbleEmitter;
mediumSplashSoundVelocity = 10.0;
hardSplashSoundVelocity = 20.0;
exitSplashSoundVelocity = 5.0;

// Controls over slope of runnable/jumpable surfaces
runSurfaceAngle  = 70;
jumpSurfaceAngle = 80;

minJumpSpeed = 20;
maxJumpSpeed = 30;
```

```
horizMaxSpeed = 68;
horizResistSpeed = 33;
horizResistFactor = 0.35;

upMaxSpeed = 80;
upResistSpeed = 25;
upResistFactor = 0.3;

footstepSplashHeight = 0.35;

// Footstep Sounds
FootSoftSound        = FootLightSoftSound;
FootHardSound        = FootLightHardSound;
FootMetalSound       = FootLightMetalSound;
FootSnowSound        = FootLightSnowSound;
FootShallowSound     = FootLightShallowSplashSound;
FootWadingSound      = FootLightWadingSound;
FootUnderwaterSound  = FootLightUnderwaterSound;

//FootBubblesSound    = FootLightBubblesSound;
//movingBubblesSound  = ArmorMoveBubblesSound;
//waterBreathSound    = WaterBreathMaleSound;

//impactSoftSound     = ImpactLightSoftSound;
//impactHardSound     = ImpactLightHardSound;
//impactMetalSound    = ImpactLightMetalSound;
//impactSnowSound     = ImpactLightSnowSound;

//impactWaterEasy     = ImpactLightWaterEasySound;
//impactWaterMedium   = ImpactLightWaterMediumSound;
//impactWaterHard     = ImpactLightWaterHardSound;

groundImpactMinSpeed   = 10.0;
groundImpactShakeFreq  = "4.0 4.0 4.0";
groundImpactShakeAmp   = "1.0 1.0 1.0";
groundImpactShakeDuration = 0.8;
groundImpactShakeFalloff = 10.0;
```

```
      //exitingWater            = ExitingWaterLightSound;

      observeParameters = "0.5 4.5 4.5";

      // Allowable Inventory Items
      maxInv[BulletAmmo] = 20;
      maxInv[HealthKit] = 1;
      maxInv[RifleAmmo] = 100;
      maxInv[CrossbowAmmo] = 50;
      maxInv[Crossbow] = 1;
      maxInv[Rifle] = 1;
};

<snip>

// datablock methods

function Armor::onCollision(%this,%obj,%col)
{
   if (%obj.getState() $= "Dead")
      return;

   // Try and pickup all items
   if (%col.getClassName() $= "Item") {
      %obj.pickup(%col);
      return;
   }

   // Mount vehicles
   if (%col.getDataBlock().className $= WheeledVehicleData && %obj.mountVehicle &&
         %obj.getState() $= "Move" && %col.mountable) {

      // Only mount drivers for now.
      %node = 0;
      %col.mountObject(%obj,%node);
      %obj.mVehicle = %col;
   }
}
```

```
function Armor::onImpact(%this, %obj, %collidedObject, %vec, %vecLen)
{
   %obj.damage(0, VectorAdd(%obj.getPosition(),%vec),
      %vecLen * %this.speedDamageScale, "Impact");
}



function Armor::damage(%this, %obj, %sourceObject, %position, %damage,
                       %damageType)
{
   if (%obj.getState() $= "Dead")
      return;
   %obj.applyDamage(%damage);
   %location = "Body";

   // Deal with client callbacks here because we don't have this
   // information in the onDamage or onDisable methods
   %client = %obj.client;
   %sourceClient = %sourceObject ? %sourceObject.client : 0;

   if (%obj.getState() $= "Dead")
      %client.onDeath(%sourceObject, %sourceClient, %damageType, %location);
}

function Armor::onDamage(%this, %obj, %delta)
{
   // This method is invoked by the ShapeBase code whenever the
   // object's damage level changes.
   if (%delta > 0 && %obj.getState() !$= "Dead") {

      // Increment the flash based on the amount.
      %flash = %obj.getDamageFlash() + ((%delta / %this.maxDamage) * 2);
      if (%flash > 0.75)
         %flash = 0.75;
      %obj.setDamageFlash(%flash);

      // If the pain is excessive, let's hear about it.
      if (%delta > 10)
         %obj.playPain();
   }
}
```

```
function Armor::onDisabled(%this,%obj,%state)
{
   // The player object sets the "disabled" state when damage exceeds
   // it's maxDamage value.  This method is invoked by ShapeBase
   // state mangement code.

   // If we want to deal with the damage information that actually
   // caused this death, then we would have to move this code into
   // the script "damage" method.
   %obj.playDeathCry();
   %obj.playDeathAnimation();
   %obj.setDamageFlash(0.75);

   // Release the main weapon trigger
   %obj.setImageTrigger(0,false);

   // Schedule corpse removal.  Just keeping the place clean.
   %obj.schedule($CorpseTimeoutValue - 1000, "startFade", 1000, 0, true);
   %obj.schedule($CorpseTimeoutValue, "delete");
}

<snip>

function Armor::onEnterLiquid(%this, %obj, %coverage, %type)
{
   switch(%type)
   {
      case 0: //Water
      case 1: //Ocean Water
      case 2: //River Water
      case 3: //Stagnant Water
      case 4: //Lava
         %obj.setDamageDt(%this, $DamageLava, "Lava");
      case 5: //Hot Lava
         %obj.setDamageDt(%this, $DamageHotLava, "Lava");
      case 6: //Crusty Lava
         %obj.setDamageDt(%this, $DamageCrustyLava, "Lava");
      case 7: //Quick Sand
   }
}
```

```
function Armor::onLeaveLiquid(%this, %obj, %type)
{
    %obj.clearDamageDt();
}

<snip>

// Player object methods

function Player::kill(%this, %damageType)
{
    %this.damage(0, %this.getPosition(), 10000, %damageType);
}

<snip>

function Player::playDeathAnimation(%this)
{
    if (%this.deathIdx++ > 11)
        %this.deathIdx = 1;
    %this.setActionThread("Death" @ %this.deathIdx);
}

function Player::playDeathCry( %this )
{
    %this.playAudio(0,DeathCrySound);
}

function Player::playPain( %this )
{
    %this.playAudio(0,PainCrySound);
}
```

At the top are a series of pseudo-constants. These establish the damage rating for the lava-type liquids. We go into this sort of thing in more detail in Chapter 12, so let's just note that they are there, and used as part of the damage system in the demo.

Moving on down, we come across another series of pseudo-constants; this time it's a list of death animations. These correspond to animation sequences that are defined along with the player character's model; in this case, the sequences can be found in

\A3D\demo\data\shapes\player\player.cs. These are here in case you want to invoke a specific sequence using the setActionThread method of the player object. The method Armor::onDisabled that you'll see later on in this code does exactly that.

After that, there are a bunch of AudioProfiles, the usual kind of thing. Some of them point to a non-existent file called replaceme.ogg. I don't know about you, but that strongly suggests to me that any profile with that filename in it needs some sound effects made for it.

Then come the player datablocks. I'm not going to explain all of the properties in these datablocks, just those that are of interest in damage management.

First is the DebrisData datablock called PlayerDebris. The job of this object is to represent the player avatar *after* the player has been killed. Therefore all of the properties are oriented around how the husk of debris bounces around or off things, and whether it eventually blows up on its own after a while, and things like that.

Then comes the PlayerData datablock, LightMaleHumanArmor. Inside here there is the property debris that points to the PlayerDebris datablock we were just talking about, and debrisShapeName that points to the shape model that will play the part of the debris. There is maxDamage, which is the overall damage variable for the player; maxEnergy does the same job for the energy side of things.

The property repairRate is an interesting one. This value does nothing on its own, but if we apply that value, or something similar, to the player object via the player object's setRepairRate, then we can have the damage be slowly (or quickly) undone.

Even more interesting is the concept raised by the property energyPerDamagePoint. It only makes sense that if you receive damage, then your energy level should suffer as well, at least for a while. The value that energyPerDamagePoint has been set to by default in the demo is 75, about three quarters of the full energy. We'll use this later on in some code that ties damage and energy together.

The rechargeRate property is used in the same way as the repairRate property, except that it is applied to the method setRechargeRate. It has a similar effect—the energy is restored over time at the given rate, not all at once.

The two properties minImpactSpeed and speedDamageScale are often used in conjunction, but not directly. There is another related property further down in the datablock called groundImpactMinSpeed. Before we get too cozy with those three variables, I want to explain something briefly.

When the collision boxes of two objects (or the bounding box, in the case of a player avatar) in the game world intersect, the Torque Engine takes note of that fact and pronounces that a collision has occurred. However, many times we are not just interested in the *fact* that the collision occurred—often we need to know how *serious* the collision is. Torque divides collisions into two types: *collisions* and *impacts*. Impacts are the more serious forms of collisions, the determination of which is based upon the closing speed of the objects. Collisions can often be trivial. Every time the player character takes a step, he is colliding with the terrain object. Trivial, but still useful to know—thus we can keep the physics portion of Torque from pulling the player through the terrain using gravity. The closing speed of the player model with the terrain is quite low, and so the collision does not take on the seriousness of an impact. However, if the player falls off of a building and hits the terrain. Wham! That's an impact, and we could then assign some damage to the player.

So, `minImpactSpeed` and `groundImpactMinSpeed` tell the engine the speeds below which it should *not* register that an impact has taken place, depending on the collided object. In the case of `groundImpactMinSpeed`, it is the terrain. In the case of `minImpactSpeed`, it is other shape objects and interiors. If you are intending to implement damage code that will translate impacts into injury, you need to take these properties into account. If the closing speeds of the objects are too slow, the engine will not register an impact, and you will not be able to use the built-in impact callback to capture the collision as an impact. The default setting of `minImpactSpeed` is 45, which is much too high to cause an impact callback to happen at normal default player running speeds. The default `maxForwardSpeed` is only 14. In the same vein, if a player falls off a high-enough building, you might get an impact with the `groundImpactSpeed` setting of 10, but that's it.

The point here is that judicious setting of the minimum impact speed variables and the various other speed properties in the player datablock is essential if you want to try to realistically model real-world-like injury due to trying to batter down a wall with your nose, and things like that.

The `speedDamageScale` property is used to modify the amount of damage inflicted based upon the collision speed, only after an impact has been established as having happened. Typically, the speed would be available to us via a velocity vector passed into the `onImpact` callback method.

The player's avatar is treated by Torque in ways slightly different than other models, and one example of that is underlined by the use of the `boundingBox` property. That property sets the x, y, and z dimensions of the player's avatar independently from the model itself. I'm not entirely sure why this is so, but when you think about it, in a networked game, collision detection is obviously one potential weakness, due to network latency and other vagaries. So it might be that this independent bounding box is somehow used to optimize player avatar collision detection. In any event, you can make your player larger or smaller for collision purposes using this setting. It will not change the visual appearance of the model, nor any of the other model-based geometries that affect gameplay—like the camera or eye heights, for example.

See for yourself. Edit the player datablock in \A3D\demo\server\scripts\player.cs and change the settings of the bounding box to something like "4.0 4.0 2.3" and try to get inside any of the orc hovels. I dare you.

Next on our plate are a series of settings that will be quite useful in the next section where we encounter hit locations: boxNormalHeadPercentage, boxNormalTorsoPercentage, boxHeadLeftPercentage, boxHeadRightPercentage, boxHeadBackPercentage, and boxHeadFrontPercentage. These properties are used to tweak the areas that are covered when the built-in hit location assessment routines in Torque make their pronouncements. The values are percentages from a base to the full extent of the measurement of the region in question. This way, the areas can be defined with regard to actual size or dimensions of the model.

For example, starting from the bottom of the bounding box at the base and moving up, the torso starts at 49 percent of the distance to the top. The torso ends and the head begins at 83 percent of the distance to the top. Similarly, when measuring from the left, the left side of the head starts at the full left extent, and the right side starts at the full right extent. The front/back proportions are measured from the back.

Moving down the datablock, the next major properties of interest are actually commented out. Starting with impactSoftSound and ending with impactWaterHard, these properties point to audio profiles that are invoked when an impact callback has occurred within the realm of the appropriate property. This is a good time to note that there are two more impact speed definition properties that don't actually appear here in this player datablock: softImpactSpeed and hardImpactSpeed. You need these two properties to be set in the datablock for the various impact-based audio profile properties to work correctly.

For example, if you set softImpactSpeed to 10 and hardImpactSpeed to 40, then anything less than 10 is soft (or easy), between 10 and 40 is medium, and greater than 40 is hard. For the record, the metal- and snow-based impacts are calculated based upon the materials encountered, and not velocities, while the water-based impacts are derived from both the impact velocity and the collided type (water).

When an impact occurs, not only can we be damaged, but our view can be messed up momentarily through the use of impact-based camera shake. Each of the properties that start with groundImpactShake… are used to define what the shaking of our 3D view should be like.

After the player datablock, there are a few damage-oriented methods. The most basic is the Armor::onCollision method. We can use this method to decide what to do when we bump into just about anything. We can pick up items or decide to mount a vehicle (meaning, get into and control the vehicle), to name two examples. Of course, we should, and will, leave any specific impact-based calculations up to the proper callback methods, which you will look at next.

Armor::onImpact is the primary impact callback. When the engine decides an impact has taken place, this method is called, and we are handed all sorts of useful information: which object we are, which object we hit, what our velocity vector was at the time of impact, and the scalar length of that vector.

In the default version, the vector is used to calculate where the impact occurred using a vector add function, and then the length of the vector is used in conjunction with the datablock's speedDamageScale property to establish how much damage was inflicted. These calculations are then passed to the damage method which merely applies the damage to our player object via the object's applyDamage method, and then works out whether or not we are dead now, and if we are, what killed us.

When the damage method applied the damage via applyDamage, the engine invoked the Armor::onDamage callback. This is where we decide what to do at the moment the damage is incurred. If the player is already dead, then we just skip the whole thing. If the player is still kicking, we flash the screen to indicate "Ouch!", and if the damage is bad enough, we play an audio sound effect version of "Ouch!"

Once a player has been killed, his character is disabled, and we end up at Armor::onDisabled where we need to do a bunch of housekeeping-like things: play a death sound effect if we have one, initiate the death animation sequence, do another damage screen flash, give up our weapon control, and schedule to have the corpse (debris) of the player removed from the scene at some later time.

We can also be damaged by liquids, either directly by things like searing hot lava or by drowning. The lava damage support already exists in the demo and is found in Armor::onEnterLiquid. It's pretty straightforward—examines the type of liquid we've encountered and acts appropriately. Like I said earlier, Armor::onEnterLiquid and Armor::onLeaveLiquid are dealt with in more detail in Chapter 12.

The ultimate damage is the death of the player. Player::kill is a straightforward, no-nonsense way to bring that about by inflicting gobs of damage on the player all at once. 'Nuff said.

Player::playDeathAnimation will select at random one of the 11 stock death animations and play it. This method is called from Armor::onDisabled.

Player::playDeathCry is also called from Armor::onDisabled, and simply plays a death-specific audio profile sound effect. Player::playPain is called from Armor::onDamage and plays the single pain sound effect. For your own game, you would be well advised to create a bunch more pain and death cries and invoke them here using a random technique like the one used in Player::playDeathAnimation.

So, I hope that gives you some understanding of how damage is handled with player objects.

Adding an Energy Bar

As I mentioned earlier, an intriguing concept is the idea of tying damage to the player's current energy level. To investigate that approach, we'll first need to enable the player's energy bar in addition to the health (damage) bar that is already in use.

Open the file \A3D\demo\client\ui\FpsGui.gui and locate the health (damage) bar control, which looks like this:

```
new GuiHealthBarHud() {
    profile = "GuiDefaultProfile";
    horizSizing = "right";
    vertSizing = "top";
    position = "14 315";
    extent = "26 138";
    minExtent = "8 8";
    visible = "1";
    fillColor = "0.000000 0.000000 0.000000 0.500000";
    frameColor = "0.000000 1.000000 0.000000 0.000000";
```

```
      damageFillColor = "0.800000 0.000000 0.0000000 0.500000";
      pulseRate = "1000";
      pulseThreshold = "0.5";
      showFill = "1";
      showFrame = "1";
      displayEnergy = "0";
         helpTag = "0";
         value = "1";
   };
```

We're going to add another control, just like that one, directly after it. This new control will be the energy bar control. Type the following code into \A3D\demo\client\ui\FpsGui.gui immediately after the closing }; of the preceding health control:

```
new GuiHealthBarHud(Energy) {
      profile = "GuiDefaultProfile";
      horizSizing = "right";
      vertSizing = "top";
      position = "50 315";
      extent = "26 138";
      minExtent = "8 8";
      visible = "1";
      fillColor = "0.000000 0.000000 0.000000 0.500000";
      frameColor = "0.000000 1.000000 0.000000 0.000000";
      damageFillColor = "0.000000 0.800000 0.000000 0.500000";
      pulseRate = "1000";
      pulseThreshold = "0.5";
      showFill = "1";
      showFrame = "1";
      displayEnergy = "1";
         helpTag = "0";
         value = "1";
   };
```

I gave the new control the name Energy and changed the position property in order to place the new control to the right of the existing control and changed the damageFillColor property to set it apart from the existing control. Then finally, the change that really matters, I set the displayEnergy property to 1, which means it will display the player's energy level and not his health (damage) level.

Next, locate the `GuiBitmapCtrl` control that surrounds the health bar. It looks like this:

```
new GuiBitmapCtrl() {
    profile = "GuiDefaultProfile";
    horizSizing = "right";
    vertSizing = "top";
    position = "11 299";
    extent = "32 172";
    minExtent = "8 8";
    visible = "1";
    bitmap = "./healthBar";
    wrap = "0";
        helpTag = "0";
};
```

We'll add another one just like that, directly after it. Type the following code into \A3D\demo\client\ui\FpsGui.gui, immediately after the closing }; of the preceding `GuiBitmapCtrl` control:

```
new GuiBitmapCtrl() {
    profile = "GuiDefaultProfile";
    horizSizing = "right";
    vertSizing = "top";
    position = "47 299";
    extent = "32 172";
    minExtent = "8 8";
    visible = "1";
    bitmap = "./healthBar";
    wrap = "0";
        helpTag = "0";
};
```

Here I just changed the `position` property in order to place the bitmap correctly in relation to the `Energy` control. That's it. Now run the demo and take a look at what you get in the play GUI, while I tidy up around here and get ready for the next phase. Your GUI should look like my GUI shown in Figure 10.2. Make sure that you exit the demo program after you finish before continuing to the next section.

Figure 10.2 Health and energy bars.

Linking Damage and Energy

First, we need to crack open the player datablock—open the file \A3D\demo\server\scripts\player.cs and locate the rechargeRate property in the player datablock, and set it to 0.1.

Next, scroll down until you find Armor::onDamage and after this line:

```
if (%delta > 0 && %obj.getState() !$= "Dead") {
```

add this code:

```
%obj.setEnergyLevel(%obj.getEnergyLevel()-(%delta*%this.energyPerDamagePoint));
```

Save your work, and then run the demo again. This time aim your crossbow at the ground by your feet, and shoot. You'll take a big damage hit, but look what happens to the energy! Notice that it dips way down (in fact 75 percent towards the bottom) and slowly recharges towards 100 percent. Now you are probably wondering how that recharge is activated. You know where the rate came from because you just set it a minute ago in the player datablock. Well go look in player.cs again and scroll down to the first method after the player datablock, called `Armor::onAdd`. It has this statement in it:

```
%obj.setRechargeRate(%this.rechargeRate);
```

Yup, that's what does it. When the player avatar is added into the scene, the recharge rate is set. Look below that and you'll see the same thing for the repair rate, except that the setting is 0, meaning that there is no ongoing damage repair happening. Does that give you any ideas? You know, we all heal, however slowly, after we get hurt…

Well, there you have it. Of course, you can really fine-tune these properties and methods to have more applicability to genres like RPGs and adventure games if you wish. The values used by default in the Torque demo are more oriented towards fast action games.

Hit Locations

Now, it's all well and good to be able to heal ourselves, restore our energy, and link energy and damage together, but good gameplay often needs more specificity than a simple damage total. Well, as mentioned earlier, we can get that with very little effort, using Torque's built-in hit location capability.

Open up our old friend, the player.cs module, and locate the `Armor::damage` method again. After these lines:

```
if (%obj.getState() $= "Dead")
   return;
```

add this code:

```
%location = %obj.getDamageLocation(%position);
%region = getword(%location,0);
%part = getword(%location,1);
switch$(%region)
{
   case "head":
     %damage = %this.maxDamage;
   case "torso":
```

```
      case "legs":
        %damage = %damage/2;
  }
  messageAll('MsgGameTest','damaged: %1 of the %2 -- severity: %3',
%part,%region,%damage);
```

Save your work.

The first line of the new code obtains the damage location string by feeding in the position value. The next two lines extract the two parts of the location string into separately checkable variables.

Then the switch statement evaluates the region of the damage and modifies the amount of damage based upon where the hit took place. A headshot is considered instant death for the sake of this example, so the damage is set to the maximum. A torso hit is considered to be the "normal" injury, while a leg hit is considered to be less debilitating, so the damage is set to a lower amount there.

Finally, the messageAll function is used here to send the details of the damage into the chat window, simply to avoid having to switch back and forth to the console. Note that the last two lines is actually the messageAll statement broken and spread across two lines. That's because it's too long for the book layout here. You can type it in exactly as you see it, and it will work, but it's better if you put the whole thing on one line.

Launch the demo and shoot at stuff close to you. Get up close to a wall and shoot above your head, at waist level, and at your feet. Watch the chat window for the messages that tell you where you are taking damage and how much it is.

This implementation is quite simple, but you can see that there is a lot of power wrapped up in this capability. I'm sure you can put it to even better use!

Bang, Bang, Boom!

Pop quiz! After crates, what's the most common piece of traditional first-person shooter furniture? For bonus points: What do you do with them?

That's right. Barrels, and we blow them up!

Figures 10.3, 10.4, and 10.5 depict a sequence of a barrel exploding after having been hit by a non-explosive crossbow bolt.

Figure 10.3 Initial explosion particles.

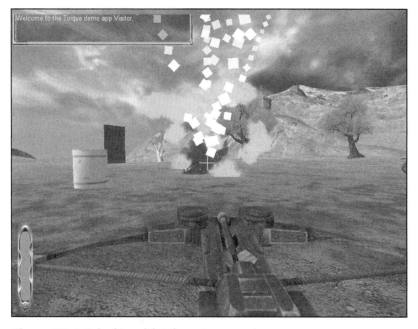

Figure 10.4 Sub-object debris bouncing around.

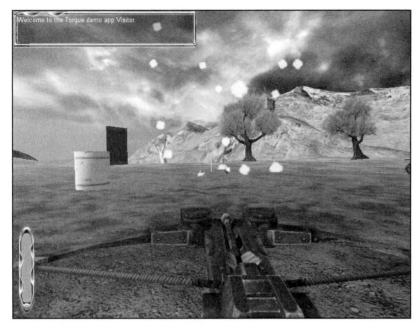

Figure 10.5 Sub-object debris at the end of their lives.

Preparation

Create a new folder called \A3D\demo\data\shapes\splody. Then locate the following files in RESOURCES\ch10 and copy them into the new splody folder:

barrel.dts

barrel.png

debris.dts

debris.png

Create another new folder, this time called \A3D\demo\data\sound\weapons. Then locate the file RESOURCES\ch10\fuel_explosion.ogg and copy it into the new weapons folder.

Now, we're going to be using the default crossbow when testing our code, and the crossbow already has an exploding bolt. That could cause confusion when trying to observe our results during testing. So what we're going to do is modify the crossbow projectile so that it *doesn't* have an exploding head.

Open the file \A3D\demo\server\scripts\crossbow.cs and locate the datablock that starts with this line:

```
datablock ProjectileData(CrossbowProjectile)
```

In that datablock locate these two lines:

```
    explosion            = CrossbowExplosion;
    waterExplosion       = CrossbowWaterExplosion;
```

and comment them out like this:

```
//  explosion            = CrossbowExplosion;
//  waterExplosion       = CrossbowWaterExplosion;
```

Then locate each of the following properties in that same datablock and set the values as shown:

```
    radiusDamage         = 0;
    lifetime             = 10000;/
    fadeDelay            = 10000;
```

Now, open the file.

Great!

Next, like you've seen before, and will see again before this book is finished, edit the file \A3D\demo\server\scripts\game.cs, and in the function onServerCreated, after this line:

```
    exec("./crossbow.cs");
```

place this line of code:

```
    exec("./barrels.cs");
```

Great! That's the resources looked after and the script modes handled. Next comes the actual code.

The Code

Create the file \A3D\demo\server\scripts\barrel.cs and insert the following code:

```
datablock AudioProfile(FuelExplosionSound)
{
filename = "~/data/sound/weapons/fuel_explosion.ogg";
description = AudioDefault3d;
preload = true;
};

datablock ParticleData(FuelExplosionSmoke)
{
   textureName         = "~/data/shapes/particles/smoke";
   dragCoeffiecient    = 100.0;
   gravityCoefficient  = -0.5;
   inheritedVelFactor  = 0.05;
   constantAcceleration = -0.30;
   lifetimeMS          = 2200;
   lifetimeVarianceMS  = 300;
   useInvAlpha =  true;
   spinRandomMin = -80.0;
   spinRandomMax =  80.0;
   colors[0]      = "0.56 0.36 0.26 1.0";
   colors[1]      = "0.7 0.7 0.7 0.9";
   colors[2]      = "0.9 0.9 0.9 0.8";
   sizes[0]       = 4.0;
   sizes[1]       = 2.5;
   sizes[2]       = 1.0;
   times[0]       = 0.0;
   times[1]       = 0.5;
   times[2]       = 1.0;
};

datablock ParticleEmitterData(FuelExplosionSmokeEmitter)
{
   ejectionPeriodMS = 10;
   periodVarianceMS = 0;
   ejectionVelocity = 8;
   velocityVariance = 2;
```

```
      thetaMin        = 0.0;
      thetaMax        = 180.0;
      lifetimeMS      = 250;
      particles = "FuelExplosionSmoke";
};


datablock ParticleData(FuelExplosionFire)
{
      textureName          = "~/data/shapes/splody/debris.dts";
      dragCoeffiecient     = 100.0;
      gravityCoefficient   = 0;
      inheritedVelFactor   = 0.1;
      constantAcceleration = 0.0;
      lifetimeMS           = 300;
      lifetimeVarianceMS   = 200;
      useInvAlpha =   false;
      spinRandomMin = -80.0;
      spinRandomMax =  80.0;
      colors[0]     = "0.9 0.9 0.9 0.9";
      colors[1]     = "0.8 0.8 0.0 0.7";
      colors[2]     = "0.7 0.3 0.0 0.9";
      sizes[0]      = 0.7;
      sizes[1]      = 0.3;
      sizes[2]      = 0.2;
      times[0]      = 0.0;
      times[1]      = 0.3;
      times[2]      = 0.6;
};


datablock ParticleEmitterData(FuelExplosionFireEmitter)
{
      ejectionPeriodMS = 10;
      periodVarianceMS = 0;
      ejectionVelocity = 0.2;
      velocityVariance = 0.05;
      thetaMin        = 0.0;
      thetaMax        = 180.0;
      lifetimeMS      = 250;
      particles = "FuelExplosionFire";
};
```

```
datablock ParticleData(FuelExplosionSparks)
{
   textureName          = "~/data/shapes/splody/debris.dts";
   dragCoefficient      = 1;
   gravityCoefficient   = 0.0;
   inheritedVelFactor   = 0.2;
   constantAcceleration = 0.0;
   lifetimeMS           = 500;
   lifetimeVarianceMS   = 350;
   colors[0]     = "0.60 0.40 0.30 1.0";
   colors[1]     = "0.60 0.40 0.30 0.8";
   colors[2]     = "1.0 0.40 0.30 0.0";
   sizes[0]      = 0.25;
   sizes[1]      = 0.15;
   sizes[2]      = 0.15;
   times[0]      = 0.0;
   times[1]      = 0.5;
   times[2]      = 1.0;
};

datablock ParticleEmitterData(FuelExplosionSparkEmitter)
{
   ejectionPeriodMS = 3;
   periodVarianceMS = 0;
   ejectionVelocity = 5;
   velocityVariance = 1;
   ejectionOffset  = 0.0;
   thetaMin        = 0;
   thetaMax        = 180;
   phiReferenceVel = 0;
   phiVariance     = 360;
   overrideAdvances = false;
   orientParticles = true;
   lifetimeMS      = 100;
   particles = "FuelExplosionSparks";
};
```

```
datablock ParticleData(FuelDebrisTrail)
{
   textureName          = "~/data/shapes/splody/debris.dts";
   dragCoefficient      = 1;
   gravityCoefficient   = 0;
   inheritedVelFactor   = 0;
   windCoefficient      = 0;
   constantAcceleration = 0;
   lifetimeMS           = 800;
   lifetimeVarianceMS   = 100;
   spinSpeed     = 0;
   spinRandomMin = -90.0;
   spinRandomMax =  90.0;
   useInvAlpha   = true;
   colors[0]     = "0.8 0.8 0.8 0.2";
   colors[1]     = "0.8 0.8 0.8 0.2";
   colors[2]     = "0.8 0.8 0.8 0.2";
   sizes[0]      = 0.2;
   sizes[1]      = 0.3;
   sizes[2]      = 0.4;
   times[0]      = 0.1;
   times[1]      = 0.2;
   times[2]      = 0.3;
};

datablock ParticleEmitterData(FuelDebrisTrailEmitter)
{
   ejectionPeriodMS = 30;
   periodVarianceMS = 0;
   ejectionVelocity = 0.0;
   velocityVariance = 0.0;
   ejectionOffset   = 0.0;
   thetaMin         = 170;
   thetaMax         = 180;
   phiReferenceVel  = 0;
   phiVariance      = 360;
   lifetimeMS       = 1000;
   particles = "FuelDebrisTrail";
};
```

```
datablock DebrisData(FuelExplosionDebris)
{
    shapeFile = "~/data/shapes/splody/debris.dts";
    emitters = "FuelDebrisTrailEmitter";
    elasticity = 0.3;
    friction = 0.7;
    numBounces = 3;
    bounceVariance = 1;
    explodeOnMaxBounce = false;
    staticOnMaxBounce = false;
    snapOnMaxBounce = false;
    minSpinSpeed = 0;
    maxSpinSpeed = 700;
    render2D = false;
    lifetime = 1;
    lifetimeVariance = 0.5;
    velocity = 100;
    velocityVariance = 60;
    fade = true;
    useRadiusMass = true;
    baseRadius = 0.25;
    gravModifier = 2.0;
    terminalVelocity = 100;
    ignoreWater = true;
};

datablock ExplosionData(FuelExplosion)
{
    soundProfile = FuelExplosionSound;
    lifeTimeMS = 1900;
    particleEmitter = FuelExplosionFireEmitter;
    particleDensity = 100;
    particleRadius = 5;
    emitter[0] = FuelExplosionSmokeEmitter;
    emitter[1] = FuelExplosionSparkEmitter;
    shakeCamera = true;
    camShakeFreq = "10.0 11.0 10.0";
    camShakeAmp = "1.0 1.0 1.0";
    camShakeDuration = 0.5;
    camShakeRadius = 10.0;
```

```
   debris = FuelExplosionDebris;
   debrisThetaMin = 0;
   debrisThetaMax = 40;
   debrisPhiMin = 0;
   debrisPhiMax = 360;
   debrisNum = 20;
   debrisNumVariance = 8;
   debrisVelocity = 4;
   debrisVelocityVariance =1;
   impulseRadius = 30;
   impulseForce = 25;
   lightStartRadius = 9;
   lightEndRadius = 4;
   lightStartColor = "0.5 0.5 0";
   lightEndColor = "0 0 0";
};

datablock StaticShapeData(BarrelA)
{
   category    = "decor";
   shapeFile    = "~/data/shapes/splody/barrel.dts";
   damageRadius     = 10;
   radiusDamage   = 50;
   damageType   = barrelAdebris;
   damageImpulse   = 200;
   maxDamage      = 30;
};

function
    BarrelA::Damage(%theDatablock,%aBarrel,%sourceObject,%pos,%damage,%damagetype)
{
  %aBarrel.applyDamage(%damage);
  if(%aBarrel.getDamageLevel() >= %theDatablock.maxDamage)
    %theDatablock.Explode( %aBarrel ,%pos);
}
```

```
function BarrelA::Explode(%theDatablock, %aBarrel, %position)
{
  if(%aBarrel.exploded)
    return;
  %aBarrel.exploded = true;
  %boom = new Explosion()
  {
    datablock = FuelExplosion;
    position  = %position;
    sourceObject = %aBarrel.sourceObject;
    sourceSlot   = %aBarrel.sourceSlot;
    client    = %aBarrel.client;
  };
  MissionCleanup.add(%boom);
  radiusDamage(%aBarrel,%position,%theDatablock.damageRadius,
               %theDatablock.radiusDamage,%source.damageType,
               %theDatablock.damageImpulse);
  %aBarrel.schedule(500, "delete");
}
```

Let's look at that code some and see what it does.

To start with, there is an audio profile that defines the sound that the exploding barrel will make, and then a bunch of particle definition datablocks. These two resource types are discussed in my first book, *3D Game Programming All in One*, so I won't go into them in detail here. There are particles for smoke, fire, sparks, and even for debris that is scattered hither and yon by the explosion.

The significant datablock is an ExplosionData one called FuelExplosion, which ties together all of the various particle emitters and assigns their general behavior, generates a shake of the camera (caused by the explosion shockwave), and defines how and where the leftover debris is handled after the explosion.

The key methods are BarrelA::Damage and BarrelA::Explode. BarrelA::Damage is called by the crossbow's projectile, believe it or not, when it detects the collision with the barrel.

If you look in C:\A3D\demo\server\scripts\crossbow.cs in the method CrossbowProjectile::onCollision, you will find this line:

```
%col.damage(%obj,%pos,%this.directDamage,"CrossbowBolt");
```

When the crossbow bolt hits the barrel, the collision detection will stuff the variable %col with the handle for the barrel. Then the barrel's damage method is called, and that just so happens to be the BarrelA::Damage method. Oh, how I love it when a plan comes together!

Ah, but if you look closely at the call to the damage method via %col.damage, and then at where the method is defined, you'll notice a discrepancy. Four parameters are passed in: %obj, %pos, %this. directDamage, and "CrossbowBolt". And you might recall that because it's the method of an object being called, the object's handle is automatically added in front of all the other parameters, so that we actually have five parameters being passed into the method. But look at the BarrelA::Damage method's parameter list:

```
(%theDatablock,%aBarrel,%sourceObject,%pos,%damage,%damagetype)
```

Six parameters! *What happen? Someone set us up the bomb?* Not hardly.

It happens because BarrelA is a StaticShape, according to its datablock. It so happens that there is already a damage method for the general ShapeBase class located in \A3D\demo\server\scripts\shapeBase.cs. Notice that the capitalizations of Damage and damage differ; it's not an issue, since TorqueScript is not case sensitive (except with respect to keywords).

Anyway, you'll see that ShapeBase::damage accepts five parameters, and then calls damage method for the shape's datablock using all five parameters. This has the effect of adding the datablock's handle onto the pile, which then gets handed to the datablock's Damage method (the one we defined in barrels.cs), and *that* accepts the six parameters.

Whew! Take the time to review that explanation and look at the code. There's a lot of useful skullduggery in there.

Anyway, once all the chicanery is behind us, we examine the damage level, and if it exceeds the maximum damage absorption capability of the barrel, we call the Explode method.

The Explode method dynamically creates a new explosion object that has all of the nifty particle effects and sound effects and stuff, and, well, obliterates the barrel. Notice the use of the function radiusDamage to cause injury or damage to nearby items or players.

Testing the Amazing Exploding Barrel

Launch the fps demo, and after spawning in, switch to camera fly mode and position yourself above the ground aiming at where you would like to place a barrel. Open the Mission Editor and in the World Editor Creator's selection list at lower right, choose Shapes, decor, and then click on BarrelA to insert the barrel at your aim point.

Exit the editor, and then return to your player character by pressing Alt+C. Now, aim carefully at the barrel and shoot it. Then duck (running won't help much).

Cool, huh?

Now, you might be thinking that you've seen better explosions, and I'm sure you are right. I've shown you everything you need to go ahead and make some really killer explosions and show me up. So do it. If you need a few hints, look at the particle definitions, specifically the velocity and particle lifetime. Better particle textures would help as well.

Tip

Don't forget to restore your crossbow projectile back to its default values before continuing with the rest of the chapter.

Hot Wheels

Dune buggy takes a licking, but alas! No more ticking.

What we're going to do is spruce up the damage handling code for the dune buggy so that if it is abused or attacked with weapons, it can be destroyed.

Buggy Code

Open the file \A3D\demo\server\scripts\car.cs and *before* this line near the top:

```
datablock AudioProfile(buggyEngineSound) datablock:
```

place this code:

```
datablock ParticleData(LightDamageParticle)
{
  textureName        = "~/data/shapes/particles/smoke";
  dragCoefficient    = 2.0;
  gravityCoefficient = -0.2;
```

```
    inheritedVelFactor   = 0.1;
    constantAcceleration = 0.0;
    lifetimeMS           = 500;
    lifetimeVarianceMS   = 500;
    colors[0]     = "0.46 0.46 0.46 0.3";
    colors[1]     = "0.46 0.46 0.26 0.3";
    sizes[0]      = 0.20;
    sizes[1]      = 0.5;
};
datablock ParticleEmitterData(LightDamageEmitter)
{
    ejectionPeriodMS = 10;
    periodVarianceMS = 0;
    ejectionVelocity = 6;
    velocityVariance = 2.0;
    ejectionOffset   = 0.0;
    thetaMin         = 25;
    thetaMax         = 35;
    phiReferenceVel  = 0;
    phiVariance      = 90;
    overrideAdvances = false;
    particles = "LightDamageParticle";
};
datablock ParticleData(HeavyDamageParticle)
{
    textureName          = "~/data/shapes/particles/smoke";
    dragCoefficient      = 2.0;
    gravityCoefficient   = -0.15;
    inheritedVelFactor   = 0.1;
    constantAcceleration = 0.0;
    lifetimeMS           = 1000;
    lifetimeVarianceMS   = 0.5;
    colors[0]     = "0.25 0.25 0.25 0.5";
    colors[1]     = "0.16 0.16 0.16 05";
    sizes[0]      = 0.50;
    sizes[1]      = 2.0;
};
datablock ParticleEmitterData(HeavyDamageEmitter)
{
    ejectionPeriodMS = 10;
    periodVarianceMS = 0;
```

```
    ejectionVelocity = 15;
    velocityVariance = 2.0;
    ejectionOffset   = 0.4;
    thetaMin         = 10;
    thetaMax         = 40;
    phiReferenceVel  = 0;
    phiVariance      = 180;
    overrideAdvances = false;
    particles = "HeavyDamageParticle";
};
datablock ParticleData(DestroyedParticle)
{
    textureName          = "~/data/shapes/particles/smoke";
    dragCoefficient      = 2.0;
    gravityCoefficient   = -0.05;
    inheritedVelFactor   = 0.1;
    constantAcceleration = 0.0;
    lifetimeMS           = 5000;
    lifetimeVarianceMS   = 0.5;
    colors[0]      = "0.0 0.0 0.0 0.8";
    colors[1]      = "0.0 0.0 0.0 0.8";
    sizes[0]       = 2.00;
    sizes[1]       = 5.0;
};
datablock ParticleEmitterData(DestroyedEmitter)
{
    ejectionPeriodMS = 10;
    periodVarianceMS = 0;
    ejectionVelocity = 25;
    velocityVariance = 3.0;
    ejectionOffset   = 0.4;
    thetaMin         = 5;
    thetaMax         = 60;
    phiReferenceVel  = 0;
    phiVariance      = 360;
    overrideAdvances = false;
    particles = "DestroyedParticle";
};
```

Next, find the vehicle datablock, which starts with this line:

```
datablock WheeledVehicleData(DefaultCar)
```

Inside the vehicle datablock, locate the following property and set it to the value shown:

```
maxDamage = 100;
```

Now add this code somewhere inside that same vehicle datablock, just before the closing brace:

```
damageEmitter[0] = LightDamageEmitter;
damageEmitter[1] = HeavyDamageEmitter;
damageEmitter[2] = DestroyedEmitter;
damageEmitterOffset[0] = "0.0 -1.0 0.5 ";
damageEmitterOffset[1] = "0.0 -2.0 0.3 ";
damageEmitterOffset[2] = "0.0 -3.0 0.0 ";
damageLevelTolerance[0] = 0.40;
damageLevelTolerance[1] = 0.60;
damageLevelTolerance[2] = 0.80;
numDmgEmitterAreas = 3;
```

And finally, add the following functions to the end of the car.cs file:

```
function DefaultCar::damage(%this, %obj, %sourceObject, %position, %dmg, %type)
{
  %obj.applyDamage(%dmg);
}

function DefaultCar::onDamage(%this, %obj, %delta)
{
  error("HIT DefaultCar::onDamage !"@%obj.getDamageLevel());
}
```

Save your work.

Okay, let's see what that was all about. First, we added a whack of particle definitions to the top of the car module. The important thing to note is that there are three kinds of emitters: light, medium, and heavy. Each emitter and particle definition is slightly different.

The code we added to the `vehicle` datablock specifies to Torque how to use each of those three kinds of particle emitters. First, we specify the maximum damage value with `maxDamage` property. Then we add a block of code that sets up a few arrays to contain pointers to the particle emitters. The properties `damageEmitterOffset[n]` specify where on the vehicle the particle emitters will originate.

The properties `damageLevelTolerance[n]` are used to set the damage level at which the various emitters are enabled. Presumably, the more damage, the worse the emitters would appear. Of course, the choice is yours.

When the vehicle takes some damage, the `DefaultCar::damage` method is called. This is where we actually apply the damage to the vehicle, and when we do that, the handler `DefaultCar::onDamage` is invoked as well, after the engine applies the damage to the object. All I'm doing here in `onDamage` is sending a message to the console to show that the method is actually invoked. This is where you can get creative with your vehicle damage routines!

Blasting the Buggy

Launch the fps demo, and after spawning in, switch to camera fly mode and position yourself above the ground aiming at where you would like to place the buggy. Open the Mission Editor and in the World Editor Creator's selection list at lower right, choose Shapes, Vehicles, and then click on DefaultCar to insert the buggy at your aim point.

When you do that, you might find the buggy stuck in the ground. If so, simply grab it by its Z-axis marker and yank it up a little until all of the wheels are clear of the ground, then let it go. It will settle down in place on the ground.

Now go back to first-person mode with your player avatar, then run over to the dune buggy. Blast away at it with the crossbow for a bit. You might have to experiment a bit to find the right parts of the buggy to hit to inflict the most damage. It all depends on where the collision box is located in the dune buggy model. Eventually, it's going to be hurt. Figure 10.6 shows the dune buggy burning furiously.

But wait! There's more! Taking enemy fire is not the only way a vehicle can be damaged, now is it?

How about collisions, driving off cliffs, getting rammed by a massive SUV, and stuff like that? Well, that's easily handled.

Figure 10.6 Hot buggy!

Open the file \A3D\demo\server\scripts\car.cs once again and add the following code at the end of the file:

```
function DefaultCar::onImpact(%this, %obj, %collidedObject, %vec, %vecLen)
{
   %obj.damage(0, VectorAdd(%obj.getPosition(),%vec),%vecLen *
                                  (%this.speedDamageScale+1), "Impact");

   if( (%obj.getDamageLevel() >= %this.maxDamage) &&
                                  (%obj.getDamageState() !$= "Destroyed"))
   {
     %obj.setDamageState(Destroyed);
   }
}
```

Save your work.

To test this addition, instead of using the fps demo, use the Multiplayer Off-Road Racing demo instead. Drive around, trying not to bang into things. If you are as good a virtual driver as I am, you'll no doubt hit every obstacle in sight while trying diligently to avoid them. Now when the buggy crashes into something, or when something crashes into it, we can apply damage to it. The amount of damage depends on the velocity difference between the buggy and the thing it crashes into. We get a velocity vector and the velocity vector's length as the second to last and last parameters to the onImpact method and use that to scale the damage appropriately. Figure 10.7 shows the buggy driving along trailing some kind of vapor or smoke—probably a busted radiator from ramming into that sign back there… Ahem.

Figure 10.7 Smokin'!

Living in Glass Houses

They say "people who live in glass houses shouldn't throw stones." Ha! What do *they* know, anyway? Isn't that what stones are for? Throwing, I mean. Perhaps they meant to say "people who live in glass houses shouldn't stow thrones." Now *that* makes sense. If you live in a crystal palace, why would you want to hide your throne? You'd probably be selling tickets to the masses to come and see your funky throne!

And besides, even if your house isn't made entirely of glass, it likely has windows. Windows rarely survive a firefight, and the sound of breaking glass adds a certain elegant flair of sophistication and breeding to what would otherwise seem like nothing more than a brawl.

Preparation

Smashing windows in Torque is not all that different from blowing up barrels. There is less emphasis required on the "exploding" and more given to what the remains look like.

Figures 10.8, 10.9, 10.10, and 10.11 depict a sequence where a window is shot out. Note the glass has been modeled opaque for the broken pieces. This simulates the crazing and fine spider-web like cracks that often happen with shattered glass. Also note that in Figure 10.11, a second window has been shot out, and the debris is different from the first window (which was the right-hand one). Finally, you can see that in Figures 10.9 and 10.10, particles are hurling about, and they are defined to render small models of glass shards.

Figure 10.8 Transparent glass window in pristine condition.

Figure 10.9 Falling glass shards.

Figure 10.10 Falling glass shards with a busted window.

Figure 10.11 Two busted windows.

So, without any further ado, let's get the resources into place.

Create a new folder called windows inside the folder \A3D\demo\data\sound. Next, find the file glassshatter.ogg in RESOURCES\ch10 and copy it to your new sound\windows folder.

Create a new folder called windows inside the folder \A3D\demo\data\shapes. Next, find the following files in RESOURCES\ch10: shards0.dts, shards1.dts, shards2.dts, shards3.dts, shards4.dts, glassdebris.dts, window.dts, and glass.dts and copy them to your new shapes\windows folder.

Next, open the file \A3D\demo\server\scripts\game.cs, and in the function onServerCreated, after this line:

```
exec("./crossbow.cs");
```

place this line of code:

```
exec("./windows.cs");
```

Next comes the main body of the script code.

The Code

Type the following code and save it as \A3D\demo\server\scripts\windows.cs:

```
datablock AudioProfile(GlassShatterSound)
{
      filename = "~/data/sound/windows/glassshatter.ogg";
      description = AudioDefault3d;
      preload = true;
};


datablock ParticleData(GlassShatterSmoke)
{
   textureName = "~/data/shapes/windows/glass.jpg";
   dragCoeffiecient    = 100.0;
   gravityCoefficient  = 1.5;
   inheritedVelFactor  = 0.05;
   constantAcceleration = -0.30;
   lifetimeMS          = 800;
   lifetimeVarianceMS  = 100;
   useInvAlpha =  false;
   spinRandomMin = -80.0;
   spinRandomMax =  80.0;

   colors[0]    = "0.8 0.8 0.8 0.2";
   colors[1]    = "0.7 0.7 0.7 0.2";
   colors[2]    = "0.9 0.9 0.9 0.2";

   sizes[0]     = 0.5;
   sizes[1]     = 0.2;
   sizes[2]     = 0.1;

   times[0]     = 0.1;
   times[1]     = 0.5;
   times[2]     = 0.3;
};
```

```
datablock ParticleEmitterData(GlassShatterSmokeEmitter)
{
   ejectionPeriodMS = 10;
   periodVarianceMS = 0;
   ejectionVelocity = 8;
   velocityVariance = 2;
   thetaMin        = 0.0;
   thetaMax        = 180.0;
   lifetimeMS      = 250;
   particles = "GlassShatterSmoke";
};

datablock ParticleData(GlassShatterFire)
{
   textureName = "~/data/shapes/windows/glass.jpg";
   dragCoeffiecient    = 100.0;
   gravityCoefficient  = 2.0;
   inheritedVelFactor  = 0.1;
   constantAcceleration = 0.0;
   lifetimeMS          = 1500;
   lifetimeVarianceMS  = 200;
   useInvAlpha =  false;
   spinRandomMin = -80.0;
   spinRandomMax =  80.0;

   colors[0]    = "0.9 0.9 0.9 0.2";
   colors[1]    = "0.8 0.8 0.0 0.2";
   colors[2]    = "0.7 0.3 0.0 0.2";

   sizes[0]     = 0.7;
   sizes[1]     = 0.3;
   sizes[2]     = 0.2;

   times[0]     = 0.0;
   times[1]     = 0.3;
   times[2]     = 0.6;
};
```

```
datablock ParticleEmitterData(GlassShatterFireEmitter)
{
   ejectionPeriodMS = 10;
   periodVarianceMS = 0;
   ejectionVelocity = 0.2;
   velocityVariance = 0.05;
   thetaMin        = 0.0;
   thetaMax        = 180.0;
   lifetimeMS      = 250;
   particles = "GlassShatterFire";
};

datablock ParticleData(GlassShatterSparks)
{
   textureName = "~/data/shapes/windows/glass.jpg";
   dragCoefficient      = 1;
   gravityCoefficient   = 0.0;
   inheritedVelFactor   = 0.2;
   constantAcceleration = 0.0;
   lifetimeMS           = 1500;
   lifetimeVarianceMS   = 350;

   colors[0]     = "0.60 0.40 0.30 0.2";
   colors[1]     = "0.60 0.40 0.30 0.2";
   colors[2]     = "1.0 0.40 0.30 0.2";

   sizes[0]      = 0.25;
   sizes[1]      = 0.15;
   sizes[2]      = 0.15;

   times[0]      = 0.3;
   times[1]      = 0.4;
   times[2]      = 0.5;
};
```

```
datablock ParticleEmitterData(GlassShatterSparkEmitter)
{
   ejectionPeriodMS = 3;
   periodVarianceMS = 0;
   ejectionVelocity = 2;
   velocityVariance = 1;
   ejectionOffset   = 0.0;
   thetaMin         = 0;
   thetaMax         = 180;
   phiReferenceVel  = 0;
   phiVariance      = 360;
   overrideAdvances = false;
   orientParticles  = true;
   lifetimeMS       = 800;
   particles = "GlassShatterSparks";
};

datablock ExplosionData(GlassSubExplosion1)
{
   offset = 0;
   emitter[0] = GlassShatterSmokeEmitter;
   emitter[1] = GlassShatterSparkEmitter;
};

datablock ExplosionData(GlassSubExplosion2)
{
   offset = 1.0;
   emitter[0] = GlassShatterSmokeEmitter;
   emitter[1] = GlassShatterSparkEmitter;
};

datablock ParticleData(GlassDebrisSpark)
{
   textureName = "~/data/shapes/windows/glass.jpg";
   dragCoefficient     = 0;
   gravityCoefficient  = 0.0;
   windCoefficient     = 0;
   inheritedVelFactor  = 0.5;
```

```
    constantAcceleration = 0.0;
    lifetimeMS           = 500;
    lifetimeVarianceMS   = 50;
    spinRandomMin = -90.0;
    spinRandomMax =  90.0;
    useInvAlpha   = false;

    colors[0]     = "0.8 0.8 0.8 0.2";
    colors[1]     = "0.8 0.8 0.8 0.2";
    colors[2]     = "0.8 0.8 0.8 0.2";

    sizes[0]      = 0.2;
    sizes[1]      = 0.3;
    sizes[2]      = 0.1;

    times[0]      = 0.1;
    times[1]      = 0.3;
    times[2]      = 0.5;
};

datablock ParticleEmitterData(GlassDebrisSparkEmitter)
{
    ejectionPeriodMS = 20;
    periodVarianceMS = 0;
    ejectionVelocity = 0.5;
    velocityVariance = 0.25;
    ejectionOffset   = 0.0;
    thetaMin         = 0;
    thetaMax         = 90;
    phiReferenceVel  = 0;
    phiVariance      = 360;
    overrideAdvances = false;
    orientParticles  = false;
    lifetimeMS       = 300;
    particles = "GlassDebrisSpark";
};
```

```
datablock ExplosionData(GlassDebrisExplosion)
{
   emitter[0] = GlassDebrisSparkEmitter;

   shakeCamera = false;
   impulseRadius = 0;
   lightStartRadius = 0;
   lightEndRadius = 0;
};

datablock ParticleData(GlassDebrisTrail)
{
   textureName         = "~/data/shapes/windows/glass.jpg";
   dragCoefficient     = 1;
   gravityCoefficient  = 2;
   inheritedVelFactor  = 0;
   windCoefficient     = 0;
   constantAcceleration = 0;
   lifetimeMS          = 200;
   lifetimeVarianceMS  = 100;
   spinSpeed     = 0;
   spinRandomMin = -90.0;
   spinRandomMax =  90.0;
   useInvAlpha   = false;

   colors[0]     = "0.8 0.8 0.8 0.2";
   colors[1]     = "0.8 0.8 0.8 0.2";
   colors[2]     = "0.8 0.8 0.8 0.2";

   sizes[0]      = 0.2;
   sizes[1]      = 0.3;
   sizes[2]      = 0.4;

   times[0]      = 0.1;
   times[1]      = 0.2;
   times[2]      = 0.3;
};
```

```
datablock ParticleEmitterData(GlassDebrisTrailEmitter)
{
   ejectionPeriodMS = 30;
   periodVarianceMS = 0;
   ejectionVelocity = 0.0;
   velocityVariance = 0.0;
   ejectionOffset   = 0.0;
   thetaMin         = 170;
   thetaMax         = 180;
   phiReferenceVel  = 0;
   phiVariance      = 360;
   lifetimeMS       = 1000;
   particles = "GlassDebrisTrail";
};

datablock DebrisData(GlassShatterDebris)
{
   shapeFile = "~/data/shapes/windows/glassdebris.dts";
   elasticity = 0.2;
   friction = 0.5;
   numBounces = 2;
   bounceVariance = 1;
   explodeOnMaxBounce = false;
   staticOnMaxBounce = false;
   snapOnMaxBounce = false;
   minSpinSpeed = 0;
   maxSpinSpeed = 700;
   render2D = false;
   lifetime = 1;
   lifetimeVariance = 0.5;
   velocity = 20;
   velocityVariance = 10;
   fade = true;
   useRadiusMass = true;
   baseRadius = 0.25;
   gravModifier = 2.0;
   terminalVelocity = 100;
   ignoreWater = true;
};
```

```
datablock ExplosionData(GlassShatter)
{
   soundProfile = GlassShatterSound;
   lifeTimeMS = 1000;
   shakeCamera = true;
   camShakeFreq = "10.0 11.0 10.0";
   camShakeAmp = "1.0 1.0 1.0";
   camShakeDuration = 0.5;
   camShakeRadius = 10.0;
   debris = GlassShatterDebris;
   debrisThetaMin = 90;
   debrisThetaMax = 270;
   debrisPhiMin = 0;
   debrisPhiMax = 360;
   debrisNum = 60;
   debrisNumVariance = 20;
   debrisVelocity = 1;
   debrisVelocityVariance =0.5;
   impulseRadius = 30;
   impulseForce = 10;
   lightStartRadius = 9;
   lightEndRadius = 4;
   lightStartColor = "0.5 0.5 0";
   lightEndColor = "0 0 0";
};

datablock StaticShapeData(WindowA)
{
   category    = "windows";
   shapeFile   = "~/data/shapes/windows/window.dts";
   damageRadius    = 10;
   radiusDamage   = 50;
   damageType   = WindowAdebris;
   maxDamage     = 5;
};
```

```
datablock StaticShapeData(Shards0)
{
   category    = "windows";
   shapeFile   = "~/data/shapes/windows/shards0.dts";
};

datablock StaticShapeData(Shards1)
{
   category    = "windows";
   shapeFile   = "~/data/shapes/windows/shards1.dts";
};

datablock StaticShapeData(Shards2)
{
   category    = "windows";
   shapeFile   = "~/data/shapes/windows/shards2.dts";
};

datablock StaticShapeData(Shards3)
{
   category    = "windows";
   shapeFile   = "~/data/shapes/windows/shards3.dts";
};

datablock StaticShapeData(Shards4)
{
   category    = "windows";
   shapeFile   = "~/data/shapes/windows/shards4.dts";
};

function WindowA::Damage(%theDatablock,%aWindow,%sourceObject,%pos,%dmg,%type)
{
     %aWindow.applyDamage(%dmg);
     if(%aWindow.getDamageLevel() >= %theDatablock.maxDamage)
     %theDatablock.Explode( %aWindow, %pos, %sourceObject);
}
```

```
function WindowA::Explode(%theDatablock, %aWindow, %position, %sourceObject)
{
      if(%aWindow.exploded)
            return;
      %aWindow.exploded = true;
      %boom = new Explosion()
      {
            datablock = GlassShatter;
            position  = %position;
      };
      MissionCleanup.add(%boom);
      radiusDamage(          %aWindow,%position,%theDatablock.damageRadius,
                            %theDatablock.radiusDamage,%sourceObject.damageType,
                            %theDatablock.damageImpulse);

  %r = GetRandom(4);
  %db = "Shards" @ %r;

      %wreckage = new StaticShape()
      {
            datablock = %db;
      };
      %wreckage.setTransform(%aWindow.getTransform());
      %wreckage.setScale(%aWindow.getScale());
      %aWindow.schedule(200, "delete");
      MissionCleanup.add(%wreckage);
}
```

The multiple debris datablocks are there so that we can toss the digital dice and put up a different appearance of broken window shards each time we bust a window. Obviously, the more you make, the more variety you will get. Most of the rest of the window code is very similar to the barrel explosion code. Indeed, we treat the breaking window *as* an explosion, albeit a smokeless and flameless one.

Also, unlike the barrel blow-up code, this time we leave behind the broken windows as glass wreckage. That calls for a second bout of dynamic shape creation—the wreckage is created almost immediately, while the original window is still there. The original window is scheduled for deletion in about 1/5 of a second (200 milliseconds).

Testing the Windows

Right then, let's see if this works.

Launch the fps demo, spawn in, and switch to camera fly mode to position yourself above the ground aiming at where you would like to place a window. Open the Mission Editor and in the World Editor Creator's selection list at lower right, choose Shapes, windows, and then click on WindowA to insert a window pane at your aim point.

Now, you will recall the earlier figures, like Figure 10.8, where I had placed the windows in the Great Hall building. You can do that too, but I suggest you just place your pane in the world at an easy to get at spot, and then save your mission. Then worry about making sure you've got your code working correctly. After everything proves to be copasetic, go ahead and start sticking window panes in buildings.

Anyway, once your window is in, get back inside your avatar's skin and let loose with the crossbow on the window. Enjoy the sound of guilt-free breaking glass! The models of the glass shards in the wreckage have a small collision box defined down at the bottom area of the shards. You might consider using some of your newfound damage management skills from earlier in the chapter to cause the player to receive some small amount of injury if he brushes against that glass.

Moving Right Along

Well, that was pretty exciting. Blowing stuff up. Breaking things. Pulling the wings off flies. Oh, okay, no one did that. Good thing, too. That would have been cruel.

But it *wasn't* cruel to pummel the player avatar with weapons until he died.

We saw how a hitpoint system can grow to be a fairly sophisticated health/energy status system.

Then we looked at linking the damage and energy systems, and saw how easy it is to create a damage system with a much higher fidelity using Torque's built-in hit location system. This approach allowed us to track damage to different parts of an object, not just the thing as a whole.

Then we blew up that barrel, over and over. We saw that particle definitions can get to be pretty unwieldy, but they bring a lot of power to bear in the realm of special effects.

Then we went around breaking windows, and learned that smashing glass can be treated just like an explosion. We just needed to modify a few particles and debris models.

Now someone just has to pay for all that damage…

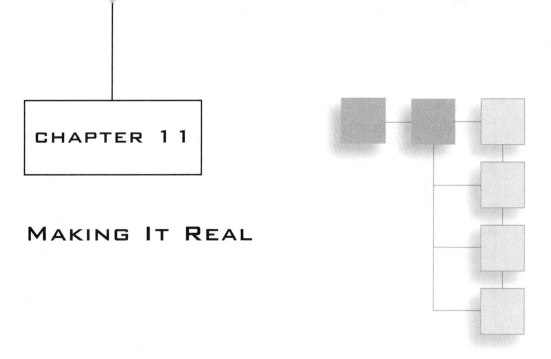

CHAPTER 11

MAKING IT REAL

Many game developers are creating games in which some level of direct correlation with the real world is required. The degree of realism necessary depends on the genre, style, and gameplay of the design, as well as the designer's vision.

There are several areas in which you can provide a great deal of realism for a small amount (relatively speaking) of effort. These include terrain, vegetation, and those seemingly insignificant and unnoticed things like litter on city streets, or collections of rocks and boulders on a streambed.

If your game involves historical events in actual locations in the world, you probably want to create terrain that reflects the area in question. Some people have enjoyed a certain measure of success by hand-building and modeling terrain based upon photographs and site visits that involved direct measurement or "eyeball" approximations of major terrain features. A more accurate and less time-consuming approach is to obtain digital terrain information and use that to create your terrain instead. In this chapter, you will learn how to do this.

When it comes to vegetation, the big problem is quantity. Unless you are in the desert, or in some other sparsely vegetated area, hundreds or thousands of trees and bushes probably surround you. Stop and look around you, and try to count how many individual trees and bushes you see, and how many varieties there are. If you happen to be in or near a forest, you'll no doubt discover pretty quickly that it's almost impossible to count them all. Oh yeah, did I mention grass? Heh. Look around—nah, don't bother. You know there are likely millions of blades of grass within your sight range.

Fortunately, there are ways to deal with all of these things without resorting to unsatisfying approaches like using terrain textures with grass textures.

Also, with methods similar to those used to include in-game vegetation, litter—the detritus of human society, or rubble—and the leavings of natural erosion and weathering processes can be introduced into a game world.

Real-World Terrain

Real-world digital terrain information is gathered by many countries and made available for free or for a modest fee. There are many different formats for the data, and the formats change to keep pace with new acquisition, storage, and display technology.

We will use the Digital Elevation Model (DEM) standard, used by the US Geological Survey (USGS), to map almost the entire world. A DEM file contains elevation data in a raster (line-by-line) form on a regularly spaced grid.

DEM Formats

DEM formatted data files contain values that represent a grid of elevation points in a quadrilateral area. The simplest and least accurate format, 1-degree DEM, contains data points comprising a rectangular grid with its sides quasi-parallel with the latitude and longitude in the local context. Longitudinal lines are never parallel since they converge at the Earth's poles, but at small scales they appear to be parallel.

The most useful and widely available standard format is 7.5-minute DEM, which presents data with a much higher resolution. Each grid is 7.5 *arc-minutes* in size, and each point in the grid is 1/3 of an arc-second, or 10 meters apart. This format is also used for 7.5-minute grids with 1 arc-second resolution—a lower resolution with fewer data points, each being 30 meters apart. Even this lower resolution data can be very useful.

An arc-minute is one-sixtieth of a degree and measures one mile in longitude. An arc-minute also measures one mile in latitude at the equator but gets progressively shorter as you move northward or southward, until you can actually cover one arc-minute with a single baby step if you are walking around at either the North or South Pole! Therefore, the 7.5-minute is about 7.5 miles on each side, which is 12 kilometers (1 mile equals about 1.6 kilometers).

One of the tricky things about 7.5-minute DEM data is that the files are created according to boundaries that follow the north-south, east-west orientation of latitude and longitude, but the actual data is usually not collected along the lengths of those boundaries. Therefore, you can have ragged edges to the data. As a consequence, datasets of adjoining areas have some substantial overlap from one to the other to ensure that all areas are covered.

In addition, the USGS has created 30-minute and 15-minute DEM datasets. Other formats are available from other nations' government agencies. For example, Canada creates its data in a CDED format derived from DEM.

Where to Get DEM Data

The biggest producer by far of DEM data is the USGS. On this book's companion CD, in the folder \A3D\RESOURCES\ch11, you will find the USGS DEM specification in the file DEM_FILE_FORMAT_2DEM0198.pdf. The Canadian CDED specification is in the same folder, called GeoBase_product_specs_CDED1_Ed2.pdf. The specifications, as well as data created by agencies of both governments, are released to the public under unrestricted use licenses.

The USGS Geographic Data Download has also been the traditional source for United States DEM data. In the past few years, this has changed and not all data, or all datasets of all types, have been made available by the USGS. Many commercial sites offer the data for download for a one-time or subscription fee, but there are several that offer the data for free, no doubt believing that publicly owned data should be freely available. Probably the most important data are the 1:24,000 SDTS 30m and 10m Digital Elevation Models (7.5-minute). These are available from two commercial sites: www.gisdatadepot.com and www.atdi-us.com. They also offer other kinds of free data in addition to their own value-added efforts.

The USGS still offers what amounts to the same data but in a different format, called the USGS Seamless Data Distribution (NED).

Canadian data can be obtained from a consortium agency, called Geobase, that brings together government agency efforts from the municipal level all the way up to the federal level. Their website is geobase.ca.

DEM to Heightmap

Included in the \A3D\Tools folder is a program called Wilbur, created by an enterprising gentleman name Joe Slayton. Joe maintains a website at www.ridgenet.net/~jslayton/.

We're going to use Wilbur to convert some DEM data into a heightmap that we can later use to create some terrain.

1. Launch Wilbur. Once it is running, select File, Open. In the Open dialog in the Type field, select the USGS DEM Surface (*.dem) type. Then browse to and open \A3D\RESOURCES\ch11\ch11.DEM. When the file loads, an image that looks like Figure11.1 will appear. Note the ragged edges, just like I mentioned earlier. Wilbur doesn't really like to have its data in this form—it can't figure out how to present it—but that's okay, because we're going to tidy it up just a wee bit.

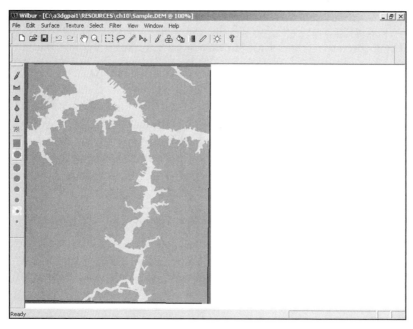

Figure 11.1 DEM data loaded in Wilbur.

2. Use the selection tool

to select a "clean" rectangular region, as shown in Figure 11.2, which excludes the ragged edges. In the screenshot, the selected region is within the dashed rectangle.

3. Next, select Surface, Crop to Selection. This will chop out the extraneous bits of the image outside the selection rectangle. The image will change and look like the one in Figure 11.3. Note the drastic change in appearance. Now Wilbur knows which way is up and can use the information to present the data in a visually interesting and informative way, with pseudo-lighting providing highlights and shading for the various elevations.

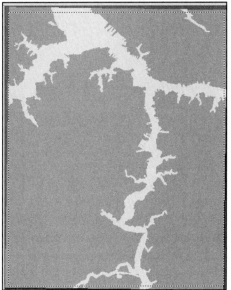

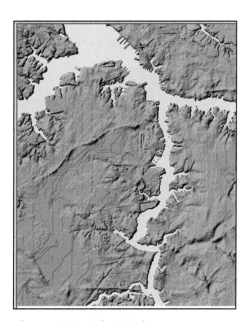

Figure 11.2 Selecting a clean region.   **Figure 11.3** Tidy DEM data.

4. Now, select Surface, Resample, Simple Resample. The Simple Resample dialog box will appear on your screen in short order, as depicted in Figure 11.4. In the New Image Size panel, enter **256** for both X Size and Y Size. Click OK.

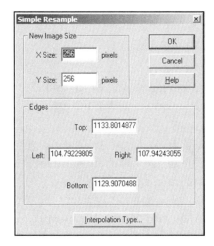

Figure 11.4 Simple Resample dialog box.

The image shown in Figure 11.5 will appear. This is still DEM data, but now the image is square with 256 units on every side.

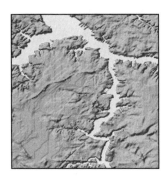

Figure 11.5 Resampled DEM data.

5. Now it's time to make the heightmap. Choose Texture, Gray Maps, Height Map. An image like that shown in Figure 11.6 will appear.

6. Save your heightmap data as mydem.png.

Figure 11.6 The heightmap.

Prep for Torque

Create the folder \A3D\common\editor\heightscripts, if it doesn't already exist. Copy mydem.png to that folder. Or, if you're lazy and can't be stirred to do the work on your own, or maybe you're just too tired after having stayed up all night reading this book, you can also try it out with the book's version, called ch11.png (which should be almost identical to your own mydem.png image).

After that, launch the Torque demo and create an FPS demo server. Go ahead and spawn into the game world.

Heightmap to Game Terrain

Once you've spawned in, move your player to inside one of the buildings or up on the roof and leave him there. Switch to camera fly mode by pressing F8 and whistle on up to a reasonable height above the ground until your player avatar is about the size of an ant.

Before we work with the heightmap, we want to prepare the world a little bit. First, we are going to make a new game mission (world definition):

1. Open the Mission Editor by pressing F11.
2. Select File, New Mission.

   You will exit the default FPS demo mission and be deposited in a new mission, with a generic, algorithmically generated terrain.
3. Choose File, Save Mission As. A Save dialog will appear.
4. Type in **ch11.mis** for your mission file name. Now you have your own mission data to work with. Not only that, but your terrain work automatically will be saved in ch11.ter whenever you save your mission file.

Now onto the heightmaps.

1. Open the Mission Editor, and then open the Terrain Terraform Editor either by choosing Window, Terrain Terraform Editor or by pressing F7. You should get the editor screen that looks like Figure 11.7.
2. On the right hand side of the editor is the Operation list, and it will have one entry, called General. Click once on this entry to select it.
3. Up above the Operation list are some entry fields for General Settings. In the Min. Terrain Height field, type in **5**, and in the Height Range field, type in **150**.

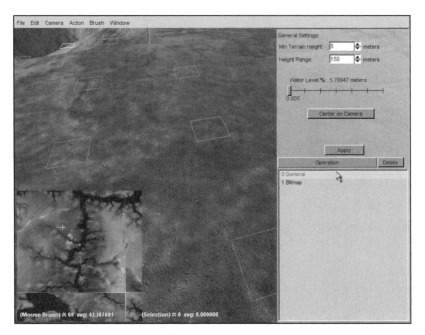

Figure 11.7 The Terrain Terraform Editor.

4. Below the General Settings on the right hand side is the Operation button. Click on it and select bitmap from the pop-up menu that appears. The Load File dialog will appear. In the file list you should see the file mydem.png (or ch11.png, if you used the file from the CD). If there are no files listed, go back to the "Prep for Torque" section of this chapter and double-check your activities.

5. Next, select mydem.png (or ch11.png, depending on what you had previously decided to do. And get your feet off the couch while you're at it, ya lazy bum) from the open dialog. Click Apply.

6. Next, Open the World Editor Creator, and in the pane on the lower right corner click Mission Objects, environment, water. When the Building Objects: WaterBlock dialog appears, just click on OK.

7. Now select File, Save Mission to save your work as ch11.mis. Exit the mission and the game.

For the next part, we could continue to use the Mission Editor, but I want to expose you to the inner workings of a mission file. So instead we will use a text editor and modify the mission file manually.

1. Open the file \A3D\demo\data\ch11.mis (this is the mission file you just created and saved) with your favorite text editor.

2. Scroll down until you find the Sky SimGroup entry. It looks like this:

```
new Sky(Sky) {
    position = "336 136 0";
    rotation = "1 0 0 0";
    scale = "1 1 1";
    materialList = "~/data/skies/sky_storm.dml";
    cloudHeightPer[0] = "7";
    cloudHeightPer[1] = "0.3";
    cloudHeightPer[2] = "0.199973";
    cloudSpeed1 = "0.002";
    cloudSpeed2 = "0.001";
    cloudSpeed3 = "0.003";
    visibleDistance = "500";
    fogDistance = "300";
    fogColor = "0.400000 0.400000 0.400000 1.000000";
    fogStorm1 = "0";
    fogStorm2 = "0";
    fogStorm3 = "0";
    fogVolume1 = "100 0 169.5";
    fogVolume2 = "0 0 0";
    fogVolume3 = "0 0 0";
    fogVolumeColor1 = "0.900000 0.900000 0.900000 1.000000";
    fogVolumeColor2 = "0.900000 0.900000 0.900000 1.000000";
    fogVolumeColor3 = "0.000000 0.000000 0.000000 1.000000";
    windVelocity = "1 1 0";
    windEffectPrecipitation = "0";
    SkySolidColor = "0.640000 0.148000 0.215000 0.000000";
    useSkyTextures = "1";
    renderBottomTexture = "0";
    noRenderBans = "0";
    locked = "true";
};
```

Some of the property values above may be different from the ones in your mission file. That's okay—we're going to change some of them, and the other ones don't really matter right now.

First, we want to increase the visibility to make it easier to see the terrain. Set the following properties in the Sky datablock to the values shown here:

```
visibleDistance = "2500";
fogDistance = "2300";
```

This means that the visual distance cutoff doesn't happen until 2500 meters away (2.5 kilometers), and the distance fog doesn't start until 2300 meters. This opens a large viewing vista. Next, change the following as shown:

```
fogColor = "0.400000 0.430000 0.450000 1.000000";
fogVolume1 = "50 0 10";
fogVolume2 = "0 0 0";
```

This removes one layer of fog that might be lurking around above ground messing up our view and adjusts the fog that's used to restrict the underwater visibility to match our new terrain. It also tweaks the fog's color slightly for use underwater.

Now scroll down until you locate the Waterblock. It looks like this:

```
new WaterBlock() {
    position = "-32 -752 164.3";
    rotation = "1 0 0 0";
    scale = "32 32 1";
    UseDepthMask = "1";
    surfaceTexture = "fps/data/water/water";
    liquidType = "OceanWater";
    density = "1";
    viscosity = "15";
    waveMagnitude = "1";
    surfaceOpacity = "0.6";
    envMapIntensity = "0.1";
    TessSurface = "15";
    TessShore = "25";
    SurfaceParallax = "0.5";
    FlowAngle = "45";
    FlowRate = "0.25";
    DistortGridScale = "0.1";
    DistortMag = "0.05";
    DistortTime = "0.5";
    ShoreDepth = "4";
```

```
        DepthGradient = "1";
        MinAlpha = "0.03";
        MaxAlpha = "1";
        removeWetEdges = "0";
        specularColor = "1.000000 0.800000 0.200000 1.000000";
        specularPower = "30";
        params0 = "0.32 -0.67 0.066 0.5";
        extent = "2000 2000 1";
        textureSize = "32 32";
        params1 = "0.63 -2.41 0.33 0.21";
        params3 = "1.21 -0.61 0.13 -0.33";
        params2 = "0.39 0.39 0.2 0.133";
        seedPoints = "1 1 1 1 1 1 1 1";
    };
```

Make sure that the Waterblock has these properties with these values:

```
    position = "0 0 10";
    scale = "2048 2048 1";
    surfaceTexture = "demo/data/water/water";
    ShoreTexture = "demo/data/water/wateredge";
    envMapOverTexture = "demo/data/skies/storm_0007";
    specularMaskTex = "demo/data/water/specmask";
    waveMagnitude = "0.5";
```

Make sure that you only edit the values and get them exactly as shown. It is possible to put the a value in the wrong place and create an error that will cause Torque to crash. If you accidentally delete a brace, semicolon, or something like that, you may end up with a situation where Torque runs, but then never actually finishes loading the mission. If you don't get the results you expect, don't forget to use the console to check for errors, or to examine console.log for clues about errors you might have made in the event that Torque crashes.

You might notice that the default Waterblock doesn't have some of the properties listed. That's okay, as long as you add them in (makes for much prettier water).

Fine, that should do it. Save the file, and then launch the Torque Demo again. Once you've spawned into the default FPS mission, open your custom mission by selecting File, Open Mission. Wander around and see what you have wrought. Look out Slartibartfast!

You should now have a world that looks like Figure 11.8.

Figure 11.8 The hills are alive, with the sound of… something.

Now you will note that the textures are wrong. Terrain-cover textures as a topic was covered in my first book, so I won't go into it here. In brief, you can use the Terrain Texture Painter (F8) to apply textures in quite a pleasant and straightforward way by painting them on! You have a variety of brush sizes and two brush shapes. You can add your own textures by creating them as square 128×128 or 256×256 PNG files and depositing them in the \A3D\demo\data\missions folder. Then you can add them to the Materials palette that appears on the right in the Terrain Texture Painter.

You will also notice some pesky details, like the fact that your spawn locations are pretty high up in the air. Use the Mission Editor and camera fly mode to locate the spawn sphere (it will be listed in the World Editor Inspector Pane under the PlayerDropPoints grouping). Simply select a spawn sphere in the Inspector Pane, then look around. You will see the selected sphere highlighted with its three axes marked in blue. Just go over to it and drag it down to about a meter above the terrain (or wherever you want to put it).

Also, the sample data used has some spikes in it caused by data acquisition errors. You should use the Terrain Editor (not the Terrain Terraform Editor) to lower these spikes to reasonable levels. The Terrain Editor has a brush similar to the Terrain

Texture Painter. Place the brush over a spike, select Action, Adjust Height, and then click and drag the mouse up or down to adjust the size of the terrain spike. If the default brush setting is too big, select a smaller size under the Brush menu. You can also select Action, Smooth as the brush mode to tidy up the area surrounding any ex-spikes.

Vegetation

Placing tree models in a game world one by one is an onerous task, especially if your intent is to create a forest. Trust me on this one, okay? Been there, done that, got the splinters.

Fortunately, Torque has some built-in capability to handle this, and it is available to use via both script and the Mission Editor. The tool is called fxShapeReplicator, which can be used for any kind of shape that needs to be placed in large numbers in a mission or game world.

The Forest

The way fxShapeReplicator works is pretty clever, and the cleverness arises from the need to maintain Torque's award-winning networking ways.

You see, if we simply place, let us say, a thousand tree shapes in a mission, then the server has to tell each client to load all those shapes and it then has to track the game state of those shapes on a continuous basis. This is very stressful for servers and gobbles up a great deal of bandwidth that could be used for other useful things, like more players in the game.

Enter fxShapeReplicator. What it does is define a *collection* of shapes. The server then sends the data for *one* object, the collection, to each client, and performs updates with only that one object. This frees up the bandwidth for 999 other objects. Now that number of one thousand is purely arbitrary. You can have any number of shapes in one collection—the only practical limit is the ability of the least capable client to render all those shapes. And, although that's something to keep in mind, it's less of a concern than it was before when there were one thousand (or however many) individual shapes being tracked by both the server and client. In addition, fxShapeReplicator has some nifty built-in *culling* features that make smart decisions about when it's useful to render shapes in a collection based upon some properties you can set.

But wait! There's more!

The shapes within a collection can have variety as well, like different sizes, different height to width ratios, and so on.

The perpetrator of this cool toy is a gentleman by the name of Melv May, and if you bump into him at an Independent Game Developer's conference somewhere, buy him a beer or something. He's earned it. After he made the tool available to the GarageGames community, GarageGames decided to adopt the tools and build it into the core Torque Engine along with a few other Melv May inventions, like `fxFoliageReplicator`, and the `Waterblock` that it now uses, and `fxSunlight`, and... oh, nevermind—I think you get the picture, and besides, Melv's head might start swelling.

Without any further ado, let's try it out. First, you are going to need a tree. Fortunately, I have a couple you can use.

1. Launch the Torque demo and spawn into the FPS mission. If you prefer, you can load your own ch11.mis file from here—that's what I've done, although it isn't entirely necessary.

2. Enter camera fly mode (F8) and face your camera toward an open area, then open the Mission Editor.

3. Enter World Editor Creator mode by pressing F4.

4. In the lower right panels, drill down to Mission Objects, environment, and then click on `fxShapeReplicator`. A `Building Object: fxShapeReplicator` dialog will appear.

5. For an object name, enter **foresta**, then press OK. An "empy" object will be placed at the spot where you are facing, surrounded by a weird rotating vortex-like blue stripe, as shown in Figure 11.9.

6. Press F3 to switch to the Inspector, and select the `fsShapeReplicator` entry at the end of the tree list.

7. In the Inspector's Edit Pane, at lower right, click on the Expand All button and then scroll down until you find the field called ShapeFile in the Media grouping.

8. In the Edit field for ShapeFile, enter **demo/data/shapes/trees/tree3.dts** (make sure you get the slashes right), and then click the Apply button. You should see a bunch of trees appear.

Fly up so that you can get a good look at the sparse forest you've made. To get a denser forest, try to change the `Shape Count` property in the Replications grouping to a larger value, like 100, or maybe even 300. Experiment, and see what works for you. When

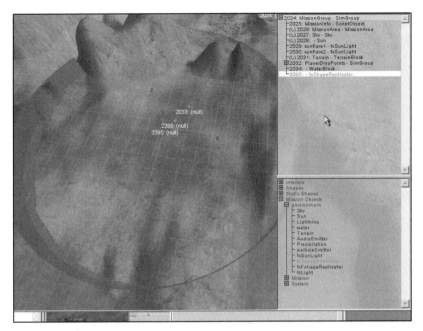

Figure 11.9 The replicator vortex.

you're finished with that, you can experiment with the other properties such as InnerRadiusX, InnerRadiusY, OuterRadiusX, and OuterRadiusY, which define the size of the area in which the replicants will appear. (Cool. I just used the word "replicants," and not in a science-fiction novel, either!)

The tree you used comes with the demo, conveniently. There are two other trees in the same folder, tree.dts and tree2.dts. Add them to the forest for a bit of variety, if you like.

The Meadow

So what about grass or wheat fields? Do we make them the same way? Well, yes and no. We use a similar technique, but with a different Melv May invention called fxFoliageReplicator.

The entire process is roughly the same as with building the forest, except instead of using a model, we use a simple texture! Most of the properties of fxFoliageReplicator are the same as fsShapeReplicator's, except that there are few specialized properties that we need.

You are also going to need an image file with the grass texture, so you can use demo/data/shapes/plants/plant1.jpg or demo/data/shapes/plants/plant2.jpg. Follow the instructions for the forest, but choose the fxFoliageReplicator instead. And then add the file name demo/data/shapes/plants/plant1 in the FoliageFile field in the Media grouping. *Do not* include the .jpg extension in the FoliageFile field. This is because the plant textures have been created with a dual jpg file technique. One jpg contains the plant texture with transparent areas rendered in black, and another file with the same name, but the extension .alpha.jpg has been created to contain the alpha mask. We can also (if we choose) create PNG files with the alpha channel built into the one file. The choice is yours, but do remember this naming rule if you use JPG images for foliage.

Finally, for the shape count, use a really big number, like maybe 1000 or more.

Figure 11.10 shows my results with two fxShapeReplicators and two fxFoliageReplicators, each using a different tree or plant.

Figure 11.10 A pleasant forest meadow.

How the Replicators Work

So how do `fxShapeReplicator` and `fxFoliageReplicator` manage to stuff so many things on the screen? Melv May (who is now a GarageGames associate) tells us himself:

"Calculate the potential foliage nodes required to achieve the selected culling resolution.

Populate quad-tree structure to depth determined by culling resolution.

A little explanation is called for here…

The approach to this problem has been chosen to make it much easier for the user to control the quad-tree culling resolution. The user enters a single world-space value `mCullResolution`, which controls the highest resolution at which the replicator will check visibility culling.

Example: If `mCullResolution` is 32 and the size of the replicated area is 128 radius (256 diameter) then this results in the replicator creating a quad-tree where there are 256/32 = 8×8 blocks. Each of these can be checked to see if they are within the viewing area, and if not, they get culled—this removes the need to parse all the billboards that occupy that region. Most of the time the culling algorithm will check the culling pyramid from the top to bottom. For example, the following blocks will be checked:

1 x 256 x 256 (All of replicated area)

4 x 128 x 128 (4 corners of above)

16 x 64 x 64 (16 x 4 corners of above)

etc.

1. First up, the replicator needs to create a fixed list of quad-tree nodes with which to work.

   To calculate this we take the largest outer-radius value set in the replicator and calculate how many quad-tree levels are required to achieve the selected `mCullResolution`. One of the initial problems is that the replicator has separate radii values for x and y. This can lead to a culling resolution smaller in one axis than in the other if there is a difference between the outer-radii. Unfortunately, we just live with this because there is not much we can do here if we still want to allow the user to have this kind of elliptical placement control.

   To calculate the number of nodes needed we use the following equation:-

   Note: We are changing the Logarithmic bases from 10 -> 2 … grrrr!

   Cr = mCullResolution

   Rs = Maximum Radii Diameter

$$\sum_{n=0}^{\mathrm{int}\left(\dfrac{\mathrm{Log10}(R_s/C_r)}{\mathrm{Log10}(2)} - 0.5\right)} 4^n$$

So basically we calculate the number of blocks in 1D at the highest resolution, then calculate the inverse exponential (base 2 - 1D) to achieve that quantity of blocks. We round that up to the next highest integer = e. We then sum 4 to the power 0>e, which gives us the correct number of nodes required. The value of e is also stored as the starting level value for populating the quad-tree (see step 3).

2. We then proceed to calculate the billboard positions as normal and calculate and assign each billboard a basic volume (rather than treat each as a point). We need to take into account possible front/back swaying as well as the basic plane dimensions here. When all the billboards have been chosen we then proceed to populate the quad-tree.

3. To populate the quad-tree we start with a box, which completely encapsulates the volume occupied by all the billboards, and enter into a recursive procedure to process that node. Processing this node involves splitting it into quadrants in x/y so it's untouched (for now). We then find candidate billboards with each of these quadrants searched using the current subset of shapes from the parent (this reduces the searching to a minimum and is very efficient).

   If a quadrant does not enclose any billboards, then the node is dropped; otherwise, it is processed again using the same procedure.

   This happens until we have recursed through the maximum number of levels as calculated using the summation max (see equation (1) above). When level 0 is reached, the current list of enclosed objects is stored within the node (for the rendering algorithm).

4. The next stage is when rendering takes place. An algorithm steps through the quad-tree from the top and does visibility culling on each box (with respect to the viewing area) and culls as appropriate. If the box is visible then the next level is checked until we reach level 0 where the node contains a complete subset of billboards enclosed by the visible box.

Using the above algorithm we can now generate *massive* quantities of billboards and (using the appropriate `mCullResolution`) only visible blocks of billboards will be processed."

—Melv

Don't Forget the Fiddly Bits

As you've no doubt figured out on your own, those two simple tools, `fxShapeReplicator` and `fxFoliageReplicator` can be used in many ways. You could use the shape replication to create a field of boulders strewn across the scene of a landslide or a beach full of washed up flotsam and jetsam after a big storm.

And, who says that the `fxFoliageReplicator` can only be used to replicate foliage? Why not replicate bits of paper, tin cans, bubble gum wrappers, and so on?

It's all these seemingly minor details that go together to make an unforgettable scene in a game.

Moving Right Along

In this chapter, you learned how to add some touches of realism to a game by importing real-world terrain data to create our terrain. You also saw how to add and adjust a waterblock and adjust the `Sky` object to suit our needs.

You also learned how to add special collections of objects and images to create large collective objects, like forests and meadows, made of many smaller objects.

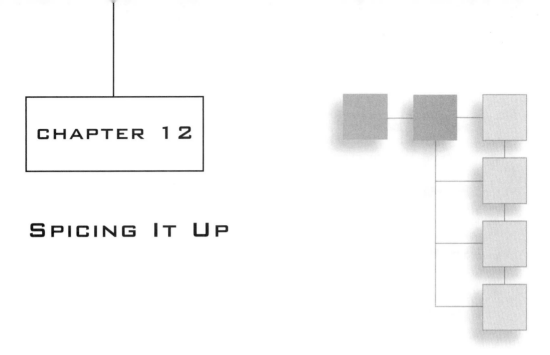

CHAPTER 12

SPICING IT UP

T here are things we can do to fancy up our surroundings, and add a little zest to the game play. Adding interesting water to our game world is an obvious way to spruce things up. We can also do things to tweak the lighting in ways that improve the appeal of our levels.

Sunshine on My Soldiers

Some of the most beautiful vistas in our lives are those we experience at either sunrise or sunset. Undoubtedly the main reason for the stunning beauty that we can sometimes encounter at those times of the day is the rich color effects. Light from the low-lying sun slices through the atmosphere at a very shallow angle. This means that the rays of light have much more air to travel through, causing changes in the color and its saturation.

Sunlight seen outside of the atmosphere is a combination of all of the wavelengths of light, so the sun looks like a white disc surrounded by the black of space. Because there are air molecules in the atmosphere, the atmosphere changes the sun light as it passes through.

The largest atmospheric effect on sun light that we experience every day is *scattering*, where light rays are deflected from their normal straight paths. Due to the relationship between the various wavelengths of light and molecular structure of the gases in the atmosphere, blue light is scattered best (therefore the most, with the greatest dispersion effect) by air molecules. This happens throughout the atmosphere—we perceive the sky to be blue because the downward scattered light rays are the blue wavelengths that have been bouncing around in the air. However, the direct sunlight has lost most of the blue wavelengths, so we no longer perceive it to be white, as it appears from space. With most of the blue light bouncing around elsewhere, most of the light our eyes see is yellowish.

When the sun gets lower in the sky, the direct beam of sunlight has to traverse a longer path through the atmosphere and there is more opportunity for scattering. More and more wavelengths other than blue begin to be affected, so that often near dawn or dusk, when the path is very long, all wavelengths except red have been removed, and a red sunset occurs. This effect also happens in the morning, although it tends not to be witnessed as often.

Another reason for red sun light around sunrise or sunset is the presence of dust in the air between our eyes and the sun. In fact, red is not the only effect—quite often there can be brownish or golden hues, caused by various kinds of dust and pollutants.

Other effects we can encounter when viewing the sun are what some people call sunflares (not solar flares) and halos. The sunflare is more like optical glare, those rays of light that seem to project away from the sun. We see the same sort of thing with car headlights at night.

A halo is just what it sounds like. A circle (or part of a circle) that surrounds the image of the sun (this also sometimes happens when we look at the moon, and even streetlights on occasion). The sun's halo is caused by ice crystals in the air deflecting some of the light rays toward our eye—light rays that otherwise would not come anywhere near us. Due to the geometry of ice crystals, there are two kinds of halos: 22-degree halos and 46-degree halos. The most common are the 22-degree variety, which are stronger (brighter, clearer, more intense) than the 46-degree flavor. The 22-degree halos also appear to be only half as far from the sun as the 46-degree halos.

It just so happens that Torque has a spiffy tool for creating these and other kinds of sun (and moon) oriented effects, called fxSunLight.

The fxSunLight object actually suffers somewhat from an embarrassment of riches. Table 12.1 shows the many, many properties that are available to be poked, prodded, tweaked, and twiddled.

Table 12.1 fxSunLight Properties

Property	Description
Enable	Turns on/off the sunlight.
LocalFlareBitmap	Sets the flare bitmap for use by the local flare effect—the effect of the camera lens. This flare uses a line-of-sight test to check whether it should be visible.
RemoteFlareBitmap	Sets the flare bitmap for use by the remote flare effect—the sun itself. This flare appears behind all scene geometry and does not use a line-of-sight test to check whether it should be visible. Leave this property blank if you don't want a remote flare.
SunAzimuth	Controls the direction of the sunlight. Azimuth is expressed in polar angles of from 0 to 359 degrees.
SunElevation	Controls the elevation of the sunlight. A value of 90 degrees is directly overhead and 0 is on the horizon.
FlareTP	Enables/disables the flare effect in a third-person view.
Colour	Colorises the flare if needed. White ("1.0 1.0 1.0 1.0") leaves the flare texture untouched. The color channels are in the form of "R G B A" where A is the alpha setting (transparency).
Brightness	Sets the flare brightness.
FlareSize	Sets the flare size. 1 is the unscaled bitmap size.
FadeTime	Fade in or out time, in seconds. When a flare appears or disappears in real life it tends to fade-in or out over time rather than instantaneously. The effect simulated here is called *blooming*. A setting of around 0.25 seconds is fairly representative.
BlendMode	Three different blending equations are used which give different results dependant upon the type of image used for the flare. A setting of between 0 and 2 (inclusive) will use one of the following OpenGL blending operations: 0 = GL_SRC_ALPHA, GL_ONE 1 = GL_SRC_ALPHA, GL_ONE_MINUS_SRC_ALPHA 2 = GL_ONE, GL_ONE
AnimColour	A flag that controls the on/off state of the color animation.
AnimBrightness	A flag that controls the on/off state of the brightness animation.
AnimRotation	A flag that controls the on/off state of the rotation animation.
AnimSize	A flag that controls the on/off state of the size animation.
AnimAzimuth	A flag that controls the on/off state of the azimuth animation.
AnimElevation	A flag that controls the on/off state of the elevation animation.

Table 12.1 fxSunLight Properties (continued)

Property	Description
LerpColour / LerpBrightness / LerpRotation / LerpSize / LerpAzimuth / LerpElevation	Linear Interpolation (LERP). fxSunLight incorporates a realtime clock to monitor its progress through animation strings. Torque will often find itself between animation key frames, and uses LERP to perform the in-between image rendering. With LERPing turned on, you get the linearly interpolated values between key frames. With it turned off you get sharp transitions. If you turn LERP off, you can create a flashing light. You could even generate a sun-like object that slowly brightens and dims over time.
LinkFlareSize	A flag that controls whether the flare size is directly proportional to its luminance. The brighter the color, the larger the flare. The flare is scaled according to its current animation (e.g. it never gets any bigger than it would with this setting off).
SingleColourKeys	When this is enabled, R,G, & B channels are controlled as a group by the R channel animation keys—RedKeys (see below).
MinColour / MaxColour	When AnimColour is on, these fields control the start/end colors used in the color animation. Note that you can animate individual rgb channels if you want.
MinBrightness / MaxBrightness	When AnimBrightness is on, these fields control the from/to brightness values used in the animation.
MinRotation / MaxRotation	When AnimRotation is on, these fields control the from/to rotation for the flare billboard.
MinSize / MaxSize	When AnimSize is on, these fields control the from/to size for the flare billboard.
MinAzimuth / MaxAzimuth	When AnimAzimuth is on, these fields control the from/to azimuth for the flare billboard.
MinElevation / MaxElevation	When AnimElevation is on, these fields control the from/to elevation for the flare billboard.
RedKeys / GreenKeys / BlueKeys	These are the key frame animation strings used to animate the color. Enter a letter character between A > Z. A corresponds to the MinColour.X value of the appropriate color channel and Z is the MaxColour.X value.
BrightnessKeys	As Colors keys but affects brightness values.
SizeKeys	As Colors keys but affects size values.
AzimuthKeys	As Colors keys but affects azimuth values.
ElevationKeys	As Colors keys but affects elevation values.
ColourTime / BrightnessTime / RotationTime / SizeTime / AzimuthTime / ElevationTime	This is the time (in seconds) to cycle through the associated animation (Colour, Brightness, Rotation, Size, Azimuth, and Elevation). Note that when the animation is complete the system starts again from the beginning of the animation string. If you want "bounce" animation (e.g from [MIN]>[MAX]-[MIN]), then you would use something like "AZA."

Note

You'll note that among the `fxSunLight` object properties, there are several properties that have the word "colour" in them, instead of "color" (the standard in this book). That's the UK English spelling and is the correct way for `fxSunLight`. Don't get caught out by that.

Let's shed some light on the situation by working with `fxSunLight` and seeing what we need to do to create some nice effects.

Sunrise, Sunset

If you are familiar with astronomy and concepts like *sidereal* motion (movement of the stars), you possibly could become a little confused by the way the properties work—especially if you are more familiar with *equatorial* telescope mounts that turn the telescope in a way that compensates for the rotation of the Earth around its polar axis. Instead of thinking in the terms of an equatorial mount, you need to think in terms of an *Alt-Az* mount, or Altitude-Azimuth telescope mount, and that requires a bit of effort.

What we do is visualize the sun rising on the horizon, at a point dictated by an angle, in degrees, from due north. This angle is the azimuth of the sun, and we can specify a starting and ending azimuth. At sunrise, the azimuth would be 90 degrees for due east. We would use 270 degrees for sunset at due west, continuing to measure the azimuth in a clockwise direction.

The `fxSunLight` effects object has a couple of properties that can be adjusted to give us dramatic sunrise and sunset effects. For our purposes, we need to work with properties that manage the color, altitude, and azimuth attribute of the sun. We are interested in these properties that operate as animation on/off *switch* controls:

- `AnimColour`
- `AnimAzimuth`
- `AnimElevation`

and these properties that operate as *motion* controls:

- `RedKeys`
- `GreenKeys`
- `BlueKeys`
- `AzimuthKeys`
- `ElevationKeys`

and these properties that operate as *limit* controls:

- MinColour
- MaxColour
- MinAzimuth
- MaxAzimuth
- MinElevation
- MaxElevation

and then these properties that function as *speed* controls:

- ColourTime
- AzimuthTime
- ElevationTime

Then there are these properties which aren't animation controls, but are nonetheless needed to define the starting position of our fxSunLight object:

- SunAzimuth
- SunElevation

The on/off switch controls are pretty straightforward. When they are set to 1 (true), then the animation is enabled, and stuff happens.

The motion controls and limit controls work together; the limit controls specify the boundaries of the motion, and the motion controls define how the animation "moves" (ie. the frames change) within those boundaries. Let's look at an example.

Let us say that we want to make the sun rise until it's directly overhead, and then we want it to move backwards until it arrives back where it started, instead of continuing across the sky like it normally would. First we would define the limits like this:

```
MaxElevation = 90;
MinElevation = 0;
```

MinElevation, when set to 0, is equal to the horizon, which may or may not be out of your line-of-sight, depending on the terrain. Not only is it the horizon, but more precisely, it's the horizon at the point where the starting azimuth (SunAzimuth) and elevation (SunElevation) are. MaxElevation is defined to be directly overhead, at 90 degrees. Our fxSunLight object will move between these two points only. By the way, our starting position is defined as SunElevation=0 and SunAzimuth=90, which is due east on the horizon.

Having defined our limits, now we need to specify how to move between those limits using the *keys*. We want our sun to start at the minimum limit and proceed to the maximum limit. With the alphabetical key system, A represents the minimum and Z represents the maximum, so the movement from horizon to overhead is written as AZ.

But remember, I also said that in our example, we will be moving the sun *back* to where it started from. So therefore, our key is written as AZA. Got that? After the sun arrives back at A, it will start the cycle over again at A and carry on. If we wanted to be even more bizarre and have the sun move back to *halfway up* the sky (ie. mid-morning position) at the end, then disappear and restart back at the horizon, we would use this key: AZAM. M!?! Well, M, because that is the 13th letter in the alphabet, halfway between A and Z. A is the horizon, Z is overhead, so M will be halfway between those points. Handy, eh?

The speed controls operate by specifying the amount of time, in seconds, it will take the object to traverse the entire key string. In the case of our previous bizarre example, that would be from A to M, so bear that in mind. To increase the speed of the elevation motion, lower the `ElevationTime` property. Or, conversely, reduce the number of keys, or even reduce the range specified by the limits properties.

Azimuth works the same way as elevation in terms of controlling it. In fact so does color, but it's not immediately obvious how.

Think in terms of starting and ending instead of minimum and maximum when thinking of color control (and the size and brightness controls as well), and you should have no problem.

Let's try a real example. A regular sunrise-to-sunset day with a red sun in the morning and evening and yellow during the rest of the day. In this example, let's not make the sun go all the way around the world, spending half of its motion on the night side. Instead, we'll start the sun just below the horizon, and end it there too, on the other side of the sky.

You can edit the mission file manually to do this, but a better approach would be to run the demo, open the World Editor Inspector, and make the changes there. The first thing you should do is disable both `sunflare1` and `sunflare2`, simply to make it easier to observe the behavior of only one object. Do this by locating the `enable` property for each of the objects and clearing the checkbox.

Then select sunflare1 and go through and set its properties as shown in Table 12.2. Set all of the properties before you hit the Apply button, just to avoid the distraction of having flares romping around your sky.

Table 12.2 sunflare1 Settings

Property	Setting
Enable	1
SunAzimuth	90
SunElevation	0
FlareTP	1
Colour	1.0 0.0 0.0 1.0
AnimColour	1
AnimAzimuth	1
AnimElevation	1
SingleColourKeys	0
MinColour	1.0 0.0 0.0 1.0
MaxColour	1.0 1.0 0.0 1.0
MinAzimuth	90
MaxAzimuth	270
MinElevation	0
MaxElevation	359
RedKeys	AZA
GreenKeys	AZA
BlueKeys	AZA
AzimuthKeys	AZ
ElevationKeys	AZ
ColourTime	15
AzimuthTime	15
ElevationTime	15

A few points about those properties: FlareTP controls whether or not the flare can be seen from a third-person point-of-view. For the sake of debugging, I always set this to 1, so I can see the flare from camera fly mode. If you don't want the flare to be visible from a third-person view, you should set FlareTP to 0 after you have the flare working the way you want.

The Colour property should be set to the same color as the ColourMin, although it doesn't really matter as long as color animation is enabled, as it is here. For the color motion controls, we use the controls for all three channels: red, green, and blue. We don't really need to do this, though. There is another property that we could set to 1 to enable, called SingleColourKeys. Enabling SingleColourKeys allows us to specify the color animation for all three channels together at the same time, simply by setting the keys in the RedKeys property. Of course, that would mean that we couldn't have separate animations for different channels. By default, SingleColourKeys is set to 1, or off. I've turned off SingleColourKeys here purely as an example that it can be done.

Notice how the color animation keys go from minimum to maximum and back to minimum again, and that the color minimum is red (1.0, 0.0, 0.0, 1.0) and the maximum is yellow (1.0, 1.0, 0.0, 1.0). That fourth parameter in the color setting is opacity. When set to 1.0, the object is fully opaque (not transparent).

Finally, take note of the fact that the time-based properties all have the same value. I want the changes to take place in a synchronized fashion, and the best way to do this is to make all animations happen over the same time period.

Your best bet is to disable (set enable to 0) both of the fxSunLight objects, then make the changes to sunflare1 only, then enable sunflare1 again. Then watch the object's behavior. If you haven't created your modified sun flare yet, go ahead and do that now, and I'll wait for you before moving on to the next effect.

Doing It with Flare

To keep things rolling along, why don't you fire up the ol' Torque demo (if it isn't running already), and pop into one of the missions, either fps or the racing one. Once you're in-game, take a look at the sun flare that's available right out of the box (see Figure 12.1).

Just sit somewhere and gaze at it for a few minutes. You can observe a lot by looking. The first thing you will notice is probably how the sun light varies as the cloud layers move in front of the sun. As you continue, you will start to notice the rays emanating from the sun itself. Then you'll notice how the rays seem to rotate around the sun.

Figure 12.1 The glaring sun.

Note

It's terminology time again! The rays around the sun generated with the two `fxSunLight` objects that are included with the demo, `sunflare1` and `sunflare2`, are often called "sun flare" or "sun glare" by the average person. In fact, there isn't any sun-based meteorological phenomenon that's goes by those names. A "solar flare" is an event that occurs on the surface of the sun, and we can't see them with the naked eye (in fact, *don't* look directly at the sun with your naked eye, *ever*).

Those rays of light happen around any bright light source, not just the sun. The intensity of the rays and other characteristics are dictated by the amount of dust or moisture in the air and the optics of the light-receiving instrument (like your eyes, or a camera). Most people are somewhat familiar with the concept of lens flare, or camera flare, which is often seen as multiple circles of light offset from the bright light source, caused by light bouncing around inside a camera body before hitting the film, or back and forth between lenses at a slightly divergent angle before striking the film.

You might first be tempted to attribute that to the interference of the cloud layers. However, that's not the case. Instead, it's the `AnimRotation` property that does that.

That "glare" or "flare" of light rays is actually created by a bitmapped image being rendered at the location of the `fxSunLight` object, believe it or don't! In fact, there are two such images that can be assigned to a single `fxSunLight` object. The *remote* flare image, and the *local* flare image. The remote image is rendered behind the cloud layers. So when you see it, you see it peeking through the transparent and translucent portions of the clouds. The local image is rendered between your "eye" or "camera" and the location of its parent `fxSunLight` object, but the image will be occluded by any intervening geometry like buildings, trees, or mountainous terrain.

Looking in the World Editor Inspector, you've probably already noticed that there are two `fxSunLight` objects, `sunflare1` and `sunflare2`. One of the objects, `sunflare1`, is a deep red, and the other, `sunflare2`, is bright yellow. Overlapping the two objects gives a nice yellow-red glare effect. When you are finished goofing around in the demo world, exit completely to the desktop. We're going to be adding a resource and will need to start the demo fresh afterwards.

We can use that ability to overlap `fxSunLight` objects to good effect. What we'll do is create the halo effect I mentioned earlier in this chapter.

The first step is to create a new custom bitmap image for use with one of the two `fxSunLight` objects, in place of the default corona bitmap. This new bitmap will be the actual halo image itself, so that we can use one of the objects to be the halo and the other to be the sun, using the default corona bitmap.

I've provided an appropriate bitmap for the halo, as shown in Figure 12.2, in RESOURCES\ch12 in the file called halo.png. Copy this file to \A3D\common\ lighting.

I've also included a bitmap you can use for the sun proper, in place of the corona bitmap, as shown in Figure 12.3. The sun bitmap image file is in RESOURCES\ch12 in the file called sun.png. Copy this file to \A3D\common\lighting as well.

Next, launch the fps demo and select `sunflare1` in the World Editor Inspector. Locate the `RemoteFlareBitmap` property, and set it to "common/lighting/halo" (with *no* extension after the filename). Then go to the `LocalFlareBitmap` property and delete the path and filename for that property. There will be no local flare because the halo effect is an atmospheric one that takes place pretty high up.

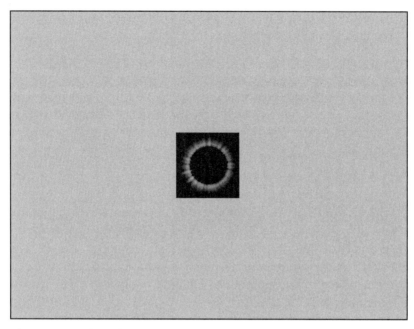

Figure 12.2 The halo bitmap.

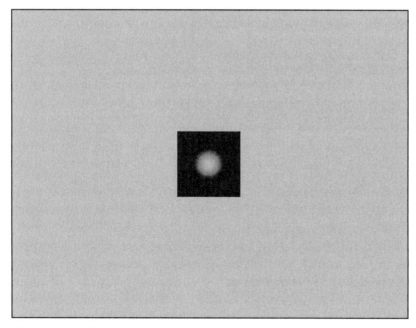

Figure 12.3 The sun bitmap.

Then replace both the `RemoteFlareBitmap` and `LocalFlareBitmap` property values with "common/lighting/sun".

Next, change the `Brightness` property of `sunflare1` to `0.8`. Now, make sure that all of the speed, position, and motion control parameters of both `fxSunLight` objects are the same.

If you have your flare objects animated for position, moving across the sky, you will probably notice that after you press the Apply button, both objects will become out of synch with each other. This is because when you press Apply, the object will be reset to whatever its starting properties dictate. So, after you make all of the settings changes, save your mission file, exit the demo program to the desktop, and restart it. That way, both objects will be started at almost exactly the same time. Note that the longer the time-base for the effects you are using (the slower the run), the more the two objects will be aligned with each other. The time base I have been working with for elevation and azimuth animation, 15 seconds, is a very fast one for sun motion. You will probably end up changing them to something much larger, like 500 or greater, in order to match the sun movement with your game needs.

A final comment about the bitmaps used to create the halo and sun images. In this context, pure black in the texture will be treated as transparent, and the transparency is graduated from black to white. This means that medium gray will be medium transparency. You should only create these images in gray scale. The color is handled by the properties. These images may be either .PNG format or .JPG. However, if you use .PNG, you also have the option of presenting your transparency in the Alpha channel that .PNG format supports. With .JPG, you must use the blackness transparency feature.

Water, Water, Everywhere!

There are times with some game designs where bodies of water, large and small, play an important role. Some game engines have no intrinsic support for water. In those cases, you will need to create water as an object, with appropriate textures containing alpha channel data for transparency. You'll then need to animate either the object or the textures on the object to achieve the visual effects you want.

Torque, and some other high-end game engines, *do* have intrinsic support for water. With the Torque there is the environmental object class called a *waterblock*.

Water Properties

Torque's waterblocks are highly configurable, and can be used for things like pools of molten lava or quicksand as well.

Figure 12.4 shows the water that is included with the standard fps Torque demo program. You can see the dock extending from the shore out into the water, and a few drying poles jutting out of the water.

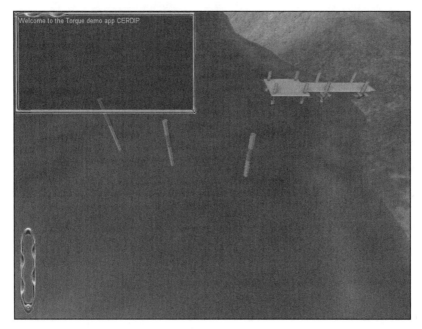

Figure 12.4 Water in a tranquil setting.

Waterblock definition code is found in the mission (.mis) file used to define your game world. Here is an example (the values of the properties vary according to settings):

```
new WaterBlock() {
    position = "-32 -752 159.5";
    rotation = "1 0 0 0";
    scale = "2048 2048 10";
    UseDepthMask = "1";
    surfaceTexture = "~/data/water/water";
    ShoreTexture = "~/data/water/wateredge";
    envMapOverTexture = "~/data/skies/storm_0007";
```

```
        specularMaskTex = "~/data/water/specmask";
        liquidType = "OceanWater";
        density = "1";
        viscosity = "15";
        waveMagnitude = "1";
        surfaceOpacity = "0.6";
        envMapIntensity = "0.1";
        TessSurface = "15";
        TessShore = "25";
        SurfaceParallax = "0.5";
        FlowAngle = "45";
        FlowRate = "0.25";
        DistortGridScale = "0.1";
        DistortMag = "0.05";
        DistortTime = "0.5";
        ShoreDepth = "4";
        DepthGradient = "1";
        MinAlpha = "0.03";
        MaxAlpha = "1";
        removeWetEdges = "0";
        specularColor = "1.000000 0.800000 0.200000 1.000000";
        specularPower = "30";
    };
```

Not all properties need to be defined. If you leave any out, Torque will simply use default values. There are also other properties that you don't see in the example. These are primarily used internally by Torque, and you will rarely, if ever, need to change them. I'm not going to list these internal-use properties here, but I mention them because if you edit a waterblock in the Mission Editor (the best place to do it), then when you save your mission, Torque will add some of these internal properties to the definition, with their default values, and write them out to the mission file. You can easily recognize them because they will be added to the end of the waterblock definition (below all of the ones you saw in the preceding example) and will be indented about four spaces.

To fiddle with a waterblock, simply open the Mission Editor in the FPS demo, and then start the World Editor Inspector. In the Inspector tree view in the upper right corner, locate the environment mission group, and click on the little plus sign to expand the list. You will see your waterblock listed there. Click on the entry and its data should appear in the pane below the tree view. Click on the Expand All button to gain access to all of the property groups.

Tables 12.3 and 12.4 contain details about the properties of a waterblock. Table 12.3 contains the *standard* waterblock properties, and Table 12.4 contains the *special* properties that come into play when the `UseDepthMask` property is set to 1.

Table 12.3 Waterblock Standard Properties

Property	Description
position	Specifies the location of the waterblock's "southwest" corner.
rotation	Has no real effect on the waterblock.
scale	Specifies the size of a waterblock. Visually, the scale is limited to a maximum of 2048 world units in the X and Y axes. At that size, adjoining waterblock copies are tiled. Scale in the Z-axis has no direct visual effect, but is used to specify the effective depth of the water.
liquidType	Used to provide a means for providing damage and visual effects. The script code that is invoked upon entering water can be modified to cause custom effects when the different types of liquid are encountered. Additionally, lava types display the submerged textures when the player's eye or camera is submerged, and the quick sand type blocks out lighting of the player character. The function `Armor::onEnterLiquid` in demo\servers\scripts\player.cs is called from the engine when you enter the liquid that allows you to customize the effects of the liquids. **Choices:** `Water`, `OceanWater`, `RiverWater`, `StagnantWater`, `Lava`, `HotLava`, `CrustyLava`, `Quicksand`.
density	Specifies a density that is used to compare against densities of shapes that might enter the water. If the water is denser than the shape, the shape will float.
viscosity	Specifies a value that will slow movement of a shape through the liquid. The higher the value, the higher the viscosity (the "thicker" the water is).
waveMagnitude	Specifies the maximum amplitude of the wave function of the waterblock in world units in the Z-axis. Note that this is the difference between the highest peak and the lowest trough.
surfaceOpacity	Controls the maximum opacity of the surface. A value of 0 means the surface is totally transparent, and a value of 1.0 means the surface is totally opaque (you can't see through it at all). This property has no effect if the `UseDepthMask` property is set to 1.
envMapIntensity	Controls the intensity of the applied environment map. A setting of 0 will show *no* environment map, while a setting of 1.0 will show the environment map at maximum intensity. Note also that setting the intensity to 0 will cause the environment map pass to be skipped thus yielding a slight performance gain.
envMapOverTexture	Specifies the environment map texture used when looking down at the surface of the water from above.
envMapUnderTexture	Specifies the environment map texture used when looking up out of the water at the surface.

Table 12.4 Waterblock Special Surface Properties

Property	Description
UseDepthMask	Also called the Melv switch. This toggle turns the depth-map features on and off. When set to 0, or off, the plain old standard surface rendering for waterblocks is used.
surfaceTexture	Specifies the texture normally used to represent the surface of the water.
ShoreTexture	Specifies the texture used to represent shallow areas of water, as defined by the ShoreDepth property.
SpecularMaskTex	Specifies the texture used to portray the specular lighting effect on the liquid surface.
TessSurface	Specifies the number of times the surface textures are repeated over the waterblock surface. Note: Setting this value too low (below about 5 or so) on a very large waterblock can result in a highly distorted surface!
TessShore	Similar to TessSurface, but for the shore textures. The same caveat applies.
SurfaceParallax	Specifies the movement speed ratio of one surface texture to the other (the liquid surface is rendered as two layers). With a value of 0.5, one surface will move at half the speed of the other.
FlowAngle	Specifies the direction of water flow using a polar-coordinate based angle.
FlowRate	Specifies the speed of apparent fluid flow. Use a value of 0 to completely stop the flow.
DistortGridScale	Specifies the distortion effect of the fluid surface, allowing you to create many different surface effects. You can distort the surface too much and get strange rendering effects, so use judiciously. DistortGridScale, which normally does not need adjusting is included because a small waterblock may not look correct when scaled to a larger size; you can fix that using this field.
DistortMag	Specifies the overall magnitude of the fluid distortion effect.
DistortTime	Specifies the speed of surface distortion.
ShoreDepth	Controls the depth at which the shore texture is applied. Larger values result in larger shore texture areas, with the shore texture visible farther away from the shoreline. If you set this value too high, you might not even see the regular surface texture.
DepthGradient	Controls the gradient that the shore textures will interpolate between the MinAlpha and MaxAlpha properties. Using a value of 1 triggers a linear-interpolation between the two properties. Using values from 0 up to (but not including) 1 triggers a fast fade-out with slow fade-in interpolation, while using values greater than 1 triggers a slow fade-out with fast fade-in (from deep to shallow).
MinAlpha	In combination with MaxAlpha, controls the alpha levels used from shore to deep fluid. MinAlpha is to prevent totally transparent areas. Note that you will *always* be able to see underneath the fluid surface. Use fog volumes in the Sky object to restrict underwater visibility.

Table 12.4 Waterblock Special Surface Properties (continued)

Property	Description
MaxAlpha	Used in conjunction with MinAlpha. See MinAlpha definition.
Specular Color	Specifies the color in RGB coordinates of the specular highlighting on the water surface.
Specular Power	Specifies the strength (the amount of "bloom") of the specular highlighting.

If you are wondering whether you should use the special properties indicated in Table 12.4, don't fret over it: the answer is **yes**, by all means. The performance penalty is almost not measurable, but the visual payoff is huge. None of the waterblock *surface* properties have any effect on run-time performance; they merely adjust the creation of the alpha-map.

To force Torque to create a new alpha-map for a waterblock's surface, click the Apply button when editing the waterblock in the Mission Editor. This way you can drag the waterblock around 'til the cows come home, and then click "Apply" when you think you are finished, making for more convenient editing.

In keeping with our earlier exploration into the fxSunLight object, take a look at Figure 12.5. The specular highlighting you see on the water in that image is caused by the Specular Power, Specular Color, and SpecularMaskTex properties of the waterblock.

Adjusting the surfaceOpacity property will change how well you can see through the water from outside. Compare Figures 12.6 and 12.7. The latter uses an opacity setting of 1.0, while the former uses an opacity setting in the area of about 0.4. Now watch out for this: Those images are taken with the useDepthMask switch clear (set to 0), so the special properties were not in effect.

If you want to adjust the opacity of the water while the useDepthMask is being used, use the MinAlpha and MaxAlpha settings. I'll explain those in a minute, but first a word about the Depth Mask feature. The Depth Mask feature is there to allow you to create more realistic transitions from shore line water to deep water. A strip of water that touches all shorelines is treated independently of the main body of the water block. That's why we have sets of properties with "Shore" in their names, while similar properties exist without "Shore" in the name.

Figure 12.5 Specular highlighting.

Figure 12.6 Translucent water.

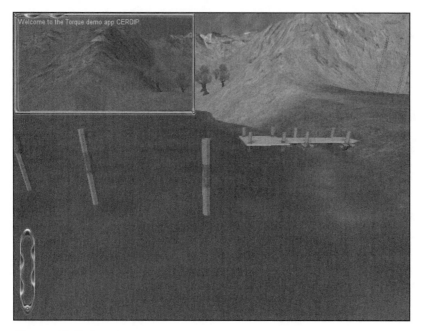

Figure 12.7 Opaque water.

The MinAlpha setting specifies the transparency in the region of the shore line, while MaxAlpha handles the deep water. The alpha setting is smoothly blended by the engine between the shore and deep water regions.

The envMapOverTexture is an environment map texture from an image file that will be rendered on the surface of the water, visible from above the water level and used to simulate reflection of things like clouds in the sky, as shown in Figure 12.8.

To achieve that level of intensity, you need to set the envMapIntensity property to around 0.8 or so.

If you have useDepthMask enabled, and have an envMapOverTexture environment map texture specified, then you can get an even more appropriate appearance of the water, especially near the shore, by using the MinAlpha and MaxAlpha settings, as you can see in Figure 12.9.

Figure 12.8 Reflections on the water.

Figure 12.9 Reflections with Alpha.

We can do the same thing for underwater views through the surface by assigning an image file to envMapUnderTexture. Normally this would be a distorted view of the above-surface world (see Figure 12.10), although I have seen in our fish tank where the surface reflects what is *under* the water.

This happens when looking up through the surface from beneath is very dark or black, and the underwater area is brightly lit. Then the surface acts like a mirror. Figure 12.11 shows this with a different texture that is very low on detail. We get some kind of muddied general sense of reflection, mixed with a view of the shoreline water foam.

Another way to modify the view underwater is to add texture for the two properties submerge0 and submerge1. I've provided two bitmap images (submerge0.jpg and submerge1.jpg) for you to play with, located in RESOURCES\ch12. Copy them both into the \A3D\demo\data\water folder, then re-launch the demo, and in the World Editor Inspector, change the waterblock's submerge0 and submerge1 properties to specify demo/data/water/submerge0 and demo/data/water/submerge1, respectively.

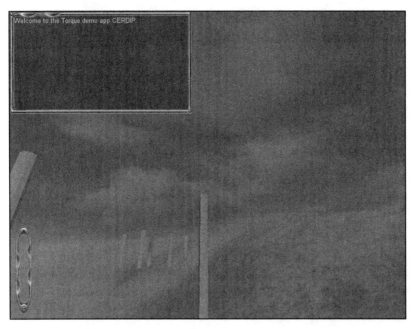

Figure 12.10 A fish's eye view.

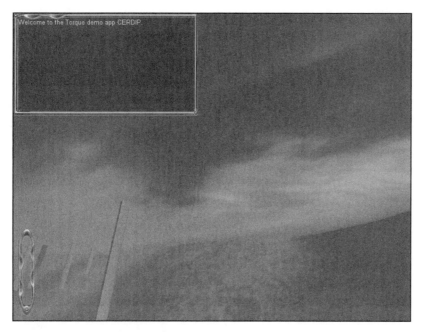

Figure 12.11 Another fish's eye view.

Now go jump in the water. Ooops, one more thing. Those textures only apply to the *Lava* liquid types. So you need to change the `liquidType` property to `Lava`, `HotLava`, or `CrustyLava`. Now go jump in the water. You will see the effects of the two overlapping submerged images quite clearly. I know that the images are nothing to write home about, but I made them with the intent to be able to clearly demonstrate the effects of each of the images. Notice the rather nauseating wavy motion. Blechh. The difference between each of the lava types boils down to the amount of damage you take when you're in the lava.

Water Damage

Water is life, and water kills. Ugh, that's too profound.

Well, profound or not, death by drowning is a necessary ingredient, in my humble opinion, in any game that allows for extensive travel underwater. So what we want to do is detect when we've entered a liquid, and then begin a series of periodic checks to ensure that our player is submerged. The player can only drown if he's been submerged, but not when he is in the wading pool.

So, let's get this party started by modifying some files.

In the file \A3D\demo\server\scripts\player.cs, near the top, after the line:

```
$DamageCrustyLava =  0.01;
```

add the following:

```
$DrowningDamage = 5;   //damage during each interval if the player is submerged
$CheckSubmergedInterval = 1000;   //interval between submerged checks
$BreathHoldDuration = 10000; // how long before player gets drowning damage.
```

Then locate the method Armor::onEnterLiquid and add a schedule call near the end so that the method looks like this:

```
function Armor::onEnterLiquid(%thisDB, %thisPlayer, %coverage, %type)
{
  switch(%type)
  {
    case 0: //Water
    case 1: //Ocean Water
    case 2: //River Water
    case 3: //Stagnant Water
    case 4: //Lava
      %thisPlayer.setDamageDt(%thisDB, $DamageLava, "Lava");
    case 5: //Hot Lava
      %thisPlayer.setDamageDt(%thisDB, $DamageHotLava, "Lava");
    case 6: //Crusty Lava
      %thisPlayer.setDamageDt(%thisDB, $DamageCrustyLava, "Lava");
    case 7: //Quick Sand
  }
    echo ("Enter ze Liquid...");
    echo ("%thisPlayer.drownCheck:"@%thisPlayer.drownCheck);
    echo ("%thisPlayer:"@%thisPlayer);
    echo ("%thisDB:"@%thisDB);
    echo ("%coverage:"@%coverage);
    echo ("%type:"@%type);
    %thisPlayer.breathHold = $BreathHoldDuration;
    %thisPlayer.SubmergedCheck();
}
```

This change schedules a periodic check to see if we are still submerged. Remember, being submerged is not the same as being in the water. We don't want to drown standing ankle deep in a puddle, and the onEnterLiquid method gets called long before our head gets submerged.

In fact, the reason why it gets called is because the engine detects that the player is in the liquid in order to determine if it needs to play splashing sound effects and particle effects. It's not concerned with drowning, although it *is* concerned that you might step in some lava. But standing knee deep in molten is far more hazardous than standing in the same amount of water. Just ask Anakin.

The upshot is, we need to differentiate being *in* water from being *submerged in* water for very good reasons.

Next up, modify the method Armor::onLeaveLiquid (located directly after the method Armor::onEnterLiquid) to look like this:

```
function Armor::onLeaveLiquid(%thisDB, %thisPlayer, %type)
{
  cancel(%thisPlayer.drownCheck);
  %thisPlayer.clearDamageDt();
  %thisPlayer.breathHold = 0;
}
```

This code disables the periodic check. We don't need the check at this point, since we aren't actually in liquid anymore.

Then, immediately following the method Armor::onLeaveLiquid, add this new method:

```
function Player::SubmergedCheck(%thisPlayer)
{
//Cast a ray from the player directly up, looking for an intersection
// with a waterblock. If we find one, then the player is still submerged.
  if (%thisPlayer.getState() $= "Dead")
  {
    echo ("Already Dead in submerge check");
    %thisPlayer.cancel(%thisPlayer.drownCheck);
  }
```

```
  else
  {
    echo ("Submerge checking...");
    %start = %thisPlayer.getEyePoint();
    %end = VectorAdd(%start, "0 0 100");
    %searchMasks = $TypeMasks::WaterObjectType;
    if(ContainerRayCast(%start, %end, %searchMasks))
    {
      if ( %thisPlayer.breathHold <= 0)
        %thisPlayer.damage(0, %thisPlayer.getPosition(), $DrowningDamage, 0);
      else
        %thisPlayer.breathHold -= $CheckSubmergedInterval;
    }
    %thisPlayer.drownCheck=%thisPlayer.schedule($CheckSubmergedInterval,
                                                 "SubmergedCheck");
  }
}
```

This method is where the grunt work gets done. Of course, it is possible to arrive at this code with our player already dead, having drowned (or maybe even having been eaten by piranhas). If that's the case, we cancel the scheduled check.

But, if we're still kicking, then we've got some drowning to do, so it's best that we check to see if we are still submerged. If we are still submerged, then check to see if we are holding our breath. If we are holding our breath, then subtract the submerge check interval time from the total of held breath time, and cycle to next check. Once the breath has been used up, then start to apply some damage to the player, and move on.

What we are doing is capturing the notification that the player has entered the water. We don't apply damage until we know that the player is actually totally submerged. And we know *that* because we've used a ray cast technique to look up from our head to well beyond where there might be a waterblock. If we don't see the waterblock, then we aren't fully submerged in it.

Walking in Water

Well, we need to test our code, so we might as well wade right in. There's really nothing to it. Launch the demo, and after you spawn in, run down to the water, and then right *into* the water, until you are completely submerged.

And wait.

And wait.

And… oops! You're running out of air—taking some damage! For the first test, just stay in the water until you die. At the moment, the parameters are set so that your player will hold his breath for 10 seconds, at which point the damage hits will start coming in every 5 seconds. The damage hit is 5 points, and the damage range is 100 points, so you will be in the water $10 + ((100/5) \times 1)$ seconds, or 30 seconds, before you succumb.

Next, after re-spawning (press the left mouse button to trigger the re-spawn), run straight over to the water, and in. Count to 5, then rapidly exit. That's a useful test to verify functionality of schedule canceling.

After a bit of that old in and out action, try staying in until the damage gets to about half, and then run out quickly. You should have stopped the accrual of damage.

Moving Right Along

So, we've spent some time with two seemingly prosaic effects systems in the Torque Engine that we've discovered can really snaz up the joint.

The fxSunLight object is a pretty powerful and versatile feature, chock-a-block full of properties that can be used to enhance a 3D scene both grossly *and* in fine detail.

There are other metrological phenomena, aside from sun glare and halos, that we could implement potentially using more fxSunLight objects in the game world, like sundogs, for example.

Then we moved on to water and waterblocks. We've learned that there are two different modes for waterblocks: the regular mode and special mode, with different sets of properties for each. Special mode (UseDepthMask mode) allows us to specify a more complete and realistic rendering of the waterblock to achieve things like specular reflection. We can manipulate how the water appears in many ways, both from above and below, through the use of various image textures.

Finally, we discovered how to use script code to easily implement a drowning damage system based on prolonged submergence in water.

CHAPTER 13

ONLINE GAME SERVICES USING PHP

The World Wide Web is everywhere these days. No doubt that's because it's so flexible and adaptable. Most people know that pages are published using a special language called Hyper Text Markup Language (HTML)—and if you didn't know that, then let me just say: "Welcome to the Planet Earth! Nice saucer you have there…"

As useful as HTML is for displaying data and text on web pages, there are capabilities that just aren't available that are a must have when it comes to creating dynamic web page content. Microsoft invented Active Server Pages (ASP), using a derivative of Visual Basic, for just such applications. Of course, as with everything webby in the world today, there is a non-Microsoft solution for dynamic content called PHP. I won't get into an argument about which is better, PHP or ASP, but we are going to be using PHP in this book.

Now I'm not going to spend any time actually teaching the ins and outs of PHP. As a language it is very similar to TorqueScript; both languages trace their lineage back to C/C++. And while TorqueScript was specifically created to make games using the Torque Game Engine, PHP was specifically created for providing dynamic web page content. Both have their own peculiarities, as well as special capabilities and functions that serve their primary purposes.

What I will do is show you where to obtain PHP, how you install it along with the Apache Web Server, and how you can use PHP as an online adjunct to your game for things like information delivery and updating (from the web), publication (to the web), and authentication. I'm not going to give you instruction on how to program in PHP, but the PHP documentation can be found in the TOOLS\PHP folder and a Windows help file for PHP in the RESOURCES\ch13 folder. I *do* provide you with functioning PHP code that will illustrate the points of this chapter and give you a leg up on how to use the Web with Torque.

The acronym PHP means *Personal Home Page*. It's a server-side scripting language that was created in order to generate HTML content for web pages. With the current direction of the World Wide Web, it is easily being adapted to write out all forms of XML content as well.

PHP was first developed as server-side modules that perform a few specific operations on small "personal" web servers. PHP capabilities have since grown well beyond the scale of one person writing some tools for his own use and into one of the most prevalent server scripting languages on the web.

Three things make PHP popular. The first is that it is easy: easy to implement, easy to learn, and easy to use. The second is that it is free. The third is that it runs on almost any web server on almost any platform currently available.

I should address the issue of databases. The techniques I'm showing can be used with any back-end database system. PHP has built-in support for several popular non-Microsoft databases. Probably the most used would be mySQL. I'm not going to address the database aspect, except to include hooks in the PHP server code that you can expand to include your own database access methods.

PHP and Apache

Most of you will be using Windows computers for your development. PHP is cross-platform, and that's goodness, but I will be focusing on the Windows platform. In case you're thinking "Windows-bigot," please disabuse yourself of that notion forthwith. And give me 50 pushups while you're at it!

You see, although you could run Microsoft Personal Web Server (PWS) or the Internet Information Server (IIS), I prefer Apache for this job for many reasons, some technical, some security-oriented, and some personal. Even better, Apache is now built into Apple's OS/X and most flavors of Linux, so it's really a slam-dunk choice anyway.

And besides that, getting "under the hood" of Apache is much easier than it is with any other HTTP server.

N o t e

On Windows platforms, both PWS and IIS have auto-installers for PHP. If you have either of those servers already installed or want to install them, then go ahead—fill your boots. Just skip the Apache-specific stuff.

In order to proceed you will need the following:

- a computer, preferably your own
- a reasonably speedy Internet connection
- a hard drive that is not totally maxed out
- (for Apache) a zip tool
- (for Apache) the Microsoft Installer (should be built into Windows on all newer computers)—unless you want to do things the hard way
- patience

Installing Apache

First, download Apache.

To download Apache 2 you want to find Apache_2.0.54-win32-x86-no_ssl.msi on the CD in the \A3D\TOOLS\Apache folder.

To install Apache from the MSIE file, double-click on the file and it should invoke the Microsoft Installer.

You should have a recent version of Microsoft Installer in order to install the software. Fortunately, if you don't have a recent installer, newer versions of Windows should automatically take you to the Microsoft download site when you try to invoke the installer. If it does not, then look on the Apache download page at http://httpd.apache.org/download.cgi for the link to important notes for Windows (Win32) users.

At the appropriate prompt screen in the install process, you will want to set the network domain and server name to `localhost`. You should also set the e-mail address to one that you use, or to `me@localhost` (or anything else at `localhost`, it's not a real e-mail address). You can leave everything else with the default settings.

Apache 2 comes with a control console, which should show up as a little icon in your system tray (that space just to the left of the clock on the task bar). Double-clicking it will open the Apache console (See Figure 13.1), where you can start and stop Apache as well as connect to remote computers and determine what local services you have running.

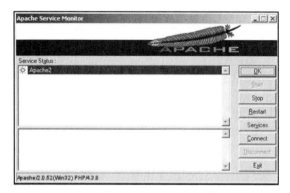

Figure 13.1 Apache 2 console.

If you installed Apache correctly, Apache and the Apache console should already be up and running. Now we just have to tweak it for your computer.

Set Up

The first thing you have to do is stop Apache. If you did not install Apache 2 and/or do not have the Apache console, you can stop Apache from the Start menu. It should be found under something like Start, All Programs, Apache HTTP Server, Control Apache. You will also find the commands to start and restart the server there.

Then you need to edit the configuration file. The Apache subfolder in the Start menu will include an edit function on one of its submenus. Otherwise, the file you want is httpd.conf and it can be found under C:\Program Files\Apache Group\Apache2\conf. Open httpd.conf in your favorite text editor.

Note there is also a file called httpd.default.conf. *Do not* modify this file in any way. You will need to use it to overwrite the configuration file back to its default settings if you mess things up.

The httpd.conf file is the file that contains all the basic configuration information for running Apache. Most of it is comments, which is anything preceded by a hash-mark (#). We need to make a few changes to this file to make sure Apache knows where to find our files.

First, you want to find the following location in the code:

```
#
# DocumentRoot: The directory out of which ...
# documents. By default, all requests are  ...
# symbolic links and aliases may be used   ...
#
DocumentRoot "C:/Program Files/Apache Group/Apache2/htdocs"
```

We want to change our document root to the name of the folder in which we are storing our web pages. For instance, I do all of my development in a folder called webdev, so my document root is:

```
DocumentRoot "C:/webdev"
```

Notice that even though it is a Windows path name, Apache is expecting forward slashes.

You also need to find the following section and change it to point to the same folder as your DocumentRoot.

```
#
# This should be changed to whatever you set DocumentRoot to.
#
<Directory "C:/Program Files/Apache Group/Apache2/htdocs">
```

If you save this file and then start Apache up again, assuming you didn't make any mistakes, you should be able to open up a web browser, type **localhost** into the address bar, and it should display the contents of the folder you specified as the DocumentRoot above. If you haven't changed the document root folder or if the DocumentRoot folder doesn't contain any web pages, then it will display an Apache welcome page.

If you have gotten this far, you are ready to add in the PHP.

Installing PHP

Installing PHP manually is not that hard, but occasionally it can call for some trial and error. We need to find PHP at \A3D\TOOLS\PHP\php-4.3.11-installer.exe, install it, configure it, and then edit the Apache httpd.conf file to tell Apache where PHP is and what to do with it.

If you are running Apache, then you want to use

PHP 4.3.0 zip package [5,811Kb]—27 December 2002.

If you are running PWS or IIS, then you can download

PHP 4.3.0 installer [1,028Kb]—27 December 2002.

The installer is a Microsoft Installer file and is self-configuring. You merely need to double-click on the installer icon and pretty much let it run. We won't worry about it here. We *will* worry about the Zip package, which you do have to configure manually.

Double-click the .zip file and unzip its contents into some folder. C:\ is probably a good one, since the installation directions that come with it assume that this is where it's going. Make sure the user folder names option is checked. Winzip unzips the archive contents to a folder called php-4.3.0-Win32. You can make your life easier by simply renaming the folder to php. Then you are ready to continue.

Take a few minutes to examine the files that are there in order to gain some familiarity, and read the installation directions included in the install.txt file. Read it over once or twice—eventually it will start to make sense to you. Then follow the directions. The rest of this section contains useful advice about following the official installation directions. One of the first decisions you will have to make is whether PHP will be used for server-side scripting, command line scripting, or client-side GUI applications. You will be doing server-side scripting.

After that, a little bit of trial and error may become necessary.

Tip

The PHP install.txt wants you to set the PATH variable, but it may not be clear how to do that. If you are using Windows XP, or Windows 2000:

1. Right-click on the My Computer icon on your desktop, and choose Properties from the pop-up menu.
2. When the Properties window opens up, click on the Advanced tab.

3. At the bottom of the Advanced tab you will find the button called Environment Variables. Click on it.

4. The Environment Variables dialog will open and display two panes: one at the top called User Variables for [your username] and one at the bottom called System Variables.

5. In the System Variables pane, scroll down until you see an entry with Path on the left side.

6. Select the Path entry, then click the Edit button.

7. Click your cursor in the lower edit box, and scroll the blinking text cursor all the way to the right, to the end of the path information that's already there.

8. Add a semicolon to the end of the path, and after the semicolon, enter the new path information you want to add. Click OK when you have entered your information.

9. Click OK again to exit the Environment Variables dialog, and then OK one final time to close the Properties box.

If you are using Windows 98:

1. Choose Start, Run.

2. Type **command** in the little edit box in the Run window. A command shell window will open.

3. Type the following command in the command shell:

```
SET PATH=%PATH%;C:\PHP
```

That's assuming that C:\PHP is the new path you want to set. You should put whatever path applies for your needs, according to the install.txt file.

4. Verify that you correctly set the path by typing **PATH**, then pressing Enter key. Check the output in the command shell window to make sure you got it right.

5. Close the command shell when you are done.

Now get back to work.

Do not copy the php.ini-dist file to the system folder. Instead, make a copy of php.ini-recommended, and call the copy php.ini. Then copy php.ini to the Apache 2 folder (C:\Program Files\Apache Group\Apache2). The php.ini-dist is the same as php.ini-recommended, except it has fewer security options set, so don't use it.

Move all the DLL files where they tell you to, paying attention to the differences between Apache and Apache2 directions. If you are uncertain of the system folder to which to move the DLL files from the dlls folder, you will either have to experiment or move them to all possible locations. If you use the second approach, when you get comfortable with the software, you can experiment with deleting them until you figure out which deletions cause the software to stop working.

The directions that follow assume that you've copied all the sapi and dll folder contents to the /php root folder.

Whether they go in windows\system, windows\system32, or c:\winnt\system32 is entirely dependent on your configuration, which may vary much more than is apparent by the installation directions. I use Windows XP where they are in the windows\system32 folder.

Setting Up PHP

Open the php.ini file in the text editor of your choice. You may have multiple copies of the file floating around by now, so make sure you are editing the one in the Apache2 folder.

First, search for the line

```
short_open_tag = On
```

and change it to

```
short_open_tag = Off
```

It will make learning to code a little easier by making the edits a little stricter. It will also make the PHP engine XML-compatible. If you plan to work with XML, you must have the short_open_tag turned off; otherwise, it will conflict with XML processing directives.

Be forewarned that the school still has short_open_tag set to on in spite of repeated protestations on my part. Fortunately, the only place that will mess you up on my PHP class is when using an XML prologue in an XHMTL document.

Next, look for the section beginning with:

```
;;;;;;;;;;;;;;;;;;;;;;;;
; Paths and Directories ;
;;;;;;;;;;;;;;;;;;;;;;;;
```

Notice the semicolon at the front of each line. The PHP configuration line uses semicolons to comment out a line.

Just below this heading you want to set the doc_root variable to the same path you set for the Apache DocumentRoot above. Unlike Apache, you can use backslashes in the path name.

For me this is

```
; The root of the PHP pages.
doc_root = c:\webdev
```

You also want to set `extension_dir` to wherever you will put your PHP extension modules. All the extensions are stored in the extensions subfolder of the PHP install, so if you accepted the default placement above, you can point directly to them with:

```
; Directory in which the loadable extensions (modules) reside.
extension_dir = c:\php\extensions\
```

If you put PHP somewhere else, you will need to use a different path.

Save your work.

Linking Apache and PHP

We now need to tell Apache where PHP is and what to do with it. So, open the C:\Program Files\Apache Group\Apache2\conf \httpd.conf file again.

Now find where it says:

```
#
# DirectoryIndex: Name of the file or files   ...
# directory index.  Separate multiple entries ...
#
<IfModule mod_dir.c>
    DirectoryIndex index.html
</IfModule>
```

This is where you tell Apache what files to look for as default files to be loaded when a file is not specified in the requested address. index.html is already listed. In a space-separated list, we are going to add a few more options. For us, the last one is the most important.

```
<IfModule mod_dir.c>
DirectoryIndex index.html index.htm index.php
</IfModule>
```

Now find the #LoadModule and #AddType sections of the configuration file and add the following lines of code to the appropriate sections:

```
LoadModule php4_module c:/php/php4apache2.dll
AddType application/x-httpd-php .php
```

The first line tells Apache to load and start up the core PHP module for use by the server. The second line says to associate files ending in a .php suffix with the PHP modules.

Save the file.

Restart Apache.

If you get no errors, you should be all set. Put the PHP hello world exercise in your document root folder, C:\webdev, and see if you can access it in a web browser using `localhost`.

If it says it is unable to start, then try moving the php.ini file around to the Windows folder and to the various system directories until Apache successfully starts.

It can be pretty annoying getting all the files placed in the right locations. There is no easy way around this with Apache, unfortunately. If you are reluctant to fiddle around with the paths to get it to work, you should probably try running PHP through PWS. You can use the PWS auto-installer, if you don't already have it installed, and the PHP auto-installer to configure PHP for PWS.

If something goes horribly, horribly wrong installing Apache, chin up! You can always just delete it all and start again. Any damage will be isolated and not liable to mess up your computer. You can also try the directions for the PHP executable; just be aware that it is a major security risk to use the PHP executable if you are online with Apache running. It is really just a development tool.

If you want some extra reading on the topic, you can also look at the Official PHP documentation, located here: http://www.php.net/docs.php.

Alternatively, you can use the PHP manual in the \A3D\RESOURCES\ch13 folder.

In-Game News Service Using the Web

Quite a number of years ago, a friend of mine, known by his *nom-de-net* as Insomniac, had an idea for an in-game news service he called the Multi-Player News Network (MPNN). He wandered around inside various servers in the *Delta Force 2* series (by Novalogic) games and gathered data on the battles, who won or lost, and various other tidbits of interesting gossip. He took copious notes and then transposed them to his web page later as original reporting. There were technical issues involved, however, that made it a difficult proposition. If he'd had the capability we're about to explore, his task would have been a whole lot easier.

In-Game Info Grabber

For pulling information, like news or update information, down from a website, the following tool is quite handy.

Create a new empty file called webServices.gui in the folder \A3D\demo\client\ui. Open webServices.gui and type in the following:

```
//--- OBJECT WRITE BEGIN ---
new GuiControl(WebDialog) {
   profile = "GuiDefaultProfile";
   horizSizing = "right";
   vertSizing = "bottom";
   position = "0 0";
   extent = "640 480";
   minExtent = "8 8";
   visible = "1";
      helpTag = "0";

   new GuiWindowCtrl() {
      profile = "GuiWindowProfile";
      horizSizing = "center";
      vertSizing = "center";
      position = "75 10";
      extent = "490 459";
      minExtent = "300 200";
      visible = "1";
      text = "Web Info Update";
      maxLength = "255";
      resizeWidth = "1";
      resizeHeight = "1";
      canMove = "1";
      canClose = "1";
      canMinimize = "1";
      canMaximize = "1";
      minSize = "50 50";
      closeCommand = "Canvas.popDialog(WebDialog);";
         helpTag = "0";
```

```
new GuiScrollCtrl() {
   profile = "GuiScrollProfile";
   horizSizing = "width";
   vertSizing = "height";
   position = "6 25";
   extent = "477 402";
   minExtent = "8 8";
   visible = "1";
   willFirstRespond = "1";
   hScrollBar = "alwaysOn";
   vScrollBar = "alwaysOn";
   constantThumbHeight = "0";
   childMargin = "0 0";
      helpTag = "0";

   new GuiMLTextCtrl(Content) {
      profile = "GuiMLTextProfile";
      horizSizing = "width";
      vertSizing = "bottom";
      position = "4 4";
      extent = "450 490";
      minExtent = "8 8";
      visible = "1";
      lineSpacing = "2";
      allowColorChars = "0";
      maxChars = "-1";
         autoSizeWidth = "1";
         helpTag = "0";
         autoSizeHeight = "1";
   };
};
new GuiButtonCtrl() {
   profile = "GuiButtonProfile";
   horizSizing = "right";
   vertSizing = "top";
   position = "169 431";
   extent = "133 21";
   minExtent = "8 8";
   visible = "1";
```

```
            command = "GetWebPage();";
            text = "Refresh";
            groupNum = "-1";
            buttonType = "PushButton";
                helpTag = "0";
        };
    };
};
//--- OBJECT WRITE END ---
```

Next, create the file webServices.cs in the folder \A3D\demo\client\scripts, and put the following control code in it:

```
function InitHTTP()
{
    $Web::HTTPHost="localhost:80";
    $Web::HTTPPath="/test/";
    $Web::HTTPInfoPage="info.php";
    $Web::HTTPTextLines="";
}


function GetInfoPageMenu()
{
    InitHTTP();
    %webpage = new HTTPObject(InfoPageMenu){};
    %webpage.get($Web::HTTPHost, $Web::HTTPPath @ $Web::HTTPInfoPage, "");
}


function InfoPageMenu::onLine( %this, %line )
{
    if(%line $= "[-]")
    {
        Content.setText($Web::HTTPTextLines);
        $Web::HTTPTextLines="";
    }
    else
    {
        Content.setText($Web::HTTPTextLines);
        $Web::HTTPTextLines=$Web::HTTPTextLines @ "\n" @ %line;
    }
}
```

```
function GuiMLTextCtrl::onURL(%this, %url)
{
        gotoWebPage( %url );
}


function InfoPageMenu::onConnectFailed()
{
        MessageBoxOK("ERROR","Couldn't connect to web server! [1]");
}


function InfoPageMenu::onConnected()
{
        echo("Connected to Items Page [1]");
}


function InfoPageMenu::onDisconnect()
{
        echo("Disconnected from Web Page [1]");
}


function GetWebInfo(%thePageName)
{
        GetInfoPageMenu();
        Canvas.pushDialog(WebDialog);
}
```

Next create the following file, name it info.php and save it in C:\webdev:

```
line 1 test
line 2 test
[-]
```

Now this next bit is very important: *Ensure* that you put a final carriage return after
the line that says [-]. In other words, there needs to be a blank line after the [-].

I have added a larger php file in RESOURCES\ch13 that you can use instead of the
simple info.php file we've used here. Just copy it to C:\webdev replacing the small
one, if it exists.

In the file \A3D\demo\client\init.cs in the function initClient, find the line that says
// Client scripts and put the following two lines in front of it:

```
exec("./ui/webServices.gui");
exec("./scripts/webServices.cs");
```

Note the path in the exec statements, and make sure the files are located in these paths: demo\client\ui and demo\client\scripts.

Now, run the Torque Demo. You can test your code from the main menu by opening the console with the tilde key, and typing in the command:

```
GetWebInfo();
```

You should then see the dialog shown in Figure 13.2 appear on your screen (you will have to close the console first).

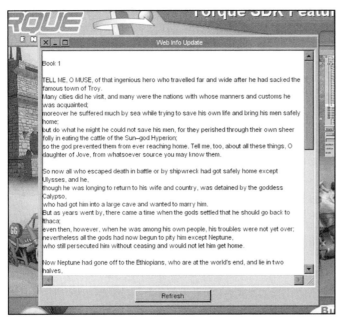

Figure 13.2 The Web Info Update dialog.

It shouldn't take too large a leap of imagination to see where you can go with this capability. The first thing that comes to my mind is a news update for players logging into a game on a persistent server.

You could also have links to a scoring system or "ladder" ranking page. Virtual news reporters is another possibility—people who wander around inside a game world, write up reports about the in-game activities, and publish the news via a web page.

Authentication

There are many ways to implement authentication services for your game. You can write a dedicated back-end Master Server in the language of your choice. You can even do it using Torque itself, running in dedicated server mode with local hooks to a database. A very elegant, secure, and modular approach would be to put a number of PHP scripts on a server that would accept name and password information from your Torque client, and upon authenticating you, would pass you the IP address of the server.

Before embarking on this exercise, I should point out that security is in your hands. It's a good idea to do some research into online security techniques and insert whatever you find to be appropriate into your authentication flow before you go live with a server on the Internet. There are a number of opinions about what passes for acceptable online security, so make sure to consult with more than one source.

The code we're going to see will cover making the website connections and obtaining the information needed for your client to connect to the game server. You'll just need to insert the appropriate security mechanisms, encryption, encoding, hashes, CRC checks, or tokens in the places appropriate for the approach you decide to take.

The PHP Authentication Code

Create the file authenticate.php and put it on your website in the webdev/test/folder. Then, insert the following code:

```
require_once("variables.php");
$auth_host = $GLOBALS['auth_host'];
$auth_user = $GLOBALS['auth_user'];
$auth_pass = $GLOBALS['auth_pass'];
$auth_dbase = $GLOBALS['auth_dbase'];
//Check if username is valid else error and exit
if(is_null($user) || $user == "" || $user == " ")
{
        echo "Auth Server - Invalid Account Name <br>";
        exit();
}
//Check password is valid else error and exit
if(is_null($passcrc) || $passcrc == "" || $passcrc == " ")
{
        echo "Auth Server - Invalid Password<br>";
        exit();
}
```

```
//Check password and username match
$home = mysql_connect($auth_host, $auth_user, $auth_pass);
mysql_select_db($auth_dbase);
$query = "select * from account where username='$user'";
$result = mysql_query($query,$home);
$row = mysql_fetch_assoc($result);
$temppass = $row['password'];
$userid = $row['userid'];
$crcpass = crc32($temppass);
if($crcpass != $password)
{
        echo "Auth Server - Incorrect Password <br>";
        exit();
}
//Advise Server of verified data
echo "Auth Server - Verified Account Details<br>";
```

The first thing the code does is extract the global variables for the session. When we post our query to the page, the variables are passed in with both their names and their values. In this case, username is exactly what the variable name implies, and passcrc is a computed crc32 check value for the password. This is a one-way encoding of the password. On the user's end, in Torque, the player types in the password. That is the only place where the password exists in unencoded form. The password crc32 is stored in the database at the time that the user creates the account (or changes the password), so no one has the ability to guess the user's password. It cannot be derived from the crc32 value.

So, when the crc32 is sent to the PHP script, it fetches the crc32 value for the user from the database. If the two values match, the user is authenticated, and the server is told that important piece of information.

The TorqueScript Code

We'll have to make some changes to the Torque scripts in order to be able to pass our username and password information up to the website.

Client Changes

First up, we are going to modify the client gui a bit and add a tiny bit of code to the client to support using a password.

Open the file C:\A3D\demo\client\ui\StartMissionGui.gui and replace its contents with the following:

```
new GuiChunkedBitmapCtrl(StartMissionGui) {
   profile = "GuiModelessDialogProfile";
   horizSizing = "right";
   vertSizing = "bottom";
   position = "0 0";
   extent = "800 600";
   minExtent = "8 2";
   visible = "1";
   useVariable = "0";
   tile = "0";
      helpTag = "0";
      title = "Play Demo Game";

   new GuiControl() {
      profile = "GuiBevelLoweredProfile";
      horizSizing = "width";
      vertSizing = "height";
      position = "30 105";
      extent = "740 390";
      minExtent = "8 2";
      visible = "1";
         helpTag = "0";

      new GuiControl() {
         profile = "GuiDefaultProfile";
         horizSizing = "right";
         vertSizing = "bottom";
         position = "14 255";
         extent = "229 95";
         minExtent = "8 2";
         visible = "1";
            helpTag = "0";

         new GuiTextCtrl() {
            profile = "GuiTextProfile";
            horizSizing = "right";
            vertSizing = "bottom";
```

```
      position = "17 10";
      extent = "63 18";
      minExtent = "8 8";
      visible = "1";
      text = "Player Name:";
      maxLength = "255";
         helpTag = "0";
   };
   new GuiTextEditCtrl() {
      profile = "GuiTextEditProfile";
      horizSizing = "right";
      vertSizing = "bottom";
      position = "88 11";
      extent = "134 18";
      minExtent = "8 8";
      visible = "1";
      variable = "pref::Player::Name";
      maxLength = "255";
      historySize = "0";
      password = "0";
      tabComplete = "0";
      sinkAllKeyEvents = "0";
         helpTag = "0";
   };
   new GuiTextCtrl() {
      profile = "GuiTextProfile";
      horizSizing = "right";
      vertSizing = "bottom";
      position = "8 67";
      extent = "71 18";
      minExtent = "8 2";
      visible = "1";
      text = "Create Server:";
      maxLength = "255";
   };
   new GuiCheckBoxCtrl(StartMissionGuiCheck) {
      profile = "GuiCheckBoxProfile";
      horizSizing = "right";
      vertSizing = "bottom";
```

```
            position = "88 63";
            extent = "18 30";
            minExtent = "8 2";
            visible = "1";
            text = " ";
            groupNum = "-1";
            buttonType = "ToggleButton";
        };
        new GuiTextEditCtrl() {
            profile = "GuiTextEditProfile";
            horizSizing = "right";
            vertSizing = "bottom";
            position = "88 40";
            extent = "134 18";
            minExtent = "8 8";
            visible = "1";
            variable = "pref::Player::Password";
            maxLength = "255";
            historySize = "0";
            password = "1";
            tabComplete = "0";
            sinkAllKeyEvents = "0";
                helpTag = "0";
        };
        new GuiTextCtrl() {
            profile = "GuiTextProfile";
            horizSizing = "right";
            vertSizing = "bottom";
            position = "24 39";
            extent = "53 18";
            minExtent = "8 8";
            visible = "1";
            text = "Password:";
            maxLength = "255";
                helpTag = "0";
        };
    };
    new GuiMLTextCtrl(StartMissionGuiText) {
        profile = "GuiMLTextProfile";
        horizSizing = "width";
        vertSizing = "bottom";
```

```
        position = "2 2";
        extent = "735 266";
        minExtent = "8 2";
        visible = "1";
        lineSpacing = "2";
        allowColorChars = "0";
        maxChars = "-1";
            fileName = "demo/client/ui/missions/start_fps.txt";
    };
  };
};
```

The only real change here is that we've added a password field, a label for the password field, and then modified the container object that the password field and its label appear in (which is the same container that the player name field and its tag are in). The password field has the password property set, which means that whenever you type a character in it, only an asterisk displays. That way, no one can look over your shoulder and steal your password. Figure 13.3 shows the new appearance of the StartMissionGui screen.

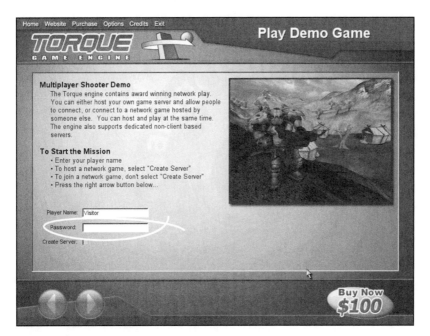

Figure 13.3 The revised StartMissionGui screen.

Server Changes

Next, we need to make a few modifications to the Torque server code. Open the file
demo/server/scripts/game.cs and enter the following code at the end of the file:

```
function GameConnection::onConnect( %client, %name, %passcrc )
{
   // Send down the connection error info, the client is
   // responsible for displaying this message if a connection
   // error occurs.
   messageClient(%client,'MsgConnectionError',"",$Pref::Server::ConnectionError);

   // Send mission information to the client
   sendLoadInfoToClient( %client );

   // if hosting this server, set this client to superAdmin
   if (%client.getAddress() $= "local") {
      %client.isAdmin = true;
      %client.isSuperAdmin = true;
   }

   // Get the client's unique id:
   // %authInfo = %client.getAuthInfo();
   // %client.guid = getField( %authInfo, 3 );
   %client.guid = 0;
   addToServerGuidList( %client.guid );
   //Store the clients passcrc
   %client.passcrc = %passcrc;
   checkClientLogin(%client, %name, %passcrc);
   //give 30 seconds for response or boot him!
   %client.loginLoop = schedule(30000, 0, "clientLoginFailed", %client);
   // Set admin status
   %client.isAdmin = false;
   %client.isSuperAdmin = false;
   // Save client preferences on the connection object for later use.
   %client.gender = "Male";
   %client.armor = "Light";
   %client.race = "Human";
   %client.skin = addTaggedString( "base" );
   %client.setPlayerName(%name);
   %client.score = 0;
```

```
$instantGroup = ServerGroup;
$instantGroup = MissionCleanup;
echo("CADD: " @ %client @ " " @ %client.getAddress());
// Inform the client of all the other clients
%count = ClientGroup.getCount();
for (%cl = 0; %cl < %count; %cl++) {
   %other = ClientGroup.getObject(%cl);
   if ((%other != %client)) {
      // These should be "silent" versions of these messages...
      messageClient(%client, 'MsgClientJoin', "",
            %other.name,
            %other,
            %other.sendGuid,
            %other.score,
            %other.isAIControlled(),
            %other.isAdmin,
            %other.isSuperAdmin);
   }
}


// Inform the client we've joined up
messageClient(%client,
   'MsgClientJoin', '\c2Welcome to the Torque demo app %1.',
   %client.name,
   %client,
   %client.sendGuid,
   %client.score,
   %client.isAiControlled(),
   %client.isAdmin,
   %client.isSuperAdmin);


// Inform all the other clients of the new guy
messageAllExcept(%client, -1, 'MsgClientJoin', '\c1%1 joined the game.',
   %client.name,
   %client,
   %client.sendGuid,
   %client.score,
   %client.isAiControlled(),
   %client.isAdmin,
   %client.isSuperAdmin);
```

```
    // If the mission is running, go ahead and download it to the client
    if ($missionRunning)
        %client.loadMission();
    $Server::PlayerCount++;
}


$AuthServer     = "localhost";    //url and port
$AuthServerPath = "/test/";       //server path

function checkClientLogin(%client, %username, %passcrc)
{
        %client.authReturned = false;
        %query          = "user="@%username@"\t"@
                          "passcrc="@%passcrc@"\r";
        %server         = $AuthServer;
        %path           = $AuthServerPath;
        %script         = %path @ "game_login.php";
        %upd = new HTTPObject(CharLogin);
        %client.sendObject = %upd;        //store object details just in case
        %upd.clientid = %client;
        %upd.get(%server, %script, %query);
}


function CharLogin::onLine( %this, %line )
{
        %client = %this.clientid;
        //Check if webpage returns the word Verified on the first line
        if(StrStr(%line, "Verified") != -1)
        {
                cancel(%client.loginLoop);
                return;
        }

        //otherwise, auth failed!
        error("- ",%line);
        clientLoginFailed(%client);
}
```

```
function CharLogin::onConnectionDied( %this )
{
        %client = %this.clientid;
        clientLoginFailed(%client);
}

function CharLogin::onDNSFailed( %this )
{
        %client = %this.clientid;
        clientLoginFailed(%client);
}

function CharLogin::onConnectFailed( %this )
{
        %client = %this.clientid;
        clientLoginFailed(%client);
}

function clientLoginFailed(%client)
{
        //Do what you want to with him.  Auth failed.
        //(This is bad code, you want to improve it)
        %client.delete();
}
```

Now code somewhat similar to this, with some of the same function and method names, can be found in common\server\clientConnection.cs. We are *overriding* that code in clientConnection.cs with this code. When the time comes, our new code will be executed instead of the original version.

Our code in game.cs accepts the player name and password embedded in the same string, as it arrives at the server from the client at connection time. Our code extracts the two pieces of information and verifies that the username is well formed and valid. It then encodes the password with the crc32 one-way encoding, creates a new HTTP object, builds the player name and password into the query, and ships it out onto the net and onto your Apache server (wherever it may be). It then waits for a response from the web server, and if it is favorable, lets the player continue onto the server to play.

The code assumes that you've already set up the server, as shown earlier in this chapter in the section "The PHP Authentication Code." Make sure to replace `localhost` with the domain name of your server, or its IP address. If you specify the IP address, make sure you also specify the port, like this: 192.168.0.2:80, where :80 indicates the port number.

Also, make sure that you have the ports 28000 open for incoming and outgoing connections on your router or firewall if you have one.

Testing

To test this, you need to run two versions of Torque, one in dedicated server mode, and one as a client. First, launch the dedicated server by creating a shortcut with the following text in the field below "Type the location of the item:"

```
demo.exe -dedicated -mod fps -mission "demo/data/missions/fps.mis"
```

You could also put that command in a batch file in the Torque demo folder, or even just type it in from a command line. When the server is up and running, it will initiate a conversation with the GarageGames master server.

Next, make sure you have Apache running on your server, and launch your Torque application into the FPS demo `StartMissionGui` screen. Make sure that the CreateServer checkbox is *not* checked. Enter your player name and password (assuming they match any database setup you've done). Then click the right arrow, locate your server from the list (if your server is running on the same computer, or on your home LAN, then click Query LAN), and then join that server.

The authentication process will happen behind the scenes, invisible to your prying eyes. You should also test it by trying an incorrect password or an invalid username, and various combinations of both.

Moving Right Along

Okay, interesting chapter! You've installed Apache and PHP on your computer, setting up your own little dynamic-content-capable web server.

You've seen how you can use web services to push information up to the Net, as well as pull it down from the Internet. You've had a glimpse at how you can use online services in a larger way for player authentication.

I'm sure your head is already buzzing with all sorts of ideas about where to go with this: online statistics sites, server locators, a replacement master server design of your own, and so on.

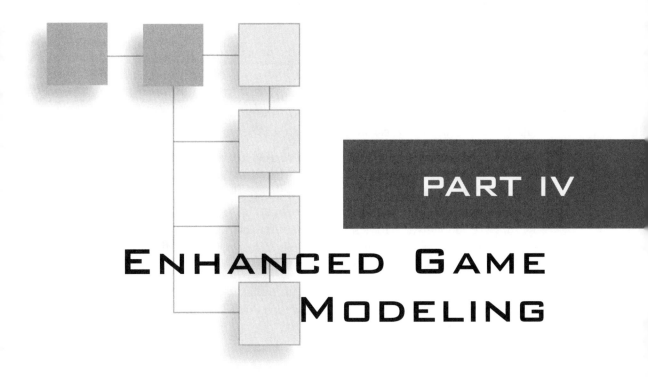

PART IV

ENHANCED GAME MODELING

I n these final chapters of the book, we are going to examine some techniques and features we can apply to our games to bring a certain degree of polish and completeness.

These include creating our models in ways that maximize the rendering performance of our game engine. In certain "low-intensity" games, where the action may not be extremely vigorous, high frame rates may not be much of an issue. In other games, like "twitchy" first-person shooters, the player's frame rate might make the difference between virtual life and death. We're going to utilize some techniques that will address the frame rate issue from a game developer's perspective.

Another area of polish is that of *content creation*. Some games, like RPGs, and certain variations of RTS and Adventure games might need a great deal of visual variety to keep players from getting bored with seeing the same things over and over again. It's rare that a game will have *completely* continuously exciting or engaging game play. During those times when the action or interest is liable to wane somewhat, if we have sufficiently varied content, we can head off incipient ennui before it has the chance to sink its grubby little claws into our players and drag them off to the TV set to watch "Dialing for Donuts" or "Survivor: Staff Meeting."

One method we can use to enhance our content variety is to mix and match models with textures both at the time of level creation and in real-time during a game session. We'll spend a chapter learning how to do that in the pages ahead.

Lighting, especially lighting indoor areas, can be used to tweak the mood and the pacing of gameplay. This is particularly effective when there are great contrasts in lighting that can be used to good effect. Imagine trying to chase down some enemy on a brightly lit sunny day—he ducks into a nearby building, you crash through the doors after him and suddenly… darkness. Ahead and to the left is a dim bulb at the end of a long dark hallway; all else is enveloped in black shadow. Where did he go? And is he still carrying that lead pipe? What do I do now?

As you'll see, lighting is also another tool we can employ to enhance variety. By reusing existing models with variations in lighting, we can create entirely new locales with a minimum of extra effort.

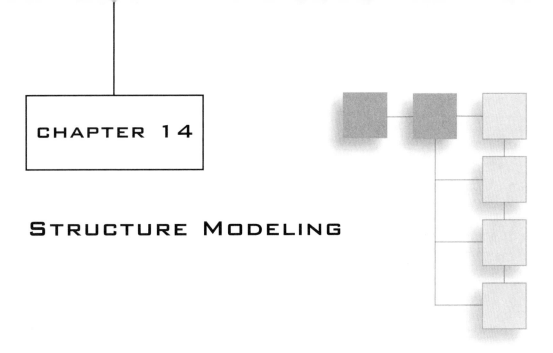

CHAPTER 14

STRUCTURE MODELING

As I've pointed out in this book, and in *3D Game Programming All in One*, and as others have said elsewhere, a large part of a game's success (outside of gameplay) derives from its ability to render scenes smoothly at fairly high frame rates.

Of course, there are several factors at play in the frame rate arena: the CPU speed of the player's computer, available system RAM, and the capabilities of the computer's video adapter, to name three hardware factors. Hardware keeps getting faster and more capable, but as it does so, game developers keep "pushing the outside of the envelope" in their attempts to deliver a more immersive and exciting game experience.

As a developer, you can't completely dictate, nor predict, the hardware configuration your game's players will have. There will certainly be a wide variation, unless you are developing console, PDA, or telephone games. But, there are some things you can do to mitigate variations in hardware to provide the best rendering performance possible and keep those frame rates up there.

In this chapter, we are going to use a technique called *LOD* (level of detail) modeling to help maintain, or even improve, our frame rates. This is an approach that is offered by most professional-grade game engines, like Torque, and supported by most of the better CSG modeling tools, like Hammer, qRadiant, and QuArK. We won't focus on any particular modeling tools here—all of the techniques can be employed in any of them. We will get into some specifics about map2dif, however; it's the conversion tool that lets us create Torque .DIF models from .MAP models that most game-oriented CSG tools can generate. Please consult the documentation for the modeling tool of your choice for guidance as needed, or visit http://www.garagegames.com/ makegames/ and ask for help in the Modeling forums.

As a courtesy, The CSG modeling tool QuArK 6.3 has been included on the CD in the TOOLS folder, along with Mini-Python (a tool that Quark needs) and a short reference document (an excerpt from a *3D Game Programming All in One* chapter). You will need to ensure that you've set up QuArK correctly for use with Torque. If you need help, go to the GarageGames forums at http://www.garagegames.com/ mg/forums/result.forum.php?qf=136.

There is also a clickable html link shortcut provided in the TOOLS\QuArK folder.

Note

More taxing terminology! In game development circles what you create are often called *rooms*. This fetches back to the early days of first-person shooter games, like *Castle Wolfenstein* and *Doom* where everything was a room. There were no outdoor areas and therefore no external terrain. Then along came *Quake* from id Software and the word *map* was introduced to describe their *levels*. Clear as mud?

GarageGames calls these creations *interiors* (which fetches back to the term *rooms* in a way) in Torque. I usually use the word *structure*, which I think is both pithy and generic at the same time. My use of structure can encompass room, map, and interior as each is used in its respective context, while still also applying to things like bridges and guard towers.

So, room = map = level = interior = structure.

In any event, the common source format for the files that most structure modelers will be dealing with is .MAP, a text file format. Although most of the modeling tools like Hammer and QuArK have their own native format, they all import and export .MAP files. The added little wrinkle is that you should check your tool's documentation to ensure that the .MAP exporter creates the output in "Valve 220" format. Hammer does this by default, and the Torque-ready version of QuArK provides a menu option to specify this format. Most other tools also support Valve 220, but you should double-check to be sure.

The compiled, game-ready version of your structure will be in .DIF, a binary format, generated by map2dif, a Torque tool that we'll look at later.

So, .MAP is our *source* format and .DIF is our *compiled* or *binary* format.

Levels of Detail

The more polygons we have in our scene, the more work the computer and the graphics adapter have to do to render the scene. There comes a point where one or both of those hardware systems begin to have trouble keeping up with the action. When this happens, the scene rendering becomes "jerky" or "twitchy."

A Demonstration

To help you get a handle on this, let's poke around in the Torque demo for a bit. Launch the demo, and run the FPS demo, making sure to check the Create Server checkbox.

Open the console window, and type **metrics(fps);** (don't forget that semicolon!), then hit Enter. Close the console window, and you will see a frame rate display in the upper left corner of your screen, as shown in Figure 14.1. Your numbers will likely be different.

Figure 14.1 The frame rate display.

On the left side, *FPS* indicates frames per second. On the right side, *mspf* indicates milliseconds per frame, with a millisecond being one one-thousandth of a second. These are two opposing views of the same information: At that time, in that scene, with that particular view, FPS and mspf indicate how quickly the Torque renderer can draw all of the visible objects in the scene, as well as perform all of the other processing it has to handle (like network requests and updates, AI computations, user inputs, and so on).

The more stuff there is for Torque to think about and draw, the lower the frame rate is going to be. Look at Figure 14.2. This screenshot is taken in a different part of the game world. You can see that there are a lot more things in the scene for Torque to handle, and you can see that the frame rate has dropped significantly—about a 30% or more reduction.

Figure 14.2 More objects—lower frame rate.

Take some time to run around the game world, and look at the effects that various views have on your frame rate. If you happen to switch into the Mission Editor, you will have to exit the Mission Editor and then turn the frame rate display back on again using the metrics(fps); command in the console.

When you've had your fill, exit the demo and the game. Now we'll set up a little of a stress test, to make the point more dramatically.

Step One

In the folder \A3D\demo\data\missions, locate the file fps.mis and rename it ofps.mis (prefixing "o" for original). Now we're going to replace it with a stressful version. In RESOURCES\ch14 find the file stress.mis and rename it to fps.mis, and then copy it into \A3D\demo\data\missions.

Step Two

Launch the demo and start the FPS demo server. You will notice that the load screen will take considerably longer, especially in the lighting phase. This is because I've put 56 additional copies of the greathall structure in the stress mission. That's the big granite building with the archways and pillars and the open courtyard inside. This was just a quick way to introduce a whole whack of polygons in the scene without a lot of fuss. It takes a while for the engine to "burn in" the shadows and stuff generated by all those buildings.

After the demo loads, press F8 to get yourself into camera fly mode, and head out to the dock on the lakeshore, look straight down, and then go backwards up into the sky until you see about three or four greathall buildings in your view below you. Now look up and back inland to where the quaint little huts are, and your scene will be chock-a-block full of greathalls. Open the console window, and use the `metrics(fps);` command to get your frame rate display up. When I did this, I got a frame rate of around 45 fps, as you can see in Figure 14.3.

Take some time to zoom around in player mode or camera fly mode, and you will see that your frame rate, for the most part, will stay within 10 or 15 percent of your initial rate. Of course, different people will get different results. An older video adapter might be somewhat lower than the 45 fps I got. The important thing here is the difference between this frame rate and what we are going to do next. When you've seen enough, exit the demo.

Step Three

In the folder \A3D\demo\data\interiors\room, locate the file greathall.dif and rename it to ogreathall.dif. In RESOURCES\ch14 find the file notsogreathall.dif and rename it to greathall.dif and copy it into \A3D\demo\data\interiors\room.

We've replaced the greathall structure with a different version.

FPS: 45.2 mspf: 22.1239 e demo app CERDIP.

Figure 14.3 Crowded scene.

Step Four

Launch the demo again. Notice how much longer the load time is. You'll have to be very patient this time. It *is* a stress test, after all. Eventually, you'll be plunked down into the game.

If you have an older video adapter you will immediately see a difference. The screen might even be slow to refresh. As you move your player around, you will notice pauses between each frame. They may be for only a fraction of a second to as long as a few seconds. If you can, make your way back over to dock and repeat the positioning maneuver: Look straight down, then go backwards to go up until you have four or five greathall buildings in your view. You might notice that when you are looking straight down your frame rate improves considerably. This is because the engine doesn't have as many objects in the scene to draw. When you get to altitude, and look back over the village, your fps should plummet again. Turn on your metrics display, and take a look.

Figure 14.4 shows my results—a measly 2.7 frames per second!

Figure 14.4 Extremely slow crowded scene.

It's pretty painful to try to operate in this environment, so as soon as you can, exit the game.

That, my friends, is a low frame rate. And of course, you are wondering, what is the difference? After all, the buildings look *exactly* the same, and the scene wasn't changed at all between the 45 fps test and the 2.7 fps test. Well, the buildings *are* exactly the same between the tests except for one important detail: In the 45 fps test, the greathall (which is the one that comes with the standard demo) had *five* levels of detail in its model, while the 2.7 fps version (one I made especially for this demonstration) had only *one*.

Levels of Detail

Here's the scoop. In the standard greathall, the artist at GarageGames who made it actually created five different versions of the hall. He started out with a fully detailed version with all the nooks and crannies. Every brush, and therefore every polygon, was present. This is the detail level 0 version. Figure 14.5 shows the model at level 0. All the brushes, portals, and lights are there. The model has 5082 faces contained in 927 brushes, with 9 different textures.

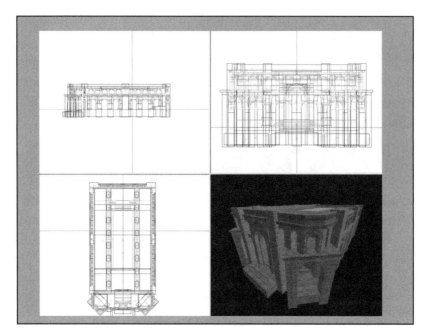

Figure 14.5 The greathall at detail level 0.

Now when we are inside wandering the hallways, or outside and nearby, this is the amount of detail that we want in the model. The more detail, the better the model, and the better the model, the more substantial the immersive effect. Both the standard greathall.dif and the notsogreathall.dif models had this detail level.

However, as you've just witnessed in the demonstration, when you get a large enough number of buildings like this in a scene at the same time—like you would get in a city, for example—all those polygons begin to drag the engine down.

The level 0 detail is the only level in notsogreathall.dif. Wherever you see the notso-greathall, you see the whole thing, even if it is so far away that you can't really make out any details; the details are still there, and still being computed and rendered by the game engine and video card.

That is not the case with the standard greathall, though. The artist has created five versions of the hall, each version with less detail than the last. As the player moves farther away from a model, the engine examines the size of the model with respect to the player's view, and swaps in the version that's appropriate for the distance. The artist specifies the maximum number of pixels in on-screen rendered height for the model that each detail level will support, and the engine uses that information to determine which model to use.

Figure 14.6 shows the level 1 version of the standard greathall. You might have some trouble figuring out where the differences are, but this version has only 4378 faces compared to the level 0 version with 5082—a difference of just over 700 faces. And because there are two triangles per face, that's around 1400 polygons. *For one model!*

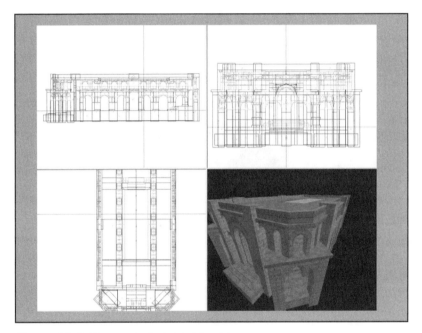

Figure 14.6 The greathall at detail level 1.

The level 0 model was created with a pixel height of 500. This means that as you move away from the model, it grows smaller in the view. When the model's apparent size on the screen shrinks to less than 500 pixels high, the engine swaps that model out and replaces it with the level 1 model. In doing so, it just relieved itself of the need to worry about approximately 700 faces.

Now, as you continue to move away, the engine knows that the level 1 model is set to a pixel height of 250. When the model gets 1 pixel smaller in height than 250, the level 2 version is swapped in. The level 2 version has only 2239 faces.

At 80 pixels in height, level 2 is dropped and level 3 is brought in, with its 1215 faces. At 40 pixels, level 3 is dropped, and the last detail level is swapped in. Detail level 4 has only 1103 faces in it. Figure 14.7 depicts the LOD 4 model. The visual difference between LOD 4 and LOD 0 is fairly obvious, whereas the differences between adjacent LODs weren't so readily detected.

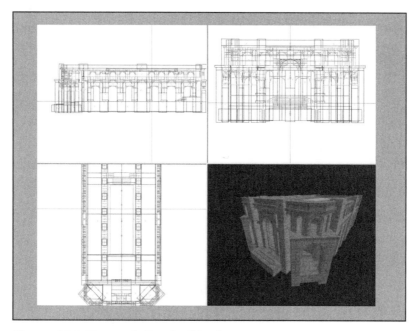

Figure 14.7 The greathall at detail level 4.

Implementation

Creating LODs for use in Torque is pretty straightforward. First, get your highest detail model right, before moving on to create your other detail levels. Once you are happy with the LOD 0 model, save your work exported as a .MAP file type (in Valve 220 format—consult your modeling tool's documentation if necessary) with a name like mymodel_0.map. Whatever filename you choose for the level 0 version, append "_0" to the end of the first part of the filename. You need to make sure that you've specified the pixel height according to your modeling tool's methods, and also that you've specified the detail index somewhere. The detail index (sometimes called the "detail number" or the "detail level") should be exactly the same as the appended number in the filename for a given model.

Then run the map2dif.exe program: To do this you will need to open a command prompt in the folder where your models are located, and either copy the map2dif.exe file from the TOOLS folder of the CD into the same folder or copy map2dif.exe to another folder on the hard drive, and make sure your Windows PATH variable has that folder in it (consult your Windows Help for the version of Windows that you are using on how to do this).

The general form of the map2dif syntax looks like this:

```
map2dif -o outputDirectory -t textureDirectory mymodel_0.map
```

The `outputDirectory` part of the command line indicates where the folder (or directory) is in which you want the processed .DIF file to be placed. It can be a full path or a relative path. If you want to specify the current directory, just use "." (a period). For the level above the current directory, use ".." (two periods).

The `textureDirectory` is the place where the map2dif tool will find your textures. Some modeling tools like Hammer use a thing called a *wad* file that has all of the textures stuffed inside it, whereas QuArK doesn't do that. If your modeling tool uses a wad file, you need to make sure you *also* have your textures available in a folder somewhere so that you can tell map2dif where to find them.

See Table 14.1 for a more detailed explanation of the map2dif command line switches.

Table 14.1 Movement Vectors

Switch	Description
-p	Include a preview bitmap in the interior file
-d	Process only the detail specified on the command line
-l	Process as a low detail shape (implies -s)
-h	Process for final build (exhaustive BSP search)
-g	Generate navigation graph info
-e	Do extrusion test
-s	Don't search for textures in parent dir
-n	Noisy error/statistic reporting
-q *ver*	Quake map file version (2, 3)
-o *dir*	Directory in which to place the .dif file
-t *dir*	Location of textures

A simple approach to setting up the folders for output and textures would be to place all of your textures in \A3D\demo\data\interiors\ and use that path as your textureDirectory argument to map2dif, and to set the outputDirectory argument to that same path or to a subfolder on the path. When TGE runs and needs to find textures for structures (models that are converted to .DIF format, also called *interiors*), it will look in the folder where the .DIF file is located, and if it doesn't find the texture, it will look in the parent folder and keep moving up to each parent until it gets to the \A3D\demo\data\interiors\ folder, or it finds the texture.

Given all of that, your command line will probably generally look like this:

```
map2dif -o \A3D\demo\data\interiors\room\ -t \A3D\demo\data\interiors\mymodel_0.map
```

But don't do anything yet! If you want to work from the models and textures I've supplied in the RESOURCES/ch14 folder, you can do that. I've included map2dif.exe in that folder. I've also included very slightly modified and renamed versions of the stock greathall files, called gh_0.map, gh_1.map, gh_2.map, gh_3.map, and gh_4.map, so that you can do this exercise without interfering with the greathall that is already included in the game world. The modification I made is there to help you see when some of the detail changes happen when using the structure in the game. To compile the gh version of the greathall with all of its detail levels for use in the demo, open a command window, change to the RESOURCES/ch14 folder, and type this command:

```
cd \A3D\RESOURCES\ch14
```

and then run map2dif:

```
map2dif -o ..\..\demo\data\interiors\room\ -t . gh_0.map
```

Because the textures are located in the ch14 folder, you only need to specify the current directory using the dot.

Tip

There is also a version of map2dif included in the TOOLS folder called map2dif_DEBUG.exe. This version provides extra information that might be useful if you are having problems with some of the .MAP files not processing correctly. However, it does run slower, and probably shouldn't be used for your finalized work. Both of these versions of map2dif are provided as part of the stock Torque Game Engine (TGE) Software Development Kit (SDK) that you get when you buy a license for the TGE SDK.

You will see a great deal of output on your command line screen; it should look like this (with blank lines omitted):

```
Successfully opened map file: gh_0.map
  Parsing mapfile...done.
  Creating BSP...done.
  Marking active zones...done
  Creating surfaces...done.
  Lightmaps: Normal...
  * Number of ambiguous planes (dropped):  13
Alarm...done.
  Resorting and Packing LightMaps...done.
  STATISTICS
   - Total brushes:      927
     + structural:       251
     + detail:           674
     + portal:           2
   - Number of zones:    2
   - Number of surfaces: 3171
  ** ***   WARNING WARNING WARNING  *** **
  *** **   WARNING WARNING WARNING  ** ***
  Errors exist in this interior.  Please use the debug rendering modes
   to find and correct the following problems:
  * Ambiguous brushes: 0
  * Orphaned Polygons: 24
  *** **   WARNING WARNING WARNING  ** ***
  ** ***   WARNING WARNING WARNING  *** **
  Exporting to runtime...done.
Successfully opened map file: gh_1.map
  Parsing mapfile...done.
  Creating BSP...done.
  Marking active zones...done
  Creating surfaces...done.
  Lightmaps: Normal...
  * Number of ambiguous planes (dropped):  7
Alarm...done.
  Resorting and Packing LightMaps...done.
  STATISTICS
   - Total brushes:      790
     + structural:       243
```

```
    + detail:          545
    + portal:          2
  - Number of zones:   3
  - Number of surfaces: 2791
  ** ***  WARNING WARNING WARNING  *** **
  *** **  WARNING WARNING WARNING  ** ***
   Errors exist in this interior.  Please use the debug rendering modes
    to find and correct the following problems:
   * Ambiguous brushes: 0
   * Orphaned Polygons: 38
  *** **  WARNING WARNING WARNING  ** ***
  ** ***  WARNING WARNING WARNING  *** **
  Exporting to runtime...done.
Successfully opened map file: gh_2.map
  Parsing mapfile...done.
  Creating BSP...done.
  Marking active zones...done
  Creating surfaces...done.
  Lightmaps: Normal...Alarm...done.
  Resorting and Packing LightMaps...done.
  STATISTICS
  - Total brushes:     396
    + structural:      234
    + detail:          160
    + portal:          2
  - Number of zones:   2
  - Number of surfaces: 1849
  ** ***  WARNING WARNING WARNING  *** **
  *** **  WARNING WARNING WARNING  ** ***
   Errors exist in this interior.  Please use the debug rendering modes
    to find and correct the following problems:
   * Ambiguous brushes: 0
   * Orphaned Polygons: 52
*** **  WARNING WARNING WARNING  ** ***
  ** ***  WARNING WARNING WARNING  *** **
  Exporting to runtime...done.
Successfully opened map file: gh_3.map
  Parsing mapfile...done.
  Creating BSP...done.
```

```
Marking active zones...done
Creating surfaces...done.
Lightmaps: Normal...Alarm...done.
Resorting and Packing LightMaps...done.
STATISTICS
 - Total brushes:      210
   + structural:       150
   + detail:           58
   + portal:           2
 - Number of zones:    5
 - Number of surfaces: 1057
 ** ***   WARNING WARNING WARNING  *** **
 *** **   WARNING WARNING WARNING  ** ***
  Errors exist in this interior.  Please use the debug rendering modes
   to find and correct the following problems:
  * Ambiguous brushes: 0
  * Orphaned Polygons: 86
*** **   WARNING WARNING WARNING  ** ***
 ** ***   WARNING WARNING WARNING  *** **
 Exporting to runtime...done.
Successfully opened map file: gh_4.map
 Parsing mapfile...done.
 Creating BSP...done.
 Marking active zones...done
 Creating surfaces...done.
 Lightmaps: Normal...Alarm...done.
 Resorting and Packing LightMaps...done.
 STATISTICS
  - Total brushes:      190
    + structural:       141
    + detail:           47
    + portal:           2
  - Number of zones:    4
  - Number of surfaces: 922
  ** ***   WARNING WARNING WARNING  *** **
  *** **   WARNING WARNING WARNING  ** ***
   Errors exist in this interior.  Please use the debug rendering modes
    to find and correct the following problems:
   * Ambiguous brushes: 0
   * Orphaned Polygons: 117
```

```
*** **  WARNING WARNING WARNING  ** ***
  ** ***  WARNING WARNING WARNING  *** **
 Exporting to runtime...done.
Writing Resource: persist..(../../demo/data/interiors/room/gh.dif) Done.
```

The key line here is the last one. If it says Writing Resource…Done, then the object was compiled and deposited in the indicated folder.

As you can see from looking at the listing, there are some errors in the model. In each detail level of the map there are some minor problems with "orphaned polygons" from some of the brushes. These don't have any serious effect on the resulting object. Orphaned polygons are those that end up not part of any brush. When they are detected, they are removed from the data stream by map2dif and so will not cause your structure any problems in the game.

The same goes for "ambiguous planes," which happens when different brushes have exactly the same surface defined. The tool picks one of them and tosses the other one overboard.

As you can see, the tool starts with the highest level of detail file, and keeps on adding LOD indices to the file name until all the files have been processed. It will combine all the levels of detail for the greathall structure, produce a single output file called gh.dif, and deposit it in the \A3D\demo\data\interiors\room folder. Let's check it out:

1. Run the FPS demo, switch to camera fly mode (F8), go up a little bit in altitude, and aim your cursor to a point in the game world where you want the gh structure to be. A good place to go would be next to the original greathall; park yourself on the side where the water is and aim your crosshair to the open area on the side.

2. Open the Mission Editor with F11.

3. Open the World Editor Creator by pressing F4.

4. From the tree list on the bottom right, open the Interiors group by clicking on the little plus sign to its left. Then drill down through the demo, data, and interiors, and you will see gh listed in blue.

5. Click once on the gh entry in the interiors group list. Your building will plop down at the spot where your cursor intersects the terrain. The building will be black, with no textures.

6. Press ALT+L. This will relight the scene, and your building's textures will appear in all their glory.

Now go and zoom around the scene in camera fly mode, keeping an eye on the gh version of the greathall that you placed. Can you see the detail levels change? Ha! You probably noticed it as soon as you planted your gh building, didn't you? Yes, I added some simple stone columns above the roof of each detail level, one column for each detail index number. Obviously, there is none for level 0, the main detail level. Figure 14.8 shows the gh structure in a good spot.

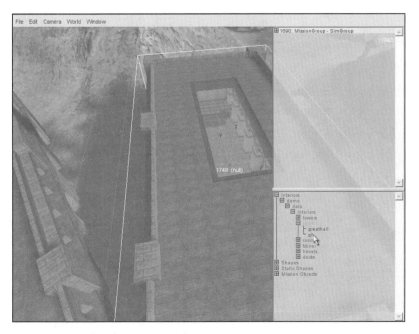

Figure 14.8 The gh structure *in loco.*

Try looking at the two buildings, the original greathall and your gh structure, from about 50 feet in the air or so, out over the docks. Then fly backwards out over the lake watching the two buildings. See if you can notice the LOD change as you back up. Of course, those honkin' great pillars on top of the gh structure obviously change, and should provide good cues about when to look. Ideally, you should not see any change at all.

You'll probably also notice that you won't see all of the detail levels before the buildings disappear in the fog.

After you've finished poking and prodding at everything and are ready to move on, make sure you quit the demo. It might be a good idea to save your mission so that your building placements are preserved.

The Devil's in the Details

Okay, so we've established that levels of detail are seriously useful things. Well, how about not so seriously useful? Can they be that?

Let's have a little fun.

Step One

Open \A3D\demo\server\scripts\game.cs and locate the function onServerCreated and add this line to the end of the function after the other statements.

```
exec("./details.cs");
```

Save your work.

Step Two

Open the file \A3D\demo\client\config.cs and then place the following lines of code at the end of the file:

```
moveMap.bindCmd(keyboard, "f", "commandToServer(\'FargleStart\');", "");
moveMap.bindCmd(keyboard, "ctrl f", "commandToServer(\'FargleStop\');", "");
```

If you want to keep these key bindings as defaults that won't get blown away when the user opens the control mapping dialog in the Options screen, then you should also place the same statements at the end of \A3D\demo\client\scripts\default.bind.cs.

Save your work.

Step Three

Next, type in the following contents, and then save as a new file, \A3D\demo\server\scripts\details.cs:

```
function findMissionGroupObject(%filename)
{
   warn ("looking for building:"@%filename);
   %count = Buildings.getCount();
   %target = 0;
```

```
   for(%i = 0; %i < %count; %i++)
   {
      %found = MissionGroup.getObject(%i);
      warn("id:"@%i@"-"@%found.interiorFile);
      if (%found.interiorFile $= %filename)
      {
      %target = %found;
      break;
      }
   }
   return %target;
}


function serverCmdFargleStart(%client)
{
   %bldg = findMissionGroupObject("demo/data/interiors/room/gh.dif");
        %bldg.fargleState=true;
   %bldg.schedule(1000, "Fargle", %bldg);
}


function serverCmdFargleStop(%client)
{
   %bldg = findMissionGroupObject ("demo/data/interiors/room/gh.dif");
        %bldg.fargleState=false;
}


function InteriorInstance::Fargle(%theDatablock, %whichBldg)
{
  error ("FFFAAAARRRGGGGLLINGGGG!!!!");
  %dl = GetRandom(%whichBldg.getNumDetailLevels());
  %whichBldg.setDetailLevel(%dl);
  if (%whichBldg.fargleState==true)
     %whichBldg.schedule(1000, "Fargle", %whichBldg);
  else
     echo("Fargle Halted. Bummer.");
}
```

Step Four

Hop into the demo. If you still don't have a gh structure placed in the FPS mission map, then add one in somewhere. Position yourself so that you can watch it.

Press the Fargle key ("F") and watch the farglin'. Press the Stop Fargling key (CTRL+F) and it stops. You can continue to start and stop it to your heart's content. Exit the demo when your heart is officially content.

The program code that you typed in has many similarities to code you've worked with elsewhere. The findMissionGroupObject function is similar to the findBuilding function you encountered back in Part I, except this time it looks for the named structure in the MissionGroup, instead of within the Building's SimGroup. You've also seen the schedule method in action for other objects, most notably the swinging and sliding doors.

The key code is where the setDetailLevel method of the InteriorInstance class is used to arbitrarily set the detail level, rather than allow it to be slaved to the relative distance of the player to the building. This simple little method opens up some gameplay potential. One quick example that comes to mind is to reserve one or two high-indexed detail levels for use as damaged or destroyed state models. If you set the index higher than your lowest usable detailed level, with a pixel height set to a ridiculously low value, like two or one, then when the building takes damage, you can fire off some particle pyrotechnics, and set the building to a reserved LOD that shows the building as destroyed.

There are other potentials as well, like animated .DIF structures: draw bridges, anyone?

Entities

Entities are parts of .MAP-type models that are not brushes. Remember that brushes are used to define our actual structure. But there are some features we want to add to the model that aren't actually structural. Portals and lights are two very common entities used by pretty much every professional game engine out there.

Portals

Portals are special solid objects inserted into the structure that are used to isolate one area of a structure from the other. This is done to help the renderer decide what to render, and how to light the brushes that it does render. A simple example is a door on a one-room building. Take a look at the two buildings in Figure 14.9.

Figure 14.9 Two buildings, one with a portal and one without.

One of these buildings has a portal in the doorway, and the other does not. Guess which is which?

The building on the right has the portal. Notice how dark the interior is. That is because the portal blocks out ambient light from the sun that lights the scene (the same light that casts the shadows on the ground beside the buildings or shades the walls depending on how they are oriented). Your modeling tool will provide you with an option to change this, to allow the ambient light to pass through the portal, and then the right-hand building's interior will look the same as the other.

But portals work with more than lighting. In fact, the reason for their invention in the first place was to help the game engine figure out what to render and what to ignore. If you have a large interior scene with lots of cool architecture and fiddly bits, you could end up with too many polygons for your poor overburdened video card.

And yet, when you are standing in one room, the renderer really doesn't need to *think* about drawing the contents of a room two doors down the corridor—nor the contents of the five floors above you that you can't see from here. Portals are used to divide the interior into areas that the engine can check easily to see if they are visible from where the player's eyeball is. Whole regions, or *zones* can be quickly eliminated from any consideration by the renderer, saving great gobs of processing time.

In general practice, it's a good idea to put a portal on every exterior door and window, and at most internal entrances or doorways, including openings in floors where stairwells go up or down. Then the engine only has to draw those polygons that absolutely *must* be drawn.

A Demonstration

C'mon, let's do a simple demonstration. In your RESOURCES\ch14 folder are the .DIF files for the two buildings I showed you in Figure 14.9, buildingA.dif and buildingB.dif. Copy them into the \A3D\demo\data\interiors\room folder (they need the textures that are found in there) and then launch the demo. Place the buildings side by side somewhere, and remember to relight the scene with the ALT+L key combination while you are still in the Mission Editor, after you've placed the buildings. Then exit the Editor and take your player over to in front of buildingA (the one that does not have a dark shadowy interior). Now turn on your fps display (open the console window with ~ and type **metrics(fps);** followed by Enter).

Notice your frame rate. Standing in front of buildingA, I got about 100 to 120 fps depending on which way I looked, as you can see in Figure 14.10. Your mileage may vary. Now run up into buildingA and look all around. You'll see that your fps stays in the same range as when you were outside. buildingA doesn't have portals. Now run out and over into buildingB. Now look back out the door from inside. Your frame rate should still be in the same ballpark as before.

Figure 14.10 Frame rate outside (left) and inside (right) buildingA.

But here it comes: Slowly turn your avatar to one side or the other while watching your frame rate. Watch what happens as soon as the door and the exterior contents of the game world visible through it move out of your view. See that? My frame rate more than *doubles* to well over 200 fps inside buildingB when I'm not looking out the door! See Figure 14.11.

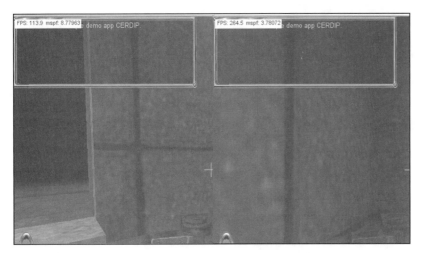

Figure 14.11 Frame rate outside (left) and inside (right) buildingB.

The advantages of portals really come to the fore when you have large interior areas, like office buildings and super-secret hidden underground bases and things like that.

Creating and Placing Portals

Portals start out as brushes that you convert into portal entities. A portal should be slightly larger than the opening that it covers. You also need to ensure that you keep your portals thin, to minimize the chances that some part of the portal will protrude into "open air" and thus cause a *light leak*. In fact, light is not the only thing that leaks if the portal is not done right—the zone division that helps the engine keep the frame rate up will also be negated. So, one must be careful when placing portals.

Figure 14.12 shows how the portal is placed in the doorway of buildingB. Note how every single edge of the solid shape that forms the portal entity is embedded inside a normal brush.

There is also a portal in the lone window in that building, as shown in Figure 14.13.

Now it may be that not all game engines require this overlap, but many do, and TGE certainly does.

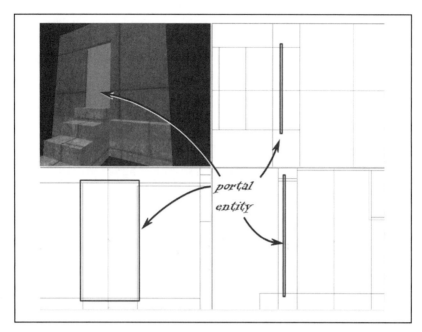

Figure 14.12 Door portal placement.

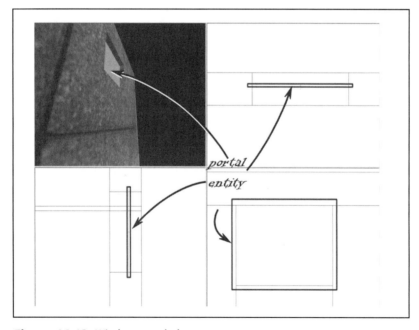

Figure 14.13 Window portal placement.

Lights

No discussion of portals in interior structures is complete without touching on the lighting. As you've seen, portals allow us to completely block out lighting from the external scene lighting source, typically the sun.

Once we've done that, we need to use interior lights to achieve the visibility and mood effects we want. There are several light types that are supported in Torque .DIF interiors; Table 14.2 lists the supported light entities with a brief description.

Table 14.2 Interior Lights

Entity	Type	Description
strobe	*animated*	Instantaneously switches between two color values at a specified rate.
flicker	*animated*	Instantaneously switches through five color values at a specified rate.
omni	*static*	Point source with light radiating in all directions (omni-directional).
pulse	*animated*	Gradually changes between two color values at a specified rate.
pulse2	*animated*	Gradually cycles through four color values at a specified rate.
runway	*animated*	Light moves in a step-wise fashion from origin to a target (and back).
spot	*static*	Projects light in a direction specified by a target.

Most of the light entities are animated—that is, they change their appearance over time. For example the `strobe` light entity can be set to behave exactly like a real life strobe light: flashing on and off in a fraction of a second or over a period of several seconds (or even longer), over and over.

There are various properties for the lights that you can set in your modeling program. All light types support `color`, `falloff1`, and `falloff2`.

`Color` is fairly obvious: it's a tuple of red-green-blue (RGB) values, each ranging from 0 to 255. If all three are zero (0 0 0), then you will end up with black. If all three are at maximum (255 255 255), then you will end up with full white. Table 14.3 shows the various basic colors and the tuples that will create them.

Table 14.3 RGB Values for Lights

Color	red-green-blue values
black	0 0 0.
white	255 255 255
red	255 0 0
green	0 255 0
blue	0 0 255
cyan	0 255 255
magenta	255 0 255
yellow	255 255 0
orange	255 128 0
pink	255 0 128
purple	128 0 255

Of course, there are many other hues and shades between those basic colors, which you can obtain by varying the RGB values using settings somewhere between 0 and 255.

The two falloff settings specify the range of space over which the lights will appear to fade. falloff1 is the distance from the light source where the maximum light intensity starts to decline, and falloff2 is the distance at which the projected light reaches zero.

For Alarm Type settings, use Normal only for Torque for all light types.

Static Lights

Static lights are light entities that do not ever automatically change. This means that they are often used to simulate natural lighting that takes place indoors, such as lighting that comes in from windows, skylights, lamps, machinery, and brightly lit work areas.

Omni

The omni light is probably the most used light type, commonly used for things like lighting the inside of open doorways, under windows, and other interior lighting purposes.

Place an omni light in your interior structure, and it will radiate light in all directions in a spherical (omni-directional) manner. Quite easy to use.

You can also place omni lights (and all other lights) outside a building, or on any other structure that does not have portals. The light won't be brightly visible, but you can use it to alter the colors of exterior textures for more variety. I like to add green-hued omni lights on the outside of castle walls to give a hint of moss.

Spot

Spot lights are directed (something like focused) light sources. You place the entity as a point source of the light, and then another entity, called a target, at a location in the direction you want the spot light to project. You specify the name of the target entity in the `target` property. Do make sure that all of your target entities in an interior structure are uniquely named or you will have problems.

The distance properties of a spot light are used to specify the spread of the light cone. The `distance1` property is the diameter of the light beam at the `falloff1` distance from the light source. `Distance1` is the diameter at the `falloff2` distance from the light source.

Spot lights can be used for any kind of indoor lighting that would have a directed beam: focused "pot" lighting, table lamps with shades, or for an opening into a brightly lit room where the light spills out into a hallway. Outside buildings, spot lights are useful for things like street lights and prison camp security lights.

Animated Lights

Lights that are categorized as "animated" can be animated in one of two ways, depending on the type. All animated lights are considered animated in the sense that their intensity and colors can be varied over time according to a set of properties. One particular type, *runway* is also animated in space, having the ability to change position according to its settings.

Animated lights can have their `Name` property set to a string value. By setting this value, you can access the light programmatically, which is goodness. This way you can activate and deactivate in a structure by name.

There is a little wrinkle, though. Each light entity can have a series of flags set. If the `Autostart` flag is set, causing the animated lights to automatically begin flashing when the game starts (which might be desirable, depending on your needs), then you cannot programmatically activate or deactivate these lights. So you need to uncheck or clear the Autostart flag when you create your model for each light you want to control with script code. Then you can check to see which lights can be activated or deactivated ("triggerable" in Torque parlance) using the following script code:

```
%theInterior.echotriggerablelights();
```

This will print the list of such lights to the console. Unfortunately, you can't use this method to return a value for you to parse looking for lights to activate. There is no return value.

You can activate a light this way:

```
%theInterior.activateLight("lightname");
```

And stop its animation this way:

```
%theInterior.deactivateLight("lightname");
```

When you stop the animation, the light reverts to the on state, whether or not it was illuminated when deactivated.

Note that some modeling tools use settings called *spawnflags* to set Autostart. If this is the case for you, you want to set bit zero of the spawnflags to enable Autostart, or clear it to enable triggered lights. Other tools just call these *flags*, and others actually name the flag Autostart.

Strobe and Pulse

The strobe light changes output intensity (and color) between two states, indicated by the setting of two properties, color1 and color2. The light will switch on and then off according to the speed setting. The speed can be very slow, slow, normal, fast, or very fast.

A pulse light is the same as a strobe light, but does not switch instantaneously between illumination states. Instead, it changes from one state to the other in a gradual way, governed by the speed setting.

Flicker and Pulse2

A flicker light is like a strobe light, but it cycles through five different states instead of between two. Again, you have the same speed settings as the strobe light.

A pulse2 light is the same as a flicker light, but like pulse, does not switch instantaneously between illumination states. It changes gradually from one state to the other, governed by the speed setting.

Runway

This is one of the coolest light types. The name comes from the idea that you can use this light type to make approach lights for a runway, like you see at airports. This is another type that requires a target setting that contains the name of a target entity. You place the runway light at one location, and the target at the other. The runway light will move from its original location to the target's location in a series of steps. You can specify the number of steps using the step property.

The speed property dictates how quickly the light moves (and blinks).

If you want the light to return to its original location in a step-wise fashion, set the pingpong property to yes (or true, or 1, depending on your modeling tool). If you set pingpong to false, then when the light reaches the target, it jumps back to its original location and starts stepping towards the target again.

Testing the Lights

I've created a structure called buildingC that contains all of the lights, as shown in Figure 14.14. There is one example each of the static lights, and then two versions of the animated lights: those with Autostart enabled (and therefore not triggerable) and those with Autostart disabled (and therefore triggerable).

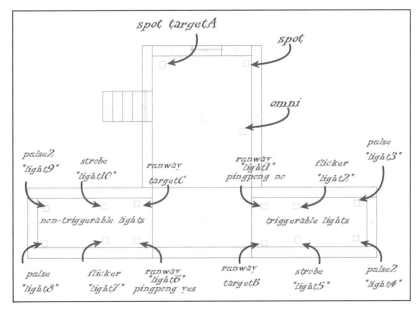

Figure 14.14 Locations of light entities in buildingC.

Copy the file buildingC.dif from the RESOURCES\ch14 folder to the \A3D\demo\ data\interiors\room folder. Then launch the FPS demo, and place the buildingC structure into the game world, in the same way that you've done with other structures in the chapter. Don't forget to use Alt+L in the Mission Editor to relight the scene.

Head on over to the building and go inside. In the foyer, to your left is the spot light. Take care to compare the locations of the spot light entity and the target entity to what you see in the room, and see the relationship. To the right in the foyer is the simple omni light. Head over to the right and you will see two rooms, left and right. On the right are non-triggerable animated lights. Note that the runway is not in ping-pong mode. On the left, all the lights are triggerable. Refer to Figure 14.14 to get their names, from light6 to light10. You might notice that some of the triggerable lights are already switched on—they just started in that default state. They aren't blinking or anything, though they still need to be activated.

Switch to camera fly mode, and then back into the Mission Editor. Zoom up above the building and select it to find out its object ID. Once you have that, go back inside the building so that you can observe the triggerable lights.

Next, open the console and get a list of the triggerable lights like this:

```
NNNN.echotriggerablelights();
```

Where NNNN is the id number of the building that you obtained.

Next, try activating each of the lights:

```
NNNN.activateLight("lightname");
```

Where lightname is one of the names from Figure 14.14.

And then try stopping their animations in this way:

```
NNNN.deactivateLight("lightname");
```

Moving Right Along

Well that was a fun-filled chapter. Lots of blinking lights and stuff.

You saw that the concept of LOD, using structures of decreasing detail, can be used to keep frame rates from suffering when large numbers of objects populate a scene.

We also saw how that same LOD feature can be used (misused?) in other interesting ways, allowing us to use program code to arbitrarily change the appearance of a structure.

You learned how to use portals to help with frame rate issues as well as to control the access of general scene lighting into a structure.

Finally, there were a plethora of light types that we could manipulate in several ways, including controlling them with TorqueScript. Next, we will look at a similar set of features for "those other" model types: Shapes.

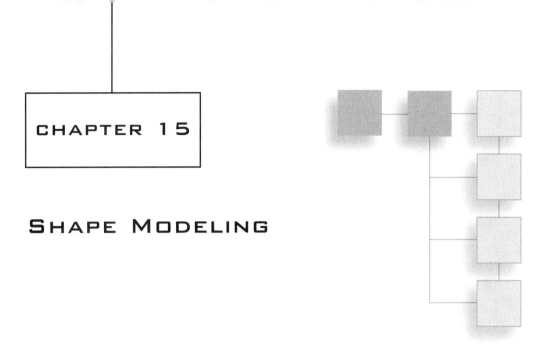

CHAPTER 15

SHAPE MODELING

I n the previous chapter, we saw, in quite dramatic fashion, how a somewhat large number of immobile objects like buildings with high polygon counts can drag down the frame rates of a game. Fortunately, with things like buildings, we can plan with a reasonable degree of certainty how many polygons will be present in a scene for any given level, and tweak them accordingly.

Note

The least complex polygon is a triangle. Most of the time, the words polygon and triangle can be interchanged. That applies to this chapter as well.

Unfortunately, not all of our game objects are as predictable. Player characters, non-player characters (AI), power-ups, and other objects that we refer to in general as *shapes* have a tendency to come and go from a scene. This variability makes it harder to plan the polygon budget.

A necessary design strategy is to prepare for the worst (or almost the worst) by calculating out your polygon needs based upon the expected number of objects in a scene. Total up the polygons for each shape, then multiply by the number of instances of the shape you expect to have in the scene, and add all the shapes together. Use the result as your limit, and implement rules and code to restrict the numbers of each shape. You will probably pretty quickly find this to be very restrictive.

Fortunately, we can turn to the same technique for shapes that we used for modeling structures: LOD.

We can create our models with varying levels of detail to ease the polygon count and raise the restrictions we calculate to higher, more useful values. This way, we can be more relaxed about how often and how many shapes move in and out of our scene.

Levels of Detail

Every game engine worth its salt supports the concept of LOD for all of its model types, just as Torque does. The differences lie mainly in how the modeling tools actually convert your models into LOD instances for use by the engine.

In the previous chapter, you saw that the map2dif tool that is provided with the Torque Game Engine (TGE) takes several different models, each of which has certain properties set to indicate their LOD level, and combines them into one model with multiple LODs.

With shapes, the story is the same, only different. Whether you are modeling your shapes with 3D Studio Max, Maya, MilkShape, Lightwave, Blender, or some other modeling tool, the approach you will take is to create all of the detail levels inside the one model as individual meshes. Contrast this with the last chapter's approach of using separate CSG-type models for each LOD and relying on the DIF compiler to combine the LODs into one model.

With shapes, each mesh is assigned properties that indicate its detail level, and then the DTS (shape file format used by TGE) exporter for the modeling tool will generate the DTS file with the appropriate detail info inside it.

Note

The latest version of MilkShape 3D, and the DTS exporter, ms3dtsExporterPlus, have been included on the companion CD to this book in the TOOLS folder. There is a basic Torque exporter included with MilkShape, from GarageGames, but it doesn't provide the necessary features that the ms2dtsExporterPlus exporter provides.

First, run the MilkShape installer, and then extract ms2dtsExporterPlus.dll from the zip file kit and put it in the MilkShape folder, wherever you installed it (usually under C:\Program Files\MilkShape 3D 1.7.4).

The exporter kit also includes documentation specific to its use that relates to the material in this chapter, so you should probably extract the entire zip file to a convenient location in order to get at the documentation in it.

An "Introduction to MilkShape" tutorial chapter from my first book (*3D Game Programming All in One*) is included in PDF form on the CD in TOOLS\MilkShape. It is there to provide some assistance in getting started with MilkShape if you have no experience but wish to use it. It is included as a courtesy. You should note that the resources and other materials that the chapter refers to are NOT included on the companion CD for this book. You will need to create your own. The chapter provides explanations for the features of the version of MilkShape that was current at the time it was written. The makers of MilkShape have added several more features since then.

You are encouraged to use your own modeling tools if you have them. All of the high-end tools have the features described in this book, and Torque exporters are available for them. Go to the GarageGames site to search for the appropriate exporter: http://www.garagegames.com/mg/projects/torque1/#art

Creating Crates

Let's dive into things with the help of a useful and ubiquitous item found in many action/shooter games: the lowly (or evil, depending on your point of view) crate. It may be a simple model, but that's to the good. It makes it easier to see where we can make reasonable LOD decisions. Fire up your favorite shape-modeling tool and let's get this party started.

LOD 0

First, make a bunch of frame-and-panel wooden sides for the crate, like the one shown in Figure 15.1. The side is made out of five boxes that form the frame, and one flatter box primitive that is the panel held inside the frame. When you join the frame pieces, make sure that the ends are angled.

Use the sides you've just made to build a six-sided crate that has the top slightly askew to indicate that the crate has been opened (see Figure 15.2).

A perusal of the model reveals that there are a total of 30 faces on each of the six boxes that comprise one side of the crate. That means there is a total of 180 faces on the whole crate. Since each face is made up of two triangles, there are 360 triangles for the whole crate. With close examination, you can see the reason for choosing boxes to build the sides of the crate: The thickness of the plywood used to make the crate is quite obvious, and appropriately so, when you are close to the crate. It's the right amount of detail.

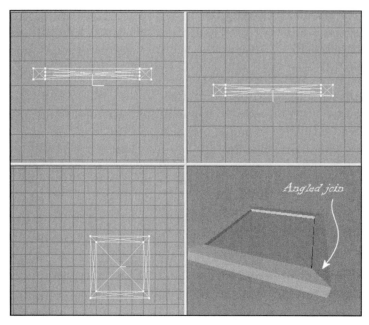

Figure 15.1 A side of a crate.

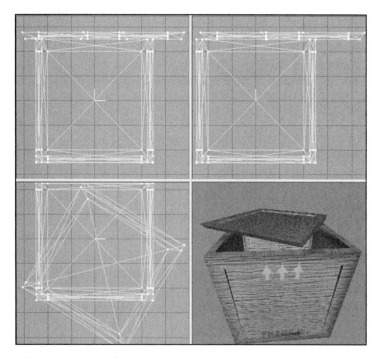

Figure 15.2 A stylish and trendy crate.

Before we go on to the next modeling step, let's export our shape to Torque's DTS format. Before we do that, we need to ensure that we have our meshes named appropriately.

The naming scheme employed for visible meshes generally follows the form *nameLOD*, like this: sidea0, where the name of the mesh is sidea and its LOD value is 0. This value represents the minimum size in pixel height for an object that will cause Torque to render all meshes within that object that have this LOD value. We use this LOD value of 0 whenever we have only one level of detail.

We've got several choices available when dealing with meshes. We could leave each side on its own as an individual mesh or object, or we could group the side meshes together and create a single mesh. Or you could group all of the meshes together into one big mesh—or any combination in between. I've opted for leaving each side as a mesh on its own. Here are my mesh names (you should use the same names for now):

    top0
    bottom0
    sidea0
    sideb0
    sidec0
    sided0

If you are using MilkShape, you need to know that MilkShape comes bundled with a DTS exporter, but unfortunately this exporter does *not* support LOD (or many other DTS features). However, the DTSExporterPlus exporter *does* support LOD. It is included in the \A3D\TOOLS\MilkShape\ms3dts Exporter Plus folder. You just need to extract the DLL ms2dtsExporterPlus.dll from ms2dtsExporterPlus.zip, and then deposit the DLL in the folder where you installed MilkShape. It will load up and appear as "Torque DTS Plus" in MilkShape's export menu.

If you are using a modeling tool other than MilkShape (like Lightwave or Maya), and it has a DTS exporter, then it has LOD support available. They all employ a numeric LOD naming scheme very similar to the one described here, but you should consult your documentation to ensure proper usage.

Use your DTS exporter to create a Torque-usable DTS file. Make sure to include at least one collision mesh—a simple box mesh the size of the crate, occupying the same space as the crate, and named Collision-1 will do fine. If you don't need collision, then you can skip that part.

Export your shape. Now create the folder \A3D\demo\data\shapes\crates, if it doesn't already exist, and copy your exported shape and the skin texture file that goes with it into that crate's folder.

Alternatively, you can use the single LOD crate I made: Just go to \A3D\ RESOURCES\ch15 and copy lod0crate.dts and lodcrate.png to the new folder you've just created called \A3D\demo\data\shapes\crates.

Then run the Torque FPS Demo. Once you've spawned in, open the Mission Editor by pressing F11, and then press F4 to enable the World Editor Creator. Drill down in the creation tree (lower-right corner) until you get to Static Shapes, demo, data, Shapes, crates where you will find the lod0crate shape you made. Click on the shape to insert it at ground level at the center of your screen. Switch out of the editor and press F8 to go into Camera Fly mode. Inspect your handiwork. Figure 15.3 shows my version of that crate.

This version of our stylish and trendy crate is the most detailed version. It's a good idea to run around and view it from all angles to get a sense of how small the crate gets in your view before it loses various details.

Figure 15.3 The stylish and trendy crate enjoys the great outdoors.

LOD 1

Now we want to establish our next level of detail. We have to watch our terminology here, because there is a trap! Previously we discussed LOD 0 and now we are discussing LOD 1. These are the detail *levels*. As you saw in the last section, there is also an LOD *value*, which is the pixel height for a given LOD level. We also saw in the previous chapter how LOD 0 was the most detailed LOD, LOD 1 was less detailed, and so on.

The trap is, with only one LOD, that LOD level is 0, and its pixel height *value* is also 0. It *could* be a larger number; all that will happen is that your model will vanish from the scene when its pixel height is equal to that number or less. However, when you have more than one LOD, LOD 0 will *always* have a much larger pixel height value, typically in the 25 to 100 pixel range (although I have seen larger pixel values used, like 250, for very complex shapes). Keep this in mind because although not all modeling tools understand the concept of LOD level numbers (MilkShape doesn't), they all *do* have some method of assigning a pixel value for establishing an LOD.

In my estimation, there are two model details that can be dispensed with next: the thickness of the sides, and the variation of the mesh between the side frames and the inner side panels.

That last detail involves the fact that the sides are made up of a four-sided frame and a center panel, totaling 60 triangles in all (six faces per frame edge box, plus six faces for the panel, times two triangles per face). If we instead build a side out of a single box, stretched and squashed to suit, we only need to use six faces for the whole side, or twelve triangles in all. That's an 80 percent reduction in polygons!

Before we build the next LOD in the model, we need to take a stab at determining *when* the LOD change will take place. As you know from Chapter 14, we do this based on the number of pixels the shape extends in the vertical dimension on the screen. So instead of just running around admiring our handiwork from all angles, let's take a more analytical approach.

At some distance from the crate, you will notice that you can't discern any real difference between the side panel inserts and the frame that surrounds them. After fiddling around for a minute or two gazing at the crate, I came up with a pixel height of 38 pixels, as shown in Figure 15.4. From many different angles, 38 pixels was where it seemed to me that the detail of the side frames became lost.

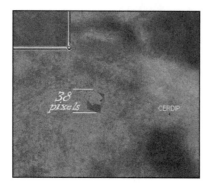

Figure 15.4 The first LOD transition distance.

Well, that works for me. So, here's what we do: First we need to rename all of our existing LOD 0 meshes to reflect the new LOD pixel value.

top0 becomes top38

bottom0 becomes bottom38

sidea0 becomes sidea38

and so on.

Next we need to create new sides that exactly overlap the original complex sides by using a box primitive and scaling it (or by dragging vertices around) until the box exactly envelops a side. If you make a box that covers the side named top38, then name the new box mesh top0, where 38 is the pixel height for the transition. Then use your modeling tool's hide function to hide top38 just to keep your view from becoming too cluttered. Repeat this process for all of the sides of the crate. The new, less-detailed meshes are our new LOD 1 meshes (with a pixel height of 0), while the original more complex meshes remain LOD 0 meshes, with a pixel height of 38.

Figure 15.5 shows my version of the LOD1 crate meshes.

Once you've done this, save your work and export your model to DTS format. I've included my own working file as \A3D\RESOURCES\ch15\lod0&1crate.ms3d and the pre-exported DTS version as lod0&1crate.dts. You can copy your DTS file, or the one I've provided, to the same crates folder you created and used in the last section.

Fire up your FPS demo, and go on in and take a look. I've deliberately left a variation in the skin mapping in my version so that you can see the changes between LODs more readily.

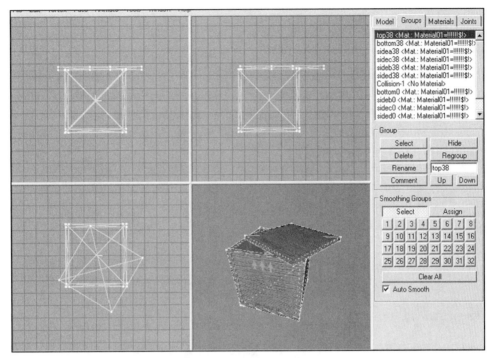

Figure 15.5 The first LOD transition distance.

LOD 2 and Beyond

Now that you know the principals and work tasks involved, get cracking and make for yourself a version of the model with an LOD 2 and a pixel value of your own choosing. Then go try it out.

Player Avatars

For games with mobs and mobs of player characters and AI players, like Real-Time Strategy (RTS) games with waves of troops (*ROME: Total War* being a good example), LOD issues can make the difference between success and failure.

Back in the day, RTS units were typically tiny things, perhaps even 2D sprites, that appeared on the battlefield. You could make out just enough detail to be able to identify and differentiate them. The trend now in 3D strategy games is to offer camera controls that allow you to zoom in to get up close and personal with the hordes of personnel that you are sending off to their doom.

So let's take a character model and apply some LOD goodness to it. And this time, we'll use a different and easier technique to generate the different LOD models. Easier perhaps, but be warned that sometimes the results might require some extra tweaking to create an acceptable LOD.

Many modeling programs come equipped with built-in automated tools for generating different LOD versions of a model. For example, 3D Studio Max has the MultiRes modifier. As before, I will use MilkShape to demonstrate an automated approach. MilkShape has the DirectX Mesh Tools plug-in bundled with it. Doubtless these same tools are available as plug-ins for other modeling tools as well, if they don't have their own built-in LOD support. Don't forget that this is not a tutorial *per se* for doing LOD in MilkShape, but rather an explanation of LOD techniques using MilkShape screen shots as a common reference point.

LOD 0

Figure 15.6 shows an old friend from *3D Game Programming All in One*: the Standard Male. We'll use him as our victim… I mean guinea pig. Well, test subject, anyway. Fortunately, he doesn't know what is about to happen to him, and it's best we keep it

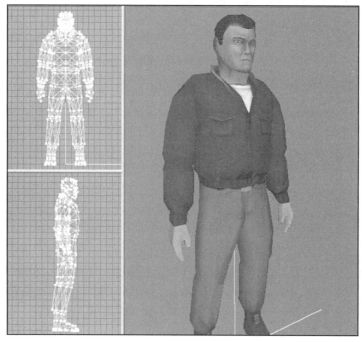

Figure 15.6 The trusty ol' standard male model.

that way. In the folder \A3D\RESOURCES\ch15, you will find the MilkShape 3D file called standardmale.ms3d. You can follow along this discussion using that model in MilkShape 3D.

The model as shown in Figure 15.6 has 1484 triangles, with 1106 vertices. He's already a pretty low poly model starting out. Before moving any farther, you should rename the mesh to mesh128. As you know by now, the 128 indicates the smallest size, in vertical pixels, at which this model will be rendered. Since this is our most detailed model, it's our LOD 0 model. After renaming the mesh, save the file as male0.ms3d.

LOD 1

The DirectX mesh tools can be found in the MilkShape Tools menu, in the section with the other plug-ins. Open up the DirectX mesh tools, and you will see a little dialog like the one shown in Figure 15.7.

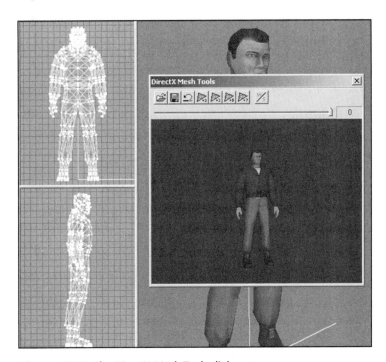

Figure 15.7 The DirectX Mesh Tools dialog.

If you click on the button at the far right in the dialog that carries the label "W/S" (for Wireframe/Shaded), you will see the model in the textured and shaded form, in miniature.

You can left-click anywhere inside the picture portion of the dialog and drag your mouse to rotate the avatar so that you can review its appearance from all sides. Notice that in Figure 15.7 the slider is all the way to the right, signifying that no change has occurred.

Now drag the slider to about roughly the middle of its range, as shown in Figure 15.8. Watch the subtle changes that take place in real time inside the little window. As you move the slider to the left, the number of polygons, triangles, and vertices in the model decreases. Now save your changes using the little floppy disk icon (second button from the left). This does *not* save your changes to disk—it merely applies the changes to the model.

This also reduces the number of triangles in the model by 50%. The resulting model, as shown in Figure 15.9, has a triangle count of 774 and a vertex count of 732.

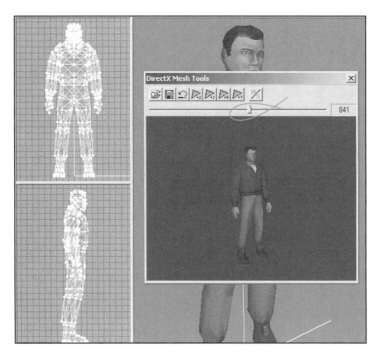

Figure 15.8 Mesh tools set to 50% of polygons.

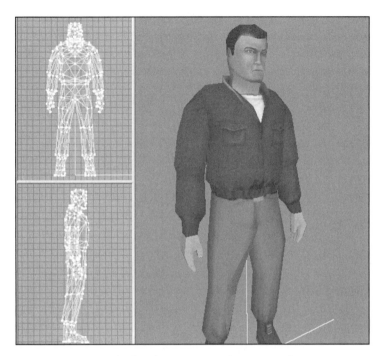

Figure 15.9 Standard male at LOD 1 with 774 triangles.

Unfortunately, on some computers with certain screen size/resolution configurations, the avatar might appear too small in that little dialog window, so it might be difficult to see what it looks like with the fewer polygons. Not to worry—once you've saved your changes in the DirectX Mesh Tools dialog, simply close the dialog, and you will see the changes implemented in your main model.

Rename your mesh to male64, and then save your new model as male1.ms3d. That was our LOD 1 model.

LOD 2 and Beyond

If you reduce the triangles by a further 50%, you will get a model like the one shown in Figure 15.10. This one will have a triangle count in the area of 360.

Rename the mesh for this model to male32, and save this LOD 2 model as male2.ms3d.

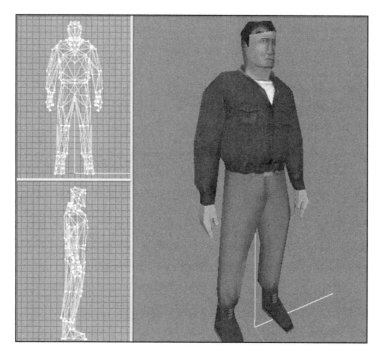

Figure 15.10 Standard male at LOD 2.

Finally, if we repeat the mesh reduction process one more time, we end up with a model that has around 160 triangles, and looks like the model in Figure 15.11.

Rename the mesh to male16 and save the model as male3.ms3d.

Figure 15.12 shows a comparison of LOD 3 and LOD 0 models, side-by-side at the distance where LOD 3 would come into play. Can you tell which one has more detail?

Merging the Detail Levels

The final step is to get all of the LOD files merged into one. That's easy enough.

Create a new empty model document in MilkShape and save it as maleLODall.ms3d. Then, use the Merge item in the File menu to select each of the four model LOD versions you created earlier: male0.ms3d, male1.ms3d, male2.ms3d, and male3.ms3d. Once you have them all merged, go through the materials list and remove the duplicates, and make sure you have the sole remaining material assigned to all four models.

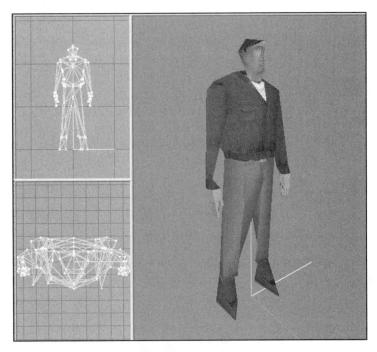

Figure 15.11 Standard male at LOD 3.

Figure 15.12 Comparison of LOD 0 and LOD 3 models.

Once the materials are straightened out, use the Torque DTS Plus exporter found under the File menu in the Export item, and export to the file maleLOD.dts. Copy this file and the texture file for the model's material to the folder \A3D\demo\data\shapes\objects. Launch the FPS demo, and in the World Editor Creator, you will find the maleLOD model in with the Static Shapes, demo, data, shapes, objects entries. Add the model to the scene, as shown in Figure 15.13 and admire your handiwork. Poke around and view the model from different angles and different distances. Make estimates about pixel heights and see if you can detect the LOD changes.

Figure 15.13 Standard male with all LOD levels in a game scene.

Moving Right Along

So that's how we handle levels of detail with shapes. You saw that it is essentially the same process as the one we covered with structures in Chapter 14, but the implementation details are slightly different. At the end of the day, I think it's a toss up which approach works best.

The key thing with LOD is understanding what changes happen and how they affect the visual appearance of your model as the model shrinks in the scene. Practiced observation is required to be able to produce seamless detail transitions.

There are times when using automated tools like the DirectX mesh tool is the best way to go. The more complex the model, the more likely you are to benefit from these automated mesh reduction tools.

However, hand-crafted detail levels can probably produce detail levels that handle the level transitions more smoothly while yielding better triangle reduction than the automated tools. Which approach to use is your call.

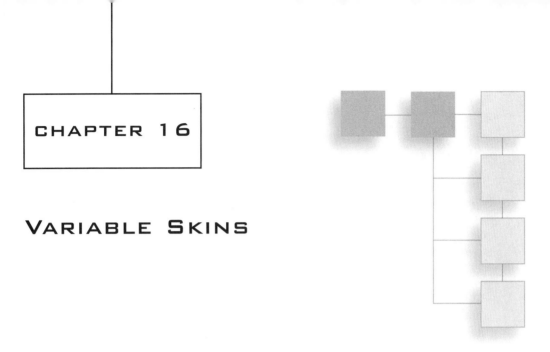

CHAPTER 16

VARIABLE SKINS

Creating content for games can be an onerous task—designing and creating models of characters, buildings, decorations, flora and fauna, vehicles, bits of garbage and debris, and so on.

The most common approach to creating a wide variety of content is to mix and match components and parts of things to create larger and more complex things. A simple, but often overlooked example is the concept of creating a library of objects that you would use to create a game level.

No one in his right mind would create a multi-level game where each level is populated only with objects and other resources that were custom made for that level, and that level *alone*. Instead, we will re-use the vast majority of our library of objects and resources, placing them within the levels in common ways, and sometimes in ways unique to the needs of the level.

It's a simple equation. Let's say that you've decided to have every level's objects be unique to that level. Furthermore, let's say that every level needs 30 different object types, and you have 20 levels. This means that you need to create 600 unique models for use in your game. That's gonna hurt!

However, let's say that with a design that has the same number of objects, and the same number of levels, you decide that you will create a *maximum* of five unique objects per level and then draw the rest of the level content from a library of common objects. This means that your library will need a minimum of 25 objects, and you will need to create 100 unique objects for use in their respective levels. That's a total of 125 models versus 600.

Not only that, but experience shows that you can get a great deal of variety by changing some of the unique models to "low-use" (but not unique) models. You could easily get your model count below 100 this way. This will go a long, long way towards helping you get your game finished.

Of course, the same approach applies to other resources, like sound effects and textures. Unless your game is about bird watching, there is no real reason that three or four different bird song sound effects couldn't be used throughout *all* of your levels. Unless, of course, your game is a space flight simulator or something. Then you will have some "splainin" to do.

Reusing textures is obviously another area where a library of textures can be spread throughout a library of models. Three models (carefully crafted to be obviously different) of a crate, with four different wood grain textures will yield 12 different in-game items, as shown in Figure 16.1. That almost cuts your texturing *and* modeling workload in half. It's like a results multiplier.

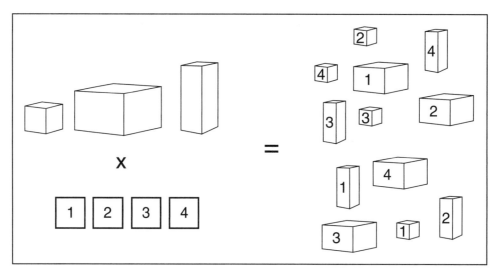

Figure 16.1 A results multiplier.

Look at this:

1. Create Textures 1, 2, 3, and 4—each with a unique visual appearance.
2. Create Model A. Assign Texture 1. Export Model A-1 for game use. Now assign Texture 2 and Export A-2, Texture 3 and Export A-3, Texture 4 and Export A-4. There you go, four different crate models.
3. Create Model B. Assign Texture 1. Export Model A-1 for game use. Now assign Texture 2 and Export B-2, Texture 3 and Export B-3, Texture 4 and Export B-4. Now you have four more different crate models.
4. Create Model C. Assign Texture 1. Export Model A-1 for game use. Now assign Texture 2 and Export C-2, Texture 3 and Export C-3, Texture 4 and Export C-4. And now you have yet again four more different crate models.

That's your target total of twelve crate items. Relatively quick and painless.

But, in fact, it can get even quicker and less, um, painful. Or more painless. Or something.

Try this:

1. Create Textures 1, 2, 3, and 4—each with a unique visual appearance.
2. Create Crates A, B, and C—each with the same base texture (let's say Texture 1).

That's three models and four textures created, the same as before. But then step three:

3. When placing each crate in a level, set a property that dictates which of the four textures the crate should use!

Huh? Can you do that? Isn't that illegal or something?

Well, no, you can't normally do that with most game engines, not even with Torque. But with a little bit of scripting magic, you can! It probably won't take you very long to realize how much work this can save you. And no, it isn't illegal. In fact, it's not even against any union rules that I'm aware of.

I call this (as do others) *variable skins*. Some people call it other names, like *variable textures*, and that's fine.

Mmmmm, Crates!

For our first simple foray into the world of variable skins, let's work with the crates we talked about. Yes, I know, crates are everywhere. Almost every shooter game, and most other action and adventure types of games have crates all over the place. Stacks of crates, exploding crates, opening crates, moving crates—crates galore. Let's hop on the crate wagon.

In fact, let's address the situation I described in the chapter introduction and create a system where we'll create one crate and a few textures, and then place that one crate in the game world, change a property, and end up with a variety of crates.

Resources and Preparation

I've made a crate model, oddly enough called crate.dts (see Figure 16.2) and some textures named base.crate.png, wood.crate.png, metal.crate.png, and mixed.crate.png (see Figure 16.3).

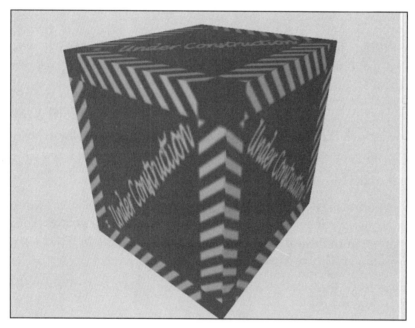

Figure 16.2 The crate model.

Figure 16.3 The crate textures.

They can be found in the folder RESOURCES\ch16. Create a folder called \A3D\demo\data\shapes\crates and copy the crate model and the crate textures into it.

Note the naming scheme employed—it's quite important, because the built-in TorqueScript skin naming capabilities use this scheme. The general form for the variable skin naming system is *variant.model.extension*. From last-to-first, the extension part of the name is the image file type, normally either .png or .jpg. The middle part of the name, delimited by a period on either side, refers to the model you are using. It doesn't *have* to match the model name. In fact, it doesn't have to match anything, but it must be the same in all the different versions of the texture you are going to use for a given model. The first part of the name, the variant portion, *must* be "base" for your initial texture. The game engine looks for this word and uses it (and the fact that the rest of the name conforms) to flag the fact that you are using the variable skin system.

Feel free to create your own models and textures, but at this stage, use the exact same names that I have used. This is so that the following program will work. Later, you can change your names if you like—just make sure you change the code to match.

Code

You will need to create a shape datablock for your crate. We need to treat the crate as something a bit more sophisticated than a simple static shape in order to achieve our goals.

Step One

Open \A3D\demo\server\scripts\game.cs and locate the function onServerCreated and add this line to the end of the function after the other statements, in the same way you've done for earlier code examples:

```
exec("./varSkinItems.cs");
```

Step Two

Next, type in the following contents, and then save as a new file, \A3D\demo\
server\scripts\varSkinItems.cs:

```
datablock ItemData(Crate)
{
  category = "VariableSkinItems";
  shapeFile = "~/data/shapes/crates/crate.dts";
};


function Crate::onAdd(%data, %obj)
{
   %obj.rotate=false;
   %obj.setSkinName(%obj.skin);
}
```

It should look mostly familiar by now. The datablock, an ItemData type, has the name
Crate. In the Crate datablock, the category property tells the Mission Editor how to
list the datablock in the Shapes branch of the tree. So, we will find it under the
VariableSkinItems branch. Of course, the shapeFile property tells the engine which
model to use, and that would be the one and only crate model.

And then we have an OnAdd method for the datablock. You've also encountered this
before: The engine calls the OnAdd method for a datablock whenever an instance of an
object that uses that datablock is added into the game world.

Since this is an ItemData object, it has the ability to rotate the object around its Z-axis
while the item sits in the game world. This is a standard feature of powerups and
other pickable items in a game. Its purpose is to help players recognize items that can
be picked up or otherwise have a special use. In this example, we don't want that feature (just because), so the OnAdd method turns off the rotation by setting the rotate
property of this particular instance of the object to false.

Finally, the key statement:

```
%obj.setSkinName(%obj.skin);
```

This statement does two things: It gets the skin property (a dynamic field that we will
add when we insert the crate into the game world) of the instance of the object placed
in the game world, and then passes that name to the setSkinName method of the object.
The skin (the texture image) will be changed instantly.

Note that this happens when the object is placed in the world. When we are building the game world and placing the items with the editor, we won't see this effect, because when we place the object, the OnAdd will be called, but we *haven't yet assigned* a skin name. This is okay—remember the naming scheme? At initial placement time, the base.crate.png image will be used. I've created an "under construction" texture for use as the base texture for exactly this reason. We can quickly look around our game world and see which of the variable skin items have their skins correctly set, and which are still showing the default skin.

Using the Variable Skin Crate

Now that we have all of our ducks in a row, let's proceed to knock them down. Launch the demo, and start the FPS mission (you can also use the racing example if you like).

1. Switch to camera fly mode by pressing F8.

2. Zoom around until you find an open space, and then open the Mission Editor by pressing F11.

3. Press F4 to invoke the World Editor Creator interface (see Figure 16.4).

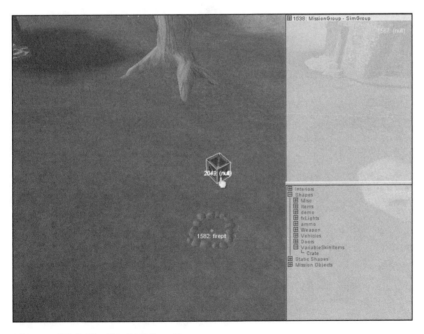

Figure 16.4 The World Editor Creator.

4. Then in the lower right pane, find the Shapes tree, and expand it by clicking on the little plus sign.

5. You will see the VariableSkinItems branch—expand it too. In the Variable-SkinItems list you will find the Crate entry, visible in Figure 16.4.

6. Aim your crosshair at the location where you want to insert the crate, then click on the Crate entry in the VariableSkinItems branch of the Shapes list. A crate with the "Under Construction" skin will appear. It should not be rotating.

7. Switch to the World Editor Inspector.

8. Select the crate by clicking on it with the hand cursor, or click-dragging the arrow cursor over it.

9. Locate the highlighted entry for the crate in the Inspector Tree view, in the upper right pane, and click on it to make its properties appear in the properties pane at the lower right corner.

10. Click on the Expand button to reveal all of the property entries.

11. Scroll to the bottom of the properties pane until you find the Add button in the Dynamic Fields area, and click it. The Add Dynamic Fields dialog box will open, as shown in Figure 16.5.

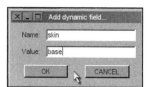

Figure 16.5 The Add Dynamic Fields dialog box.

12. In the Name field, type **skin**.

13. In the Value field, type **wood**, and then click OK.

14. Press the Apply button at the top of the properties pane. You will see your crate where you left it, and it won't appear to be any different. Don't fret about it. That's expected behavior.

15. Repeat the above steps, placing two more crates, naming one of the new crates "metal" and the other "mixed."

16. Choose File, Save Mission. Then press F11 to exit the Editor and Escape to quit the mission level. Then click on the Exit button at the top of the screen to exit the game completely.

17. Now relaunch the demo as before, and re-enter the mission in which you added the crates.

18. Well? What are you waiting for? Go take a look at your crates! Notice how when you placed them, they all had the construction skin, but now they have their assigned skins. Three different crates, using only one model.

But wait! There's even more game programming goodness to be had! Do this:

1. Open the Mission Editor in World Editor Inspector mode.

2. Select one of the crates—it doesn't matter which.

3. Locate its entry in the Inspector Tree in the upper right pane, and note the object handle (the number on the left side). You can also see the handle number floating near or in the object itself in the Game World view, as shown in Figure 16.6. Let's say the handle of the object you selected was 1600 (yours will most likely be different).

4. Open the console with the tilde key (~) and type in **1600.setSkinName('wood');** and press Enter. Don't forget that final semi-colon! Take a look at the crate. Ha! The skin has changed to the wood texture.

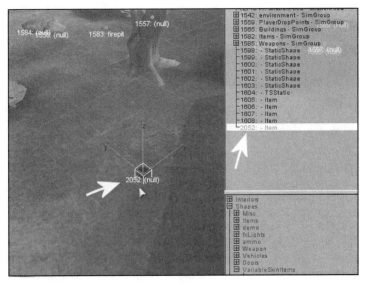

Figure 16.6 Locating the object handle.

I think you can see that there are many possibilities opened up here in terms of game-play. Figure 16.7 shows the herd of wild crates in their natural habitat.

Figure 16.7 Herd of wild crates.

Oh, and one more thing. If you selected the wood crate, and then set it to the wood texture, umm, well, I think it's obvious you won't see very much of a change in the crate. If that was the case, try one of the other skins, like metal or mixed. You can even set it back to base if you like.

One more thing: It's absolutely essential that you use the single-quote (') in the setSkinName function call, and **not** the double quotes.

Ready, Set, Go!

Crates are cool, as far as they go, I suppose, but there's more to games than crates—even though some big-name game companies don't seem to realize that.

Let's examine the ubiquitous traffic light. Traffic lights have three colors. (In most places in the Western world—some regions use just two colors, in certain situations.) We'll use the straightforward, red-yellow-green system where only one color shows at any one time. There are several techniques that could be used for the traffic light. Here are three:

- Use four models, each having a texture displaying one of the three standard light combinations, and one for no lights showing (power failure, maybe). Swap one model for another as needed.

- Use one model and an animated (IFL) texture with four animation sequences, one for each color. Select the appropriate animation thread for the light combination you want.

- Use one model with four textures, one for each combination. Swap the textures as dictated by the state of the traffic light.

Method three is the one we will take, of course. You might want to eliminate the "power failure" mode, and stick with only three textures, or use more combinations. For example, one might opt to use the red-yellow combination found in Germany, which is used as a warning that the light is about to turn green (so wake up goofball, and put your eyes on the road!).

Ready…

First, as always, we need to get our resources in order. I've created a traffic light model (see Figure 16.8) called trafficlight.dts that you can find in the RESOURCES\ch16 folder. The source file, in MilkShape's .ms3d format is also in there, so you can fiddle with the model to your heart's content.

Also in the ch16 folder are the four textures I created for use with the model: base.light.jpg, red.light.jpg, yellow.light.jpg, and green.light.jpg, as shown in Figure 16.9.

Create a folder called \A3D\demo\data\shapes\traffic and copy the traffic light model and the four traffic light textures into it.

Set…

Okay, now for the code. It's essentially an expansion of the code we used for the crates, but fleshed out a bit, with some automated sequencing to change the lights. And unlike with the crates, we don't bother setting a dynamic skin property with the World Editor Inspector, although such a property is used.

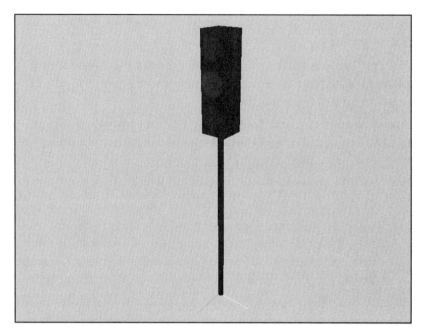

Figure 16.8 Traffic light model.

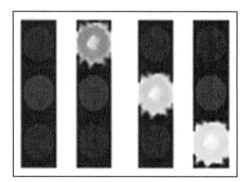

Figure 16.9 The traffic light's textures.

All we need to do is add the new datablock, some functions, and some pseudo-constant variables to the existing code in \A3D\demo\server\scripts\varSkinItems.cs, so type in the following at the end of that module:

```
$OFF_STATE      = 0;
$GREEN_STATE    = 1;
$YELLOW_STATE   = 2;
$RED_STATE      = 3;

datablock ItemData(TrafficLight)
{
  category = "VariableSkinItems";
  shapeFile = "~/data/shapes/traffic/trafficlight.dts";

DELAY[$OFF_STATE]    = 10;
DELAY[$GREEN_STATE]  = 15 * 1000;
DELAY[$YELLOW_STATE] = 2 * 1000;
DELAY[$RED_STATE]    = 10 * 1000;

SKIN[$OFF_STATE]     = "base";
SKIN[$GREEN_STATE]   = "green";
SKIN[$YELLOW_STATE]  = "yellow";
SKIN[$RED_STATE]     = "red";

};

function TrafficLight::onAdd(%theDatablock, %whichLightPole)
{
  %whichLightPole.rotate = false;
  %whichLightPole.state = $OFF_STATE;
  %whichLightPole.setSkinName(%theDatablock.SKIN[$OFF_STATE]);
  %theDatablock.schedule(%theDatablock.DELAY[%whichLightPole.state],
                                    "Sequence", %whichLightPole);
}
```

```
function TrafficLight::Sequence(%theDatablock, %whichLightPole)
{
  %whichLightPole.state++;
  if (%whichLightPole.state > $RED_STATE)
    %whichLightPole.state = $GREEN_STATE;
  %whichLightPole.setSkinName(%theDatablock.SKIN[%whichLightPole.state]);
  %theDatablock.schedule(%theDatablock.DELAY[%whichLightPole.state],
                                    "Sequence", %whichLightPole);
}
```

At the top of the module, you will find the pseudo-constants that are used to indicate the various states of the lights, including the "off" state.

Next is the datablock that defines the traffic light. Notice that I've included some properties that look like the pseudo-constants. This is to show you another way of doing the same thing as the constants, how these pseudo-constant properties, if you will, are "hidden" within the datablock and not accessible without using the datablock. It's another useful technique, and since the values these properties contain are only suitable for use by the traffic light, it's wholly appropriate. Notice how I use the global pseudo-constants to index the arrays rather than the actual numbers (or "magic" numbers). This helps me keep track of what goes where and why, especially if I have to come back later and puzzle out what the code does after having forgotten all about it. Also, note the use of the expression 15 * 1000. I do it this way, rather than as 15,000, because these values will be passed to a schedule method later, and they need to be expressed in milliseconds. I break it apart into seconds times milliseconds per second to make it easier to read. If I were to schedule for something on the order of minutes in duration, I would do something like 5 * 60 * 1000 for a five minute delay value, rather than 300,000. It's just easier on the brain.

The ::onAdd method is very similar to the one used for the crates as well, except we do a bit more. The property that tracks the state is set to the "off" state, and the skin is set to the "base" skin, which has been assigned to the "off" state.

Then we schedule a call to a datablock method I created, ::Sequence.

::Sequence is where all the light management activity takes place. The first thing it does is increment the state property to the next state, and check to make sure it's a valid state. If we've passed beyond the red light state, then we reset the state to the green state. The sequence is, of course, green-yellow-red-green-yellow... and so on, ad infinitum.

Then we set the skin name, but this time we get all fancy and everything. The second argument to this method is the handle of the instance of the light object we are addressing at this moment, %whichLightPole. Using that handle, we access its state variable and use it as an index into the datablock's array of skin names. The name that we find at the state's index is the one we pass into the setSkinName method. The skin will change instantly to the next color.

Finally, we reschedule a call to this same function using the state value to index into an array of delay values held in the datablock. And around and around we go.

Go!

All right, this is where the rubber hits the road, so to speak. Everything's in place, let's see some exciting traffic light action!

Launch the demo, and start the racing mission (you could use the FPS example if you like, but orcs don't understand what traffic lights mean). Once you've spawned into the world do the following:

1. Switch to camera fly mode by pressing F8.

2. Zoom around until you find an appropriate place on the race track, and then open the Mission Editor with F11.

3. Press F4 to invoke the World Editor Creator interface.

4. In the lower right pane, find the Shapes tree, and expand it by clicking on the little plus sign.

5. You will see the VariableSkinItems branch—expand it. In the Variable-SkinItems list you will find the TrafficLight entry.

6. Aim your crosshair at the location where you want to insert the traffic light, then click on the TrafficLight entry in the VariableSkinItems branch of the Shapes list. A light pole with the "off" skin will appear. This is the skin that has no particular light lit up. It should not be rotating.

7. You might have to select the pole and drag it up a little bit to align the bottom with the ground level. You also might need to rotate the pole around the Z-axis to get it facing in the direction you want. After you finish lining up the pole, you should see that one of the lights is now lit up, and if you wait long enough, you will see the lights change. Once it turns green, you may go.

...mber, slow down and prepare to stop if the light is yellow when you approach. ...stop in the intersection (if you can find it) and do not run any red lights. Drive safely. Figure 16.10 shows the traffic light in action in the three "on" states: red, yellow, and green.

Figure 16.10 The traffic light in action.

Swapping on the Fly

Crates and traffic lights are, of course, the pinnacle of fun and frivolity when it comes to computer games. But let's try something more staid and serious.

Figure 16.11 depicts an interesting character I fondly refer to as Mr. Box. A complex character, Mr. Box has a few nasty habits. One of the more interesting ones is his habit of changing color when he bumps into things, somewhat like a demented chameleon.

Yes, of course, we are going to change his skins on the fly, to accommodate the character's inner needs.

Setup

In the RESOURCES\ch16 folder, locate the files mrbox.dts, base.lmale.png, 0.lmale.png, 1.lmale.png, 2.lmale.png, 3.lmale.png, and 4.lmale.png and copy them to the folder \A3D\demo\data\shapes\player.

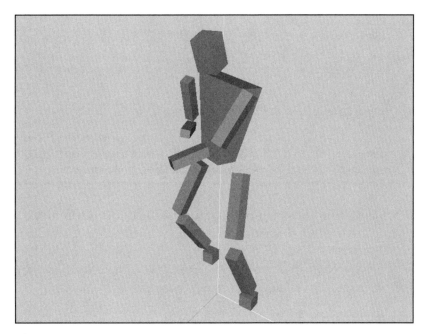

Figure 16.11 Mr. Box.

Code

Now we are going to make a few slight modifications to the player character's data-block. Open the file \A3D\demo\server\scripts\player.cs and scroll down until you find this statement (near the top):

```
exec("~/data/shapes/player/player.cs");
```

and replace it with this statement:

```
exec("~/data/shapes/player/mrbox_animation_map.cs");
```

Note

If you happened to notice that the file you are editing here is called player.cs, and there is a statement inside it (albeit one that you are changing) that contains a reference to player.cs, and are tempted to freak out, go ahead. I'll watch. Far be it for me to stop you from enjoying yourself.

Once you've regained your composure, I'll point out that, no, you aren't imagining things. This file, player.cs, really does run an exec operation on the file player.cs, but a different file. And this is one of my little pet peeves about the default file organization for the Torque demo.

> The file you are editing is server-side code. The file in the exec statement you are changing is both server- and client-side code, and has a completely different job from the server-side-only version of player.cs. The server- and client-side file contains a mapping of the player model's animation sequence files, so that your client will know which sequences to execute when the server tells it to animate. The server-side-only version of player.cs contains the player datablock—all of its related definitions, profiles, and methods. Two different beasts. But they have the same name, and I hate that.
>
> By happy coincidence, we need to change the file name used in that exec statement anyway, because we are going to be using a different model for the following activity. Therefore, I get to name the model's animation mapping file the way I want to, hence the change.

The file referenced in the exec statement contains a mapping of the player model's animation sequence files to a numeric index. The server will send an index number to the client when it needs the client to change to a particular animation. This animation mapping file is the link between what the server deals with (indices) and the client deals with (file names). It's all quite clever and civilized.

Next, scroll down until you find the datablock definition:

```
datablock PlayerData(LightMaleHumanArmor)
```

Inside this definition, about four lines down, you will find the line with the shapeFile property. Comment this line out by putting two forward slashes at the front of the line, like this:

```
//  shapeFile = "~/data/shapes/player/player.dts";
```

Then, below the commented line, put this version of the line instead:

```
   shapeFile = "~/data/shapes/player/mrbox.dts";
```

What we've done is merely told the datablock that we are going to use the Mr. Box model instead of the Ugly Orc model that normally lurks around these parts.

Next, scroll down until you encounter this statement (still in the LightMaleHumanArmor datablock definition).

```
   minImpactSpeed = 45;
```

and change it to this:

```
   minImpactSpeed = 10;
```

We've lowered the speed at which the player object receives some damage from an impact. At a setting of 45, you can run straight into the side of a house at top speed and simply bounce off without any ill effects. The last time I did something like that myself, I broke my nose and bled all over everything. That certainly counts as an ill effect on the planet I come from.

You can fiddle with the minimum impact speed as much as you like, but watch out. If you set the minimum impact speed to too low a value, then you will take damage when your character simply spawns in. Not useful.

Now scroll down until you find the function definition:

```
function Armor::onImpact(%this, %obj, %collidedObject, %vec, %vecLen)
```

It's down around line 804 or so (yeah I know, it's a very big file).

Add the following code after the first brace in the function:

```
%name = getRandom(4);
%obj.setSkinName(%name);
```

What this does is when the player bumps into something, the onImpact method for this class of character is invoked (because of the changed minImpactSpeed value). Inside the onImpact method, we've stuck some statements that pick a random number between 0 and 4. You may recall that our skins all have the variant portions of their names as numbers. Well, when we get our random number, that becomes the variant portion of the skin name!

We simply pass in the number to the setSkinName call to our object, and wait to see what color Mr. Box ends up with.

Finally, we need to create the animation sequence mapping file. Type in the following and save it as \A3D\demo\data\shapes\player\mrbox_animation_map.cs:

```
datablock TSShapeConstructor(PlayerDts)
{
   baseShape = "./mrbox.dts";
   sequence0 = "./player_root.dsq root";
   sequence1 = "./player_forward.dsq run";
   sequence2 = "./player_back.dsq back";
   sequence3 = "./player_side.dsq side";
   sequence4 = "./player_lookde.dsq look";
   sequence5 = "./player_head.dsq head";
```

```
    sequence6 = "./player_fall.dsq fall";
    sequence7 = "./player_land.dsq land";
    sequence8 = "./player_jump.dsq jump";
    sequence9  = "./player_diehead.dsq death1";
    sequence10 = "./player_diechest.dsq death2";
    sequence11 = "./player_dieback.dsq death3";
    sequence12 = "./player_diesidelf.dsq death4";
    sequence13 = "./player_diesidert.dsq death5";
    sequence14 = "./player_dieleglf.dsq death6";
    sequence15 = "./player_dielegrt.dsq death7";
    sequence16 = "./player_dieslump.dsq death8";
    sequence17 = "./player_dieknees.dsq death9";
    sequence18 = "./player_dieforward.dsq death10";
    sequence19 = "./player_diespin.dsq death11";
    sequence20 = "./player_looksn.dsq looksn";
    sequence21 = "./player_lookms.dsq lookms";
    sequence22 = "./player_scoutroot.dsq scoutroot";
    sequence23 = "./player_headside.dsq headside";
    sequence24 = "./player_recoilde.dsq light_recoil";
    sequence25 = "./player_sitting.dsq sitting";
    sequence26 = "./player_celsalute.dsq celsalute";
    sequence27 = "./player_celwave.dsq celwave";
    sequence28 = "./player_standjump.dsq standjump";
    sequence29 = "./player_looknw.dsq looknw";
    sequence30 = "./player_dance.dsq dance";
    sequence31 = "./player_range.dsq range";
};
```

As you can see, it's a datablock definition for the model itself. The key line is

```
    baseShape = "./mrbox.dts";
```

It tells Torque which model file the animation sequences will be used with. All of the rest of the datablock is a list where each line maps a sequence identifier (used as an index pointer) to a file name and a sequence name, like this example:

```
    sequence0 = "./player_root.dsq root";
```

A few things to know about this datablock. The sequence identifiers need to be laid out in order, from lowest (sequence0) to highest (sequence31 in this case, but you can have more). The names that appear after the file names in the string (ie. "root" in the preceding example) must appear as written. The file names must be properly exported sequence files (.dsq), but can have any naming scheme you like, as long as they correctly correspond to the sequence names they were created for.

Note also that although I am using the Mr. Box model, I'm still using the sequence files created for the orc! Now that's flexibility.

Abusing Mr. Box

Now comes the fun part. Launch the demo into the FPS mission. Hit the Tab key to switch into third-person point-of-view mode.

Now just race around the map, banging into things! It's a smashing lot of fun. Watch Mr. Box change colors. Heh. When it comes to computer characters, I can be a wee bit ornery. On the odd occasion you will notice that the color doesn't change. This is purely the luck of the draw. Every now and then, randomly, the same number can be picked twice, or even three times in a row!

Moving Right Along

In this chapter, you learned how to change the textures, or skins, of various objects and types of shapes in the game using TorqueScript.

Starting with simple crates, we've seen how we can use variable skins as a results multiplier, helping to create a wide variety of visual appearances with a minimal amount of modeling and texture creation.

Then we looked at changing skins under program control in a sequence fashion simulating a traffic light.

Finally, we played with poor Mr. Box, slamming him into all manner of immovable objects, giggling with glee as we saw him change colors as a result of the impacts.

Final Thoughts

Here endeth the book. By now I think you probably have a head full of things you want to do with your new game ideas.

As you've moved through the chapters, you may have slowly started to form the concepts for what might be the Next Killer Game. Or you may have developed some nifty new ideas to use in a game or program already underway. Or you might be dreaming up new and interesting ways to abuse Mr. Box. Who knows?

One thing is certain though, whatever you do, have fun while you are doing it. It *can* be all fun and games, you know!

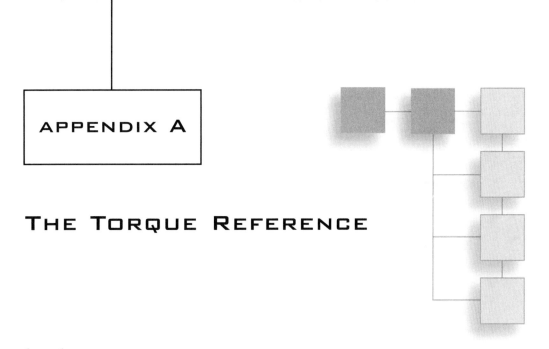

APPENDIX A

THE TORQUE REFERENCE

The following tables refer to the Torque Game Engine release version 1.3 engine build. Some notes about the functions:

- Some functions are available for use on the client only. For the most part, this is very obvious. For example, any hardware-related functions are client-only. However, for other functions this may not be so obvious. These functions are marked "client-only."

- Torque is not case-sensitive with respect to identifiers, like variables and function names. (Although TorqueScript keywords like *if*, *function*, *while* and so on are case-sensitive. See Table A.3 for a list TorqueScript keywords.) The Torque functions in this list all begin with lowercase letters, even though in many programming circles it is conventional for function identifiers to begin with capitals. The reference is written to conform to the Torque internal representation, but you can capitalize the functions if you need to to match your programming standards.

Note

TorqueScript is both a compiled and an interpreted language. Most of the functions in this reference can be used in real-time through the Torque console window by directly typing in the function with the appropriate parameters and correct syntax with proper usage, and all of them can be used script programs.

Because of this duality, the word *function* may be supplanted by the word *command*, depending on the usage context. They both mean the same thing—they both refer to TorqueScript executable statements that invoke a block of code defined elsewhere in script or in the Torque engine itself. However, when we write script programs, we use *function* to describe such a program statement. When we type in the statement directly using the console, we call it a *command*.

If you choose not to worry about the context, then feel free to call them all functions, or call them all commands—whatever twists your crank. However, take note that the keyword *function* has a specific meaning and usage, as described in Chapter 2.

So if you see code that looks like this:

```
function Fubar()
{
   echo("tarfu");
}
```

You can NOT substitute the word "command" for the word "function," since "command" is not a keyword. But you can still *call* Fubar a command when speaking or writing about it, and not be wrong.

TorqueScript Function Reference

activateDirectInput()

Parameters: none

Return: nothing

Description: Activates direct input device polling

Usage: `activateDirectInput();`

activateKeyboard()

Parameters: none

Return: numeric   1 = success, 0 = fail.

Description: Enables DirectInput polling of the keyboard

Usage: `%result = activateKeyboard();`

activatePackage(name)

Parameters: name   String containing the name of the package

Return: nothing

Description: Tells Torque to start using the package specified by *name*

Usage: `activatePackage(Show);`

addCardProfile(vendor, renderer, safeMode, lockArray, subImage, fogTexture, noEnvColor, clipHigh, deleteContext, texCompress, interiorLock, skipFirstFog, only16, noArraysAlpha, profile)

Parameters:	*vendor*	Name of card vendor
	renderer	Name of renderer
	safeMode	true or false
	lockArray	true or false
	subImage	true or false
	fogTexture	true or false
	noEnvColor	true or false
	clipHigh	true or false
	deleteContext	true or false
	texCompress	true or false
	interiorLock	true or false
	skipFirstFog	true or false
	only16	true or false
	noArraysAlpha	true or false
	profile	Name of profile
Return:	nothing	
Description:	Creates a profile of features of a video card for later reference	
Usage:	addCardProfile(%vendor, %renderer, true, true, true, true, true, false, false, true, true, false, false, false,"")	

addMaterialMapping(material, sound, color)

Parameters:	*material*	Name string to identify the material
	sound	Name of sound profile to attach to material
	color	Color specification to attach to material
Return:	nothing	
Description:	Adds sound and dust color to specified material	
Usage:	addMaterialMapping("sand", "sound:0", "color:0.3 0.3 0.5 0.4 0.0");	

addOSCardProfile(vendor,renderer,allowOpenGL,allowD3D, preferOpenGL)

Parameters:	*vendor*	Name of card vendor
	Renderer	Name of renderer
	AllowOpenGL	true or false
	allowD3D	true or false
	preferOpenGL	true or false
Return:	*nothing*	
Description:	Stores certain aspects of a video card for later usage	
Usage:	addOSCardProfile(%vendor,%renderer,true,true,true);	

addTaggedString (string)

Parameters:	*string*	Normal string to be added
Return:	*numeric*	The tag
Description:	Adds a string to the tagged string list (NetStringTable)	
Usage:	%tagname = AddTaggedString(%name);	

aiAddPlayer(name, AIClass)

Parameters:	*name*	AI character's name
	AIClass	Character class or namespace
Return:	*numeric*	New AIPlayer handle
Description:	Adds an AI Player to the game	
Usage:	%handle=aiAddPlayer("Boss",RTSUnit);	

aiConnect(id)

Parameters:	*id*	ID reference number (0 to 20) of the AI bot
Return:	*numeric*	New object handle
Description:	Creates a new uncontrolled AI connection. The AI is treated the same as a player.	
Usage:	aiConnect(1);	

alGetListener3f(ALenum)

Parameters:	*ALenum*	The enum string. Choices:
		"AL_VELOCITY"
		"AL_POSITION"
		"AL_DIRECTION"

Return: *numeric*

Description: Queries the value of the *ALenum*

Usage: `%direction = alGetListener3f("AL_DIRECTION");`

alGetListeneri(ALenum)

Parameters:	*ALenum*	The enum string. Choices:
		"AL_CONE_INNER_ANGLE"
		"AL_CONE_OUTER_ANGLE"
		"AL_LOOPING"
		"AL_STREAMING"
		"AL_BUFFER"

Return: *numeric*

Description: Queries the value of the *ALenum*

Usage: `%looping = alGetListeneri("AL_LOOPING");`

alGetString(ALenum)

Parameters:	*string*	The enum string. Choices:
		"AL_VENDOR"
		"AL_VERSION"
		"AL_RENDERER"
		"AL_EXTENSIONS"

Return: *string*

Description: Obtains the string specified

Usage: `%vendor = alGetString("AL_VENDOR");`

alListener3f(ALenum, ["x y z"] I [x,y,z])

Parameters:	ALenum	The enum string. Choices:
		"AL_VELOCITY"
		"AL_POSITION"
		"AL_DIRECTION"
	"x y z"	The string contains a tuple indicating where to place the enumed property in 3D world space.
	x,y,z	(alternative) If "x y z" isn't used, then this is a tuple indicating where to place the audio object in 3D world space. *Note:* These are three numerics, not a string!
Return:	nothing	
Description:	Sets the *ALenum* to *value* for the listener (the player, who "hears" a sound)	
Usage:	`alListener3f("AL_GAIN_LINEAR", $pref::Audio::masterVolume);`	

allowConnections(switch)

Parameters:	switch	1 (or `true`) = enable, 0 (or `false`) = disable.
Return:	nothing	
Description:	Enables and disables connections to the game server	
Usage:	`allowConnections(true);`	

alxCreateSource({ profile, [x,y,z] } I { description, filename, [x,y,z] })

Parameters:	profile	Descriptor string
	x,y,z	If *profile* is used, this is a tuple indicating where to place the audio object. *Note:* These are three numerics, not a string!
	description	(alternative) If *profile* isn't used, then this is an audio object description string.
	filename	If *description* is used, then this string specifies the audio file to use for the sound.
	x,y,z	If *description* is used, this is a tuple indicating where to place the audio object. *Note:* These are three numerics, not a string!

Return: *numeric*   Handle to audio object

Description: Loads an audio source file into memory and initializes it for use

Usage: `$handle =alxCreateSource("Audio0","~/data/sounds/test.wav");`

alxGetChannelVolume(channel)

Parameters: *channel*   Channel ID number

Return: *numeric*

Description: Queries the volume of *channel*

Usage: `%vol = alxGetChannelVolume(%channel);`

alxGetListenerf(ALenum)

Parameters: *ALenum*   The enum string. Choices:
                                      "AL_GAIN"
                                      "AL_GAIN_LINEAR"

Return: *numeric*

Description: Queries the value of the *ALenum*

Usage: `%gain = alxGetListenerf("AL_GAIN");`

alxGetSource3f(handle, ALenum)

Parameters: *handle*   Handle to audio object

                ALenum   The enum string. Choices:
                                      "AL_VELOCITY"
                                      "AL_POSITION"
                                      "AL_DIRECTION"

Return: *string*   "x y z"

Description: Obtains the value of *ALenum* for the specified *handle*

Usage: `%pos = alxGetSource3f(%handle[%sender], "AL_POSITION");`

alxGetSourcef(handle, ALenum)

Parameters: *handle*   Handle to audio object

ALenum   The enum string. Choices:

"AL_PITCH"

"AL_REFERENCE_DISTANCE"

"AL_MAX_DISTANCE"

"AL_CONE_OUTER_GAIN"

"AL_GAIN"

"AL_GAIN_LINEAR"

Return: numeric

Description: Obtains the value of *ALenum* for the specified *handle*

Usage: `%gain = alxGetSourcef(%handle[%sender], "AL_GAIN");`

alxGetSourcei(handle, ALenum)

Parameters: *handle*   Handle to audio object

ALenum   The enum string. Choices:

"AL_CONE_INNER_ANGLE"

"AL_CONE_OUTER_ANGLE"

"AL_LOOPING"

"AL_STREAMING"

"AL_BUFFER"

Return: numeric   *The pitch value*

Description: Obtains the value of *ALenum* for the specified *handle*

Usage: `%pitch = alxGetSourcei((%handle[%sender], "AL_LOOPING");`

alxGetWaveLen(fileName)

Parameters: *string*   fileName

Return: numeric   length of file in milliseconds

Description: Obtains the length in milliseconds of the .wav file specified by *fileName*

Usage: `%len = alxGetWaveLen (%pathToWaveFile);`

alxIsPlaying(handle)

Parameters:	*handle*	Handle to audio object
Return:	*numeric*	1 = true, 0 = false
Description:	Queries if a *handle* is currently playing	
Usage:	%isPlaying = alxIsPlaying(%handle);	

alxListenerf(ALenum,value)

Parameters:	*ALenum*	The enum string. Choices:
		"AL_GAIN"
		"AL_GAIN_LINEAR"
	value	Numeric gain value
Return:	*nothing*	
Description:	Sets the *ALenum* to *value* for the Listener (the player, who "hears" a sound)	
Usage:	alxListenerf("AL_GAIN_LINEAR", %vol);	

alxPlay([handle] | [profile [, x,y,z]])

Parameters:	*handle*	Handle to audio object
	profile	(alternative) Descriptor string
	x,y,z	If *profile* is used, this is a tuple indicating where to place the audio object. *Note:* These are three numerics, not a string! (optional)
Return:	*numeric*	Returns object handle if profile is used.
Description:	Begins audio playback with audio object specified by *handle*. Alternatively, if *profile* is used, this function creates an object, begins playback at optional *x,y,z* coordinates and then returns a handle to the created object.	
Usage:	%handle0 = alxCreateSource("Audio0", "~/data/sounds/test.wav");	
	alxPlay(%handle0);	
	%handle1 = alxPlay("Audio1", "100, 100, 10");	

alxSetChannelVolume(channel, volume)

Parameters:	*channel*	Channel ID number
	volume	Volume value
Return:	*numeric*	1 = success, 0 = fail
Description:	Sets the *channel* to *volume*	
Usage:	`%result = alxSetChannelVolume(%channel, %volume);`	

alxSource3f(handle,ALenum, ["x y z"] | [x,y,z])

Parameters:	*handle*	Handle to audio object
	ALenum	The enum string. Choices:
		"AL_VELOCITY"
		"AL_POSITION"
		"AL_DIRECTION"
	"x y z"	String containing a tuple indicating where to place the enumed property in 3D world space
	x,y,z	(alternative) If "xyz" isn't used, then this is a tuple indicating where to place the audio object in 3D world space. *Note:* These are three numerics, not a string!
Return:	*nothing*	
Description:	Sets *ALenum* for the specified *handle* to 3D	
Usage:	`alxSource3f(%handle[%sender], "AL_POSITION", "100 100 20");`	

alxSourcef(handle, ALenum, value)

Parameters:	*handle*	Handle to audio object
	ALenum	The enum string. Choices:
		"AL_PITCH"
		"AL_REFERENCE_DISTANCE"
		"AL_MAX_DISTANCE"
		"AL_CONE_OUTER_GAIN"
		"AL_GAIN"
		"AL_GAIN_LINEAR"
	value	Numeric (floating point) value to set *ALenum* to

Return:	*nothing*	
Description:	Sets *ALenum* for the specified *handle* to the floating-point *value*	
Usage:	`alxSourcef(%handle[%sender], "AL_GAIN", %gain);`	

alxSourcei(handle, ALenum, value)

Parameters:	*handle*	Handle to audio object
	ALenum	The enum string. Choices:
		"AL_CONE_INNER_ANGLE"
		"AL_CONE_OUTER_ANGLE"
		"AL_LOOPING"
		"AL_STREAMING"
		"AL_BUFFER"
	value	Numeric value to set *ALenum* to.
Return:	*nothing*	
Description:	Sets *ALenum* for the specified *handle* to the floating-point *value*	
Usage:	`alxSourcei(%handle[%sender], "AL_LOOPING", true);`	

alxStop(handle)

Parameters:	*handle*	Handle to audio object
Return:	*nothing*	
Description:	Stops the playback from *handle*	
Usage:	`alxStop(%handle[%sender]);`	

alxStopAll()

Parameters:	*none*	
Return:	*nothing*	
Description:	Stops the playback on all registered channels	
Usage:	`alxStopAll();`	

backtrace()

Parameters: none

Return: nothing

Description: Enables echo of script call stack to console

Usage: `backtrace();`

buildTaggedString(string, format)

Parameters: *string*   Normal string to be added

format   Format specifying string

Return: *string*

Description: Builds and adds a tagged string using *string* with specified *format.*

Usage: `%tagstring = buildTaggedString(%name, %format);`

calcExplosionCoverage(location, handle, mask)

Parameters: *location*   Where the target object is

handle   Target object

mask   Object type mask of objects that may block the explosion

Return: *numeric*   1 = affected, 0 = unaffected

Description: Determines if an object at a location was affected by an explosion. Listed object types will be taken into consideration in the calculation if they would block the explosion force.

Usage: `%coverage = calcExplosionCoverage(%location, %targetObject,`

`$TypeMasks::InteriorObjectType | $TypeMasks::TerrainObjectType`

`| $TypeMasks::VehicleObjectType);`

call(function [,args ...])

Parameters: *function*   String containing name of function

args   Zero or more arguments as needed by *function*

Return: *string*   *Function*'s return value embedded in a string

Description: Executes the function with the name *function* with supplied arguments, *args*

Usage: `%result = call(%func, %arg1, %arg2);`

cancel(id)

Parameters: *id*   ID number of supposed event

Return: *nothing*

Description: Cancels the event specified by *id*

Usage: `cancel($eventid);`

cancelServerQuery()

Parameters: *none*

Return: *nothing*

Description: Cancels the current query and drops anything outstanding in the ping list

Usage: `cancelServerQuery();`

clearServerPaths()

Parameters: *none*

Return: *none*

Description: Clears all stored paths held by the path manager and releases the memory used

Usage: `clearServerPaths();`

clearTextureHolds()

Parameters: *none*

Return: *numeric*   Amount of memory released

Description: Releases any textures not being used, and frees the memory

Usage: `%clearedMem=clearTextureHolds();`

cls()

Parameters: none

Return: none

Description: Clears the console screen

Usage: `cls();`

collapseEscape(text)

Parameters: text   String

Return: string   The resultant string

Description: Removes escaped characters in text. For example, \\n becomes \n.

Usage: `%coltext = collapseEscape(%text);`

commandToClient(client, function [,arg1,...argn])

Parameters: client   Handle of target client

    function   Function on the server to be executed

    arg1,...argn   Arguments for the function

Return: nothing

Description: Tells client to execute the command or function specified by *function* and passes it the arguments. On the client, the function is declared in the following format:

```
function clientCmdfunction(arg1,...argn) { … }
```

The identifier fragment `clientCmd` is prepended to the function name.

Usage: `commandToClient( %client, 'SyncClock', %time);`

commandToServer(function [,arg1,...argn])

Parameters: function   Function on the server to be executed

    arg1,...argn   Arguments for the function

Return: nothing

Description: Tells the server to execute the command or function specified by *function*, and passes it the arguments. On the server, the function is declared in the following format:

```
function serverCmdfunction(%client, arg1,...argn) { … }
```

The identifier `serverCmd` is prepended to the function name. The first parameter is always the handle of the client that sent the command, and the actual command arguments follow.

Usage: `commandToServer('ToggleCamera');`

compile(fileName)

Parameters: *filename*   String containing filename

Return: *numeric*   1 = success, 0 = fail

Description: Compiles the source script file *filename*

Usage: `%result = compile("/common/default.cs");`

containerBoxEmpty(mask, loc, rad [,yrad, zrad])

Parameters: *mask*   Object type mask

loc   Coordinate tuple

rad   Radius distance (or X-axis distance)

yrad   Optional distance in Y-axis

zrad   Optional distance in Z-axis

Return: *numeric*

Description: Returns `true` if any objects of given types exist in a sphere of the specified extent *rad* and `false` otherwise. If *yrad* is specified, then *rad* is the X-axis extent, and *yrad* is the Y-axis extent. If *zrad* is specified, it becomes the Z-axis extent.

Usage: `%isAny = containerBoxEmpty(ItemObjectType,"10.0 10.0 100.0", 100);`

containerFindFirst(type, point, x, y, z)

Parameters:	*type*	The type mask of objects to find
	point	Location of container
	x, y,z	Numeric bounds of container specified. Not a string.
Return:	*numeric*	Handle of object found

Description: Finds objects of *type* within the box specified with *x,y,z* at the given point *point*. Returns the handle of the first object found.

Usage: `%objectHandle = containerFindFirst(type, point, x, y, z);`

containerFindNext()

Parameters:	*none*	
Return:	*numeric*	Handle of object found

Description: Finds the next object in the container specified immediately preceding call to `containerFindFirst`, and gets its handle.

Usage: `%objectHandle = containerFindNext();`

containerRayCast (start, end, mask, [exclude])

Parameters:	*start*	Starting coordinate tuple
	end	Ending coordinate tuple
	mask	Object type mask
	exclude	List of handles
Return:	*string*	Hit list

Description: Finds a list of objects of type *mask* between the two cords supplied. A list of object handles can be included in the *exempt* parameter that will not be returned in the hit list.

Usage: `%tgt = containerRayCast (%cameraPoint, %rangeEnd, ItemObjectType);`

containerSearchCurrDist()

Parameters: none

Return: numeric

Description: Gets the current container search distance

Usage: `%dist = containerSearchCurrDist();`

containerSearchCurrRadiusDist()

Parameters: none

Return: numeric

Description: Gets the current container search radius distance

Usage: `%rad = containerSearchCurrRadiusDist();`

containerSearchNext()

Parameters: none

Return: numeric

Description: Gets the next object in a container search

Usage: `%nc = containerSearchNext();`

createCanvas(title)

Parameters: title   String containing title of the window

Return: numeric   1 = success, 0 = fail

Description: Creates a graphics "canvas" in a window

Usage: `%result = createCanvas("My Game");`

dbgSetParameters (port, pw)

Parameters: port   Connection port

                pw   Password

Return: nothing

Description: Initializes telnet debug connection request parameters

Usage: `dbgSetParameters(1130, "games");`

deactivateDirectInput()

Parameters: *none*

Return: *nothing*

Description: Disables DirectInput device polling (mouse, keyboard, joystick)

Usage: deactivateDirectInput();

deactivateKeyboard()

Parameters: *none*

Return: *nothing*

Description: Disables DirectInput polling of the keyboard

Usage: deactivateKeyboard();

deactivatePackage(name)

Parameters: *name*   String containing the name of the package

Return: *nothing*

Description: Tells Torque to stop using the package specified by *name*

Usage: deactivatePackage(Show);

debug()

Parameters: *none*

Return: *nothing*

Description: Enables debug mode

Usage: debug();

debug_debugbreak()

Parameters: *none*

Return: *nothing*

Description: *Windows:*   Displays a crash dialog box

Linux: Causes a *segfault*

Usage: debug_debugbreak();

debug_testx86unixmutex()

Parameters: *none*

Return: *nothing*

Description: *Linux only:* Check if OS can create a mutex

Usage: `debug_testx86unixmutex();`

decreaseFSAA()

Parameters: *none*

Return: *nothing*

Description: Decrements FSAA level by 1

Usage: `decreaseFSAA ()`

deleteDataBlocks()

Parameters: *none*

Return: *nothing*

Description: Unloads and removes all registered data blocks from the game

Usage: `deleteDataBlocks();`

deleteVariables(wildcard)

Parameters: *wildcard*   Match string to specify variables

Return: *nothing*

Description: Deletes global variables specified by *wildcard*. The wildcard string supports "*" to match any number of any characters and "?" to match any single character.

Usage: `deleteVariables("*");`

detag(tstring)

Parameters: *tstring*   Tagged string

Return: *string*   String value for the tagged string

Description: Detags a tagged string

Usage: `%name = detag(%test.name);`

disableJoystick()

Parameters: *none*

Return: *nothing*

Description: Disables DirectInput polling of the joystick device

Usage: `disableJoystick();`

disableLocking()

Parameters: *none*

Return: *nothing*

Description: Disables UNIX/Linux lock mechanism

Usage: `disableLocking();`

disableMouse()

Parameters: *none*

Return: *nothing*

Description: Disables DirectInput polling of the mouse device

Usage: `disableMouse();`

dnetSetLogging(switch)

Parameters: *switch*   1 (or `true`) = enable, 0 (or `false`) = disable

Return: *nothing*

Description: Enables network packet logging to the console

Usage: `dnetSetLogging(1);`

dumpConsoleClasses()

Parameters: *none*

Return: *nothing*

Description: Dumps all registered console classes to the console

Usage: `dumpConsoleClasses();`

dumpMemSnapshot(filename)

Parameters: *filename*   String containing filename

Return: *nothing*

Description: Dumps memory statistics to the file

Usage: `dumpMemSnapshot("dump.txt");`

dumpNetStringTable()

Parameters: *none*

Return: *nothing*

Description: Dumps the `NetStringTable` stats to the console

Usage: `dumpNetStringTable();`

dumpResourceStats();

Parameters: *none*

Return: *nothing*

Description: Dumps texture information to the console in the following format: `path, resource, lockCount`

Usage: `dumpResourceStats();`

dumpTextureStats()

Parameters: *none*

Return: *nothing*

Description: Dumps texture information to the console in the following format: `type, refCount, holding` (yes or no), `textureSpace, texFileName`

Usage: `dumpTextureStats();`

echo(text)

Parameters: *text*   String

Return: *nothing*

Description: Prints *text* to the console with the standard font. Text can be formatted according to the string rules.

Usage: `echo( "Hello World");`

echoInputState()

Parameters: *none*

Return: *nothing*

Description: Displays the current state of DirectInput (mouse, keyboard, and joystick)

Usage: `echoInputState();`

enableJoystick()

Parameters: *none*

Return: *nothing*

Description: Enables DirectInput polling of the joystick device

Usage: `enableJoystick();`

enableLocking()

Parameters: *none*

Return: *nothing*

Description: Enables UNIX/Linux lock mechanism

Usage: `enableLocking();`

enableMouse()

Parameters: *none*

Return: *numeric*   1 = success, 0 = fail

Description: Enables DirectInput polling of the mouse device

Usage: `%result = enableMouse();`

enableWinConsole(switch)

Parameters: *switch*   1 enables, 0 disables

Return: *nothing*

Description: Displays the console window

Usage: `enableWinConsole(true);`

error(text)

Parameters:	text	String
Return:	nothing	

Description: Prints *text* to the console with red font. Text can be formatted according to the string rules.

Usage: `error("I'm sorry, Dave, I'm afraid I can't do that.");`

eval(string)

Parameters:	string	String containing script code
Return:	string	

Description: Executes functions, assigns variables, and loads packages and data blocks contained within the *string* parameter.

Usage: `%result = eval( %MissionInfoObject );`

exec(fileName [, nocalls [,journalScript]])

Parameters:	filename	String containing filename
	nocalls	When set to `true`, prevents functions from being called
	journalScript	When set to `true`, indicates that *filename* is a journal script
Return:	string	

Description: Compiles, executes functions, assigns variables, and loads packages and data blocks read from contents of the file *filename*. If *nocalls* is set to `true`, functions are not executed, but the other operations still take place.

Usage: `%result = exec("/common/default.cs");`

expandEscape(text)

Parameters:	text	String
Return:	string	The resultant string

Description: Escapes all of the escape characters in *text*. For example, \n becomes \\n. In this case the \n would be printed to the console instead of the new line it would otherwise cause.

Usage: `%extext = expandEscape(%text);`

expandFilename(filename)

Parameters: *filename*   String containing filename

Return: *string*

Description: Obtains the actual OS-specific absolute path of *filename*

Usage: `%fullmissionpath = expandFilename("~/data/missions/test.mis");`

export(searchString [, fileName [,append]])

Parameters: *search*   Prefix of variables to search for

                   filename   String containing filename

                   append   Indicates whether to append to file or overwrite

Return: *nothing*

Description: Saves the values of variables starting with *search* to the filenamed *filename*. When *append* is set to `true`, the file is appended; when set to `false`, the file is overwritten. The search string supports "*" to match any number of any characters and "?" to match any single character.

Usage: `%result = export("$Pref::Game::*", "./game/prefs.cs", False);`

fileBase(filename)

Parameters: *filename*   String containing full filename

Return: *string*   String containing the base name

Description: Gets the base name of the file specified by *filename*

Usage: `%base = fileBase("/common/server/script.cs");`

fileExt(filename)

Parameters: *filename*   String containing full filename

Return: *string*   String containing extension

Description: Gets the extension of the file specified by *filename*

Usage: `%name = fileExt("script.cs");`

fileName(filename)

Parameters:	*filename*	String containing full filename
Return:	*string*	String containing the name
Description:	Gets the name of the file specified by *filename*	
Usage:	`%name = fileName("scripts.cs");`	

filePath(filename)

Parameters:	*filename*	String containing full filename
Return:	*string*	String containing the path
Description:	Gets the path of the file specified by *filename*	
Usage:	`%path = filePath("/common/server/script.cs");`	

findFirstFile (pattern)

Parameters:	*pattern*	String pattern
Return:	*string*	The file's name
Description:	Finds the name of the first file in the TorqueScript filename buffer matching the given *pattern*. Supports "*" to match any number of any characters and "?" to match any single character.	
Usage:	`%result = findFirstFile("/common/*.cs");`	

findNextFile (pattern)

Parameters:	*pattern*	String pattern
Return:	*string*	The file's name
Description:	Finds the name of the next file in the TorqueScript filename buffer matching the search by the call immediately preceding `findFirstFile`. Supports "*" to match any number of any characters and "?" to match any single character.	
Usage:	`%result = findNextFile("/common/*.cs");`	

firstWord(text)

Parameters: *text*   String with space-delimited words

Return: *string*   The resultant string

Description: Gets the first word-string within *text*

Usage: `%tgt = firstWord(%text);`

flushTextureCache()

Parameters: *none*

Return: *nothing*

Description: Deletes cached textures from memory.

Usage: `flushTextureCache();`

freeMemoryDump()

Parameters: *none*

Return: *nothing*

Description: Prints free memory statistics

Usage: `freeMemoryDump();`

getBoxCenter(box)

Parameters: *box*   String containing two 3D tuples defining the box

Return: *string*

Description: Computes the center of a box

Usage: `%c = getBoxCenter("10,10,10,50,50,50");`

getBuildString()

Parameters: *none*

Return: *string*

Description: Obtains the BUILD type (Release or Debug) of the current build

Usage: `%bs = getBuildString();`

getClipboard()

Parameters: *none*

Return: *string*   *clipboard contents*

Description: Extracts the text contained in the current OS clipboard (this is the clipboard that the OS uses for copy/paste operations)

Usage: `%text = getClipboard ();`

getCompileTimeString()

Parameters: *none*

Return: *string*

Description: Obtains the compile time and date of the current build

Usage: `%ct = getCompileTimeString();`

getControlObjectAltitude()

Parameters: *none*

Return: *numeric*

Description: Client-only. Obtains the altitude of the player object.

Usage: `%altitude = getControlObjectAltitude();`

getControlObjectSpeed()

Parameters: *none*

Return: *numeric*

Description: Client-only. Obtains the speed of the player object.

Usage: `%speed = getControlObjectSpeed();`

getDesktopResolution()

Parameters: *none*

Return: *string*

Description: Reports the current desktop resolution

Usage: `%res = getDesktopResolution():`

getDisplayDeviceList()

Parameters: *none*

Return: *string*

Description: Obtains the device name for each display device

Usage: `%name = getDisplayDeviceList();`

getField(text, index)

Parameters: *text*   String with field-delimited words

                     index   Field-based offset into the text string

Return: *string*   Contains the found field-string

Description: Gets the field-string at *index* within *text*. In the usage example that follows, if %text equaled "Of Mice and Men", then %word would be set to "and" when the function returned.

Usage: `%field = getField(%text, 0);`

getFieldCount (text)

Parameters: *text*   String with field-delimited words

Return: *numeric*

Description: Gets the number of field-strings within *text*

Usage: `%count = getFieldCount( %text );`

getFields(text, first [, last])

Parameters: *text*   String with space-delimited fields

                     first   Field-based offset into the text string specifying the first field to extract

                     last   Field-based offset into the text string specifying the last field to extract

Return: *string*   Contains the found fields

Description: Gets one or more field-strings at *index* within *text*. If *count* is specified, gets *count* number of field-strings.

Usage: `%position    = getFields(%obj.getTransform(), 0, 2);`

getFileCount (pattern)

Parameters:	*pattern*	String pattern
Return:	*numeric*	

Description: Gets the number of files in the TorqueScript filename buffer that match *pattern*

Usage: `%count = getFileCount("/common/server/*.cs");`

getFileCRC(filename)

Parameters:	*filename*	String containing full filename
Return:	*numeric*	The *Cyclic Redundancy Check* (CRC) value

Description: Gets the CRC value of the file specified by *filename*

Usage: `%crc = getFileCRC("/common/server/script.cs");`

getJoystickAxes(instance)

Parameters:	*instance*	The joystick object
Return:	*string*	

Description: Obtains the current axes of the joystick pointed to by *instance*

Usage: `%joyAxes = getJoystickAxes( 3 );`

getMaxFrameAllocation()

Parameters:	*none*
Return:	*numeric*

Description: Gets the Max Frame Allocation unit

Usage: `%maxFrameAlloc = getMaxFrameAllocation();`

getModPaths()

Parameters:	*none*
Return:	*string*

Description: Gets the current Mod path

Usage: `$mp = getModPaths();`

getRandom([[max]|[min,max]])

Parameters:	*max*	High limit (optional)
	min	Low limit (optional)
Return:	*numeric*	Ranged from 0 to 1, exclusive, if no parameters given, otherwise, see description

Description: Computes a pseudo-random number. If *min* is not included, then 0 is the minimum. If *max* is not included, then 4,294,967,295 (highest 32-bit number minus 1) is the maximum.

Usage: `%random = getRandom(1,99);`

getRandomSeed()

Parameters:	*none*
Return:	*numeric*

Description: Obtains the current random seed

Usage: `%seed = getRandomSeed();`

getRealTime()

Parameters:	*none*
Return:	*numeric*

Description: Gets the real time (in milliseconds) since this computer started

Usage: `%rt = getRealTime();`

getRecord(text, index)

Parameters:	*text*	String with new line-delimited records
	index	Record-based offset into the text string
Return:	*string*	Contains the found record-string

Description: Gets the record-string at *index* within *text*. In the usage example that follows, if `%text` equaled "Of Mice and Men\nGrapes of Wrath\nCannery Row", then `%record` would be set to "Grapes of Wrath" when the function returned.

Usage: `%record = getRecord(%text, 1);`

getRecordCount(text)

Parameters:	*text*	String with new line-delimited records
Return:	*numeric*	

Description: Get the number of record-strings within *text*

Usage: `%count = getRecordCount(%text );`

getRecords(text, first [, last])

Parameters:	*text*	String with new line-delimited records
	first	Record-based offset into the text string specifying the first record to extract
	last	Record-based offset into the text string specifying the last record to extract
Return:	*string*	Contains the found records

Description: Gets one or more record-strings at *index* within *text*. If *count* is specified, gets *count* number of record-strings.

Usage: `%books    = getRecords(%obj.getTransform(), 0, 2);`

getRes()

Parameters:	*none*	
Return:	*string*	*"w h bpp"*
	w: width	
	h: height	
	bpp: bits per pixel	

Description: Gets the width, height, and bit depth of the screen

Usage: `%res = getRes():`

getResolutionList(devicename)

Parameters:	*devicename*	Name of the device to query
Return:	*string*	

Description: Obtains all available resolutions for the specified device

Usage: `%rl = getResolutionList(%device);`

getServerCount()

Parameters: none

Return: numeric

Description: Gets the number of available servers from the master server

Usage: `%sc = getServerCount();`

getSimTime()

Parameters: none

Return: numeric

Description: Gets the current game time

Usage: `%st = GetSimTime();`

getSubStr(str, loc, count)

Parameters:	*str*	String to be processed
	loc	Offset into *str* to get start of substring from
	count	Number of characters to get
Return:	*string*	The processed resultant string

Description: Gets the substring of *string* that begins at *loc*, continuing for *count* characters or to the end of the string, whichever comes first

Usage: `%sub = getSubStr(%text, 5, 99);`

getTag(tstring)

| *Parameters:* | *tstring* | Tagged string |
| | *Return:* | *string* |

Description: Gets the tag for the tagged string *tstring*

Usage: `%tag = getTag(%variable);`

getTaggedString(tag)

Parameters:	*tag*	Numeric tag of string to be removed
Return:	*string*	
Description:	Gets the string associated with *tag*	
Usage:	`%name = getTaggedString( %tagname );`	

getTerrainHeight(pos)

Parameters:	*pos*	2D coordinate
Return:	*numeric*	
Description:	Gets the terrain height at the specified position	
Usage:	`%height = getTerrainHeight(%pos);`	

getVersionNumber()

Parameters:	*none*
Return:	*numeric*
Description:	Obtains the hard-coded engine version number of the current build
Usage:	`%vn = getVersionNumber();`

getVersionString()

Parameters:	*none*
Return:	*string*
Description:	Obtains the hard-coded engine version string of the current build
Usage:	`%vs = getVersionString ();`

getVideoDriverInfo()

Parameters:	*none*
Return:	*string*
Description:	Gets device driver information
Usage:	`%info = getVideoDriverInfo();`

getWord(text, index)

Parameters:	*text*	String with space-delimited words
	index	Word-based offset into the text string
Return:	*string*	Contains the found word-string

Description: Gets the word-string at *index* within *text*. In the usage example that follows, if %text equaled "Of Mice and Men", then %word would be set to "and" when the function returned.

Usage: `%word = getWord(%text, 2);`

getWordCount(text)

Parameters:	*text*	String with space-delimited words
Return:	*numeric*	

Description: Gets the number of word-strings within *text*

Usage: `%count = getWordCount( %text );`

getWords(text, first [, last])

Parameters:	*text*	String with space-delimited words
	first	Word-based offset into the text string specifying the first word to extract
	last	Word-based offset into the text string specifying the last word to extract
Return:	*string*	Contains the found words

Description: Gets one or more word-strings at *index* within *text*. If *count* is specified, gets *count* number of word-strings.

Usage: `%position = getWords(%obj.getTransform(), 0, 2);`

GLEnableLogging(switch)

Parameters:	*switch*	1 enables, 0 disables
Return:	*nothing*	

Description: Enables OpenGL logging to gl_log.txt

Usage: `GLEnableLogging(true);`

GLEnableMetrics(switch)

Parameters:	*switch*	1 enables, 0 disables
Return:	*nothing*	
Description:	Tracks metrics data for OpenGL features	
Usage:	`GLEnableMetrics(1);`	

GLEnableOutline(switch)

Parameters:	*switch*	1 enables, 0 disables
Return:	*nothing*	
Description:	Enables OpenGL wire-frame mode	
Usage:	`GLEnableOutline(true);`	

gotoWebPage(address)

Parameters:	*address*	URL of web page
Return:	*nothing*	
Description:	Opens default browser with specified address	
Usage:	`gotoWebPage("http://www.tubettiworld.com/");`	

increaseFSAA()

Parameters:	*none*	
Return:	*nothing*	
Description:	Increments FSAA level by 1	
Usage:	`increaseFSAA()`	

initContainerRadiusSearch (loc, radius, mask)

Parameters:	*loc*	3D coordinate
	radius	To be searched
	mask	Mask of object type to look for
Return:	*nothing*	
Description:	Searches for objects of type *mask* within a radius around the location	
Usage:	`initContainerRadiusSearch("0 450 76", %somerad, DebrisObjectType);`	

inputLog(filename)

Parameters: *filename*   String containing filename

Return: *nothing*

Description: *Windows Only:* Enables or disables logging of DirectInput events to log
file specified by string.

Usage: `inputLog(DI.log);`

isDemoRecording()

Parameters: *none*

Return: *numeric*   1 (or `true`) = enable, 0 (or `false`) = disable

Description: Queries if a demo is currently being recorded

Usage: `%state = isDemoRecording();`

isDeviceFullScreenOnly(devicename)

Parameters: *devicename*   Name of device to query

Return: *numeric*   1 = yes, 0 = no

Description: Queries if device is capable of full screen only

Usage: `isDeviceFullScreenOnly(%devicename);`

isEventPending(%id)

Parameters: *id*   ID number to check

Return: *numeric*   1 = `true`, 0 = `false`

Description: Queries if an event is pending with an ID number of *id*

Usage: `%status =isEventPending($eventid);`

isFile(filename)

Parameters: *filename*   String containing full filename

Return: *numeric*   1 = `true`, 0 = `false`

Description: Queries if the file exists in the TorqueScript filename buffer

Usage: `%result = isFile("/common/server/script.cs");`

isFullScreen()

Parameters:	none	
Return:	numeric	1 = yes, 0 = no
Description:	Queries whether screen mode is set to full screen	
Usage:	`%result = isFullScreen();`	

isJoystickDetected()

Parameters:	none	
Return:	numeric	1 = true, 0 = false
Description:	Determines if a joystick is present	
Usage:	`%jd = isJoystickDetected();`	

isKoreanBuild()

Parameters:	none	
Return:	string	
Description:	Korean registry key checker	
Usage:	`%kb = isKoreanBuild();`	

isObject(handle)

Parameters:	*handle*	Handle of supposed object
Return:	numeric	1 = true, 0 = false
Description:	Queries if *handle* is an object	
Usage:	`%status = isObject(%chopper);`	

isPackage(name)

Parameters:	*name*	String containing the name of the package
Return:	numeric	1 = true, 0 = false
Description:	Queries if *name* is a registered package	
Usage:	`%status = isPackage(Show);`	

isPointInside(point)

Parameters:	*point*	"x y"
Return:	*numeric*	1 = true, 0 = false
Description:	Queries if *point* is coincident with the interior of any object	
Usage:	%status = isPointInside("123 345 25");	

isWriteableFileName(filename)

Parameters:	*filename*	String containing full filename
Return:	*numeric*	1 = true, 0 = false
Description:	Queries if file specified by *filename* is writeable	
Usage:	%result = isWriteableFileName("/common/server/script.cs");	

lightScene(completion)

Parameters:	*completion*	Completion callback
Return:	*numeric*	Function handle
Description:	Lights the current mission using the callback function pointed to by *completion* when mission lighting is finished	
Usage:	%result = lightScene("CompletionCallback")	

lockMouse(switch)

Parameters:	*switch*	1 (or true) = lock, 0 (or false) = unlock
Return:	*nothing*	
Description:	Toggles the mouse state	
Usage:	lockMouse(true);	

ltrim(str)

Parameters:	*str*	String to be processed
Return:	*string*	The processed resultant string
Description:	Strips any white space from *str* from the left side (before any other characters) of *str*. White space is defined as space, carriage returns, or new line characters.	
Usage:	%tidystring = ltrim(%yuckystring);	

mAbs(x)

Parameters: *x*   Operand. Can be an integer or a floating point.

Return: *numeric*

Description: Computes the absolute value of x

Usage: `%val = mAbs(76.3);`

mAcos(x)

Parameters: *x*   Radians. Can be an integer or a floating point.

Return: *numeric*

Description: Computes the arc cosine

Usage: `%val = mAcos(2.0);`

makeTestTerrain(filename)

Parameters: *filename*   String containing filename

Return: *nothing*

Description: Makes a test terrain file

Usage: `makeTestTerrain("testfile");`

mAsin(x)

Parameters: *x*   Radian. Can be an integer or a floating point.

Return: *numeric*

Description: Computes the arc sine

Usage: `%val = mAsin(1.5);`

mAtan(x,y)

Parameters: *x*   Radian. Can be an integer or a floating point.

                 y   Radians. Can be an integer or a floating point.

Return: *numeric*

Description: Computes the arc tangent

Usage: `%val = mAtan(-1.667,2);`

mathInit(mode)

Parameters: *mode*   The string specifier. Choices:
                                        "DETECT"
                                        "C"
                                        "FPU"
                                        "MMX"
                                        "3DNOW"
                                        "SSE"

Return: *nothing*

Description: Enables math extensions based on CPU type

Usage: `mathInit("DETECT");`

matrixCreate(vector, angledvector)

Parameters: *vector*   "x y z"

               angledvector   "x y z angle"

Return: *string*

Description: Generates a matrix from the specified values

Usage: `%mtx = matrixCreate("10 10 30", "30 40 50 10");`

matrixCreateFromEuler (valstring)

Parameters: *valstring*   "x y z"

Return: *string*

Description: Generates a matrix from given arguments

Usage: `%val = matrixCreateFromEuler("5.5 90 200");`

matrixMulPoint(matrix, point)

Parameters: *matrix*

               point

Return: *string*

Description: Multiplies a matrix by a point

Usage: `%mtx = matrixMulPoint(%matrix,%point);`

matrixMultiply(matrixA, matrixB)

Parameters: *matrixA*

                matrixB

Return: *string*

Description: Multiplies two matrices

Usage: `%mtx = matrixMultiply(matrix1,matrix2);`

matrixMulVector(matrix, vector)

Parameters: *matrix*

                vector

Return: *string*

Description: Multiplies a matrix by a vector

Usage: `%mtx = matrixMulVector(matrix,vector);`

matrixReloaded()

Parameters: *none*

Return: *none*

Description: **Hah!** Got ya! No such function. Yet.

Usage: `there isn't any :-)`

mCeil(x)

Parameters: *x*   Operand. Can be an integer or a floating point.

Return: *numeric*

Description: Finds the smallest integral value greater than or equal to the operand.

Usage: `%val = mCeil(%dialogHeight / %textHeight);`

mCos(x)

Parameters: *x*   Radian. Can be an integer or a floating point.

Return: *numeric*

Description: Computes the cosine

Usage: `%val = mCos(69);`

mDegToRad(degrees)

Parameters: *degrees*   Degrees to be converted. Can be an integer or a floating point.

Return: *numeric*

Description: Converts degrees to radians

Usage: `%rads = mDegToRad(90);`

mFloatLength(x, len)

Parameters: *x*   Operand. Can be an integer or a floating point.

               len   Number of decimal places

Return: *numeric*

Description: Returns *x* as a floating-point value with *len* decimal places

Usage: `%mypi = mFloatLength((21/7),8);`

mFloor(x)

Parameters: *x*   Operand. Can be an integer or a floating point.

Return: *numeric*

Description: Finds the largest integral value less than or equal to the operand

Usage: `%val = mFloor(%dialogHeight / %textHeight);`

mLog(x)

Parameters: *x*   Radian. Can be an integer or a floating point.

Return: *numeric*

Description: Computes the natural logarithm

Usage: `%val = mLog(7654.98);`

mPow(x,y)

Parameters: *x*   Base. Can be an integer or a floating point.

               y   Exponent. Can be an integer or a floating point.

Return: *numeric*

Description: Computes *x* raised to the power of *y*

Usage: `%val = mPow(2,4);`

mRadToDeg(radians)

Parameters: *radians*   Radians to be converted. Can be integers or floating points.

Return: *numeric*

Description: Converts radians to degrees

Usage: `%degs = mRadToDeg(1);`

msg(handle,message)

Parameters: *handle*   Handle of object to receive message

                 message   String containing message

Return: *nothing*

Description: Sends *message* to the object specified by *handle*

Usage: `msg(%objhandle, %msg);`

mSin(x)

Parameters: *x*   Radian. Can be an integer or a floating point.

Return: *numeric*

Description: Computes the sine

Usage: `%val = mSin(65);`

mSolveCubic(a,b,c,d)

Parameters: *a,b,c,d*   Operands. Can be integers or floating points.

Return: *string*

Description: Computes a cubic solution for *x*. $ax^3 + bx^2 + cx + d = 0$

Usage: `%val = mSolveCubic(a,b,c,d);`

mSolveQuadratic(a,b,c)

Parameters: *a,b,c*   Operands. Can be integers or floating points.

Return: *string*

Description: Computes a quadratic solution for *x*. $ax^2 + bx + c = 0$

Usage: `%val = mSolveQuadratic(a,b,c);`

mSolveQuartic(a,b,c,d,e)

Parameters: a,b,c,d,e   Operands. Can be integers or floating points.

Return: string

Description: Computes a quartic solution for x. $ax^4 + bx^3 + cx^2 + dx + e = 0$

Usage: `%val = mSolveQuartic(a,b,c,d,e);`

mSqrt(x)

Parameters: x   Operand. Can be an integer or a floating point.

Return: numeric

Description: Computes the square root of x

Usage: `%val = mSqrt(81);`

mTan(x)

Parameters: x   Radian. Can be an integer or a floating point.

Return: numeric

Description: Computes the tangent

Usage: `%val = mTan(45.0);`

nameToID(name)

Parameters: name   String containing the name of the object

Return: nothing

Description: Gets the ID number of the named object

Usage: `nameToID(%chopper);`

nextResolution()

Parameters: none

Return: numeric   1 = success, 0 = fail

Description: Increases next highest resolution

Usage: `%result = nextResolution ();`

nextToken (str,token,delim)

Parameters:	str	Initializes tokenizer when set to a valid string variable. Uses an empty string ("") to specify follow-up operation on the same string.
	token	Reference handle to the variable that will receive the found token. *Note:* When passing a variable by reference to a function, such as with this parameter, you do not prefix the variable name with % or $.
	delim	Specifies the character that delimits the tokens
Return:	string	Balance of the string after the found token

Description: Sets *token* to the next substring in *str* delimited by *delim*. The initial call to this function specifies *str*; subsequent calls to this function that operate on the same string must pass the empty string ("").

Usage: `%str = nextToken("one,two,three", number, ",");`

openALInitDriver()

Parameters: none

Return: numeric

Description: Initializes the sound driver

Usage: `openALInitDriver();`

openALShutdownDriver()

Parameters: none

Return: nothing

Description: Disables the sound driver

Usage: `openALShutdownDriver();`

panoramaScreenShot(filename)

Parameters: *filename*   String containing filename

Return: *nothing*

Description: Captures the panoramic screen view and saves it to the file specified by *filename.* The engine will take the panoroma shot as a sequence of three screen captures, looking left, center, then right.

Usage: panoramaScreenShot("myPanorama");

pathOnMissionLoadDone()

Parameters: *none*

Return: *nothing*

Description: Sets the Mod path that will be active when a mission is finished loading

Usage: pathOnMissionLoadDone("missE/mission");

permDisableMouse()

Parameters: *none*

Return: *nothing*

Description: Permanently disables DirectInput polling of the mouse device

Usage: permDisableMouse();

playDemo(filename)

Parameters: *filename*   String containing filename

Return: *nothing*

Description: Plays back a demo saved in *filename*

Usage: playDemo(MyNiftyDemo);

playJournal(name,[break])

Parameters:	*name*	String containing filename of journal
	break	If true, then stops playback after each event
Return:	*nothing*	

Description: Plays back saved journal specified by *name*

Usage: `playJournal("myjrnl.jnl");`

png2jpg(filename,quality)

Parameters:	*filename*	String containing filename of PNG file to convert
	quality	Conversion quality, numeric range 0 to 100
Return:	*numeric*	-1 = failure, 0 = success

Description: Converts the PNG formatted file specified by *filename* to JPG format and writes resulting image file to disk with same name and path as *filename* but with JPG extension instead of PNG.

Usage: `png2jpg("image1.png", 100);`

prevResolution()

Parameters:	*none*	
Return:	*numeric*	1 = success, 0 = fail

Description: Decreases next highest resolution

Usage: `%result = prevResolution();`

profilerDump()

Parameters:	*none*
Return:	*nothing*

Description: Dumps NetStringTable statistics to the console

Usage: `profilerDump();`

profilerDumpToFile(filename)

Parameters: *filename*   String containing filename

Return: *nothing*

Description: Dumps `NetStringTable` statistics to the file specified by *filename*

Usage: `profilerDumpToFile(dump.txt);`

profilerEnable(switch)

Parameters: *switch*   1 enables, 0 disables

Return: *nothing*

Description: Enables or disables profiling

Usage: `profilerEnable(false);`

profilerMarkerEnable(markerName, switch)

Parameters: *markerName*   Name of profile marker

               switch   1 enables, 0 disables

Return: *nothing*

Description: Enables or disables profiling for `markerName`

Usage: `profilerMarkerEnable(mark,true);`

profilerReset()

Parameters: *none*

Return: *nothing*

Description: Resets the profiler, clearing all of its data

Usage: `profilerReset ();`

purgeResources()

Parameters: *none*

Return: *nothing*

Description: Purges all resources used by the game through the resource manager

Usage: `purgeResources();`

queryLANServers (port, flags, gametype, missiontype, minplayers, maxplayers, maxbots, regionmask, maxping, filterflags, mincpu)

Parameters: *port*   Host server port

               flags   The query flags. Choices:

                                       0x00 = online query

                                       0x01 = offline query

                                       0x02 = no string compression

               gametype   Game type string

               missiontype   Mission type string

               minplayers   Minimum number of players for viable game

               maxplayers   Maximum allowable players

               maxbots   Maximum allowable connected AI bots

               regionmask   Numeric discriminating mask

               maxping   Maximum ping for connecting clients; 0 means no maximum.

               mincpu   Minimum specified CPU capability

               filterflags   Server filters. Choices:

                                       0×00 = dedicated

                                       0×01 = not password protected

                                       0×02 = Linux

                                       0×80 = current version

Return: *nothing*

Description: Queries all computers found in the LAN, examining the port specified with *port*. The responses are accessible from the ServerList array.

Usage:
```
queryLANServers(

28000, 0, $Client::GameTypeQuery, Client::MissionTypeQuery,

0, 100, 0, 2, 0, 100, 0);
```

queryMasterServer (port, flags, gametype, missiontype, minplayers, maxplayers, maxbots, regionmask, maxping, filterflags, mincpu)

Parameters:	*flags*	The query flags. Choices:
		0x00 = online query
		0x01 = offline query
		0x02 = no string compression
	gametype	Game type string
	missiontype	Mission type string
	minplayers	Minimum number of players for viable game
	maxplayers	Maximum allowable players
	maxbots	Maximum allowable connected AI bots
	regionmask	Numeric discriminating mask
	maxping	Maximum ping for connecting clients; 0 means no maximum.
	mincpu	Minimum specified CPU capability
	filterflags	Server filters. Choices:
		0x00 = dedicated
		0x01 = not password protected
		0x02 = Linux
		0x80 = current version

Return: *nothing*

Description: Queries a master server looking for specified information. The responses are accessible from the ServerList array.

Note: *buddycount* and *buddylist* are obsolete arguments and no longer included or used.

Usage:
```
queryMasterServer(
    28000, 0, $Client::GameTypeQuery, Client::MissionTypeQuery,
    0, 100, 0, 2, 0, 100, 0);
```

querySingleServer(address, flags)

Parameters:	*address*	IP address of server
	flags	The query flags. Choices:
		0x00 = online query
		0x01 = offline query
		0x02 = no string compression

Return: *nothing*

Description: Queries a single server looking for a game being served. The responses are accessible from the ServerList array.

Usage: querySingleServer ("192.168.100.1",0);

quit()

Parameters: *none*

Return: *nothing*

Description: Quits the game

Usage: quit();

redbookClose()

Parameters: *none*

Return: *numeric*   1 = success, 0 = fail

Description: Closes the currently open redbook (CD) device

Usage: %result = redbookClose();

redbookGetDeviceCount()

Parameters: *none*

Return: *numeric*

Description: Queries for the number of redbook (CD) devices

Usage: %count = redbookGetDeviceCount();

redbookGetDeviceName(idx)

Parameters: *idx*   Device index

Return: *string*

Description: Queries the device name of redbook (CD) at the specified device index

Usage: `%name = redbookGetDeviceName(1);`

redbookGetLastError()

Parameters: *none*

Return: *string*

Description: Queries for the last error from a redbook (CD) device

Usage: `%error = redbookGetLastError();`

redbookGetTrackCount()

Parameters: *none*

Return: *numeric*

Description: Queries the number of redbook (CD) tracks

Usage: `%tracks = redbookGetTrackCount();`

redbookGetVolume()

Parameters: *none*

Return: *numeric*

Description: Queries the current volume level of a redbook (CD) device

Usage: `%volume = redbookGetVolume();`

redbookOpen([name])

Parameters: *name*   If non-null, specifies the device

Return: *numeric*   1 = success, 0 = fail

Description: Opens a redbook (CD) device

Usage: `%result = redbookOpen();`

redbookPlay(track)

Parameters: *track*   Index of track

Return: *numeric*   1 = success, 0 = fail

Description: Plays a track on a redbook (CD) device

Usage: `%result = redbookPlay(2);`

redbookSetVolume(volume)

Parameters: *volume*   Volume setting

Return: *numeric*   1 = success, 0 = fail

Description: Sets the volume of a redbook (CD) device

Usage: `%result = redbookSetVolume(%volume);`

redbookStop()

Parameters: *none*

Return: *numeric*   1 = success, 0 = fail

Description: Stops playing on the current redbook (CD) device

Usage: `%result = redbookStop();`

removeField(text, index)

Parameters: *text*   String with field-delimited words

                index   Field-based offset into the text string

Return: *string*   The resultant string

Description: Removes the field-string at *index* from *text*

Usage: `%result = removeField(%text, 0);`

removeRecord(text, index)

Parameters: *text*   String with new line-delimited records

                index   Record-based offset into the text string

Return: *string*   The resultant string

Description: Removes the record-string at *index* from *text*

Usage: `%str = removeRecord(%text, 0);`

removeTaggedString(tag)

Parameters: *tag*   Numeric tag of string to be removed

Return: *nothing*

Description: Removes a tagged string from the list

Usage: `removeTaggedString(%tagname);`

removeWord(text, index)

Parameters: *text*   String with space-delimited words

                index   Word-based offset into the text string

Return: *string*   The resultant string

Description: Removes the word-string at *index* from *text*

Usage: `%str = removeWord(%text, 0);`

resetLighting()

Parameters: *none*

Return: *nothing*

Description: Resets the current lighting

Usage: `resetLighting();`

restWords(text)

Parameters: *text*   String with space-delimited words

Return: *string*   The resultant string

Description: Returns the words remaining after the first word in *text*

Usage: `%data = restWords(%text);`

rtrim(str)

Parameters: *str*   String to be processed

Return: *string*   The processed resultant string

Description: Strips any white space from *str* from the right side (after all other characters) of *str*. White space is defined as space, carriage returns, or new line characters.

Usage: `%tidystring = rtrim(%yuckystring);`

saveJournal(name)

Parameters:	*name*	String containing filename of journal
Return:	*nothing*	

Description: Save a journal to file specified by *name*

Usage: `saveJournal("myjrnl.jnl");`

schedule(time, reference, function, <arg1...argN>)

Parameters:	*time*	Time to wait for trigger, in milliseconds
	reference	Handle of object to attach schedule to, or 0
	function	Function to execute
	arg1...argN	Arguments to accompany function (optional)
Return:	*numeric*	Event ID

Description: Schedules an event that will trigger in *time* milliseconds and execute *function*, with *args*. If *reference* is not 0, then it must be a valid object handle. If the object is deleted, the scheduled event is discarded.

Usage: `$evt = schedule(5000, 0, "updateRadar");`

screenShot(filename)

Parameters:	*filename*	String containing filename
Return:	*nothing*	

Description: Captures the screen view and saves it to file specified by *filename*

Usage: `screenShot("myScreen");`

setClipboard(string)

Parameters:	*string*	String containing text
Return:	*nothing*	

Description: Inserts the contents of *string* into the OS copy/paste clipboard

Usage: `setClipboard("A string of text");`

setDefaultFov(fov)

Parameters:	*fov*	Numeric in degrees
Return:	*nothing*	
Description:	Sets the default field of view	
Usage:	`setDefaultFov(60);`	

setDisplayDevice(deviceName[, width[, height[, bpp[, fullScreen]]]])

Parameters:	*deviceName*	Name of target device driver
	width	Screen width
	height	Screen height
	bpp	Bits per pixel
	fullScreen	1 enables, 0 disables
Return:	*numeric*	1 = success, 0 = fail
Description:	Sets up the display device with specified values	
Usage:	`%result = setDisplayDevice("OpenGL", 800, 600, 32, true);`	

setEchoFileLoads(switch)

Parameters:	*switch*	1 (or `true`) enables, 0 (or `false`) disables
Return:	*nothing*	
Description:	Enables or disables File Load echo to console	
Usage:	`setEchoFileLoads(1);`	

setField(text, index, subst)

Parameters:	*text*	String with field-delimited words
	index	Field-based offset into the text string
	subst	Substitute string
Return:	*string*	The resultant string
Description:	Substitutes the field-string *sub* for the word-string found at *index* in the string *text*	
Usage:	`%rec = setField(%text, 0, "blah");`	

setFov(val)

Parameters:	*val*	The field of view (degrees)
Return:	*nothing*	
Description:	Sets the current field of view	
Usage:	`setFov(90);`	

setFSAA(switch, level)

Parameters:	*switch*	1 enables, 0 disables
	level	Target level
Return:	*nothing*	
Description:	Enables or disables Full Screen Anti-Aliasing at specified *level*	
Usage:	`setFSAA(%newstate,%lvl)`	

setInteriorFocusedDebug(which)

Parameters:	*which*	Handle of interior for focus. If *which* has a value, then debugging is enabled; if *which* is empty (not passed), then debugging is disabled.
Return:	*nothing*	
Description:	Enables debug mode for interior focused objects	
Usage:	`setInteriorFocusedDebug();`	

setInteriorRenderMode(mode)

Parameters:	*mode*	
Return:	*nothing*	
Description:	Sets the detail render level for interiors	
Usage:	`setInteriorRenderMode(7);`	

setLogMode(mode)

Parameters:	*mode*	The numeric mode value. Choices:
		0 = no logging
		1 = logging on, append mode
		2 = logging on, overwrite mode
Return:	*nothing*	
Description:	Enables or disables error logging to disk into the file name "console.log"	
Usage:	`setLogMode(1);`	

setModPaths(path)

Parameters:	*path*	String containing path
Return:	*nothing*	
Description:	Set Mod path. This specifies which folders will be visible to the scripts and the resource engine.	
Usage:	`setModPaths("common;game");`	

setNetPort(port)

Parameters:	*port*	Port number
Return:	*numeric*	1 = success, 0 = fail
Description:	Sets the network port	
Usage:	`%result = setNetPort(1313);`	

setOpenGLAnisotropy(level)

Parameters:	*level*	0=trilinear, 1=bilinear
Return:	*nothing*	
Description:	Sets the level of anisotropy	
Usage:	`setOpenGLAnisotropy(0);`	

setOpenGLInteriorMipReduction(level)

Parameters: *level*   Mipmap level (0 = minimum detail, 5 = maximum detail)

Return: *nothing*

Description: Sets interior texture detail

Usage: `setOpenGLInteriorMipReduction(2);`

setOpenGLMipReduction(level)

Parameters: *level*   Mipmap level (0 = minimum detail, 5 = maximum detail)

Return: *nothing*

Description: Sets shape texture detail to *level*

Usage: `setOpenGLMipReduction(2);`

setOpenGLSkyMipReduction(level)

Parameters: *level*   Mipmap level (0 = minimum detail, 5 = maximum detail)

Return: *nothing*

Description: Sets skybox and cloud texture detail

Usage: `setOpenGLMipReduction(2);`

setOpenGLTextureCompressionHint(hint)

Parameters: *hint*   The compression level hint. Choices:

                                        GL_DONT_CARE

                                        GL_FASTEST

                                        GL_NICEST

Return: *nothing*

Description: Suggests texture compression mode

Usage: `setOpenGLTextureCompressionHint(GL_NICEST);`

setPowerAudioProfiles(up, down)

Parameters:	*up*	power up profile
	down	power down profile
Return:	*nothing*	
Description:	Set the ambient audio manager's power up/down profiles	
Usage:	`setPowerAudioProfiles(AudioPowerUpProfile, AudioPowerDownProfile);`	

setRandomSeed([seed])

Parameters:	*seed*	Starting point
Return:	*nothing*	
Description:	Sets the current starting point for generating a series of pseudo-random numbers	
Usage:	`setRandomSeed();`	

setRecord (text, index, subst)

Parameters:	*text*	String with new line-delimited records
	index	Record-based offset into the text string
	subst	Substitute string
Return:	*string*	The resultant string
Description:	Substitutes the record-string *sub* for the record-string found at *index* in the string *text*	
Usage:	`%str = setRecord(%text, 0, "blah");`	

setRes(width, height, bpp)

Parameters:	*width*	Screen width
	height	Screen height
	bpp	Bits per pixel
Return:	*numeric*	1 = success, 0 = fail
Description:	Sets the screen resolution to specified values	
Usage:	`%result = setRes(640,480,32);`	

setScreenMode(width, height, bpp, fullScreen)

Parameters: *width*   Screen width

               height   Screen height

               bpp   Bits per pixel

               fullScreen   1 enables, 0 disables

Return: *numeric*   1 = success, 0 = fail

Description: Sets up the screen with specified values

Usage: `%result = setScreenMode(800, 600, 32, true);`

setServerInfo(index)

Parameters: *index*   Row of interest in the server list

Return: *numeric*   1 = success, 0 = fail

Description: Changes our indexed reference into the `ServerList`

Usage: `%result = setServerInfo(%index);`

setShadowDetailLevel(level)

Parameters: *level*   Numeric range 0.0 to 1.0

Return: *nothing*

Description: Sets the level of detail for shadows

Usage: `setShadowDetailLevel(1.0);`

setVerticalSync(switch)

Parameters: *switch*   1 enables, 0 disables

Return: *numeric*   1 = true, 0 = `false`

Description: Enables or disables the use of Vertical Sync

Usage: `setVerticalSync(true);`

setWord(text, index, subst)

Parameters:	*text*	String with space-delimited words
	index	Word-based offset into the text string
	subst	Substitute string
Return:	*string*	The resultant string

Description: Substitutes the word-string *sub* for the word-string found at *index* in the string *text*

Usage: `%str = setWord(%text, 0, "blah");`

setZoomSpeed(speed)

Parameters:	*speed*	Transition speed. Ranges from 0 to 2,000 milliseconds.
Return:	*nothing*	

Description: Sets the transition speed when changing field of view

Usage: `setZoomSpeed( speed );`

startHeartbeat()

Parameters: *none*

Return: *nothing*

Description: Begins periodic messages to the master server that show that this server is still alive

Usage: `schedule(0,0,startHeartbeat);`

startClientReplication()

Parameters: *none*

Return: *nothing*

Description: Starts the client-side shape replicator running. Note that you must actually have the right kind of shapes (`fxShapeReplicator`) applied in a mission for this function to actually do anything.

Usage: `startClientReplication();`

startFoliageReplication()

Parameters: none

Return: nothing

Description: Starts the client-side foliage replicator. This works the same way as the shape replicator described in startShapeReplication.

Usage: startShapeReplication();

startRecording(filename)

Parameters: *filename* String containing filename

Return: nothing

Description: Records a demo and saves it as *filename*

Usage: startRecording(myDemo);

stopHeartbeat()

Parameters: none

Return: nothing

Description: Stops the heartbeat messages

Usage: stopHeartbeat();

stopRecording()

Parameters: none

Return: nothing

Description: Stops the currently recording demo

Usage: stopRecording();

stopServerQuery()

Parameters: none

Return: nothing

Description: Cancels the current query and marks outstanding pings as finished

Usage: stopServerQuery();

strchr(str, char)

Parameters:	*str*	String to be processed
	char	String containing the character to be found
Return:	*string*	

Description: Finds the first substring in the string that begins with *char*

Usage: `%file = strchr("data/file.dat", "/" );`

strcmp(str1, str2)

Parameters:	*str1*	First string
	str2	Second string
Return:	*numeric*	< 0 *str1* is less than (also not equal to) *str2*.
		0 *str1* is equal to *str2*.
		> 0 *str1* is greater than (also not equal to) *str2*.

Description: Case-*sensitive* comparison of two strings: *str1* and *str2*

Usage: `if(strcmp(%weaponName,"candlestick")==0) return %weaponFound;`

stricmp(str1, str2)

Parameters:	*str1*	First string
	str2	Second string
Return:	*numeric*	< 0 *str1* is less than (also not equal to) *str2*.
		0 *str1* is equal to *str2*.
		> 0 *str1* is greater than (also not equal to) *str2*.

Description: Case-*insensitive* comparison of two strings: *str1* and *str2*

Usage: `if(stricmp(%weaponName,"CandleStick")==0) return %weaponFound;`

stripChars(str, chars)

Parameters:	*str*	String to be processed
	chars	String containing characters to be stripped
Return:	*string*	The processed resultant string

Description: Removes all characters in the string *chars* from the string *str*

Usage: `%stripped = stripChars(%value, "~" );`

stripMLControlChars(string)

Parameters: *string*

Return: *string*

Description: Strips ML special control characters from string

Usage: `%text = stripMLControlChars(%string);`

stripTrailingSpaces(string)

Parameters: *string*   Input string

Return: *string*

Description: Strips trailing spaces and underscores from string to be used for player name

Usage: `%name = stripTrailingSpaces(strToPlayerName( %name ) );`

strlen(str)

Parameters: *str*   String

Return: *numeric*

Description: Obtains the number of characters in *str*

Usage: `%len = strlen(%weaponName);`

strlwr(str)

Parameters: *str*   String to be processed

Return: *string*   The processed resultant string

Description: Converts all characters in *str* to lowercase

Usage: `%var = strlwr(%value);`

strpos(str, target[, offset])

Parameters:	*str*	String to be searched
	target	String to find
	offset	Starts search at offset (optional)
Return:	*numeric*	

Description: Finds the first occurrence of the target string in the search string, with optional starting offset. *Note:* This function is identical to strstr when *offset* isn't used.

Usage: %pos = strpos(%weaponName, "gun") ;

strreplace(str, target, subst)

Parameters:	*str*	String to be processed
	target	Target string to be replaced
	subst	Substitute string
Return:	*string*	The processed resultant string

Description: Replaces all instances of *target* and replaces with *subst*

Usage: %dospath = strreplace(%path, "/", "\");

strstr(str, target)

Parameters:	*str*	String to be tested
	target	Target substring to find
Return:	*numeric*	Offset within *str* where *target* was found

Description: Finds first occurrence of a *target* within *string*

Usage: %loc = strstr(%weaponName, "stick");

strToPlayerName(string);

Parameters:	*string*	Player name string
Return:	*string*	

Description: Converts name string to properly formatted player name string. Proper formatting means the player name is limited to 16 characters in length. Leading and trailing spaces are trimmed; reserved characters are removed.

Usage: %newname = strToPlayerName(%name);

strupr(str)

Parameters:	*str*	String to be processed
Return:	*string*	The processed resultant string
Description:	Converts all characters in *str* to uppercase	
Usage:	`%var = strupr(%value);`	

switchBitDepth()

Parameters:	*none*	
Return:	*numeric*	1 = success, 0 = fail
Description:	Switches between 16 and 32 bits per pixel in full-screen mode	
Usage:	`%result = switchBitDepth();`	

telnetSetParameters(port, consolePW, listenPW)

Parameters:	*port*	Connection port
	consolePW	Console password
	listenPW	"Listener" password
Return:	*nothing*	
Description:	Initializes telnet connection request parameters	
Usage:	`telnetSetParameters(4123, "garage", "games");`	

toggleFullScreen()

Parameters:	*none*	
Return:	*numeric*	1 = success, 0 = fail
Description:	Switches between windowed mode and full-screen mode	
Usage:	`%result = toggleFullScreen();`	

toggleInputState()

Parameters:	*none*	
Return:	*nothing*	
Description:	Toggles DirectInput state between *enabled* and *disabled*. Also prints the new input state (same as `echoInputState`) to the console.	
Usage:	`toggleInputState();`	

toggleLocking()

Parameters: *none*

Return: *nothing*

Description: Toggles UNIX/linux locking mechanism

Usage: `ToggleLocking();`

trace(switch)

Parameters: *switch*   1 (or `true`) enables, 0 (or `false`) disables

Return: *nothing*

Description: Turns execution trace on or off

Usage: `Trace(true);`

trim(str)

Parameters: *str*   String to be processed

Return: *string*   The processed resultant string

Description: Strips any white space from *str* from the left or right sides (before and after all other characters) of *str*. White space is defined as space, carriage returns, or new line characters.

Usage: `%tidystring = trim(%yuckystring);`

validateMemory()

Parameters: *none*

Return: *nothing*

Description: Ensures sufficient memory available for the program

Usage: `validateMemory();`

vectorAdd(vector1, vector2)

Parameters: *vector1*   "x y z"

           vector2   "x y z"

Return: *string*

Description: Adds *vector2* to *vector1*

Usage: `%result = vectorAdd("87.21 54.11 10.0", "9.99 12.6 6.00");`

vectorCross(vector1, vector2)

Parameters:	*vector1*	"x y z"
	vector2	"x y z"
Return:	*string*	
Description:	Computes the cross product between two vectors	
Usage:	`%product = vectorCross("x y z","x y z");`	

vectorDist(vector1, vector2)

Parameters:	*vector1*	"x y z"
	vector2	"x y z"
Return:	*string*	
Description:	Computes the distance between two vectors	
Usage:	`%delta = vectorDist(%vector1, %vector2);`	

vectorDot(vector1, vector2)

Parameters:	*vector1*	"x y z"
	vector2	"x y z"
Return:	*string*	
Description:	Computes the dot product between two vectors	
Usage:	`%product = vectorDot("0 0 1",%eye);`	

vectorLen(vector)

Parameters:	*vector*	"x y z"
Return:	*string*	
Description:	Computes the length of the vector	
Usage:	`%len = vectorLen(vector);`	

vectorNormalize(vector)

Parameters: *vector*   "x y z"

Return: *string*

Description: Normalizes a vector

Usage: `%nvector = vectorNormalize("5 10 30");`

vectorOrthoBasis(vector)

Parameters: *vector*   "x y z"

Return: *string*

Description: Computes the orthogonal normal for a vector

Usage: `%normal = vectorOrthoBasis("x y z angle");`

vectorScale(vector, scalar)

Parameters: *vector*   "x y z"

                scalar   Can be an integer or a floating point

Return: *string*

Description: Computes the result of the vector sized by the scale

Usage: `%svector = vectorScale("5 10 30", 100);`

vectorSub(vector1, vector2)

Parameters: *vector1*   "x y z"

                vector2   "x y z"

Return: *string*

Description: Subtracts *vector2* from *vector1*

Usage: `%result = vectorSub("34.0989 989.3249 100.00", %position);`

videoSetGammaCorrection(gamma)

Parameters: *gamma*   Gamma correction setting

Return: *nothing*

Description: Sets the gamma correction

Usage: `videoSetGammaCorrection(0.5);`

warn(text)

Parameters: *text*   String

Return: *nothing*

Description: Prints *text* to the console with light gray font. Text can be formatted according to the string rules.

Usage: `warn("Danger, Will Robinson!!");`

Torque Reference Tables

Table A.1 TorqueScript Object Type Masks

Mask Identifier	Number	Mask Bit Position
DefaultObjectType	0	0
StaticObjectType	1	1
EnvironmentObjectType	2	2
TerrainObjectType	4	3
InteriorObjectType	8	4
WaterObjectType	16	5
TriggerObjectType	32	6
MarkerObjectType	64	7
unassigned	128	8
unassigned	256	9
DecalManagerObjectType	512	10
GameBaseObjectType	1024	11
ShapeBaseObjectType	2048	12
CameraObjectType	4096	13
StaticShapeObjectType	8192	14
PlayerObjectType	16384	15
ItemObjectType	32768	16
VehicleObjectType	65536	17
VehicleBlockerObjectType	131072	18
ProjectileObjectType	262144	19
ExplosionObjectType	524288	20
unassigned	2097152	21
CorpseObjectType	1048576	22
DebrisObjectType	4194304	23

Table A.1 TorqueScript Object Type Masks (continued)

Mask Identifier	Number	Mask Bit Position
PhysicalZoneObjectType	8388608	24
unassigned	33554432	25
StaticTSObjectType	16777216	26
StaticRenderedObjectType	67108864	27
unassigned	268435456	28
unassigned	536870912	29
unassigned	1073741824	30
unassigned	2147483648	31

Table A.2 Torque Object Methods

Object Class	Method
AIPlayer	.moveForward()
	.walk()
	.run()
	.stop()
	.setMoveSpeed(float)
	.setTargetObject(object)
	.getTargetObject()
	.targetInSight()
	.aimAt(point)
	.getAimLocation()
BanList	.add(id, TA, banTime)
	.addAbsolute(id, TA, banTime)
	.removeBan(id, TA)
	.isBanned(id, TA)
	.export(filename)
Camera	.getPosition()
	.setOrbitMode(obj, xform,min-dist,max-dist, cur-dist)
	.setFlyMode()
DbgBreakPointView	.set(file, line,,,)
	.remove(file, line)
	.condition(clear, passct, condition)

Object Class	Method
(continued)	.isSet(file, line)
	.clear()
DbgCallStackView	.add(file, line, function)
	.getFrame()
	.clear()
DbgFileView	.setBreak(line)
	.removeBreak(line)
	.findString(Text)
DbgWatchView	.set(expression)
	.update(queryId,
	.edit(newValue)
	.remove()
	.queryAll()
	.clear()
Debris	.init(position, velocity)
DebugView	.addLine(startPt, endPt, color)
	.clearLines()
	.SetText(line, text [, colorF])
	.ClearText()
EditTSCtrl	.renderSphere(pos, radius,=)
	.renderCircle(pos, normal, radius,=)
	.renderTriangle(pnt, pnt, pnt)
	.renderLine(start, end)
FileObject	.openForRead(fileName)
	.openForWrite(fileName)
	.openForAppend(fileName)
	.writeLine(text)
	.isEOF()
	.readLine()
	.close()
FlyingVehicle	.setCreateHeight(bool)
GameBase	.getDataBlock()
	.setDataBlock(DataBlock)
GameConnection	.chaseCam(size)
	.setControlCameraFov(fov)
	.getControlCameraFov()
	.transmitDataBlocks(seq)

Table A.2 Torque Object Methods (continued)

Object Class	Method
(continued)	.activateGhosting()
	.resetGhosting()
	.setControlObject(%obj)
	.getControlObject()
	.isAIControlled()
	.play2D(AudioProfile)
	.play3D(AudioProfile,Transform)
	.isScopingCommanderMap()
	.scopeCommanderMap(bool)
	.listenEnabled()
	.getListenState(clientId)
	.canListen(clientId)
	.listenTo(clientId, true|false)
	.listenToAll()
	.listenToNone()
	.setVoiceChannels(0-3)
	.setVoiceDecodingMask(mask)
	.setVoiceEncodingLevel(codecLevel)
	.setBlackOut(fadeTOBlackBool, timeMS)
	.setMissionCRC(crc)
GuiBitmapCtrl	.setBitmap(blah)
	.setValue(xAxis, yAxis)
GuiCanvas	.renderFront(bool)
	.setContent(ctrl)
	.getContent()
	.pushDialog(ctrl)
	.popDialog()
	.popLayer()
	.cursorOn()
	.cursorOff()
	.setCursor(cursor)
	.hideCursor()
	.showCursor()
	.repaint()
	.reset()
	.isCursorOn()

Object Class	Method
(continued)	.getCursorPos()
	.setCursorPos(pos)
GuiControl	.getPosition()
	.getExtent()
	.getMinExtent()
	.resize(x, y, w, h)
	.setValue(value)
	.getValue()
	.setActive(value)
	.isActive()
	.setVisible(value)
	.isVisible()
	.isAwake()
	.setProfile(profileI)
	.makeFirstResponder(value)
GuiEditCtrl	.addNewCtrl(ctrl)
	.select(ctrl)
	.setRoot(root)
	.setCurrentAddSet(ctrl)
	.toggle()
	.justify(mode)
	.bringToFront()
	.pushToBack()
	.deleteSelection()
GuiFilterCtrl	.getValue()
	.setValue(f1, f2,...)
	.identity()
GuiFrameSetCtrl	.frameBorder(index, enable)
	.frameMovable(index, enable)
	.frameMinExtent(index, w, h)
GuiInspector	.inspect(obj)
	.apply(newName)
GuiMessageVectorCtrl	.attach(MessageVectorId)
	.detach()
GuiPopUpMenuCtrl	.sort()
	.add(name,idNum{,scheme})
	.addScheme(id, fontColor, fontColorHL, fontColorSEL)
	.getText()

Table A.2 Torque Object Methods (continued)

Object Class	Method
(continued)	.setText(text)
	.getValue()
	.setValue(text)
	.clear()
	.forceOnAction()
	.forceClose()
	.getSelected()
	.setSelected(id)
	.getTextById(id)
	.setEnumContent(class, enum)
	.findText(text)
	.size()
	.replaceText(bool)
GuiSliderCtrl	.getValue()
GuiTerrPreviewCtrl	.reset()
	.setRoot()
	.getRoot()
	.setOrigin(x, y)
	.getOrigin()
	.getValue()
	.getValue(t)
GuiTextListCtrl	.getSelectedId()
	.setSelectedById(id)
	.setSelectedRow(index)
	.clearSelection()
	.clear()
	.addRow(id,text,index)
	.setRow(id,text)
	.getRowId(index)
	.removeRowById(id)
	.getRowTextById(id)
	.getRowNumById(id)
	.getRowText(index)
	.removeRow(index)
	.rowCount()
	.scrollVisible(index)

Object Class	Method
(continued)	.sort(colId{,increasing})
	.sortNumerical(colId{, increasing})
	.findText(text)
	.setRowActive(id)
	.isRowActive(id)
GuiTreeViewCtrl	.open(obj)
HTTPObject	.get(addr, request-uri)
	.post(addr, request-uri, query, post)
InteriorInstance	.activateLight()
	.deactivateLight()
	.echoTriggerableLights()
	.getNumDetailLevels()
	.setDetailLeve(level)
Item	.isStatic()
	.isRotating()
	.setCollisionTimeout(object)
	.getLastStickyPos()
	.getLastStickyNormal()
Lightning	.warningFlashes()
	.strikeRandomPoint()
	.strikeObject(id)
MessageVector	.deleteLine(DeletePos)
	.clear()
	.dump(filename{, header})
	.getNumLines()
	.getLineText(Line)
	.getLineTag(Line)
	.getLineTextByTag(Tag)
	.getLineIndexByTag(Tag)
PhysicalZone	.activate()
	.deactivate()
Player	.setActionThread(sequenceName)
	.setControlObject(obj)
	.getControlObject()
	.clearControlObject()
	.getDamageLocation(pos)
Precipitation	.setPercentage(percentage <1.0 to 0.0>)
	.stormPrecipitation(percentage <0 to 1>, Time)

Table A.2 Torque Object Methods (continued)

Object Class	Method
SceneObject	.getScale()
	.getWorldBox()
	.getWorldBoxCenter()
	.getObjectBox()
	.getForwardVector()
ShapeBase	.setShapeName(tag)
	.getShapeName()
	.playAudio(slot,AudioProfile)
	.playAudio(slot)
	.playThread(thread)
	.setThreadDir(thread,bool)
	.stopThread(thread)
	.pauseThread(thread)
	.mountObject(object,node)
	.unmountObject(object)
	.unmount()
	.isMounted()
	.getObjectMount()
	.getMountedObjectCount()
	.getMountedObjectNode(index)
	.getMountedObject(index)
	.getMountNodeObject(node)
	.mountImage(DataBlock,slot,[loaded=true],[skinTag])
	.unmountImage(slot)
	.getMountedImage(slot)
	.getPendingImage(slot)
	.isImageFiring(slot)
	.isImageMounted(DataBlock)
	.getMountSlot(DataBlock)
	.getImageSkinTag(slot)
	.getImageState(slot)
	.getImageTrigger(slot)
	.setImageTrigger(slot,bool)
	.getImageAmmo(slot)
	.setImageAmmo(slot,bool)
	.getImageTarget(slot)

Object Class	Method
(continued)	.setImageTarget(slot,bool)
	.getImageLoaded(slot)
	.setImageLoaded(slot,bool)
	.getMuzzleVector(slot)
	.getMuzzlePoint(slot)
	.getSlotTransform(slot)
	.getAIRepairPoint()
	.getVelocity()
	.setVelocity(Vector)
	.applyImpulse(Pos,Vector)
	.getEyeVector()
	.getEyeTransform()
	.setEnergyLevel(value)
	.getEnergyLevel()
	.getEnergyPercent()
	.setDamageLevel(value)
	.getDamageLevel()
	.getDamagePercent()
	.setDamageState(state)
	.getDamageState()
	.isDestroyed()
	.isDisabled()
	.isEnabled()
	.applyDamage(value)
	.applyRepair(value)
	.setRepairRate(value)
	.getRepairRate()
	.setRechargeRate(value)
	.getRechargeRate()
	.getControllingClient()
	.getControllingObject()
	.canCloak()
	.setCloaked(true|false)
	.isCloaked()
	.setDamageFlash(flash level)
	.getDamageFlash()
	.setWhiteOut(flash level)
	.getWhiteOut()

Table A.2 Torque Object Methods (continued)

Object Class	Method
(continued)	.setInvincibleMode(time, speed)
	.getCameraFov()
	.setCameraFov(fov)
	.hide(bool)
	.isHidden()
	.startFade(U32, U32,bool)
	.setDamageVector(vec)
ShapeBaseData	.checkDeployPos(xform)
	.getDeployTransform(pos, normal)
SimpleNetObject	.setMessage(msg)
Sky	sky.stormCloudsOn(0 or 1,Time)
	sky.stormFogOn(Percentage <0 to 1>, Time)
	sky.realFog(0 or 1, max, min, speed)
	sky.getWindVelocity()
	sky.setWindVelocity(x, y, z)
	sky.stormCloudsShow(bool)
	sky.stormFogShow(bool)
StaticShape	.setPoweredState(bool)
	.getPoweredState(bool)
TCPObject	.listen(port)
	.send(string,...)
	.connect(addr)
	.disconnect()
Terraformer	.canyon(dst, freq, turb, seed)
	.preview(dst_gui, src)
	.previewScaled(dst_gui, src)
	.clearRegister(r)
	.fBm(r, freq, 0.0-1.0{roughness}, detail, seed)
	.smoothRidges(src,dst,0-1{factor},iterations)
	.setTerrain(r)
Trigger	.getNumObjects()
	.getNumObjects(Object Index)
TriggerData	.enterTrigger(Trigger, ObjectId)
	.leaveTrigger(Trigger, ObjectId)
	.tickTrigger(Trigger)
WaterBlock	.toggleWireFrame()
WorldEditor	.redirectConsole(objID

Table A.3 TorqueScript Keywords

Keyword	Description
break	Breaks execution out of a loop
case	Indicates a choice in a switch block
continue	Causes execution to continue at top of loop
datablock	Indicates that the following code block defines a data block
default	Indicates the choice to make in a switch block when no cases match
do	Indicates start of a do-while type loop block
else	Indicates alternative execution path in an if statement
false	Evaluates to 0, the opposite of true
for	Indicates start of a for loop
function	Indicates that the following code block is a callable function
if	Indicates start of a conditional (comparison) statement
new	Creates a new object data block
package	Indicates that the following code block encompasses a package
return	Indicates return from a function
switch	Indicates start of a switch selection block
true	Evaluates to 1, the opposite of false
while	Indicates the start of a while loop

Table A.4 TorqueScript Operators

Symbol	Meaning
+	Add
-	Subtract
•	Multiply
/	Divide
%	Modulus
++	Increment by 1
--	Decrement by 1
+=	Addition totalizer
-=	Subtraction totalizer
*=	Multiplication totalizer
/=	Division totalizer
%=	Modulus totalizer
@	String append

Table A.4 TorqueScript Operators (continued)

Symbol	Meaning
( )	Parentheses—operator precedence promotion
[ ]	Brackets—array index delimiters
{ }	Braces—start and end of code blocks
SPC	Space append macro (same as @ " " @)
TAB	Tab append macro (same as @ "\t" @)
NL	New line append (same as @ "\n" @)
~	(Bitwise NOT) Flips the bits of its operand
|	(Bitwise OR) Returns a 1 in a bit if bits of either operand is 1
&	(Bitwise AND) Returns a 1 in each bit position if bits of both operands are 1s
^	(Bitwise XOR) Returns a 1 in a bit position if bits of one but not both operands are 1
<<	(Left-shift) Shifts its first operand in binary representation the number of bits to the left specified in the second operand, shifting in 0s from the right
>>	(Sign-propagating right-shift) Shifts the first operand in binary representation the number of bits to the right specified in the second operand, discarding bits shifted off
|=	Bitwise OR with result assigned to the first operand
&=	Bitwise AND with result assigned to the first operand
^=	Bitwise XOR with result assigned to the first operand
<<=	Left-shift with result assigned to the first operand
>>=	Sign-propagating right-shift with result assigned to the first operand
!	Evaluates the opposite of the value specified
&&	Requires both values to be true for the result to be true
||	Requires only one value to be true for the result to be true
==	Left-hand value and right-hand value are equal
!=	Left-hand value and right-hand value are not equal
<	Left-hand value is less than right-hand value
>	Left-hand value is greater than right-hand value
<=	Left-hand value is less than or equal to right-hand value
>=	Left-hand value is greater than or equal to right-hand value
$=	Left-hand string is equal to right-hand string
!$=	Left-hand string is not equal to right-hand string
//	Comment operator—ignore all text from here to the end of the line
;	Statement terminator
.	Object/data block method or property delimiter

Table A.5 TorqueScript Operator Precedence

High Priority					Low Priority		
(	)	*	/	%	+	-	=

Table A.6 TorqueScript Tokens

Token	Description
string literal	A sequence of alphanumeric characters bracketed by single or double quotes.
variable	Prefixed with % for local variable or $ for global variable, which is then always followed by a letter character. After the initial letter character, there can be a series of alphanumeric characters, underscores, or colons; a variable cannot end with a colon.
identifier	An initial letter character followed by an optional sequence of alphanumeric characters or underscores.
number	A decimal integer or floating-point number. Hexadecimal numbers can be used if the token begins with 0x (zero-x).

Table A.7 TorqueScript String Formatting Codes (Escape Sequences)

Code	Description
\r	Embeds a carriage return character
\n	Embeds a new line character
\t	Embeds a tab character
\x$hh$	Embeds an ASCII character specified by the hex number (hh) that follows the x
\c	Embeds a color code for strings that will be displayed on-screen
\cr	Resets the display color to the default
\cp	Pushes the current display color onto a stack
\co	Pops the current display color off the stack
\c$n$	Uses n as an index into color table defined by GUIControlProfile.fontColors

Table A.8 Torque Data Blocks

Data Block	Parent
AudioDescription	SimDataBlock
AudioEnvironment	SimDataBlock
AudioProfile	SimDataBlock
AudioSampleEnvironment	SimDataBlock
CameraData	ShapeBaseData
DebrisData	GameBaseData
DecalData	SimDataBlock
ExplosionData	GameBaseData
FlyingVehicleData	VehicleData
fxLightData	GameBaseData
GameBaseData	SimDataBlock
HoverVehicleData	VehicleData
ItemData	ShapeBaseData
LightningData	GameBaseData
MissionMarkerData	ShapeBaseData
ParticleData	SimDataBlock
ParticleEmitterData	GameBaseData
ParticleEmitterNodeData	GameBaseData
PathCameraData	ShapeBaseData
PathedInteriorData	GameBaseData
PlayerData	ShapeBaseData
PrecipitationData	GameBaseData
ProjectileData	GameBaseData
ShapeBaseData	GameBaseData
ShapeBaseImageData	GameBaseData
SimDataBlock	*none*
SplashData	GameBaseData
StaticShapeData	ShapeBaseData
TSShapeConstructor	SimDataBlock
TriggerData	GameBaseData
VehicleData	ShapeBaseData
WheeledVehicleData	VehicleData
WheeledVehicleSpring	SimDataBlock
WheeledVehicleTire	SimDataBlock

Table A.9 Torque Console Objects

Object	Parent	Object	Parent
ActionMap	SimObject	GuiNoMouseCtrl	GuiControl
AIClient	AIConnection	GuiPlayerView	GuiTSCtrl
AIConnection	GameConnection	GuiPopUpMenuCtrl	GuiTextCtrl
AIPlayer	Player	GuiProgressCtrl	GuiControl
AudioDescription	publicSimDataBlock	GuiRadioCtrl	GuiCheckBoxCtrl
AudioEmitter	SceneObject	GuiScrollCtrl	GuiControl
AudioEnvironment	SimDataBlock	GuiShapeNameHud	GuiControl
AudioProfile	publicSimDataBlock	GuiSliderCtrl	GuiControl
AudioSampleEnvironment	SimDataBlock	GuiSpeedometerHud	GuiBitmapCtrl
Camera	publicShapeBase	GuiTerrPreviewCtrl	GuiControl
ConsoleLogger	SimObject	GuiTextCtrl	GuiControl
CreatorTree	GuiArrayCtrl	GuiTextEditCtrl	GuiTextCtrl
DbgFileView	GuiArrayCtrl	GuiTextEditSliderCtrl	GuiTextEditCtrl
Debris	GameBase	GuiTextListCtrl	GuiArrayCtrl
DebugView	GuiTextCtrl	GuiTreeViewCtrl	GuiArrayCtrl
DecalManager	SceneObject	GuiTSCtrl	GuiControl
EditManager	GuiControl	GuiWindowCtrl	GuiTextCtrl
EditTSCtrl	GuiTSCtrl	HoverVehicle	Vehicle
FileObject	SimObject	HTTPObject	TCPObject
FlyingVehicle	publicVehicle	InteriorInstance	SceneObject
fxLight	GameBase	Item	publicShapeBase
fxShapeReplicator	SceneObject	Lightning	GameBase
fxSunLight	SceneObject	Marker	SceneObject
GameBase	SceneObject	MaterialPropertyMap	SimObject
GameConnection	NetConnection	MessageVector	SimObject
GameTSCtrl	GuiTSCtrl	MirrorSubObject	InteriorSubObject
GuiArrayCtrl	GuiControl	MissionAreaEditor	GuiBitmapCtrl
GuiAviBitmapCtrl	GuiControl	MissionMarker	ShapeBase
GuiBackgroundCtrl	GuiControl	NetConnection	ConnectionProtocol, SimGroup
GuiBitmapBorderCtrl	GuiControl	ParticleEmitterNode	GameBase
GuiBitmapButtonCtrl	GuiButtonCtrl	Path	SimGroup
GuiBitmapButtonTextCtrl	GuiBitmapButtonCtrl	PathCamera	publicShapeBase
GuiBitmapCtrl	GuiControl	PathedInterior	GameBase
GuiBorderButtonCtrl	GuiButtonBaseCtrl	PhysicalZone	SceneObject
GuiBubbleTextCtrl	GuiTextCtrl	Player	publicShapeBase

Table A.9 Torque Console Objects (continued)

Object	Parent	Object	Parent
GuiButtonBaseCtrl	GuiControl	Precipitation	GameBase
GuiButtonCtrl	GuiButtonBaseCtrl	Projectile	GameBase
GuiCanvas	GuiControl	ScopeAlwaysShape	StaticShape
GuiCheckBoxCtrl	GuiButtonBaseCtrl	ScriptGroup	SimGroup
GuiChunkedBitmapCtrl	GuiControl	ScriptObject	SimObject
GuiClockHud	GuiControl	ShapeBase	GameBase
GuiConsole	GuiArrayCtrl	ShowTSCtrl	GuiTSCtrl
GuiConsoleEditCtrl	GuiTextEditCtrl	SimGroup	publicSimSet
GuiConsoleTextCtrl	GuiControl	SimObject	ConsoleObject
GuiControl	SimGroup	SimSet	publicSimObject
GuiControlListPopUp	GuiPopUpMenuCtrl	Sky	SceneObject
GuiControlProfile	SimObject	SpawnSphere	MissionMarker
GuiCrossHairHud	GuiBitmapCtrl	Splash	GameBase
GuiCursor	SimObject	StaticShape	publicShapeBase
GuiEditCtrl	GuiControl	TCPObject	SimObject
GuiEditorRuler	GuiControl	Terraformer	publicSimObject
GuiFadeinBitmapCtrl	GuiBitmapCtrl	TerrainBlock	SceneObject
GuiFilterCtrl	GuiControl	TerrainEditor	EditTSCtrl
GuiFrameSetCtrl	GuiControl	Trigger	GameBase
GuiGraphCtrl	GuiControl	TSShapeConstructor	SimDataBlock
GuiHealthBarHud	GuiControl	TSStatic	SceneObject
GuiInputCtrl	GuiControl	Vehicle	publicShapeBase
GuiInspector	GuiControl	VehicleBlocker	SceneObject
GuiMenuBar	GuiControl	WaterBlock	SceneObject
GuiMessageVectorCtrl	GuiControl	WayPoint	MissionMarker
GuiMLTextCtrl	GuiControl	WheeledVehicle	publicVehicle
GuiMLTextEditCtrl	GuiMLTextCtrl	WorldEditor	EditTSCtrl
GuiMouseEventCtrl	GuiControl		

Table A.10 Torque Net Objects

Data Block	Parent
AudioDescription	SimDataBlock
AudioEnvironment	SimDataBlock
AudioProfile	SimDataBlock
AudioSampleEnvironment	SimDataBlock
CameraData	ShapeBaseData
DebrisData	GameBaseData
DecalData	SimDataBlock
ExplosionData	GameBaseData
FlyingVehicleData	VehicleData
fxLightData	GameBaseData
GameBaseData	SimDataBlock
HoverVehicleData	VehicleData
ItemData	ShapeBaseData
LightningData	GameBaseData
MissionMarkerData	ShapeBaseData
ParticleData	SimDataBlock
ParticleEmitterData	GameBaseData
ParticleEmitterNodeData	GameBaseData
PathCameraData	ShapeBaseData
PathedInteriorData	GameBaseData
PlayerData	ShapeBaseData
PrecipitationData	GameBaseData
ProjectileData	GameBaseData
ShapeBaseData	GameBaseData
ShapeBaseImageData	GameBaseData
SimDataBlock	*none*
SplashData	GameBaseData
StaticShapeData	ShapeBaseData
TSShapeConstructor	SimDataBlock
TriggerData	GameBaseData
VehicleData	ShapeBaseData
WheeledVehicleData	VehicleData
WheeledVehicleSpring	SimDataBlock
WheeledVehicleTire	SimDataBlock

Table A.11 Torque Engine-Sourced Preference Variables

Identifier	Parent
$Pref::CloudOutline	$Pref::OpenGL::forcePalettedTexture
$Pref::CloudsOn	$Pref::OpenGL::gammaCorrection
$Pref::Decal::decalTimeout	$Pref::OpenGL::lightingAmbientColor
$Pref::Decal::maxNumDecals	$Pref::OpenGL::materialAmbientColor
$Pref::decalsOn	$Pref::OpenGL::materialDiffuseColor
$Pref::Editor::visibleDistance	$Pref::OpenGL::maxHardwareLights
$Pref::environmentMaps	$Pref::OpenGL::mipReduction
$Pref::Interior::detailAdjust	$Pref::OpenGL::noDrawArraysAlpha
$Pref::Interior::DynamicLights	$Pref::OpenGL::noEnvColor
$Pref::Interior::LightUpdatePeriod	$Pref::OpenGL::textureAnisotropy
$Pref::Interior::lockArrays	$Pref::OpenGL::textureTrilinear
$Pref::Interior::ShowEnvironmentMaps	$Pref::Player::renderMyItems
$Pref::Interior::TexturedFog	$Pref::Player::renderMyPlayer
$Pref::Interior::VertexLighting	$Pref::SkyOn
$Pref::Net::LagThreshold	$Pref::Terrain::dynamicLights
$Pref::Net::PacketRateToClient	$Pref::Terrain::enableDetails
$Pref::Net::PacketRateToServer	$Pref::Terrain::enableEmbossBumps
$Pref::Net::PacketSize	$Pref::Terrain::screenError
$Pref::NumCloudLayers	$Pref::Terrain::texDetail
$Pref::OpenGL::allowCompression	$Pref::Terrain::textureCacheSize
$Pref::OpenGL::anisotropy	$Pref::TS::autoDetail
$Pref::OpenGL::disableARBMultitexture	$Pref::TS::detailAdjust
$Pref::OpenGL::disableARBTextureCompression	$Pref::TS::fogTexture
$Pref::OpenGL::disableEXTCompiledVertexArray	$Pref::TS::screenError
$Pref::OpenGL::disableEXTFogCoord	$Pref::TS::skipFirstFog
$Pref::OpenGL::disableEXTPalettedTexture	$Pref::TS::skipLoadDLs
$Pref::OpenGL::disableEXTTexEnvCombine	$Pref::TS::skipRenderDLs
$Pref::OpenGL::disableSubImage	$Pref::TS::UseTriangles
$Pref::OpenGL::force16BitTexture	$Pref::visibleDistanceMod

Table A.12 Torque Engine-Sourced Console Variables

Variable	Variable
$TSControl::frameCount	$mvYawRightSpeed
$Camera::movementSpeed	$OpenGL::primCount0
$cameraFov	$OpenGL::primCount1
$Collision::boxSize	$OpenGL::primCount2
$Collision::depthRender	$OpenGL::primCount3
$Collision::depthSort	$OpenGL::triCount0
$Collision::renderAlways	$OpenGL::triCount1
$Collision::testClippedPolyList	$OpenGL::triCount2
$Collision::testDepthSortList	$OpenGL::triCount3
$Collision::testExtrudedPolyList	$Player::maxPredictionTicks
$Collision::testPolytope	$Player::maxWarpTicks
$debugControlSync	$Player::minWarpTicks
$farDistance	$SB::DFDec
$firstPerson	$SB::WODec
$frameSkip	$SceneLighting::lightingProgress
$GameBase::boundingBox	$SceneLighting::terminateLighting
$Interior::DontRestrictOutside	$screenSize
$Item::maxWarpTicks	$showBackwardAction
$Item::minWarpTicks	$showDownAction
$MacConsoleEnabled	$showForwardAction
$movementSpeed	$showLeftAction
$mvBackwardAction	$showMovementSpeed
$mvDownAction	$showPitch
$mvForwardAction	$showRightAction
$mvFreeLook	$showUpAction
$mvLeftAction	$showYaw
$mvPitch	$specialFog
$mvPitchDownSpeed	$Stats::netBitsReceived
$mvPitchUpSpeed	$Stats::netBitsSent
$mvRightAction	$Stats::netGhostUpdates
$mvRoll	$T2::dynamicTextureCount
$mvRollLeftSpeed	$T2::staticTextureCount
$mvRollRightSpeed	$timeAdvance
$mvUpAction	$timeScale
$mvYaw	$Video::numTexelsLoaded
$mvYawLeftSpeed	$Video::numTexelsLoaded

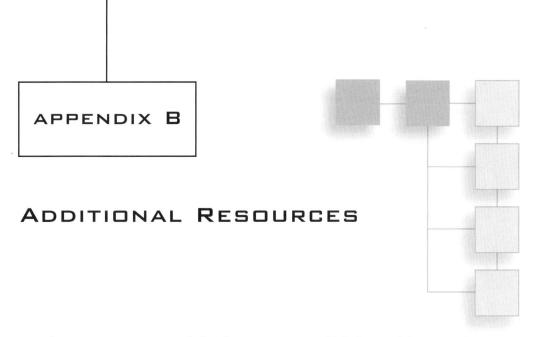

APPENDIX B

ADDITIONAL RESOURCES

Code Resources Added to TGE Build for This Book

The following information is provided to allow you to locate and procure your own copies of the custom resources used in this book. If you obtain a Torque license, you will be able to build these resources into your own build of Torque.

HitBoxes

Josh Albrecht's version:

> http://www.garagegames.com/index.php?sec=mg&mod=resource&page=
> view&qid=3374

Joshua Taylor's version:

> http://www.garagegames.com/index.php?sec=mg&mod=resource&page=
> view&qid=3981

- (Alternatively, go to www.garagegames.com, click on the "Make Games" button, then perform a search with "Resources" selected in the Search pull-down menu. Search for the resource authors by name)

Game Development Resources on the Internet

The following World Wide Web resources are extracted from my personal bookmarks, and those of my friends and associates. Most of these sites have been available for years, and few suffer from "link rot."

Torque-Related Web Sites

ActionRPG
RPG-related enhancements for Torque.
http://www.actionrpg.com

BraveTree Productions
ThinkTanks home.
http://www.bravetree.com

GarageGames
Home of the Torque Engine.
http://www.garagegames.com

Gnometech
Torque modeling and other resources.
http://www.gnometech.com

Hall of Worlds
Torque development notes and tips.
http://www.hallofworlds.com

Holodeck: Virtual Reality Computing for Design
Torque and QuArK tutorials.
http://holodeck.st.usm.edu/vrcomputing/vrc_t

PlanetTribes—Torque
Source for Torque-related files and content.
http://www.planettribes.com/torque

Realm Wars Development Site
Cooperative game development project.
http://www.realmwarsgame.com

Game Development Web Sites

3D Café

3D models and resources.

http://www.3dcafe.com

3D Today Magazine

3D modeling tutorials, resources, and articles.

http://3dtoday.com

3Dup.com

2D and 3D models and resources.

http://www.3dup.com

AngelCode

Game development and more.

http://www.angelcode.com

Art Institute of Toronto

Game Art & Design Program.

http://wherecreativitygoestoschool.ca/

CFXweb

Game design, tutorials, and resources.

http://www.cfxweb.net

CodeGuru

Programming news, tutorials, and links.

http://www.codeguru.com

Dictionary of Algorithms and Data Structures

National Institute of Standards and Technology resource.

http://www.nist.gov/dads

Doctor Dobb's Journal

Programming news, articles, and links.

http://www.ddj.com

flipCode

Game development news and resources.

http://www.flipcode.com

Gamasutra

Game development news, articles, and resources.

http://www.gamasutra.com

Game Developer Magazine

Game development news, articles, and resources.

http://www.gdmag.com

Game Developers Conference

GDC news and promotional information.

http://www.gdconf.com

GameDev.net

Game development news, articles, and resources.

http://www.gamedev.net

Game Institute

Professional training in the fields of video game production and development.

http://www.gameinstitute.com

Gamer's Technical Resources

Game development news, articles, and resources. By Gamers, For Gamers.

http://www.gamerstech.org/forum

iDevGames

Game development news, articles, and resources.

http://www.idevgames.com

insert credit

Gaming news, articles, reviews, and resources.

http://www.insertcredit.com

International Game Developers Association

Game development news, articles, and resources for independent developers.

http://www.igda.com

Linux Game Development Center

Game development news, articles, and resources.

http://lgdc.sunsite.dk

Linux Game Tome

Game development news, articles, and resources.

http://www.happypenguin.org

Machinima.com

Real-time 3D animation.

http://www.machinima.com

MathWorld

Math tutorials, articles, and resources.

http://mathworld.wolfram.com

Mesh Factory

Source for 3D models.

http://www.meshfactory.com

Monster Studios

Home of the Reaction Engine.

http://www.monsterstudios.com

NeHe Productions

Game technology articles and tutorials.

http://nehe.gamedev.net

NeXe

Game technology articles and tutorials.

http://nexe.gamedev.net

Oxford Dynamics

FastCar library—fast, precise, and simple library for vehicle simulation in games.

http://www.oxforddynamics.co.uk

Polycount

Game development articles, resources, and tutorials.

http://www.planetquake.com/polycount

Prefabland

Freeware 3D models source.

http://www.ejoop.com/pfl

Programmers Heaven

Programming articles, resources, and tutorials.

http://www.programmersheaven.com

Psionic 3D Design

3D modeling resources.

http://www.psionic3d.co.uk

SourceForge.net

Open Source software development Web site; large repository of Open Source code.

http://sourceforge.net

Steering Behaviors for Autonomous Characters

Paper by Craig Reynolds.

http://www.red3d.com/cwr/steer

Wotsit's Format

Programming articles, resources, and tutorials.

http://www.wotsit.org

Game Development Tool Reference

All of the tools listed in this appendix are for Windows platforms. Some of the listed tools are available also for the Macintosh and Linux systems. For more information on Macintosh and Linux game development tools, see Table B.1 and Table B.2.

Table B.1 Linux Tool Sources on the Web

Site	Link
Linux Game Development Center	http://lgdc.sunsite.dk
Linux Game Tome	http://www.happypenguin.org
Tucows/Linux	http://download.tucows.com/perl/Linux.html

Table B.2 Macintosh Tool Sources on the Web

Site	Link
iDevGames	http://www.idevgames.com
Mac Central	http://www.macworld.com/
Tucows/Macintosh	http://download.tucows.com/perl/Mac.html

Shareware and Freeware Tools

Modeling

Blender

3D modeling

Multiplatform: Windows, Linux, Irix, Sun Solaris, FreeBSD, or Mac OS X.

Free software: Open Source/GPL.

http://www.blender3d.org

gmax

3D modeling

Stripped-down version of 3ds max. Requires exporters to be useful.

Free (Caveat: Few exporters are available; exporter developers must pay a very high fee)

http://www.discreet.com/products/gmax

Hammer/Worldcraft

3D modeling—maps or levels

Worldcraft (later renamed Hammer) was written for creating Half-Life maps. Plug-ins available for Torque .DIF format. Windows only.

Free (to be used only for creating Half-Life levels or for use by developers using the Torque Engine)

http://collective.valve-erc.com/

MilkShape 3D

3D modeling

Supports Torque using exporter plug-in. Windows only.

INCLUDED ON COMPANION CD

http://www.swissquake.ch/chumbalum-soft

QuArK

3D modeling—maps or levels

Originally written for creating Quake maps (Quake Army Knife). Supports Torque .DIF format. Windows only.

INCLUDED ON COMPANION CD

http://dynamic.gamespy.com/~quark

Programming Editing

UltraEdit-32

Text editing

Includes project and workspace features as well as macros.

INCLUDED ON COMPANION CD

http://www.ultraedit.com/

jEdit

Programmer's Text Editing

Projects, workspace features, macros, as well as a Torque-specific add-on available (see TIDE).

Free software: Open Source/GPL

http://www.jedit.org/

TIDE

Programmer's Text Editing Add-on

Torque-specific (TorqueIDE) add-on for jEdit.

Free software: Open Source/GPL

http://torqueide.sourceforge.net/

Audio Editing

SoundEdit Pro

Audio editing and sound processing

Allows manual editing of sound files and conversion between many types.

$39.95

http://www.rmbsoft.com/sep.asp

Audacity

Audio editing and sound processing

Allows manual editing of sound files, recording, and wave manipulation.

Free software: Open Source/GPL

http://audacity.sourceforge.net/

Other

UVMapper

3D UV texture mapping utility

Allows user to completely remap the model textures of a Wavefront (obj) model.

Free software

http://www.uvmapper.com

Wilbur

Terrain editing software

Handy for converting DEM data to other formats

Free software

http://www.ridgenet.net/%7Ejslayton/software.html

Retail Tools

3ds max

3D modeling

Popular commercial 3D modeling software for Windows.

$3,000 (Price is approximate—may vary according to reseller and discount eligibility.)

http://www.discreet.com

Adobe Audition

Audio editing and sound processing

Fully featured audio recording, processing, and editing and conversion tool.

$299

http://www.adobe.com

Adobe Photoshop

Image editing

Popular fully featured image processing, painting, and editing tool.

$649

http://www.adobe.com

Corel Painter

Image editing

Popular commercial paint program for Windows.

$299 (Price varies—sometimes lower with special offers.)

http://www.corel.com

Deep Paint 3D

Image editing

Popular commercial paint program for Windows.

$995

http://www.righthemisphere.com

Deep UV

3D UV texture-mapping utility

Fully featured commercial product targeted to professionals.

$649.99

http://www.righthemisphere.com

Maya

3D modeling

Popular commercial 3D modeling software for Windows.

$1,999 to $6,999 (Price depends on product set.)

http://www.alias.com

Paint Shop Pro

Image editing

Fully featured image processing, painting, and editing tool.

$129.00 (Price varies—sometimes lower with special offers)

http://www.jasc.com

Poser

3D animation editing

Fully featured commercial product with rendering and automated tools.

$249

http://www.curiouslabs.com

GNU General Public License

The software packages Audacity and QuArK, listed in this appendix and included on the companion CD, are distributed under the terms of the GNU General Public License (GPL).

The text of the GPL is as follows:

GNU GENERAL PUBLIC LICENSE

Version 2, June 1991

Copyright (C) 1989, 1991 Free Software Foundation, Inc.

59 Temple Place, Suite 330, Boston, MA 02111-1307 USA

Everyone is permitted to copy and distribute verbatim copies of this license document, but changing it is not allowed.

Preamble

The licenses for most software are designed to take away your freedom to share and change it. By contrast, the GNU General Public License is intended to guarantee your freedom to share and change free software—to make sure the software is free for all its users. This General Public License applies to most of the Free Software Foundation's software and to any other program whose authors commit to using it. (Some other Free Software Foundation software is covered by the GNU Library General Public License instead.) You can apply it to your programs, too.

When we speak of free software, we are referring to freedom, not price. Our General Public Licenses are designed to make sure that you have the freedom to distribute copies of free software (and charge for this service if you wish), that you receive source code or can get it if you want it, that you can change the software or use pieces of it in new free programs; and that you know you can do these things.

To protect your rights, we need to make restrictions that forbid anyone to deny you these rights or to ask you to surrender the rights. These restrictions translate to certain responsibilities for you if you distribute copies of the software, or if you modify it.

For example, if you distribute copies of such a program, whether gratis or for a fee, you must give the recipients all the rights that you have. You must make sure that they, too, receive or can get the source code. And you must show them these terms so they know their rights.

We protect your rights with two steps: (1) copyright the software, and (2) offer you this license which gives you legal permission to copy, distribute and/or modify the software.

Also, for each author's protection and ours, we want to make certain that everyone understands that there is no warranty for this free software. If the software is modified by someone else and passed on, we want its recipients to know that what they have is not the original, so that any problems introduced by others will not reflect on the original authors' reputations.

Finally, any free program is threatened constantly by software patents. We wish to avoid the danger that redistributors of a free program will individually obtain patent licenses, in effect making the program proprietary. To prevent this, we have made it clear that any patent must be licensed for everyone's free use or not licensed at all.

The precise terms and conditions for copying, distribution and modification follow.

GNU GENERAL PUBLIC LICENSE

TERMS AND CONDITIONS FOR COPYING, DISTRIBUTION AND MODIFICATION

0. This License applies to any program or other work which contains a notice placed by the copyright holder saying it may be distributed under the terms of this General Public License. The "Program", below, refers to any such program or work, and a "work based on the Program" means either the Program or any derivative work under copyright law: that is to say, a work containing the Program or a portion of it, either verbatim or with modifications and/or translated into another language. (Hereinafter, translation is included without limitation in the term "modification".) Each licensee is addressed as "you".

Activities other than copying, distribution and modification are not covered by this License; they are outside its scope. The act of running the Program is not restricted, and the output from the Program is covered only if its contents constitute a work based on the Program (independent of having been made by running the Program). Whether that is true depends on what the Program does.

1. You may copy and distribute verbatim copies of the Program's source code as you receive it, in any medium, provided that you conspicuously and appropriately publish on each copy an appropriate copyright notice and disclaimer of warranty; keep intact all the notices that refer to this License and to the absence of any warranty; and give any other recipients of the Program a copy of this License along with the Program.

You may charge a fee for the physical act of transferring a copy, and you may at your option offer warranty protection in exchange for a fee.

2. You may modify your copy or copies of the Program or any portion of it, thus forming a work based on the Program, and copy and distribute such modifications or work under the terms of Section 1 above, provided that you also meet all of these conditions:

   a) You must cause the modified files to carry prominent notices stating that you changed the files and the date of any change.

   b) You must cause any work that you distribute or publish, that in whole or in part contains or is derived from the Program or any part thereof, to be licensed as a whole at no charge to all third parties under the terms of this License.

c) If the modified program normally reads commands interactively when run, you must cause it, when started running for such interactive use in the most ordinary way, to print or display an announcement including an appropriate copyright notice and a notice that there is no warranty (or else, saying that you provide a warranty) and that users may redistribute the program under these conditions, and telling the user how to view a copy of this License. (Exception: if the Program itself is interactive but does not normally print such an announcement, your work based on the Program is not required to print an announcement.)

These requirements apply to the modified work as a whole. If identifiable sections of that work are not derived from the Program, and can be reasonably considered independent and separate works in themselves, then this License, and its terms, do not apply to those sections when you distribute them as separate works. But when you distribute the same sections as part of a whole which is a work based on the Program, the distribution of the whole must be on the terms of this License, whose permissions for other licensees extend to the entire whole, and thus to each and every part regardless of who wrote it.

Thus, it is not the intent of this section to claim rights or contest your rights to work written entirely by you; rather, the intent is to exercise the right to control the distribution of derivative or collective works based on the Program.

In addition, mere aggregation of another work not based on the Program with the Program (or with a work based on the Program) on a volume of a storage or distribution medium does not bring the other work under the scope of this License.

3. You may copy and distribute the Program (or a work based on it, under Section 2) in object code or executable form under the terms of Sections 1 and 2 above provided that you also do one of the following:

a) Accompany it with the complete corresponding machine-readable source code, which must be distributed under the terms of Sections 1 and 2 above on a medium customarily used for software interchange; or,

b) Accompany it with a written offer, valid for at least three years, to give any third party, for a charge no more than your cost of physically performing source distribution, a complete machine-readable copy of the corresponding source code, to be distributed under the terms of Sections 1 and 2 above on a medium customarily used for software interchange; or,

c) Accompany it with the information you received as to the offer to distribute corresponding source code. (This alternative is allowed only for noncommercial distribution and only if you received the program in object code or executable form with such an offer, in accord with Subsection b above.)

The source code for a work means the preferred form of the work for making modifications to it. For an executable work, complete source code means all the source code for all modules it contains, plus any associated interface definition files, plus the scripts used to control compilation and installation of the executable. However, as a special exception, the source code distributed need not include anything that is normally distributed (in either source or binary form) with the major components (compiler, kernel, and so on) of the operating system on which the executable runs, unless that component itself accompanies the executable.

If distribution of executable or object code is made by offering access to copy from a designated place, then offering equivalent access to copy the source code from the same place counts as distribution of the source code, even though third parties are not compelled to copy the source along with the object code.

4. You may not copy, modify, sublicense, or distribute the Program except as expressly provided under this License. Any attempt otherwise to copy, modify, sublicense or distribute the Program is void, and will automatically terminate your rights under this License. However, parties who have received copies, or rights, from you under this License will not have their licenses terminated so long as such parties remain in full compliance.

5. You are not required to accept this License, since you have not signed it. However, nothing else grants you permission to modify or distribute the Program or its derivative works. These actions are prohibited by law if you do not accept this License. Therefore, by modifying or distributing the Program (or any work based on the Program), you indicate your acceptance of this License to do so, and all its terms and conditions for copying, distributing or modifying the Program or works based on it.

6. Each time you redistribute the Program (or any work based on the Program), the recipient automatically receives a license from the original licensor to copy, distribute or modify the Program subject to these terms and conditions. You may not impose any further restrictions on the recipients' exercise of the rights granted herein. You are not responsible for enforcing compliance by third parties to this License.

7. If, as a consequence of a court judgment or allegation of patent infringement or for any other reason (not limited to patent issues), conditions are imposed on you (whether by court order, agreement or otherwise) that contradict the conditions of this License, they do not excuse you from the conditions of this License. If you cannot distribute so as to satisfy simultaneously your obligations under this License and any other pertinent obligations, then as a consequence you may not distribute the Program at all. For example, if a patent license would not permit royalty-free redistribution of the Program by all those who receive copies directly or indirectly through you, then the only way you could satisfy both it and this License would be to refrain entirely from distribution of the Program.

If any portion of this section is held invalid or unenforceable under any particular circumstance, the balance of the section is intended to apply and the section as a whole is intended to apply in other circumstances.

It is not the purpose of this section to induce you to infringe any patents or other property right claims or to contest validity of any such claims; this section has the sole purpose of protecting the integrity of the free software distribution system, which is implemented by public license practices. Many people have made generous contributions to the wide range of software distributed through that system in reliance on consistent application of that system; it is up to the author/donor to decide if he or she is willing to distribute software through any other system and a licensee cannot impose that choice.

This section is intended to make thoroughly clear what is believed to be a consequence of the rest of this License.

8. If the distribution and/or use of the Program is restricted in certain countries either by patents or by copyrighted interfaces, the original copyright holder who places the Program under this License may add an explicit geographical distribution limitation excluding those countries, so that distribution is permitted only in or among countries not thus excluded. In such case, this License incorporates the limitation as if written in the body of this License.

9. The Free Software Foundation may publish revised and/or new versions of the General Public License from time to time. Such new versions will be similar in spirit to the present version, but may differ in detail to address new problems or concerns.

Each version is given a distinguishing version number. If the Program specifies a version number of this License which applies to it and "any later version", you have the option of following the terms and conditions either of that version or of any later version published by the Free Software Foundation. If the Program does not specify a version number of this License, you may choose any version ever published by the Free Software Foundation.

10. If you wish to incorporate parts of the Program into other free programs whose distribution conditions are different, write to the author to ask for permission. For software which is copyrighted by the Free Software Foundation, write to the Free Software Foundation; we sometimes make exceptions for this. Our decision will be guided by the two goals of preserving the free status of all derivatives of our free software and of promoting the sharing and reuse of software generally.

NO WARRANTY

11. BECAUSE THE PROGRAM IS LICENSED FREE OF CHARGE, THERE IS NO WARRANTY FOR THE PROGRAM, TO THE EXTENT PERMITTED BY APPLICABLE LAW. EXCEPT WHEN OTHERWISE STATED IN WRITING THE COPYRIGHT HOLDERS AND/OR OTHER PARTIES PROVIDE THE PROGRAM "AS IS" WITHOUT WARRANTY OF ANY KIND, EITHER EXPRESSED OR IMPLIED, INCLUDING, BUT NOT LIMITED TO, THE IMPLIED WARRANTIES OF MERCHANTABILITY AND FITNESS FOR A PARTICULAR PURPOSE. THE ENTIRE RISK AS TO THE QUALITY AND PERFORMANCE OF THE PROGRAM IS WITH YOU. SHOULD THE PROGRAM PROVE DEFECTIVE, YOU ASSUME THE COST OF ALL NECESSARY SERVICING, REPAIR OR CORRECTION.

12. IN NO EVENT UNLESS REQUIRED BY APPLICABLE LAW OR AGREED TO IN WRITING WILL ANY COPYRIGHT HOLDER, OR ANY OTHER PARTY WHO MAY MODIFY AND/OR REDISTRIBUTE THE PROGRAM AS PERMITTED ABOVE, BE LIABLE TO YOU FOR DAMAGES, INCLUDING ANY GENERAL, SPECIAL, INCIDENTAL OR CONSEQUENTIAL DAMAGES ARISING OUT OF THE USE OR INABILITY TO USE THE PROGRAM (INCLUDING BUT NOT LIMITED TO LOSS OF DATA

OR DATA BEING RENDERED INACCURATE OR LOSSES SUSTAINED BY YOU OR THIRD PARTIES OR A FAILURE OF THE PROGRAM TO OPERATE WITH ANY OTHER PROGRAMS), EVEN IF SUCH HOLDER OR OTHER PARTY HAS BEEN ADVISED OF THE POSSIBILITY OF SUCH DAMAGES.

END OF TERMS AND CONDITIONS

How to Apply These Terms to Your New Programs

If you develop a new program, and you want it to be of the greatest possible use to the public, the best way to achieve this is to make it free software which everyone can redistribute and change under these terms.

To do so, attach the following notices to the program. It is safest to attach them to the start of each source file to most effectively convey the exclusion of warranty; and each file should have at least the "copyright" line and a pointer to where the full notice is found.

<one line to give the program's name and a brief idea of what it does.>

Copyright (C) 19yy <name of author>

This program is free software; you can redistribute it and/or modify it under the terms of the GNU General Public License as published by the Free Software Foundation; either version 2 of the License, or (at your option) any later version.

This program is distributed in the hope that it will be useful, but WITHOUT ANY WARRANTY; without even the implied warranty of MERCHANTABILITY or FITNESS FOR A PARTICULAR PURPOSE. See the GNU General Public License for more details.

You should have received a copy of the GNU General Public License along with this program; if not, write to the Free Software Foundation, Inc., 59 Temple Place, Suite 330, Boston, MA 02111-1307 USA

Also add information on how to contact you by electronic and paper mail.

If the program is interactive, make it output a short notice like this when it starts in an interactive mode:

Gnomovision version 69, Copyright (C) 19yy name of author

Gnomovision comes with ABSOLUTELY NO WARRANTY; for details type `show w'.

This is free software, and you are welcome to redistribute it under certain conditions; type `show c' for details.

The hypothetical commands `show w' and `show c' should show the appropriate parts of the General Public License. Of course, the commands you use may be called something other than `show w' and `show c'; they could even be mouse-clicks or menu items—whatever suits your program.

You should also get your employer (if you work as a programmer) or your school, if any, to sign a "copyright disclaimer" for the program, if necessary. Here is a sample; alter the names:

Yoyodyne, Inc., hereby disclaims all copyright interest in the program `Gnomovision' (which makes passes at compilers) written by James Hacker.

<signature of Ty Coon>, 1 April 1989

Ty Coon, President of Vice

This General Public License does not permit incorporating your program into proprietary programs. If your program is a subroutine library, you may consider it more useful to permit linking proprietary applications with the library. If this is what you want to do, use the GNU Library General Public License instead of this License.

Gamedev.net

The most comprehensive game development resource

- The latest news in game development
- The most active forums and chatrooms anywhere, with insights and tips from experienced game developers
- Links to thousands of additional game development resources
- Thorough book and product reviews
- Over 1,000 game development articles!
  Game design
  Graphics
  DirectX
  OpenGL
  AI
  Art
  Music
  Physics
  Source Code
  Sound
  Assembly
  And More!

 Gamedev.net

License Agreement/Notice of Limited Warranty